Python Algorithms

Mastering Basic Algorithms
in the Python Language

Second Edition

Magnus Lie Hetland

Python Algorithms: Mastering Basic Algorithms in the Python Language

ISBN-13 (pbk): 978-1-4842-0056-8

ISBN-13 (electronic): 978-1-4842-0055-1

Publisher: Heinz Weinheimer
Lead Editor: Steve Anglin
Technical Reviewer: Stefan Turalski
Editorial Board: Steve Anglin, Mark Beckner, Ewan Buckingham, Gary Cornell, Louise Corrigan, James T. DeWolf, Jonathan Gennick, Robert Hutchinson, Michelle Lowman, James Markham, Matthew Moodie, Jeff Olson, Jeffrey Pepper, Douglas Pundick, Ben Renow-Clarke, Dominic Shakeshaft, Gwenan Spearing, Matt Wade, Steve Weiss
Development Editor: Kenyon Brown
Coordinating Editor: Anamika Panchoo
Copy Editor: Kim Wimpsett
Compositor: SPi Global
Indexer: SPi Global
Artist: SPi Global
Cover Designer: Anna Ishchenko
Photo Credit: Kai T. Dragland

Distributed to the book trade worldwide by Springer Science+Business Media New York, 233 Spring Street, 6th Floor, New York, NY 10013. Phone 1-800-SPRINGER, fax (201) 348-4505, e-mail orders-ny@springer-sbm.com, or visit www.springeronline.com. Apress Media, LLC is a California LLC and the sole member (owner) is Springer Science + Business Media Finance Inc (SSBM Finance Inc). SSBM Finance Inc is a Delaware corporation.

For information on translations, please e-mail rights@apress.com, or visit www.apress.com.

Apress and friends of ED books may be purchased in bulk for academic, corporate, or promotional use. eBook versions and licenses are also available for most titles. For more information, reference our Special Bulk Sales–eBook Licensing web page at www.apress.com/bulk-sales.

Any source code or other supplementary material referenced by the author in this text is available to readers at www.apress.com. For detailed information about how to locate your book's source code, go to www.apress.com/source-code/.

For JV, the silliest girl I know.

Contents at a Glance

Contents

About the Author

Magnus Lie Hetland is an experienced Python programmer, having used the language since the late 1990s. He is also an associate professor of algorithms at the Norwegian University of Science and Technology and has taught algorithms for more than a decade. Hetland is the author of *Beginning Python*.

About the Technical Reviewer

Stefan Turalski is just another coder who is perfectly happy delivering pragmatic, not necessarily software, solutions and climbing the impassable learning curve.

He has more than a decade of experience building solutions in such diverse domains as knowledge management, embedded networking, healthcare, power and gas trading, and, in the last few years, finance.

Focusing on code optimization and systems integration, he has dabbled (or almost drowned) in quite a few programming languages and has abused a number of open source and commercial software frameworks, libraries, servers, and so on.

Stefan is currently working on a highly scalable, low-latency, intraday risk valuation system at a financial institution in London. His latest interests revolve around functional and reactive programming, F#, Clojure, Python, OpenCL, and WebGL.

He still cannot believe that he was trusted enough to help on the second edition of Magnus Lie Hetland's superb book. Stefan hopes that his (and your) brain cells injured while studying the algorithmic problems covered by the author will recover stronger and wiser!

Acknowledgments

Thanks to everyone who contributed to this book, either directly or indirectly. This certainly includes my algorithm mentors, Arne Halaas and Bjørn Olstad, as well as the entire crew at Apress and my brilliant tech editors, Alex Martelli (for the first edition) and Stefan Turalski. Thanks to all the readers who pointed out errors in the first edition; I hope I have corrected most of them. I'd especially like to thank Gerald Senarclens de Grancy, who supplied an extensive, well-annotated list of errata covering the entire book. Thanks to Nils Grimsmo, Jon Marius Venstad, Ole Edsberg, Rolv Seehuus, and Jorg Rødsjø for useful input; to my girlfriend, Janne Varvára Seem, my parents, Kjersti Lie and Tor M. Hetland, and my sister, Anne Lie-Hetland, for their interest and support; and to my uncle Axel, for checking my French. Finally, a big thank-you to the Python Software Foundation for their permission to reproduce parts of the Python standard library and to Randall Munroe for letting me include some of his wonderful XKCD comics.

Preface

This book is a marriage of three of my passions: algorithms, Python programming, and explaining things. To me, all three of these are about aesthetics—finding just the right way of doing something, looking until you uncover a hint of elegance, and then polishing that until it shines (or at least until it is a bit shinier). Of course, when there's a lot of material to cover, you may not get to polish things quite as much as you want. Luckily, though, most of the content in this book is prepolished because I'm writing about really beautiful algorithms and proofs, as well as one of the cutest programming languages out there. As for the third part, I've tried hard to find explanations that will make things seem as obvious as possible. Even so, I'm sure I have failed in many ways, and if you have suggestions for improving the book, I'd be happy to hear from you. Who knows, maybe some of your ideas could make it into a future edition. For now, though, I hope you have fun with what's here and that you take any newfound insight and run with it. If you can, use it to make the world a more awesome place, in whatever way seems right.

CHAPTER 1

■ ■ ■

Introduction

1. Write down the problem.
2. Think real hard.
3. Write down the solution.

— "The Feynman Algorithm"
as described by Murray Gell-Mann

Consider the following problem: You are to visit all the cities, towns, and villages of, say, Sweden and then return to your starting point. This might take a while (there are 24,978 locations to visit, after all), so you want to minimize your route. You plan on visiting each location exactly once, following the shortest route possible. As a programmer, you certainly don't want to plot the route by hand. Rather, you try to write some code that will plan your trip for you. For some reason, however, you can't seem to get it right. A straightforward program works well for a smaller number of towns and cities but seems to run forever on the actual problem, and improving the program turns out to be surprisingly hard. How come?

Actually, in 2004, a team of five researchers[1] found such a tour of Sweden, after a number of other research teams had tried and failed. The five-man team used cutting-edge software with lots of clever optimizations and tricks of the trade, running on a cluster of 96 Xeon 2.6GHz workstations. Their software ran from March 2003 until May 2004, before it finally printed out the optimal solution. Taking various interruptions into account, the team estimated that the total CPU time spent was about *85 years*!

Consider a similar problem: You want to get from Kashgar, in the westernmost region of China, to Ningbo, on the east coast, following the shortest route possible.[2] Now, China has 3,583,715 km of roadways and 77,834 km of railways, with millions of intersections to consider and a virtually unfathomable number of possible routes to follow. It might seem that this problem is related to the previous one, yet this *shortest path* problem is one solved routinely, with no appreciable delay, by GPS software and online map services. If you give those two cities to your favorite map service, you should get the shortest route in mere moments. What's going on here?

You will learn more about both of these problems later in the book; the first one is called the *traveling salesman* (or *salesrep*) *problem* and is covered in Chapter 11, while so-called shortest path problems are primarily dealt with in Chapter 9. I also hope you will gain a rather deep insight into why one problem seems like such a hard nut to crack while the other admits several well-known, efficient solutions. More importantly, you will learn something about how to deal with algorithmic and computational problems in general, either solving them efficiently, using one of the several techniques and algorithms you encounter in this book, or showing that they are too hard and that approximate solutions may be all you can hope for. This chapter briefly describes what the book is about—what you can expect and what is expected of you. It also outlines the specific contents of the various chapters to come in case you want to skip around.

---

[1]David Applegate, Robert Bixby, Vašek Chvátal, William Cook, and Keld Helsgaun
[2]Let's assume that flying isn't an option.

What's All This, Then?

This is a book about algorithmic problem solving for Python programmers. Just like books on, say, object-oriented patterns, the problems it deals with are of a general nature—as are the solutions. For an algorist, there is more to the job than simply implementing or executing an existing algorithm, however. You are expected to come up with *new* algorithms—new *general solutions* to hitherto unseen, general problems. In this book, you are going to learn principles for constructing such solutions.

This is not your typical algorithm book, though. Most of the authoritative books on the subject (such as Knuth's classics or the industry-standard textbook by Cormen et al.) have a heavy formal and theoretical slant, even though some of them (such as the one by Kleinberg and Tardos) lean more in the direction of readability. Instead of trying to replace any of these excellent books, I'd like to *supplement* them. Building on my experience from teaching algorithms, I try to explain as clearly as possible how the algorithms work and what common principles underlie many of them. For a programmer, these explanations are probably enough. Chances are you'll be able to understand why the algorithms are correct and how to adapt them to new problems you may come to face. If, however, you need the full depth of the more formalistic and encyclopedic textbooks, I hope the foundation you get in this book will help you understand the theorems and proofs you encounter there.

■ **Note**   One difference between this book and other textbooks on algorithms is that I adopt a rather conversational tone. While I hope this appeals to at least some of my readers, it may not be your cup of tea. Sorry about that—but now you have, at least, been warned.

There is another genre of algorithm books as well: the "(Data Structures and) Algorithms in *blank*" kind, where the *blank* is the author's favorite programming language. There are quite a few of these (especially for *blank* = Java, it seems), but many of them focus on relatively basic data structures, to the detriment of the meatier stuff. This is understandable if the book is designed to be used in a basic course on data structures, for example, but for a Python programmer, learning about singly and doubly linked lists may not be all that exciting (although you *will* hear a bit about those in the next chapter). And even though techniques such as hashing are highly important, you get hash tables for free in the form of Python dictionaries; there's no need to implement them from scratch. Instead, I focus on more high-level algorithms. Many important concepts that are available as black-box implementations either in the Python language itself or in the standard library (such as sorting, searching, and hashing) are explained more briefly, in special "Black Box" sidebars throughout the text.

There is, of course, another factor that separates this book from those in the "Algorithms in Java/C/C++/C#" genre, namely, that the *blank* is Python. This places the book one step closer to the language-independent books (such as those by Knuth,[3] Cormen et al., and Kleinberg and Tardos, for example), which often use *pseudocode*, the kind of fake programming language that is designed to be readable rather than executable. One of Python's distinguishing features is its readability; it is, more or less, executable pseudocode. Even if you've never programmed in Python, you could probably decipher the meaning of most basic Python programs. The code in this book is designed to be readable exactly in this fashion—you need not be a Python expert to understand the examples (although you might need to look up some built-in functions and the like). And if you want to pretend the examples are actually pseudocode, feel free to do so. To sum up ...

---

[3]Knuth is also well-known for using assembly code for an abstract computer of his own design.

What the book is about:

- Algorithm analysis, with a focus on asymptotic running time
- Basic principles of algorithm design
- How to represent commonly used data structures in Python
- How to implement well-known algorithms in Python

What the book covers only briefly or partially:

- Algorithms that are directly available in Python, either as part of the language or via the standard library
- Thorough and deep formalism (although the book has its share of proofs and proof-like explanations)

What the book *isn't* about:

- Numerical or number-theoretical algorithms (except for some floating-point hints in Chapter 2)
- Parallel algorithms and multicore programming

As you can see, "implementing things in Python" is just part of the picture. The design principles and theoretical foundations are included in the hope that they'll help you design your *own* algorithms and data structures.

Why Are You Here?

When working with algorithms, you're trying to solve problems *efficiently*. Your programs should be fast; the wait for a solution should be short. But what, exactly, do I mean by efficient, fast, and short? And why would you care about these things in a language such as Python, which isn't exactly lightning-fast to begin with? Why not rather switch to, say, C or Java?

First, Python is a lovely language, and you may not *want* to switch. Or maybe you have no choice in the matter. But second, and perhaps most importantly, algorists don't primarily worry about *constant* differences in performance.[4] If one program takes twice, or even ten times, as long as another to finish, it may still be *fast enough*, and the slower program (or language) may have other desirable properties, such as being more readable. Tweaking and optimizing can be costly in many ways and is not a task to be taken on lightly. What *does* matter, though, no matter the language, is how your program *scales*. If you double the size of your input, what happens? Will your program run for twice as long? Four times? More? Will the running time double even if you add just *one measly bit* to the input? These are the kind of differences that will easily trump language or hardware choice, if your problems get big enough. And in some cases "big enough" needn't be all that big. Your main weapon in whittling down the growth of your running time is—you guessed it—a solid understanding of algorithm design.

Let's try a little experiment. Fire up an interactive Python interpreter, and enter the following:

```
>>> count = 10**5
>>> nums = []
>>> for i in range(count):
...     nums.append(i)
...
>>> nums.reverse()
```

---

[4]I'm talking about constant multiplicative factors here, such as doubling or halving the execution time.

Not the most useful piece of code, perhaps. It simply appends a bunch of numbers to an (initially) empty list and then reverses that list. In a more realistic situation, the numbers might come from some outside source (they could be incoming connections to a server, for example), and you want to add them to your list in reverse order, perhaps to prioritize the most recent ones. Now you get an idea: instead of reversing the list at the end, couldn't you just insert the numbers at the beginning, as they appear? Here's an attempt to streamline the code (continuing in the same interpreter window):

```
>>> nums = []
>>> for i in range(count):
...     nums.insert(0, i)
```

Unless you've encountered this situation before, the new code might look promising, but try to run it. Chances are you'll notice a distinct slowdown. On my computer, the second piece of code takes around 200 times as long as the first to finish.[5] Not only is it slower, but it also *scales* worse with the problem size. Try, for example, to increase count from 10**5 to 10**6. As expected, this increases the running time for the first piece of code by a factor of about ten … but the second version is slowed by roughly *two* orders of magnitude, making it more than *two thousand times slower* than the first! As you can probably guess, the discrepancy between the two versions only increases as the problem gets bigger, making the choice between them ever more crucial.

■ **Note** This is an example of linear vs. quadratic growth, a topic dealt with in detail in Chapter 3. The specific issue underlying the quadratic growth is explained in the discussion of vectors (or dynamic arrays) in the "Black Box" sidebar on list in Chapter 2.

Some Prerequisites

This book is intended for two groups of people: Python programmers, who want to beef up their algorithmics, and students taking algorithm courses, who want a supplement to their plain-vanilla algorithms textbook. Even if you belong to the latter group, I'm assuming you have a familiarity with programming in general and with Python in particular. If you don't, perhaps my book *Beginning Python* can help? The Python web site also has a lot of useful material, and Python is a really easy language to learn. There is some math in the pages ahead, but you don't have to be a math prodigy to follow the text. You'll be dealing with some simple sums and nifty concepts such as polynomials, exponentials, and logarithms, but I'll explain it all as we go along.

Before heading off into the mysterious and wondrous lands of computer science, you should have your equipment ready. As a Python programmer, I assume you have your own favorite text/code editor or integrated development environment—I'm not going to interfere with that. When it comes to Python versions, the book is written to be reasonably version-independent, meaning that most of the code should work with both the Python 2 and 3 series. Where backward-incompatible Python 3 features are used, there will be explanations on how to implement the algorithm in Python 2 as well. (And if, for some reason, you're still stuck with, say, the Python 1.5 series, most of the code should still work, with a tweak here and there.)

---

[5]See Chapter 2 for more on benchmarking and empirical evaluation of algorithms.

GETTING WHAT YOU NEED

In some operating systems, such as Mac OS X and several flavors of Linux, Python should already be installed. If it is not, most Linux distributions will let you install the software you need through some form of package manager. If you want or need to install Python manually, you can find all you need on the Python web site, http://python.org.

What's in This Book

The book is structured as follows:

Chapter 1: Introduction. You've already gotten through most of this. It gives an overview of the book.

Chapter 2: The Basics. This covers the basic concepts and terminology, as well as some fundamental math. Among other things, you learn how to be sloppier with your formulas than ever before, and still get the right results, using asymptotic notation.

Chapter 3: Counting 101. More math—but it's really fun math, I promise! There's some basic combinatorics for analyzing the running time of algorithms, as well as a gentle introduction to recursion and recurrence relations.

Chapter 4: Induction and Recursion … and Reduction. The three terms in the title are crucial, and they are closely related. Here we work with induction and recursion, which are virtually mirror images of each other, both for designing new algorithms and for proving correctness. We'll also take a somewhat briefer look at the idea of reduction, which runs as a common thread through almost all algorithmic work.

Chapter 5: Traversal: A Skeleton Key to Algorithmics. Traversal can be understood using the ideas of induction and recursion, but it is in many ways a more concrete and specific technique. Several of the algorithms in this book are simply augmented traversals, so mastering this idea will give you a real jump start.

Chapter 6: Divide, Combine, and Conquer. When problems can be decomposed into independent subproblems, you can recursively solve these subproblems and usually get efficient, correct algorithms as a result. This principle has several applications, not all of which are entirely obvious, and it is a mental tool well worth acquiring.

Chapter 7: Greed is Good? Prove It! Greedy algorithms are usually easy to construct. It is even possible to formulate a general scheme that most, if not all, greedy algorithms follow, yielding a plug-and-play solution. Not only are they easy to construct, but they are usually very efficient. The problem is, it can be hard to show that they are correct (and often they aren't). This chapter deals with some well-known examples and some more general methods for constructing correctness proofs.

Chapter 8: Tangled Dependencies and Memoization. This chapter is about the design method (or, historically, the problem) called, somewhat confusingly, dynamic programming. It is an advanced technique that can be hard to master but that also yields some of the most enduring insights and elegant solutions in the field.

Chapter 9: From A to B with Edsger and Friends. Rather than the design methods of the previous three chapters, the focus is now on a specific problem, with a host of applications: finding shortest paths in networks, or graphs. There are many variations of the problem, with corresponding (beautiful) algorithms.

Chapter 10: Matchings, Cuts, and Flows. How do you match, say, students with colleges so you maximize total satisfaction? In an online community, how do you know whom to trust? And how do you find the total capacity of a road network? These, and several other problems, can be solved with a small class of closely related algorithms and are all variations of the maximum flow problem, which is covered in this chapter.

Chapter 11: Hard Problems and (Limited) Sloppiness. As alluded to in the beginning of the introduction, there are problems we don't know how to solve efficiently and that we have reasons to think won't be solved for a long time—maybe never. In this chapter, you learn how to apply the trusty tool of reduction in a new way: not to *solve* problems but to show that they are *hard*. Also, we take a look at how a bit of (strictly limited) sloppiness in the optimality criteria can make problems a lot easier to solve.

Appendix A: Pedal to the Metal: Accelerating Python. The main focus of this book is asymptotic efficiency—making your programs scale well with problem size. However, in some cases, that may not be enough. This appendix gives you some pointers to tools that can make your Python programs go faster. Sometimes a *lot* (as in hundreds of times) faster.

Appendix B: List of Problems and Algorithms. This appendix gives you an overview of the algorithmic problems and algorithms discussed in the book, with some extra information to help you select the right algorithm for the problem at hand.

Appendix C: Graph Terminology and Notation. Graphs are a really useful structure, both in describing real-world systems and in demonstrating how various algorithms work. This chapter gives you a tour of the basic concepts and lingo, in case you haven't dealt with graphs before.

Appendix D: Hints for Exercises. Just what the title says.

Summary

Programming isn't just about software architecture and object-oriented design; it's also about solving algorithmic problems, some of which are really hard. For the more run-of-the-mill problems (such as finding the shortest path from A to B), the algorithm you use or design can have a huge impact on the time your code takes to finish, and for the hard problems (such as finding the shortest route through A–Z), there may not even *be* an efficient algorithm, meaning that you need to accept approximate solutions.

This book will teach you several well-known algorithms, along with general principles that will help you create your own. Ideally, this will let you solve some of the more challenging problems out there, as well as create programs that scale gracefully with problem size. In the next chapter, we get started with the basic concepts of algorithmics, dealing with terms that will be used throughout the entire book.

If You're Curious …

This is a section you'll see in all the chapters to come. It's intended to give you some hints about details, wrinkles, or advanced topics that have been omitted or glossed over in the main text and to point you in the direction of further information. For now, I'll just refer you to the "References" section, later in this chapter, which gives you details about the algorithm books mentioned in the main text.

Exercises

As with the previous section, this is one you'll encounter again and again. Hints for solving the exercises can be found in Appendix D. The exercises often tie in with the main text, covering points that aren't explicitly discussed there but that may be of interest or that deserve some contemplation. If you want to really sharpen your algorithm design skills, you might also want to check out some of the myriad of sources of programming puzzles out there. There are, for example, lots of programming contests (a web search should turn up plenty), many of which post problems that you can play with. Many big software companies also have qualification tests based on problems such as these and publish some of them online.

Because the introduction doesn't cover that much ground, I'll just give you a couple of exercises here—a taste of what's to come:

1-1. Consider the following statement: "As machines get faster and memory cheaper, algorithms become less important." What do you think; is this true or false? Why?

1-2. Find a way of checking whether two strings are anagrams of each other (such as "debit card" and "bad credit"). How well do you think your solution scales? Can you think of a naïve solution that will scale poorly?

References

Applegate, D., Bixby, R., Chvátal, V., Cook, W., and Helsgaun, K. Optimal tour of Sweden. www.math.uwaterloo.ca/tsp/sweden/. Accessed April 6, 2014.

Cormen, T. H., Leiserson, C. E., Rivest, R. L., and Stein, C. (2009). *Introduction to Algorithms*, second edition. MIT Press.

Dasgupta, S., Papadimitriou, C., and Vazirani, U. (2006). *Algorithms*. McGraw-Hill.

Goodrich, M. T. and Tamassia, R. (2001). *Algorithm Design: Foundations, Analysis, and Internet Examples*. John Wiley & Sons, Ltd.

Hetland, M. L. (2008). *Beginning Python: From Novice to Professional*, second edition. Apress.

Kleinberg, J. and Tardos, E. (2005). *Algorithm Design*. Addison-Wesley Longman Publishing Co., Inc.

Knuth, D. E. (1968). Fundamental Algorithms, volume 1 of *The Art of Computer Programming*. Addison-Wesley.

———. (1969). Seminumerical Algorithms, volume 2 of *The Art of Computer Programming*. Addison-Wesley.

———. (1973). *Sorting and Searching*, volume 3 of *The Art of Computer Programming*. Addison-Wesley.

———. (2011). *Combinatorial Algorithms, Part 1*, volume 4A of *The Art of Computer Programming*. Addison-Wesley.

Miller, B. N. and Ranum, D. L. (2005). *Problem Solving with Algorithms and Data Structures Using Python*. Franklin Beedle & Associates.

CHAPTER 2

■ ■ ■

The Basics

Tracey: I didn't know you were out there.

Zoe: Sort of the point. Stealth—you may have heard of it.

Tracey: I don't think they covered that in basic.

— From "The Message," episode 14 of *Firefly*

Before moving on to the mathematical techniques, algorithmic design principles, and classical algorithms that make up the bulk of this book, we need to go through some basic principles and techniques. When you start reading the following chapters, you should be clear on the meaning of phrases such as "directed, weighted graph without negative cycles" and "a running time of $\Theta(n \lg n)$." You should also have an idea of how to implement some fundamental structures in Python.

Luckily, these basic ideas aren't at all hard to grasp. The main two topics of the chapter are asymptotic notation, which lets you focus on the essence of running times, and ways of representing trees and graphs in Python. There is also practical advice on timing your programs and avoiding some basic traps. First, though, let's take a look at the abstract machines we algorists tend to use when describing the behavior of our algorithms.

Some Core Ideas in Computing

In the mid-1930s the English mathematician Alan Turing published a paper called "On computable numbers, with an application to the Entscheidungsproblem"[1] and, in many ways, laid the groundwork for modern computer science. His abstract *Turing machine* has become a central concept in the theory of computation, in great part because it is intuitively easy to grasp. A Turing machine is a simple abstract device that can read from, write to, and move along an infinitely long strip of paper. The actual behavior of the machines varies. Each is a so-called finite state machine: It has a finite set of states (some of which indicate that it has finished), and every symbol it reads potentially triggers reading and/or writing and switching to a different state. You can think of this machinery as a set of *rules*. ("If I am in state 4 and see an *X*, I move one step to the left, write a *Y*, and switch to state 9.") Although these machines may seem simple, they can, surprisingly enough, be used to implement any form of computation anyone has been able to dream up so far, and most computer scientists believe they encapsulate the very essence of what we think of as computing.

An *algorithm* is a procedure, consisting of a finite set of steps, possibly including loops and conditionals, that solves a given problem. A Turing machine is a formal description of exactly what problem an algorithm solves,[2] and

---

[1]The *Entscheidungsproblem* is a problem posed by David Hilbert, which basically asks whether an algorithm exists that can decide, in general, whether a mathematical statement is true or false. Turing (and Alonzo Church before him) showed that such an algorithm cannot exist.

[2]There are also Turing machines that don't solve any problems—machines that simply never stop. These still represent what we might call *programs*, but we usually don't call them algorithms.

the formalism is often used when discussing which problems can be solved (either at all or in reasonable time, as discussed later in this chapter and in Chapter 11). For more fine-grained analysis of algorithmic efficiency, however, Turing machines are not usually the first choice. Instead of scrolling along a paper tape, we use a big chunk of memory that can be accessed *directly*. The resulting machine is commonly known as the *random-access machine*.

While the formalities of the random-access machine can get a bit complicated, we just need to know something about the limits of its capabilities so we don't cheat in our algorithm analyses. The machine is an abstract, simplified version of a standard, single-processor computer, with the following properties:

- We don't have access to any form of concurrent execution; the machine simply executes one instruction after the other.

- Standard, basic operations such as arithmetic, comparisons, and memory access all take constant (although possibly different) amounts of time. There are no more complicated basic operations such as sorting.

- One computer word (the size of a value that we can work with in constant time) is not unlimited but is big enough to address all the memory locations used to represent our problem, plus an extra percentage for our variables.

In some cases, we may need to be more specific, but this machine sketch should do for the moment.

We now have a bit of an intuition for what algorithms are, as well as the abstract hardware we'll be running them on. The last piece of the puzzle is the notion of a *problem*. For our purposes, a problem is a relation between input and output. This is, in fact, much more precise than it might sound: A *relation*, in the mathematical sense, is a set of pairs—in our case, which outputs are acceptable for which inputs—and by specifying this relation, we've got our problem nailed down. For example, the problem of sorting may be specified as a relation between two sets, A and B, each consisting of sequences.[3] Without describing how to *perform* the sorting (that would be the algorithm), we can specify which output sequences (elements of B) that would be acceptable, given an input sequence (an element of A). We would require that the result sequence consisted of the same elements as the input sequence and that the elements of the result sequence were in increasing order (each bigger than or equal to the previous). The elements of A here—that is, the inputs—are called *problem instances*; the relation itself is the actual problem.

To get our machine to work with a problem, we need to *encode* the input as zeros and ones. We won't worry too much about the details here, but the idea is important, because the notion of running time complexity (as described in the next section) is based on knowing how *big* a problem instance is, and that size is simply the amount of memory needed to encode it. As you'll see, the exact nature of this encoding usually won't matter.

Asymptotic Notation

Remember the append versus insert example in Chapter 1? Somehow, adding items to the end of a list scaled better with the list size than inserting them at the front; see the nearby "Black Box" sidebar on list for an explanation. These built-in operations are both written in C, but assume for a minute that you reimplement list.append in pure Python; let's say arbitrarily that the new version is 50 times slower than the original. Let's also say you run your slow, pure-Python append-based version on a really slow machine, while the fast, optimized, insert-based version is run on a computer that is *1,000 times* faster. Now the speed advantage of the insert version is a factor of 50,000. You compare the two implementations by inserting 100,000 numbers. What do you think happens?

Intuitively, it might seem obvious that the speedy solution should win, but its "speediness" is just a constant factor, and its running time grows faster than the "slower" one. For the example at hand, the Python-coded version running on the slower machine will, actually, finish in half the time of the other one. Let's increase the problem size a bit, to 10 million numbers, for example. Now the Python version on the slow machine will be *2,000 times faster* than the C version on the fast machine. That's like the difference between running for about a minute and running almost a day and a half!

---

[3]Because input and output are of the same type, we could actually just specify a relation between A and A.

This distinction between *constant factors* (related to such things as general programming language performance and hardware speed, for example) and the *growth* of the running time, as problem sizes increase, is of vital importance in the study of algorithms. Our focus is on the big picture—the implementation-independent properties of a given way of solving a problem. We want to get rid of distracting details and get down to the core differences, but in order to do so, we need some formalism.

BLACK BOX: LIST

Python lists aren't really lists in the traditional computer science sense of the word, and that explains the puzzle of why append is so much more efficient than insert. A classical list—a so-called linked list—is implemented as a series of *nodes*, each (except for the last) keeping a reference to the next. A simple implementation might look something like this:

```
class Node:
    def __init__(self, value, next=None):
        self.value = value
        self.next = next
```

You construct a list by specifying all the nodes:

```
>>> L = Node("a", Node("b", Node("c", Node("d"))))
>>> L.next.next.value
'c'
```

This is a so-called singly linked list; each node in a doubly linked list would also keep a reference to the previous node.

The underlying implementation of Python's list type is a bit different. Instead of several separate nodes referencing each other, a list is basically a single, contiguous slab of memory—what is usually known as an *array*. This leads to some important differences from linked lists. For example, while iterating over the contents of the list is equally efficient for both kinds (except for some overhead in the linked list), directly accessing an element at a given index is much more efficient in an array. This is because the position of the element can be calculated, and the right memory location can be accessed directly. In a linked list, however, one would have to traverse the list from the beginning.

The difference we've been bumping up against, though, has to do with insertion. In a linked list, once you know where you want to insert something, insertion is cheap; it takes roughly the same amount of time, no matter how many elements the list contains. That's not the case with arrays: An insertion would have to move all elements that are to the right of the insertion point, possibly even moving *all* the elements to a larger array, if needed. A specific solution for *appending* is to use what's often called a *dynamic* array, or *vector*.[4] The idea is to allocate an array that is too big and then to reallocate it in linear time whenever it overflows. It might seem that this makes the append just as bad as the insert. In both cases, we risk having to move a large number of elements. The main difference is that it happens less often with the append. In fact, if we can ensure that we always move to an array that is bigger than the last by a fixed percentage (say 20 percent or even 100 percent), the *average* cost, amortized over many appends, is constant.

---

[4]For an "out-of-the-box" solution for inserting objects at the *beginning* of a sequence, see the black-box sidebar on deque in Chapter 5.

It's Greek to Me!

Asymptotic notation has been in use (with some variations) since the late 19th century and is an essential tool in analyzing algorithms and data structures. The core idea is to represent the resource we're analyzing (usually time but sometimes also memory) as a function, with the input size as its parameter. For example, we could have a program with a running time of $T(n) = 2.4n + 7$.

An important question arises immediately: What are the units here? It might seem trivial whether we measure the running time in seconds or milliseconds or whether we use bits or megabytes to represent problem size. The somewhat surprising answer, though, is that not only is it trivial, but it actually will not affect our results at all. We could measure time in Jovian years and problem size in kilograms (presumably the mass of the storage medium used), and it *will not matter*. This is because our original intention of ignoring implementation details carries over to these factors as well: The asymptotic notation ignores them all! (We do normally assume that the problem size is a positive integer, though.)

What we often end up doing is letting the running time be the number of times a certain basic operation is performed, while problem size is either the number of items handled (such as the number of integers to be sorted, for example) or, in some cases, the number of bits needed to encode the problem instance in some reasonable encoding.

Forgetting. Of course, the assert doesn't work. (http://xkcd.com/379)

■ **Note** Exactly how you encode your problems and solutions as bit patterns usually has little effect on the asymptotic running time, as long as you are reasonable. For example, avoid representing your numbers in the unary number system (1=1, 2=11, 3=111…).

The asymptotic notation consists of a bunch of operators, written as Greek letters. The most important ones, and the only ones we'll be using, are O (originally an omicron but now usually called "Big Oh"), Ω (omega), and Θ (theta). The definition for the O operator can be used as a foundation for the other two. The expression $O(g)$, for some function $g(n)$, represents a *set* of functions, and a function $f(n)$ is in this set if it satisfies the following condition: There exists a natural number n_0 and a positive constant c such that

$$f(n) \leq cg(n)$$

for all $n \geq n_0$. In other words, if we're allowed to tweak the constant c (for example, by running the algorithms on machines of different speeds), the function g will eventually (that is, at n_0) grow bigger than f. See Figure 2-1 for an example.

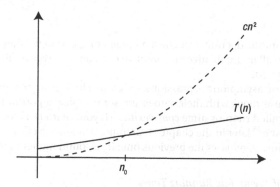

Figure 2-1. *For values of n greater than n_0, T(n) is less than cn^2, so T(n) is $O(n^2)$*

This is a fairly straightforward and understandable definition, although it may seem a bit foreign at first. Basically, $O(g)$ is the set of functions that *do not grow faster than g*. For example, the function n^2 is in the set $O(n^2)$, or, in set notation, $n^2 \in O(n^2)$. We often simply say that n^2 is $O(n^2)$.

The fact that n^2 does not grow faster than itself is not particularly interesting. More useful, perhaps, is the fact that neither $2.4n^2 + 7$ nor the linear function n does. That is, we have both

$2.4n^2 + 7 \in O(n^2)$

and

$n \in O(n^2)$.

The first example shows us that we are now able to represent a function without all its bells and whistles; we can drop the 2.4 and the 7 and simply express the function as $O(n^2)$, which gives us just the information we need. The second shows us that O can be used to express loose limits as well: Any function that is better (that is, doesn't grow faster) than g can be found in $O(g)$.

How does this relate to our original example? Well, the thing is, even though we can't be sure of the details (after all, they depend on both the Python version and the hardware you're using), we can describe the operations asymptotically: The running time of appending n numbers to a Python list is $O(n)$, while inserting n numbers at its beginning is $O(n^2)$.

The other two, Ω and Θ, are just variations of O. Ω is its complete opposite: A function f is in $\Omega(g)$ if it satisfies the following condition: There exists a natural number n_0 and a positive constant c such that

$f(n) \geq cg(n)$

for all $n \geq n_0$. So, where O forms a so-called asymptotic upper bound, Ω forms an asymptotic *lower* bound.

■ **Note** Our first two asymptotic operators, O and Ω, are each other's inverses: If f is $O(g)$, then g is $\Omega(f)$. Exercise 2-3 asks you to show this.

The sets formed by Θ are simply intersections of the other two, that is, $\Theta(g) = O(g) \cap \Omega(g)$. In other words, a function f is in $\Theta(g)$ if it satisfies the following condition: There exists a natural number n_0 and *two* positive constants c_1 and c_2 such that

$c_1 g(n) \leq f(n) \leq c_2 g(n)$

for all $n \geq n_0$. This means that f and g have *the same asymptotic growth*. For example, $3n^2 + 2$ is $\Theta(n^2)$, but we could just as well write that n^2 is $\Theta(3n^2 + 2)$. By supplying an upper bound and a lower bound at the same time, the Θ operator is the most informative of the three, and I will use it when possible.

Rules of the Road

While the definitions of the asymptotic operators can be a bit tough to use directly, they actually lead to some of the simplest math ever. You can drop all multiplicative and additive constants, as well as all other "small parts" of your function, which simplifies things a lot.

As a first step in juggling these asymptotic expressions, let's take a look at some typical asymptotic classes, or *orders*. Table 2-1 lists some of these, along with their names and some typical algorithms with these asymptotic running times, also sometimes called running-time *complexities*. (If your math is a little rusty, you could take a look at the sidebar "A Quick Math Refresher" later in the chapter.) An important feature of this table is that the complexities have been ordered so that each row *dominates* the previous one: If *f* is found higher in the table than *g*, then *f* is $O(g)$.[5]

Table 2-1. *Common Examples of Asymptotic Running Times*

Complexity	Name	Examples, Comments
$\Theta(1)$	Constant	Hash table lookup and modification (see "Black Box" sidebar on dict).
$\Theta(\lg n)$	Logarithmic	Binary search (see Chapter 6). Logarithm base unimportant.[7]
$\Theta(n)$	Linear	Iterating over a list.
$\Theta(n \lg n)$	Loglinear	Optimal sorting of arbitrary values (see Chapter 6). Same as $\Theta(\lg n!)$.
$\Theta(n^2)$	Quadratic	Comparing n objects to each other (see Chapter 3).
$\Theta(n^3)$	Cubic	Floyd and Warshall's algorithms (see Chapters 8 and 9).
$O(nk)$	Polynomial	k nested for loops over n (if k is a positive integer). For any constant $k > 0$.
$\Omega(kn)$	Exponential	Producing every subset of n items ($k = 2$; see Chapter 3). Any $k > 1$.
$\Theta(n!)$	Factorial	Producing every ordering of n values.

■ **Note** Actually, the relationship is even stricter: *f* is *o*(*g*), where the "Little Oh" is a stricter version if "Big Oh." Intuitively, instead of "doesn't grow faster than," it means "grows slower than." Formally, it states that $f(n)/g(n)$ converges to zero as *n* grows to infinity. You don't really need to worry about this, though.

Any polynomial (that is, with any power $k > 0$, even a fractional one) dominates *any* logarithm (that is, with any base), and *any* exponential (with any base $k > 1$) dominates *any* polynomial (see Exercises 2-5 and 2-6). Actually, all logarithms are asymptotically equivalent—they differ only by constant factors (see Exercise 2-4). Polynomials and exponentials, however, have different asymptotic growth depending on their exponents or bases, respectively. So, n^5 grows faster than n^4, and 5^n grows faster than 4^n.

The table primarily uses Θ notation, but the terms *polynomial* and *exponential* are a bit special, because of the role they play in separating *tractable* ("solvable") problems from *intractable* ("unsolvable") ones, as discussed in Chapter 11. Basically, an algorithm with a polynomial running time is considered feasible, while an exponential one is generally useless. Although this isn't entirely true in practice, ($\Theta(n^{100})$ is no more practically useful than $\Theta(2n)$); it is, in many cases, a useful distinction.[6] Because of this division, any running time in $O(n^k)$, for any $k > 0$,

---

[5]For the "Cubic" and "Polynomial" row, this holds only when $k \geq 3$.

[6]Interestingly, once a problem is shown to have a polynomial solution, an *efficient* polynomial solution can quite often be found as well.

[7]I'm using lg rather than log here, but either one is fine.

is called polynomial, even though the limit may not be tight. For example, even though binary search (explained in the "Black Box" sidebar on bisect in Chapter 6) has a running time of $\Theta(\lg n)$, it is still said to be a polynomial-time (or just polynomial) algorithm. Conversely, any running time in $\Omega(kn)$—even one that is, say, $\Theta(n!)$—is said to be exponential.

Now that we have an overview of some important orders of growth, we can formulate two simple rules:

- In a sum, only the dominating summand matters.

  For example, $\Theta(n^2 + n^3 + 42) = \Theta(n^3)$.

- In a product, constant factors don't matter.

  For example, $\Theta(4.2n \lg n) = \Theta(n \lg n)$.

In general, we try to keep the asymptotic expressions as simple as possible, eliminating as many unnecessary parts as we can. For O and Ω, there is a third principle we usually follow:

- Keep your upper or lower limits tight.

  In other words, we try to make the upper limits low and the lower limits high. For example, although n^2 might technically be $O(n^3)$, we usually prefer the tighter limit, $O(n^2)$. In most cases, though, the best thing is to simply use Θ.

A practice that can make asymptotic expressions even more useful is that of using them *instead of actual values*, in arithmetic expressions. Although this is technically incorrect (each asymptotic expression yields a set of functions, after all), it is quite common. For example, $\Theta(n^2) + \Theta(n^3)$ simply means $f + g$, for some (unknown) functions f and g, where f is $\Theta(n^2)$ and g is $\Theta(n^3)$. Even though we cannot find the exact sum $f + g$, because we don't know the exact functions, we *can* find the asymptotic expression to cover it, as illustrated by the following two "bonus rules:"

- $\Theta(f) + \Theta(g) = \Theta(f + g)$

- $\Theta(f) \cdot \Theta(g) = \Theta(f \cdot g)$

Exercise 2-8 asks you to show that these are correct.

Taking the Asymptotics for a Spin

Let's take a look at some simple programs and see whether we can determine their asymptotic running times. To begin with, let's consider programs where the (asymptotic) running time varies only with the problem size, not the specifics of the instance in question. (The next section deals with what happens if the actual contents of the instances matter to the running time.) This means, for example, that if statements are rather irrelevant for now. What's important is loops, in addition to straightforward code blocks. Function calls don't really complicate things; just calculate the complexity for the call and insert it at the right place.

■ **Note**   There is one situation where function calls can trip us up: when the function is recursive. This case is dealt with in Chapters 3 and 4.

The loop-free case is simple: we are executing one statement before another, so their complexities are added. Let's say, for example, that we know that for a list of size n, a call to append is $\Theta(1)$, while a call to insert at position 0 is $\Theta(n)$. Consider the following little two-line program fragment, where nums is a list of size n:

```
nums.append(1)
nums.insert(0,2)
```

We know that the line first takes constant time. At the time we get to the second line, the list size has changed and is now $n + 1$. This means that the complexity of the second line is $\Theta(n + 1)$, which is the same as $\Theta(n)$. Thus, the total running time is the sum of the two complexities, $\Theta(1) + \Theta(n) = \Theta(n)$.

Now, let's consider some simple loops. Here's a plain for loop over a sequence with n elements (numbers, say; for example, seq = range(n)):[8]

```
s = 0
for x in seq:
    s += x
```

This is a straightforward implementation of what the sum function does: It iterates over seq and adds the elements to the starting value in s. This performs a single constant-time operation (s += x) for each of the n elements of seq, which means that its running time is linear, or $\Theta(n)$. Note that the constant-time initialization (s = 0) is dominated by the loop here.

The same logic applies to the "camouflaged" loops we find in list (or set or dict) comprehensions and generator expressions, for example. The following list comprehension also has a linear running-time complexity:

```
squares = [x**2 for x in seq]
```

Several built-in functions and methods also have "hidden" loops in them. This generally applies to any function or method that deals with every element of a container, such as sum or map, for example.

Things get a little bit (but not a lot) trickier when we start nesting loops. Let's say we want to sum up all possible products of the elements in seq; here's an example:

```
s = 0
for x in seq:
    for y in seq:
        s += x*y
```

One thing worth noting about this implementation is that each product will be added twice. If 42 and 333 are both in seq, for example, we'll add both 42*333 and 333*42. That doesn't really affect the running time; it's just a constant factor.

What's the running time now? The basic rule is easy: The complexities of code blocks executed one after the other are just added. The complexities of nested loops are *multiplied*. The reasoning is simple: For each round of the outer loop, the inner one is executed in full. In this case, that means "linear times linear," which is quadratic. In other words, the running time is $\Theta(n \cdot n) = \Theta(n^2)$. Actually, this multiplication rule means that for further levels of nesting, we will just increment the power (that is, the exponent). Three nested linear loops give us $\Theta(n^3)$, four give us $\Theta(n^4)$, and so forth.

The sequential and nested cases can be mixed, of course. Consider the following slight extension:

```
s = 0
for x in seq:
    for y in seq:
        s += x*y
    for z in seq:
        for w in seq:
            s += x-w
```

---

[8]If the elements are ints, the running time of each += is constant. However, Python also support big integers, or longs, which automatically appear when your integers get big enough. This means you can break the constant-time assumption by using really huge numbers. If you're using floats, that won't happen (but see the discussion of float problems near the end of the chapter).

It may not be entirely clear what we're computing here (I certainly have no idea), but we should still be able to find the running time, using our rules. The z-loop is run for a linear number of iterations, and it contains a linear loop, so the total complexity there is quadratic, or $\Theta(n^2)$. The y-loop is clearly $\Theta(n)$. This means that the code block inside the x-loop is $\Theta(n + n^2)$. This entire block is executed for each round of the x-loop, which is run n times. We use our multiplication rule and get $\Theta(n(n + n^2)) = \Theta(n^2 + n^3) = \Theta(n^3)$, that is, cubic. We could arrive at this conclusion even more easily by noting that the y-loop is dominated by the z-loop and can be ignored, giving the inner block a quadratic running time. "Quadratic times linear" gives us cubic.

The loops need not all be repeated $\Theta(n)$ times, of course. Let's say we have two sequences, seq1 and seq2, where seq1 contains n elements and seq2 contains m elements. The following code will then have a running time of $\Theta(nm)$.

```
s = 0
for x in seq1:
    for y in seq2:
        s += x*y
```

In fact, the inner loop need not even be executed the *same number of times* for each iteration of the outer loop. This is where things can get a bit fiddly. Instead of just multiplying two iteration counts, such as n and m in the previous example, we now have to *sum* the iteration counts of the inner loop. What that means should be clear in the following example:

```
seq1 = [[0, 1], [2], [3, 4, 5]]
s = 0
for seq2 in seq1:
    for x in seq2:
        s += x
```

The statement s += x is now performed $2 + 1 + 3 = 6$ times. The length of seq2 gives us the running time of the inner loop, but because it varies, we cannot simply multiply it by the iteration count of the outer loop. A more realistic example is the following, which revisits our original example—multiplying every combination of elements from a sequence:

```
s = 0
n = len(seq)
for i in range(n-1):
    for j in range(i+1, n):
        s += seq[i] * seq[j]
```

To avoid multiplying objects with themselves or adding the same product twice, the outer loop now avoids the last item, and the inner loop iterates over the items only *after* the one currently considered by the outer one. This is actually a lot less confusing than it might seem, but finding the complexity here requires a little bit more care. This is one of the important cases of counting that is covered in the next chapter.[9]

---

[9]Spoiler: The complexity of this example is still $\Theta(n^2)$.

Three Important Cases

Until now, we have assumed that the running time is completely deterministic and dependent only on input size, not on the actual contents of the input. That is not particularly realistic, however. For example, if you were to construct a sorting algorithm, you might start like this:

```
def sort_w_check(seq):
    n = len(seq)
    for i in range(n-1):
        if seq[i] > seq[i+1]:
            break
    else:
        return
    ...
```

A check is performed before getting into the actual sorting: If the sequence is already sorted, the function simply returns.

■ **Note** The optional else clause on a loop in Python is executed if the loop has not been ended prematurely by a break statement.

This means that no matter how inefficient our main sorting is, the running time will always be linear if the sequence is already sorted. No sorting algorithm can achieve linear running time in general, meaning that this "best-case scenario" is an anomaly—and all of a sudden, we can't reliably predict the running time anymore. The solution to this quandary is to be more specific. Instead of talking about a problem in general, we can specify the input more narrowly, and we often talk about one of three important cases:

- **The best case.** This is the running time you get when the input is optimally suited to your algorithm. For example, if the input sequence to sort_w_check were sorted, we would get the best-case running time, which would be linear.

- **The worst case.** This is usually the most useful case—the worst possible running time. This is useful because we normally want to be able to give some guarantees about the efficiency of our algorithm, and this is the best guarantee we can give in general.

- **The average case.** This is a tricky one, and I'll avoid it most of the time, but in some cases it can be useful. Simply put, it's the expected value of the running time, for random input, with a given probability distribution.

In many of the algorithms we'll be working with, these three cases have the same complexity. When they don't, we'll often be working with the worst case. Unless this is stated explicitly, however, no assumptions can be made about which case is being studied. In fact, we may not be restricting ourselves to a single kind of input *at all*. What if, for example, we wanted to describe the running time of sort_w_check *in general*? This is still possible, but we can't be quite as precise.

Let's say the main sorting algorithm we're using after the check is loglinear; that is, it has a running time of $\Theta(n \lg n)$). This is typical and, in fact, optimal in the general case for sorting algorithms. The *best-case* running time of our algorithm is then $\Theta(n)$, when the check uncovers a sorted sequence, and the *worst-case* running time is $\Theta(n \lg n)$. If we want to give a description of the running time in general, however—for any kind of input—we cannot use the Θ notation at all. There is no single function describing the running time; different types of inputs have different running time functions, and these have different asymptotic complexity, meaning we can't sum them up in a single Θ expression.

The solution? Instead of the "twin bounds" of Θ, we supply only an upper or lower limit, using O or Ω. We can, for example, say that sort_w_check has a running time of $O(n \lg n)$. This covers both the best and worst cases. Similarly, we could say it has a running time of $\Omega(n)$. Note that these limits are as tight as we can make them.

■ **Note**   It is perfectly acceptable to use either of our asymptotic operators to describe either of the three cases discussed here. We could very well say that the worst-case running time of sort_w_check is $\Omega(n \lg n)$, for example, or that the best case is $O(n)$.

Empirical Evaluation of Algorithms

The main focus of this book is *algorithm design* and its close relative, *algorithm analysis*. There is, however, another important discipline of algorithmics that can be of vital importance when building real-world systems, and that is *algorithm engineering*, the art of efficiently *implementing* algorithms. In a way, algorithm design can be seen as a way of achieving low asymptotic running time by designing efficient algorithms, while algorithm engineering is focused on reducing the hidden constants in that asymptotic complexity.

Although I may offer some tips on algorithm engineering in Python here and there, it can be hard to predict exactly which tweaks and hacks will give you the best performance for the specific problems you're working on—or, indeed, for your hardware or version of Python. These are exactly the kind of quirks asymptotics are designed to avoid. And in some cases, such tweaks and hacks may not be needed at all, because your program may be fast enough as it is. The most useful thing you can do in many cases is simply to try and see. If you have a tweak you *think* will improve your program, try it! Implement the tweak, and run some experiments. Is there an improvement? And if the tweak makes your code less readable and the improvement is small, is it really worth it?

■ **Note**   This section is about evaluating your programs, not on the engineering itself. For some hints on speeding up Python programs, see Appendix A.

While there are theoretical aspects of so-called experimental algorithmics—that is, experimentally evaluating algorithms and their implementations—that are beyond the scope of this book, I'll give you some practical starting tips that should get you pretty far.

■ **Tip 1**   If possible, don't worry about it.

Worrying about asymptotic complexity can be important. Sometimes, it's the difference between a *solution* and what is, in practice, a *non*solution. Constant factors in the running time, however, are often not all that critical. Try a straightforward implementation of your algorithm first and see whether that's good enough. Actually, you might even try a naïve algorithm first; to quote programming guru Ken Thompson, "When in doubt, use brute force." Brute force, in algorithmics, generally refers to a straightforward approach that just tries every possible solution, running time be damned! If it works, it works.

■ **Tip 2**   For timing things, use timeit.

The `timeit` module is designed to perform relatively reliable timings. Although getting truly trustworthy results, such as those you'd publish in a scientific paper, is a lot of work, `timeit` can help you get "good enough in practice" timings easily. Here's an example:

```
>>> import timeit
>>> timeit.timeit("x = 2 + 2")
0.034976959228515625
>>> timeit.timeit("x = sum(range(10))")
0.92387008666992188
```

The actual timing values you get will quite certainly not be exactly like mine. If you want to time a function (which could, for example, be a test function wrapping parts of your code), it may be even easier to use `timeit` from the shell command line, using the `-m` switch:

```
$ python -m timeit -s"import mymodule as m" "m.myfunction()"
```

There is one thing you should be careful about when using `timeit`. Avoid side effects that will affect repeated execution. The `timeit` function will run your code multiple times for increased precision, and if earlier executions affect later runs, you are probably in trouble. For example, if you time something like `mylist.sort()`, the list would get sorted only the *first* time. The other thousands of times the statement is run, the list will already be sorted, making your timings unrealistically low. The same caution would apply to anything involving generators or iterators that could be exhausted, for example. You can find more details on this module and how it works in the standard library documentation.[10]

■ **Tip 3** To find bottlenecks, use a profiler.

It is a common practice to guess which part of your program needs optimization. Such guesses are quite often wrong. Instead of guessing wildly, let a profiler find out for you! Python comes with a few profiler variants, but the recommended one is cProfile. It's as easy to use as `timeit` but gives more detailed information about where the execution time is spent. If your main function is `main`, you can use the profiler to run your program as follows:

```
import cProfile
cProfile.run('main()')
```

This should print out timing results about the various functions in your program. If the cProfile module isn't available on your system, use `profile` instead. Again, more information is available in the library reference. If you're not so interested in the details of your *implementation* but just want to empirically examine the behavior of your *algorithm* on a given problem instance, the `trace` module in the standard library can be useful—it can be used to count the number of times each statement is executed. You could even visualize the calls of your code using a tool such as Python Call Graph.[11]

■ **Tip 4** Plot your results.

---

[10]https://docs.python.org/library/timeit.html
[11]http://pycallgraph.slowchop.com

Visualization can be a great tool when figuring things out. Two common plots for looking at performance are graphs,[12] for example of problem size versus running time, and *box plots*, showing the distribution of running times. See Figure 2-2 for examples of these. A great package for plotting things with Python is matplotlib (available from http://matplotlib.org).

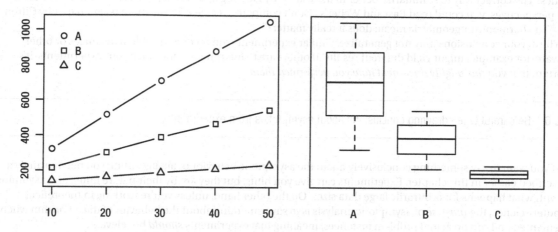

Figure 2-2. Visualizing running times for programs A, B, and C and problem sizes 10–50

■ **Tip 5** Be careful when drawing conclusions based on timing comparisons.

This tip is a bit vague, but that's because there are so many pitfalls when drawing conclusions about which way is better, based on timing experiments. First, any differences you observe may be because of random variations. If you're using a tool such as timeit, this is less of a risk, because it repeats the statement to be timed many times (and even runs the whole experiment multiple times, keeping the best run). Still, there will be random variations, and if the difference between two implementations isn't greater than what can be expected from this randomness, you can't really conclude that they're different. (You can't conclude that they *aren't*, either.)

■ **Note** If you need to draw a conclusion when it's a close call, you can use the statistical technique of *hypothesis testing*. However, for practical purposes, if the difference is so small you're not sure, it probably doesn't matter which implementation you choose, so go with your favorite.

This problem is compounded if you're comparing more than two implementations. The number of pairs to compare increases *quadratically* with the number of versions, as explained in Chapter 3, *drastically* increasing the chance that at least two of the versions will appear freakishly different, just by chance. (This is what's called the *problem of multiple comparisons*.) There are statistical solutions to this problem, but the easiest practical way around it is to repeat the experiment with the two implementations in question. Maybe even a couple of times. Do they still look different?

---

[12]No, not the network kind, which is discussed later in this chapter. The other kind—plots of some measurement for every value of some parameter.

Second, there are issues when comparing averages. At least, you should stick to comparing averages of actual timings. A common practice to get more meaningful numbers when performing timing experiments is to normalize the running time of each program, dividing it by the running time of some standard, simple algorithm. This can indeed be useful but can in some cases make your results less than meaningful. See the paper "How not to lie with statistics: The correct way to summarize benchmark results" by Fleming and Wallace for a few pointers. For some other perspectives, you could read Bast and Weber's "Don't compare averages," or the more recent paper by Citron et al., "The harmonic or geometric mean: does it really matter?"

Third, your conclusions may not generalize. Similar experiments run on other problem instances or other hardware, for example, might yield different results. If others are to interpret or reproduce your experiments, it's important that you *thoroughly document how you performed them.*

■ **Tip 6**   Be careful when drawing conclusions about asymptotics from experiments.

If you want to say something conclusively about the asymptotic behavior of an algorithm, you need to analyze it, as described earlier in this chapter. Experiments can give you hints, but they are by their nature finite, and asymptotics deal with what happens for arbitrarily large data sizes. On the other hand, unless you're working in theoretical computer science, the *purpose* of asymptotic analysis is to say something about the behavior of the algorithm when implemented and run on actual problem instances, meaning that experiments *should* be relevant.

Suppose you *suspect* that an algorithm has a quadratic running time complexity, but you're unable to conclusively prove it. Can you use experiments to support your claim? As explained, experiments (and algorithm engineering) deal mainly with constant factors, but there *is a way*. The main problem is that your hypothesis isn't really testable through experiments. If you claim that the algorithm is, say, $O(n^2)$, no data can confirm or refute this. However, if you make your hypothesis *more specific*, it becomes testable. You might, for example, based on some preliminary results, believe that the running time will never exceed $0.24n^2 + 0.1n + 0.03$ seconds in your setup. Perhaps more realistically, your hypothesis might involve the number of times a given operation is performed, which you can test with the trace module. This *is* a testable—or, more specifically, *refutable*—hypothesis. If you run lots of experiments and you aren't able to find any counter-examples, that supports your hypothesis to some extent. The neat thing is that, indirectly, you're also supporting the claim that the algorithm is $O(n^2)$.

Implementing Graphs and Trees

The first example in Chapter 1, where we wanted to navigate Sweden and China, was typical of problems that can expressed in one of the most powerful frameworks in algorithmics—that of *graphs*. In many cases, if you can formulate what you're working on as a graph problem, you're at least halfway to a solution. And if your problem instances are in some form expressible as *trees*, you stand a good chance of having a really *efficient* solution.

Graphs can represent all kinds of structures and systems, from transportation networks to communication networks and from protein interactions in cell nuclei to human interactions online. You can increase their expressiveness by adding extra data such as *weights* or *distances*, making it possible to represent such diverse problems as playing chess or matching a set of people to as many jobs, with the best possible use of their abilities. Trees are just a special kind of graphs, so most algorithms and representations for graphs will work for them as well. However, because of their special properties (they are connected and have no cycles), some specialized and quite simple versions of both the representations and algorithms are possible. There are plenty of practical structures, such as XML documents or directory hierarchies, that can be represented as trees,[13] so this "special case" is actually quite general.

---

[13]With IDREFs and symlinks, respectively, XML documents and directory hierarchies are actually general graphs.

If your memory of graph nomenclature is a bit rusty or if this is all new to you, take a look at Appendix C. Here are the highlights in a nutshell:

- A graph $G = (V, E)$ consists of a set of *nodes*, V, and *edges* between them, E. If the edges have a direction, we say the graph is *directed*.

- Nodes with an edge between them are *adjacent*. The edge is then *incident* to both. The nodes that are adjacent to v are the *neighbors* of v. The *degree* of a node is the number of edges incident to it.

- A *subgraph* of $G = (V, E)$ consists of a subset of V and a subset of E. A *path* in G is a subgraph where the edges connect the nodes in a sequence, without revisiting any node. A *cycle* is like a path, except that the last edge links the last node to the first.

- If we associate a *weight* with each edge in G, we say that G is a *weighted graph*. The *length* of a path or cycle is the sum of its edge weights, or, for unweighted graphs, simply the number of edges.

- A *forest* is a cycle-free graph, and a connected forest is a *tree*. In other words, a forest consists of one or more trees.

While phrasing your problem in graph terminology gets you far, if you want to implement a solution, you need to represent the graphs as data structures somehow. This, in fact, applies even if you just want to design an algorithm, because you must know what the running times of different operations on your graph representation will be. In some cases, the graph will already be present in your code or data, and no separate structure will be needed. For example, if you're writing a web crawler, automatically collecting information about web sites by following links, the graph is the Web itself. If you have a Person class with a friends attribute, which is a list of other Person instances, then your object model itself is a graph on which you can run various graph algorithms. There are, however, specialized ways of implementing graphs.

In abstract terms, what we are generally looking for is a way of implementing the neighborhood function, $N(v)$, so that N[v] is some form of container (or, in some cases, merely an iterable object) of the neighbors of v. Like so many other books on the subject, I will focus on the two most well-known representations, *adjacency lists* and *adjacency matrices*, because they are highly useful and general. For a discussion of alternatives, see the section "A Multitude of Representations" later in this chapter.

BLACK BOX: DICT AND SET

One technique covered in detail in most algorithm books, and usually taken for granted by Python programmers, is *hashing*. Hashing involves computing some often seemingly random integer value from an arbitrary object. This value can then be used, for example, as an index into an array (subject to some adjustments to make it fit the index range).

The standard hashing mechanism in Python is available through the hash function, which calls the __hash__ method of an object:

```
>>> hash(42)
42
>>> hash("Hello, world!")
-1886531940
```

This is the mechanism that is used in dictionaries, which are implemented using so-called hash tables. Sets are implemented using the same mechanism. The important thing is that the hash value can be constructed in essentially constant time. It's constant with respect to the hash table size but linear as a function of the size of the object being hashed. If the array that is used behind the scenes is large enough, accessing it using a hash value is also $\Theta(1)$ in the average case. The worst-case behavior is $\Theta(n)$, unless we know the values beforehand and can write a custom hash function. Still, hashing is extremely efficient in practice.

What this means to us is that accessing elements of a `dict` or `set` can be assumed to take constant expected time, which makes them highly useful building blocks for more complex structures and algorithms.

Note that the `hash` function is specifically used for use in hash tables. For other uses of hashing, such as in cryptography, there is the standard library module `hashlib`.

Adjacency Lists and the Like

One of the most intuitive ways of implementing graphs is using adjacency lists. Basically, for each node, we can access a list (or set or other container or iterable) of its neighbors. Let's take the simplest way of implementing this, assuming we have *n* nodes, numbered $0 \ldots n{-}1$.

■ **Note**   Nodes can be any objects, of course, or have arbitrary labels or names. Using integers in the range $0 \ldots n{-}1$ can make many implementations easier, though, because the node numbers can easily be used as indices.

Each adjacency (or neighbor) list is then just a list of such numbers, and we can place the lists themselves into a main list of size *n*, indexable by the node numbers. Usually, the ordering of these lists is arbitrary, so we're really talking about using lists to implement adjacency *sets*. The term *list* in this context is primarily historical. In Python we're lucky enough to have a separate set type, which in many cases is a more natural choice.

For an example that will be used to illustrate the various graph representations, see Figure 2-3.

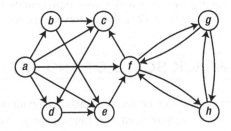

Figure 2-3. *A sample graph used to illustrate various graph representations*

■ **Tip**   For tools to help you visualize your own graphs, see the sidebar "Graph Libraries" later in this chapter.

To begin with, assume that we have numbered the nodes, that is, $a = 0$, $b = 1$, and so forth. The graph can then be represented in a straightforward manner, as shown in Listing 2-1. Just as a convenience, I have assigned the node numbers to variables with the same names as the node labels in the figure. You can, of course, just work with the numbers directly. Which adjacency set belongs to which node is indicated by the comments. If you want, take a minute to confirm that the representation does, indeed, correspond to the figure.

Listing 2-1. A Straightforward Adjacency Set Representation

```
a, b, c, d, e, f, g, h = range(8)
N = [
    {b, c, d, e, f},    # a
    {c, e},             # b
    {d},                # c
    {e},                # d
    {f},                # e
    {c, g, h},          # f
    {f, h},             # g
    {f, g}              # h
]
```

■ **Note**   In Python versions prior to 2.7 (or 3.0), you would write set literals as set([1, 2, 3]) rather than {1, 2, 3}. Note that an empty set is still written set() because {} is an empty dict.

The name N has been used here to correspond with the *N* function discussed earlier. In graph theory, $N(v)$ represents the set of *v*'s neighbors. Similarly, in our code, N[v] is now a set of v's neighbors. Assuming you have defined N as earlier in an interactive interpreter, you can now play around with the graph:

```
>>> b in N[a]   # Neighborhood membership
True
>>> len(N[f])   # Degree
3
```

■ **Tip**   If you have some code in a source file, such as the graph definition in Listing 2-1, and you want to explore it interactively as in the previous example, you can run python with the -i switch, like this:

```
python -i listing_2_1.py
```

This will run the source file and start an interactive interpreter that continues where the source file left of, with any global definitions available for your experimentation.

Another possible representation, which can have a bit less overhead in some cases, is to replace the adjacency sets with actual adjacency *lists*. For an example of this, see Listing 2-2. The same operations are now available, except that membership checking is now $\Theta(n)$. This is a significant slowdown, but that is a problem only if you actually need it, of course. (If all your algorithm does is iterate over neighbors, using set objects would not only be pointless; the overhead would actually be detrimental to the constant factors of your implementation.)

Listing 2-2. Adjacency Lists

```
a, b, c, d, e, f, g, h = range(8)
N = [
    [b, c, d, e, f],    # a
    [c, e],             # b
    [d],                # c
```

```
    [e],                # d
    [f],                # e
    [c, g, h],          # f
    [f, h],             # g
    [f, g]              # h
]
```

It might be argued that this representation is really a collection of *adjacency arrays*, rather than adjacency *lists* in the classical sense, because Python's list type is really a dynamic array behind the covers; see earlier "Black Box" sidebar about list. If you wanted, you could implement a linked list type and use that, rather than a Python list. That would allow you asymptotically cheaper inserts at arbitrary points in each list, but this is an operation you probably will not need, because you can just as easily append new neighbors at the end. The advantage of using list is that it is a well-tuned, fast data structure, as opposed to any list structure you could implement in pure Python.

A recurring theme when working with graphs is that the best representation depends on what you need to *do* with your graph. For example, using adjacency lists (or arrays) keeps the overhead low and lets you efficiently iterate over $N(v)$ for any node v. However, checking whether u and v are neighbors is linear in the minimum of their degrees, which can be problematic if the graph is *dense*, that is, if it has many edges. In these cases, adjacency sets may be the way to go.

■ **Tip** We've also seen that deleting objects from the middle of a Python list is costly. Deleting from the *end* of a list takes constant time, though. If you don't care about the order of the neighbors, you can delete arbitrary neighbors in constant time by overwriting them with the one that is currently last in the adjacency list, before calling the pop method.

A slight variation on this would be to represent the neighbor sets as *sorted lists*. If you aren't modifying the lists much, you can keep them sorted and use bisection (see the "Black Box" sidebar on bisect in Chapter 6) to check for membership, which might lead to slightly less overhead in terms of memory use and iteration time but would lead to a membership check complexity of $\Theta(\lg k)$, where k is the number of neighbors for the given node. (This is still very low. In practice, though, using the built-in set type is a lot less hassle.)

Yet *another* minor tweak on this idea is to use dicts instead of sets or lists. The neighbors would then be keys in this dict, and you'd be free to associate each neighbor (or out-edge) with some extra value, such as an edge weight. How this might look is shown in Listing 2-3, with arbitrary edge weights added.

Listing 2-3. Adjacency dicts with Edge Weights

```
a, b, c, d, e, f, g, h = range(8)
N = [
    {b:2, c:1, d:3, e:9, f:4},    # a
    {c:4, e:3},                   # b
    {d:8},                        # c
    {e:7},                        # d
    {f:5},                        # e
    {c:2, g:2, h:2},              # f
    {f:1, h:6},                   # g
    {f:9, g:8}                    # h
]
```

The adjacency dict version can be used just like the others, with the additional edge weight functionality:

```
>>> b in N[a]   # Neighborhood membership
True
>>> len(N[f])   # Degree
3
>>> N[a][b]     # Edge weight for (a, b)
2
```

If you want, you can use adjacency dicts even if you *don't* have any useful edge weights or the like, of course (using, perhaps, None, or some other placeholder instead). This would give you the main advantages of the adjacency sets, but it would also work with very, very old versions of Python, which don't have the set type.[14]

Until now, the main collection containing our adjacency structures—be they lists, sets, or dicts—has been a list, indexed by the node number. A more flexible approach, allowing us to use arbitrary, hashable, node labels, is to use a dict as this main structure.[15] Listing 2-4 shows what a dict containing adjacency sets would look like. Note that nodes are now represented by characters.

Listing 2-4. A dict with Adjacency Sets

```
N = {
    'a': set('bcdef'),
    'b': set('ce'),
    'c': set('d'),
    'd': set('e'),
    'e': set('f'),
    'f': set('cgh'),
    'g': set('fh'),
    'h': set('fg')
}
```

■ **Note** If you drop the set constructor in Listing 2-4, you end up with adjacency *strings*, which would work as well, as immutable adjacency lists of characters, with slightly lower overhead. It's a seemingly silly representation, but as I've said before, it depends on the rest of your program. Where are you getting the graph data from? Is it already in the form of text, for example? How are you going to use it?

Adjacency Matrices

The other common form of graph representation is the adjacency matrix. The main difference is the following: Instead of listing all neighbors for each node, we have a row (an array) with one position for each *possible* neighbor (that is, one for each node in the graph), and store a value, such as True or False, indicating whether that node is indeed a neighbor. Again, the simplest implementation is achieved using nested lists, as shown in Listing 2-5. Note that this, again, requires the nodes to be numbered from 0 to $V-1$. The truth values used are 1 and 0 (rather than True and False), simply to make the matrix more readable.

---

[14]Sets were introduced in Python 2.3, in the form of the sets module. The built-in set type has been available since Python 2.4.
[15]This, a dictionary with adjacency lists, is what Guido van Rossum uses in his article "Python Patterns—Implementing Graphs," which is found online at https://www.python.org/doc/essays/graphs/.

Listing 2-5. An Adjacency Matrix, Implemented with Nested Lists

```
a, b, c, d, e, f, g, h = range(8)

#     a b c d e f g h

N = [[0,1,1,1,1,1,0,0], # a
     [0,0,1,0,1,0,0,0], # b
     [0,0,0,1,0,0,0,0], # c
     [0,0,0,0,1,0,0,0], # d
     [0,0,0,0,0,1,0,0], # e
     [0,1,0,0,0,0,1,1], # f
     [0,0,0,0,0,1,0,1], # g
     [0,0,0,0,0,1,1,0]] # h
```

The way we'd use this is slightly different from the adjacency lists/sets. Instead of checking whether b is in N[a], you would check whether the matrix cell N[a][b] is true. Also, you can no longer use len(N[a]) to find the number of neighbors, because all rows are of equal length. Instead, use sum:

```
>>> N[a][b]     # Neighborhood membership
1
>>> sum(N[f])  # Degree
3
```

Adjacency matrices have some useful properties that are worth knowing about. First, as long as we aren't allowing self-loops (that is, we're not working with pseudographs), the diagonal is all false. Also, we often implement undirected graphs by adding edges in both directions to our representation. This means that the adjacency matrix for an undirected graph will be symmetric.

Extending adjacency matrices to allow for edge weights is trivial: Instead of storing truth values, simply store the weights. For an edge (u, v), let N[u][v] be the edge weight $w(u, v)$ instead of True. Often, for practical reasons, we let nonexistent edges get an *infinite* weight. This is to guarantee that they will not be included in, say, shortest paths, as long as we can find a path along existent edges. It isn't necessarily obvious how to represent infinity, but we do have some options.

One possibility is to use an illegal weight value, such as None, or -1 if all weights are known to be non-negative. Perhaps more useful in many cases is using a really large value. For integral weights, you could use sys.maxint, even though it's not guaranteed to be the greatest possible value (long ints can be greater). There is, however, one value that is designed to represent infinity among floats: inf. It's not available directly under that name in Python, but you can get it with the expression float('inf').[16]

Listing 2-6 shows what a weight matrix, implemented with nested lists, might look like. I'm using the same weights as I did in Listing 2-3, with inf = float('inf'). Note that the diagonal is still all zero, because even though we have no self-loops, weights are often interpreted as a form of distance, and the distance from a node to itself is customarily zero.

---

[16]This expression is guaranteed to work from Python 2.6 onward. In earlier versions, special floating-point values were platform-dependent, although float('inf') or float('Inf') should work on most platforms.

Listing 2-6. A Weight Matrix with Infinite Weight for Missing Edges

```
a, b, c, d, e, f, g, h = range(8)
inf = float('inf')

#      a    b    c    d    e    f    g    h

W = [[   0,   2,   1,   3,   9,   4, inf, inf], # a
     [ inf,   0,   4, inf,   3, inf, inf, inf], # b
     [ inf, inf,   0,   8, inf, inf, inf, inf], # c
     [ inf, inf, inf,   0,   7, inf, inf, inf], # d
     [ inf, inf, inf, inf,   0,   5, inf, inf], # e
     [ inf, inf,   2, inf, inf,   0,   2,   2], # f
     [ inf, inf, inf, inf, inf,   1,   0,   6], # g
     [ inf, inf, inf, inf, inf,   9,   8,   0]] # h
```

Weight matrices make it easy to access edge weights, of course, but membership checking and finding the degree of a node, for example, or even iterating over neighbors must be done a bit differently now. You need to take the infinity value into account. Here's an example:

```
>>> W[a][b] < inf    # Neighborhood membership
True
>>> W[c][e] < inf    # Neighborhood membership
False
>>> sum(1 for w in W[a] if w < inf) - 1 # Degree
5
```

Note that 1 is subtracted from the degree sum because we don't want to count the diagonal. The degree calculation here is $\Theta(n)$, whereas both membership and degree could easily be found in constant time with the proper structure. Again, you should always keep in mind how you are going to *use* your graph and represent it accordingly.

SPECIAL-PURPOSE ARRAYS WITH NUMPY

The NumPy library has a lot of functionality related to multidimensional arrays. We don't really need much of that for graph representation, but the NumPy array type is quite useful, for example, for implementing adjacency or weight matrices.

Where an empty list-based weight or adjacency matrix for *n* nodes is created, for example, like this

```
>>> N = [[0]*10 for i in range(10)]
```

in NumPy, you can use the zeros function:

```
>>> import numpy as np
>>> N = np.zeros([10,10])
```

The individual elements can then be accessed using comma-separated indices, as in A[u,v]. To access the neighbors of a given node, you use a single index, as in A[u].

If you have a relatively sparse graph, with only a small portion of the matrix filled in, you could save quite a bit of memory by using an even more specialized form of *sparse* matrix, available as part of the SciPy distribution, in the scipy.sparse module.

The NumPy package is available from http://www.numpy.org. You can get SciPy from http://www.scipy.org.

Note that you need to get a version of NumPy that will work with your Python version. If the most recent release of NumPy has not yet "caught up" with the Python version you want to use, you can compile and install directly from the source repository.

You can find more information about how to download, compile, and install NumPy, as well as detailed documentation on its use, on the web site.

Implementing Trees

Any general graph representation can certainly be used to represent trees because trees are simply a special kind of graph. However, trees play an important role on their own in algorithmics, and many special-purpose tree structures have been proposed. Most tree algorithms (even operations on search trees, discussed in Chapter 6) can be understood in terms of general graph ideas, but the specialized tree structures can make them easier to implement.

It is easiest to specialize the representation of rooted trees, where each edge is pointed downward, away from the root. Such trees often represent hierarchical *partitionings* of a data set, where the root represents all the objects (which are, perhaps, kept in the leaf nodes), while each internal node represents the objects found as leaves in the tree rooted at that node. You can even use this intuition directly, making each subtree a list containing its child subtrees. Consider the simple tree shown in Figure 2-4.

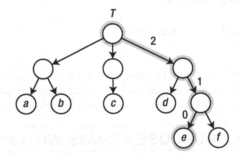

Figure 2-4. A sample tree with a highlighted path from the root to a leaf

We could represent that tree with lists of lists, like this:

```
>>> T = [["a", "b"], ["c"], ["d", ["e", "f"]]]
>>> T[0][1]
'b'
>>> T[2][1][0]
'e'
```

Each list is, in a way, a neighbor (or child) list of the anonymous internal nodes. In the second example, we access the third child of the root, the second child of that child, and finally the first child of that (path highlighted in the figure).

In some cases, we may know the maximum number of children allowed in any internal node. For example, a *binary* tree is one where each internal node has a maximum of two children. We can then use other representations, even objects with an attribute for each child, as shown in Listing 2-7.

Listing 2-7. A Binary Tree Class

```
class Tree:
    def __init__(self, left, right):
        self.left = left
        self.right = right
```

You can use the Tree class like this:

```
>>> t = Tree(Tree("a", "b"), Tree("c", "d"))
>>> t.right.left
'c'
```

You can, for example, use None to indicate missing children, such as when a node has only one child. You are, of course, free to combine techniques such as these to your heart's content (for example, using a child list or child set in each node instance).

A common way of implementing trees, especially in languages that don't have built-in lists, is the "first child, next sibling" representation. Here, each tree node has two "pointers," or attributes referencing other nodes, just like in the binary tree case. However, the first of these refers to the first child of the node, while the second refers to its next sibling, as the name implies. In other words, each tree node refers to a linked list of siblings (its children), and each of these siblings refers to a linked list of its own. (See the "Black Box" sidebar on list, earlier in this chapter, for a brief introduction to linked lists.) Thus, a slight modification of the binary tree in Listing 2-7 gives us a multiway tree, as shown in Listing 2-8.

Listing 2-8. A Multiway Tree Class

```
class Tree:
    def __init__(self, kids, next=None):
        self.kids = self.val = kids
        self.next = next
```

The separate val attribute here is just to have a more descriptive name when supplying a value, such as 'c', instead of a child node. Feel free to adjust this as you want, of course. Here's an example of how you can access this structure:

```
>>> t = Tree(Tree("a", Tree("b", Tree("c", Tree("d")))))
>>> t.kids.next.next.val
'c'
```

And here's what that tree looks like:

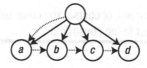

The kids and next attributes are drawn as dotted arrows, while the implicit edges of the trees are drawn solid. Note that I've cheated a bit and not drawn separate nodes for the strings "a", "b", and so on; instead, I've treated them as labels on their parent nodes. In a more sophisticated tree structure, you might have a separate value field in addition to kids, instead of using one attribute for both purposes.

31

Normally, you'd probably use more elaborate code (involving loops or recursion) to traverse the tree structure than the hard-coded path in this example. You'll find more on that in Chapter 5. In Chapter 6, you'll also see some discussion about multiway trees and tree balancing.

THE BUNCH PATTERN

When prototyping or even finalizing data structures such as trees, it can be useful to have a flexible class that will allow you to specify arbitrary attributes in the constructor. In these cases, the Bunch pattern (named by Alex Martelli in the *Python Cookbook*) can come in handy. There are many ways of implementing it, but the gist of it is the following:

```
class Bunch(dict):
    def __init__(self, *args, **kwds):
        super(Bunch, self).__init__(*args, **kwds)
        self.__dict__ = self
```

There are several useful aspects to this pattern. First, it lets you create and set arbitrary attributes by supplying them as command-line arguments:

```
>>> x = Bunch(name="Jayne Cobb", position="Public Relations")
>>> x.name
'Jayne Cobb'
```

Second, by subclassing dict, you get lots of functionality for free, such as iterating over the keys/attributes or easily checking whether an attribute is present. Here's an example:

```
>>> T = Bunch
>>> t = T(left=T(left="a", right="b"), right=T(left="c"))
>>> t.left
{'right': 'b', 'left': 'a'}
>>> t.left.right
'b'
>>> t['left']['right']
'b'
>>> "left" in t.right
True
>>> "right" in t.right
False
```

This pattern isn't useful only when building trees, of course. You could use it for any situation where you'd want a flexible object whose attributes you could set in the constructor.

A Multitude of Representations

Even though there are a host of graph representations in use, most students of algorithms learn only the two types covered (with variations) so far in this chapter. Jeremy P. Spinrad writes, in his book *Efficient Graph Representations*, that most introductory texts are "particularly irritating" to him as a researcher in computer representations of graphs. Their formal definitions of the most well-known representations (adjacency matrices and adjacency lists) are mostly adequate, but the more general explanations are often faulty. He presents, based on misstatements from several texts, the following *strawman's*[17] comments on graph representations:

There are two methods for representing a graph in a computer: adjacency matrices and adjacency lists. It is faster to work with adjacency matrices, but they use more space than adjacency lists, so you will choose one or the other depending on which resource is more important to you.

These statements are problematic in several ways, as Spinrad points out. First, there are *many* interesting ways of representing graphs, not just the two listed here. For example, there are *edge lists* (or *edge sets*), which are simply lists containing all edges as node pairs (or even special edge objects); there are *incidence matrices*, indicating which edges are incident on which nodes (useful for multigraphs); and there are specialized methods for graph types such as trees (described earlier) and interval graphs (not discussed here). Take a look at Spinrad's book for more representations than you will probably ever need. Second, the idea of space/time trade-off is quite misleading: There are problems that can be solved faster with adjacency lists than with adjacency arrays, and for random graphs, adjacency lists can actually use *more* space than adjacency matrices.

Rather than relying on simple, generalized statements such as the previous strawman's comments, you should consider the specifics of your problem. The main criterion would probably be the asymptotic performance for what you're doing. For example, looking up the edge (u, v) in an adjacency matrix is $\Theta(1)$, while iterating over u's neighbors is $\Theta(n)$; in an adjacency list representation, both operations will be $\Theta(d(u))$, that is, on the order of the number of neighbors the node has. If the asymptotic complexity of your algorithm is the same regardless of representation, you could perform some empirical tests, as discussed earlier in this chapter. Or, in many cases, you should simply choose the representation that makes your code clear and easily maintainable.

An important type of graph implementation not discussed so far is more of a nonrepresentation: Many problems have an inherent graphical structure—perhaps even a tree structure—and we can apply graph (or tree) algorithms to them without explicitly constructing a representation. In some cases, this happens when the representation is external to our program. For example, when parsing XML documents or traversing directories in the file system, the tree structures are just there, with existing APIs. In other cases, we are constructing the graph ourselves, but it is *implicit*. For example, if you want to find the most efficient solution to a given configuration of Rubik's Cube, you could define a cube state, as well as operators for modifying that state. Even though you don't explicitly instantiate and store all possible configurations, the *possible states* form an implicit graph (or node set), with the change operators as edges. You could then use an algorithm such as A* or Bidirectional Dijkstra (both discussed in Chapter 9) to find the shortest path to the solved state. In such cases, the neighborhood function $N(v)$ would compute the neighbors on the fly, possibly returning them as a collection or some other form of iterable object.

The final kind of graph I'll touch upon in this chapter is the *subproblem graph*. This is a rather deep concept that I'll revisit several times, when discussing different algorithmic techniques. In short, most problems can be decomposed into *subproblems*: smaller problems that often have quite similar structure. These form the nodes of the subproblem graph, and the dependencies (that is, which subproblems depend on which) form the edges. Although we rarely apply graph algorithms directly to such subproblem graphs (they are more of a conceptual or mental tool), they do offer significant insights into such techniques as divide and conquer (Chapter 6) and dynamic programming (Chapter 8).

---

[17]That is, the comments are inadequate and are presented to demonstrate the problem with most explanations.

GRAPH LIBRARIES

The basic representation techniques described in this chapter will probably be enough for most of your graph algorithm coding, especially with some customization. However, there are some advanced operations and manipulations that can be tricky to implement, such as temporarily hiding or combining nodes, for example. There are third-party libraries out there that take care of some of these things, and several of them are even implemented as C extensions, potentially leading to a performance increase as a bonus. They can also be quite convenient to work with, and some of them have several graph algorithms available out of the box. While a quick web search will probably turn up the most actively supported graph libraries, here are a few to get you started:

- *NetworkX*: `http://networkx.lanl.gov`

- *python-graph*: `http://code.google.com/p/python-graph`

- *Graphine*: `https://gitorious.org/graphine/pages/Home`

- *Graph-tool*: `http://graph-tool.skewed.de`

There is also Pygr, a graph database (`https://github.com/cjlee112/pygr`); Gato, a graph animation toolbox (`http://gato.sourceforge.net`); and PADS, a collection of graph algorithms (`http://www.ics.uci.edu/~eppstein/PADS`).

Beware of Black Boxes

While algorists generally work at a rather abstract level, actually implementing your algorithms takes some care. When programming, you're bound to rely on components that you did not write yourself, and relying on such "black boxes" without any idea of their contents is a risky business. Throughout this book, you'll find sidebars marked "Black Box," briefly discussing various algorithms available as part of Python, either built into the language or found in the standard library. I've included these because I think they're instructive; they tell you something about how Python works, and they give you glimpses of a few more basic algorithms.

However, these are not the only black boxes you'll encounter. Not by a long shot. Both Python and the machinery it rests on use many mechanisms that can trip you up if you're not careful. In general, the more important your program, the more you should mistrust such black boxes and seek to find out what's going on under the covers. I'll show you two traps to be aware of in the following sections, but if you take nothing else away from this section, remember the following:

- When performance is important, rely on actual profiling rather than intuition. You may have hidden bottlenecks, and they may be nowhere near where you suspect they are.

- When correctness is critical, the best thing you can do is calculate your answer more than once, using separate implementations, preferably written by separate programmers.

The latter principle of redundancy is used in many performance-critical systems and is also one of the key pieces of advice given by Foreman S. Acton in his book *Real Computing Made Real*, on preventing calculating errors in scientific and engineering software. Of course, in every scenario, you have to weigh the costs of correctness and performance against their value. For example, as I said before, if your program is fast *enough*, there's no need to optimize it.

The following two sections deal with two rather different topics. The first is about hidden performance traps: operations that seem innocent enough but that can turn a linear operation into a quadratic one. The second is about a topic that is not often discussed in algorithm books, but it is important to be aware of, that is, the many traps of computing with floating-point numbers.

Hidden Squares

Consider the following two ways of looking for an element in a list:

```
>>> from random import randrange
>>> L = [randrange(10000) for i in range(1000)]
>>> 42 in L
False
>>> S = set(L)
>>> 42 in S
False
```

They're both pretty fast, and it might seem pointless to create a set from the list—unnecessary work, right? Well, it depends. If you're going to do *many* membership checks, it might pay off, because membership checks are *linear* for lists and *constant* for sets. What if, for example, you were to gradually add values to a collection and for each step check whether the value was already added? This is a situation you'll encounter repeatedly throughout the book. Using a list would give you *quadratic* running time, whereas using a set would be linear. That's a huge difference. The lesson is that it's important to pick the right built-in data structure for the job.

The same holds for the example discussed earlier, about using a deque rather than inserting objects at the beginning of a list. But there are some examples that are less obvious that can cause just as many problems. Take, for example, the following "obvious" way of gradually building a string, from a source that provides us with the pieces:

```
>>> s = ""
>>> for chunk in string_producer():
...     s += chunk
```

It works, and because of some really clever optimizations in Python, it actually works pretty well, up to a certain size—but then the optimizations break down, and you run smack into quadratic growth. The problem is that (without the optimizations) you need to create a new string for every += operation, copying the contents of the previous one. You'll see a detailed discussion of why this sort of thing is quadratic in the next chapter, but for now, just be aware that this is risky business. A better solution would be the following:

```
>>> chunks = []
>>> for chunk in string_producer():
...     chunks.append(chunk)
...
>>> s = ''.join(chunks)
```

You could even simplify this further like so:

```
>>> s = ''.join(string_producer())
```

This version is efficient for the same reason that the earlier append examples were. Appending allows you to overallocate with a percentage so that the available space grows exponentially, and the append cost is constant when averaged (amortized) over all the operations.

There are, however, quadratic running times that manage to hide even better than this. Consider the following solution, for example:

```
>>> s = sum(string_producer(), '')
Traceback (most recent call last):
    ...
TypeError: sum() can't sum strings [use ''.join(seq) instead]
```

Python complains and asks you to use `''.join()` instead (and rightly so). But what if you're using lists?

```
>>> lists = [[1, 2], [3, 4, 5], [6]]
>>> sum(lists, [])
[1, 2, 3, 4, 5, 6]
```

This works, and it even looks rather elegant, but it really isn't. You see, under the covers, the sum function doesn't know all too much about what you're summing, and it has to do one addition after another. That way, you're right back at the quadratic running time of the += example for strings. Here's a better way:

```
>>> res = []
>>> for lst in lists:
...     res.extend(lst)
```

Just try timing both versions. As long as `lists` is pretty short, there won't be much difference, but it shouldn't take long before the `sum` version is thoroughly beaten.

The Trouble with Floats

Most real numbers have no exact finite representation. The marvelous invention of floating-point numbers makes it *seem* like they do, though, and even though they give us a lot of computing power, they can also trip us up. Big time. In the second volume of *The Art of Computer Programming*, Knuth says, "Floating point computation is by nature inexact, and programmers can easily misuse it so that the computed answers consist almost entirely of 'noise.'"[18]

Python is pretty good at hiding these issues from you, which can be a good thing if you're seeking reassurance, but it may not help you figure out what's really going on. For example, in current version of Python, you'll get the following reasonable behavior:

```
>>> 0.1
0.1
```

It certainly *looks* like the number 0.1 is represented exactly. Unless you know better, it would probably surprise you to learn that it's *not*. Try an earlier version of Python (say, 2.6), where the black box was slightly more transparent:

```
>>> 0.1
0.10000000000000001
```

Now we're getting somewhere. Let's go a step further (feel free to use an up-to-date Python here):

```
>>> sum(0.1 for i in range(10)) == 1.0
False
```

Ouch! That's not what you'd expect without previous knowledge of floats.

The thing is, integers can be represented exactly in any number system, be it binary, decimal, or something else. Real numbers, though, are a bit trickier. The official Python tutorial has an excellent section on this,[19] and David Goldberg has written a great and thorough tutorial paper. The basic idea should be easy enough to grasp if you consider how you'd represent 1/3 as a decimal number. You can't do it exactly, right? If you were using the *ternary* number system, though (base 3), it would be easily represented as 0.1.

---

[18]This kind of trouble has led to disaster more than once (see, for example, `www.ima.umn.edu/~arnold/455.f96/disasters.html`).
[19]`http://docs.python.org/tutorial/floatingpoint.html`.

The first lesson here is to never compare floats for equality. It generally doesn't make sense. Still, in many applications such as computational geometry, you'd very much like to do just that. Instead, you should check whether they are *approximately* equal. For example, you could take the approach of assertAlmostEqual from the unittest module:

```
>>> def almost_equal(x, y, places=7):
...     return round(abs(x-y), places) == 0
...
>>> almost_equal(sum(0.1 for i in range(10)), 1.0)
True
```

There are also tools you can use if you need exact decimal floating-point numbers, for example the decimal module.

```
>>> from decimal import *
>>> sum(Decimal("0.1") for i in range(10)) == Decimal("1.0")
True
```

This module can be essential if you're working with financial data, for example, where you need exact calculations with a certain number of decimals. In certain mathematical or scientific applications, you might find tools such as Sage useful:[20]

```
sage: 3/5 * 11/7 + sqrt(5239)
13*sqrt(31) + 33/35
```

As you can see, Sage does its math symbolically, so you get exact answers, although you can also get decimal approximations, if needed. This sort of symbolic math (or the decimal module) is *nowhere near* as efficient as using the built-in hardware capabilities for floating-point calculations, though.

If you find yourself doing floating-point calculations where accuracy is key (that is, you're not just sorting them or the like), a good source of information is Acton's book, mentioned earlier. Let's just briefly look at an example of his: You can easily lose significant digits if you subtract two nearly equal subexpressions. To achieve higher accuracy, you'll need to rewrite your expressions. Consider, for example, the expression sqrt(x+1)-sqrt(x), where we assume that x is very big. The thing to do would be to get rid of the risky subtraction. By multiplying and dividing by sqrt(x+1)+sqrt(x), we end up with an expression that is mathematically equivalent to the original but where we have eliminated the subtraction: 1.0/(sqrt(x+1)+sqrt(x)). Let's compare the two versions:

```
>>> from math import sqrt
>>> x = 8762348761.13
>>> sqrt(x + 1) - sqrt(x)
5.341455107554793e-06
>>> 1.0/(sqrt(x + 1) + sqrt(x))
5.3414570026237696e-06
```

As you can see, even though the expressions are equivalent mathematically, they give different answers (with the latter being more accurate).

---

[20]Sage is a tool for mathematical computation in Python and is available from http://sagemath.org.

A QUICK MATH REFRESHER

If you're not entirely comfortable with the formulas used in Table 2-1, here is a quick rundown of what they mean: A *power*, like x^y (x to the power of y), is basically x times itself y times. More precisely, x occurs as a factor y times. Here, x is called the *base*, and y is the *exponent* (or sometimes the *power*). So, for example, $3^2 = 9$. Nested powers simply have their exponents multiplied: $(3^2)^4 = 3^8$. In Python, you write powers as x**y.

A *polynomial* is just a sum of several powers, each with its own constant factor. For example, $9x^5 + 2x^2 + x + 3$.

You can have *fractional powers*, too, as a kind of inverse: $(x^y)^{1/y} = x$. These are sometimes called *roots*, such as *the square root* for the inverse of squaring. In Python you can get square roots either using the sqrt function from the math module or simply using x**0.5.

Roots are inverses in that they "undo" the effects of powers. Logarithms are another kind of inverse. Each logarithm has a fixed base; the most common one in algorithmics is the base-2 logarithm, written $\log_2$ or simply lg. (The base-10 logarithm is conventionally written simply log, while the so-called natural logarithm, with base e, is written ln). The logarithm gives us the exponent we need for the given base, so if $n = 2^k$, then lg $n = k$. In Python, you can use the log function of the math module to get logarithms.

The factorial, or $n!$, is calculated as $n \times (n-1) \times (n-2) \ldots 1$. It can be used, among other things, to calculate the number of possible orderings of n elements. There are n possibilities for the first position, and for each of those there are $n-1$ remaining for the second, and so forth.

If this is still about as clear as mud, don't worry. You'll encounter powers and logarithms repeatedly throughout the book, in rather concrete settings, where their meanings should be understandable.

Summary

This chapter started with some important foundational concepts, defining somewhat loosely the notions of algorithms, abstract computers, and problems. This was followed by the two main topics, asymptotic notation and graphs. Asymptotic notation is used to describe the growth of a function; it lets us ignore irrelevant additive and multiplicative constants and focus on the dominating part. This allows us evaluate the salient features of the running time of an algorithm in the abstract, without worrying about the specifics of a given implementation. The three Greek letters O, Ω, and Θ give us upper, lower, and combined asymptotic limits, and each can be used on either of the best-case, worst-case, or average-case behavior of an algorithm. As a supplement to this theoretical analysis, I gave you some brief guidelines for testing your program.

Graphs are abstract mathematical objects, used to represent all kinds of network structures. They consist of a set of nodes, connected by edges, and the edges can have properties such as direction and weight. Graph theory has an extensive vocabulary, and a lot of it is summed up in Appendix C. The second part of the chapter dealt with representing these structures in actual Python programs, primarily using variations of adjacency lists and adjacency matrices, implemented with various combinations of list, dict, and set.

Finally, there was a section about the dangers of black boxes. You should look around for potential traps—things you use without knowing how they work. For example, some rather straightforward uses of built-in Python functions can give you a quadratic running time rather than a linear one. Profiling your program can, perhaps, uncover such performance problems. There are traps related to accuracy as well. Careless use of floating-point numbers, for example, can give you inaccurate answers. If it's critical to get an accurate answer, the best solution may be to calculate it with two separately implemented programs, comparing the results.

If You're Curious …

If you want to know more about Turing machines and the basics of computation, you might like *The Annotated Turing* by Charles Petzold. It's structured as an annotated version of Turing's original paper, but most of the contents are Petzold's explanations of the main concepts, with lots of examples. It's a great introduction to the topic. For an fundamental textbook on computation, you could take a look at *Elements of the Theory of Computation* by Lewis and Papadimitriou. For an easy-to-read, wide-ranging popular introduction to the basic concepts of algorithmics, I recommend *Algorithmic Adventures: From Knowledge to Magic* by Juraj Hromkovič. For more specifics on asymptotic analysis, a solid textbook, such as one of those discussed in Chapter 1, would probably be a good idea. The book by Cormen et al. is considered a good reference work for this sort of thing. You can certainly also find a lot of good information online, such as in Wikipedia,[21] but you should double-check the information before relying on it for anything important, of course. If you want some historical background, you could read Donald Knuth's paper "Big Omicron and big Omega and big Theta," from 1976.

For some specifics on the perils and practices of algorithmic experiments, there are several good papers, such as "Towards a discipline of experimental algorithmics," "On comparing classifiers," "Don't compare averages," "How not to lie with statistics," "Presenting data from experiments in algorithmics," "Visual presentation of data by means of box plots," and "Using finite experiments to study asymptotic performance" (details in the "References" section). For visualizing data, take a look at *Beginning Python Visualization* by Shai Vaingast.

There are many textbooks on graph theory—some are rather technical and advanced (such as those by Bang-Jensen and Gutin, Bondy and Murty, or Diestel, for example), and some are quite readable, even for the novice mathematician (such as the one by West). There are even specialized books on, say, types of graphs (Brandstädt et al., 1999) or graph representations (Spinrad, 2003). If this is a topic that interests you, you shouldn't have any trouble finding lots of material, either in books or online. For more on best practices when using floating-point numbers, take a look at Foreman S. Acton's *Real Computing Made Real: Preventing Errors in Scientific Engineering Calculations*.

Exercises

2-1. When constructing a multidimensional array using Python lists, you need to use `for` loops (or something equivalent, such as list comprehension). Why would it be problematic to create a 10×10 array with the expression `[[0]*10]*10`?

2-2. Assume perhaps a bit unrealistically that allocating a block of memory takes constant time, as long as you leave it uninitialized (that is, it contains whatever arbitrary "junk" was left there the last time it was used). You want an array of n integers, and you want to keep track of whether each entry is unitialized or whether it contains a number you put there. This is a check you want to be able to do in constant time for any entry. How would you do this with only constant time for initialization? And how could you use this to initialize an empty adjacency array in constant time, thereby avoiding an otherwise obligatory quadratic minimum running time?

2-3. Show that O and Ω are inverses of one another; that is, if f is $O(g)$, then g is $\Omega(f)$, and vice versa.

2-4. Logarithms can have different bases, but algorists don't usually care. To see why, consider the equation $\log_b n = (\log_a n)/(\log_a b)$. First, can you see why this is true? Second, why does this mean that we usually don't worry about bases?

2-5. Show that any increasing exponential ($\Theta(k^n)$ for $k > 1$) asymptotically dominates any polynomial ($\Theta(n^j)$ for $j > 0$).

---

[21]http://wikipedia.org

2-6. Show that any polynomial (that is, $\Theta(n^k)$, for any constant $k > 0$) asymptotically dominates any logarithm (that is, $\Theta(lg\ n)$). (Note that the polynomials here include, for example, the square root, for $k = 0.5$.)

2-7. Research or conjecture the asymptotic complexity of various operations on Python lists, such as indexing, item assignment, reversing, appending, and inserting (the latter two discussed in the "Black Box" sidebar on list). How would these be different in a linked list implementation? What about, for example, list.extend?

2-8. Show that the expressions $\Theta(f) + \Theta(g) = \Theta(f + g)$ and $\Theta(f) \cdot \Theta(g) = \Theta(f \cdot g)$ are correct. Also, try your hand at $\max(\Theta(f), \Theta(g)) = \Theta(\max(f, g)) = \Theta(f + g)$.

2-9. In Appendix C, you'll find a numbered list of statements about trees. Show that they are equivalent.

2-10. Let T be an arbitrary rooted tree with at least three nodes, where each internal node has exactly two children. If T has n leaves, how many internal nodes does it have?

2-11. Show that a directed acyclic graph (DAG) can have any underlying structure whatsoever. Put differently, any undirected graph can be the underlying graph for a DAG, or, given a graph, you can always orient its edges so that the resulting digraph is a DAG.

2-12. Consider the following graph representation: You use a dictionary and let each key be a pair (tuple) of two nodes, with the corresponding value set to the edge weight. For example W[u, v] = 42. What would be the advantages and disadvantages of this representation? Could you supplement it to mitigate the downsides?

References

Acton, F. S. (2005). *Real Computing Made Real: Preventing Errors in Scientific and Engineering Calculations*. Dover Publications, Inc.

Bang-Jensen, J. and Gutin, G. (2002). *Digraphs: Theory, Algorithms and Applications*. Springer.

Bast, H. and Weber, I. (2005). Don't compare averages. In Nikoletseas, S. E., editor, WEA, volume 3503 of Lecture Notes in Computer Science, pages 67–76. Springer.

Bondy, J. A. and Murty, U. S. R. (2008). *Graph Theory*. Springer.

Brandstädt, A., Le, V. B., and Spinrad, J. P. (1999). Graph Classes: A Survey. SIAM Monographs on Discrete Mathematics and Applications. Society for Industrial and Applied Mathematics.

Citron, D., Hurani, A., and Gnadrey, A. (2006). The harmonic or geometric mean: Does it really matter? ACM SIGARCH Computer Architecture News, 34(4):18–25.

Diestel, R. (2005). *Graph Theory*, third edition. Springer.

Fleming, P. J. and Wallace, J. J. (1986). How not to lie with statistics: The correct way to summarize benchmark results. Commun. ACM, 29(3):218–221.

Goldberg, D. (1991). What every computer scientist should know about floating-point arithmetic. *ACM Computing Surveys* (CSUR), 23(1):5–48. http://docs.sun.com/source/806-3568/ncg_goldberg.html.

Hromkovič, J. (2009). *Algorithmic Adventures: From Knowledge to Magic*. Springer.

Knuth, D. E. (1976). Big Omicron and big Omega and big Theta. ACM SIGACT News, 8(2):18–24.

Lewis, H. R. and Papadimitriou, C. H. (1998). *Elements of the Theory of Computation*, second edition. Prentice Hall, Inc.

Martelli, A., Ravenscroft, A., and Ascher, D., editors (2005). *Python Cookbook*, second edition. O'Reilly & Associates, Inc.

Massart, D. L., Smeyers-Verbeke, J., Capron, X., and Schlesier, K. (2005). Visual presentation of data by means of box plots. *LCGC Europe*, 18:215–218.

McGeoch, C., Sanders, P., Fleischer, R., Cohen, P. R., and Precup, D. (2002). Using finite experiments to study asymptotic performance. *Lecture Notes in Computer Science*, 2547:94–126.

Moret, B. M. E. (2002). Towards a discipline of experimental algorithmics. In Data Structures, Near Neighbor Searches, and Methodology: Fifth and Sixth DIMACS Implementation Challenges, volume 59 of DIMACS: Series in Discrete Mathematics and Theoretical Computer Science, pages 197–214. Americal American Mathematical Society.

Petzold, C. (2008). *The Annotated Turing: A Guided Tour Through Alan Turing's Historic Paper on Computability and the Turing Machine*. Wiley Publishing, Inc.

Salzberg, S. (1997). On comparing classifiers: Pitfalls to avoid and a recommended approach. *Data Mining and Knowledge Discovery*, 1(3):317–328.

Sanders, P. (2002). Presenting data from experiments in algorithmics. *Lecture Notes in Computer Science*, 2547:181–196.

Spinrad, J. P. (2003). *Efficient Graph Representations*. Fields Institute Monographs. American Mathematical Society.

Turing, A. M. (1937). On computable numbers, with an application to the Entscheidungsproblem. *Proceedings of the London Mathematical Society*, s2-42(1):230–265.

Vaingast, S. (2009). *Beginning Python Visualization: Crafting Visual Transformation Scripts*. Apress.

West, D. B. (2001). *Introduction to Graph Theory*, second edition. Prentice Hall, Inc.

■ ■ ■

## CHAPTER 3

Counting 101

The greatest shortcoming of the human race is our inability to understand the exponential function.

— Dr. Albert A. Bartlett, World Population Balance
Board of Advisors

At one time, when the famous mathematician Carl Friedrich Gauss was in primary school, his teacher asked the pupils to add all the integers from 1 to 100 (or, at least, that's the most common version of the story). No doubt, the teacher expected this to occupy his students for a while, but Gauss produced the result almost immediately. This might seem to require lightning-fast mental arithmetic, but the truth is, the actual calculation needed is quite simple; the trick is really understanding the problem.

After the previous chapter, you may have become a bit jaded about such things. "Obviously, the answer is $\Theta(1)$," you say. Well, yes ... but let's say we were to sum the integers from 1 to n? The following sections deal with some important problems like this, which will crop up again and again in the analysis of algorithms. The chapter may be a bit challenging at times, but the ideas presented are crucial and well worth the effort. They'll make the rest of the book that much easier to understand. First, I'll give you a brief explanation of the concept of sums and some basic ways of manipulating them. Then come the two major sections of the chapter: one on two fundamental sums (or combinatorial problems, depending on your perspective) and the other on so-called recurrence relations, which you'll need to analyze recursive algorithms later. Between these two is a little section on subsets, combinations, and permutations.

■ **Tip** There's quite a bit of math in this chapter. If that's not your thing, you might want to skim it for now and come back to it as needed while reading the rest of the book. (Several of the ideas in this chapter will probably make the rest of the book easier to understand, though.)

The Skinny on Sums

In Chapter 2, I explained that when two loops are nested and the complexity of the inner one varies from iteration to iteration of the outer one, you need to start summing. In fact, sums crop up all over the place in algorithmics, so you might as well get used to thinking about them. Let's start with the basic notation.

More Greek

In Python, you might write the following:

```
x*sum(S) == sum(x*y for y in S)
```

With mathematical notation, you'd write this:

$$x \cdot \sum_{y \in S} y = \sum_{y \in S} xy$$

Can you see why this equation is true? This capital sigma can seem a bit intimidating if you haven't worked with it before. It is, however, no scarier than the sum function in Python; the syntax is just a bit different. The sigma itself indicates that we're doing a sum, and we place information about what to sum above, below, and to the right of it. What we place to the right (in the previous example, y and xy) are the values to sum, while we put a description of which items to iterate over below the sigma.

Instead of just iterating over objects in a set (or other collection), we can supply limits to the sum, like with range (except that both limits are inclusive). The general expression "sum $f(i)$ for $i = m$ to n" is written like this:

$$\sum_{i=m}^{n} f(i)$$

The Python equivalent would be as follows:

```
sum(f(i) for i in range(m, n+1))
```

It might be even easier for many programmers to think of these sums as a mathematical way of writing loops:

```
s = 0
for i in range(m, n+1):
    s += f(i)
```

The more compact mathematical notation has the advantage of giving us a better overview of what's going on.

Working with Sums

The sample equation in the previous section, where the factor x was moved inside the sum, is just one of several useful "manipulation rules" you're allowed to use when working with sums. Here's a summary of two of the most important ones (for our purposes):

$$c \cdot \sum_{i=m}^{n} f(i) = \sum_{i=m}^{n} c \cdot f(i)$$

Multiplicative constants can be moved in or out of sums. That's also what the initial example in the previous section illustrated. This is the same rule of *distributivity* that you've seen in simpler sums many times: $c(f(m) + \ldots + f(n)) = cf(m) + \ldots + cf(n)$.

$$\sum_{i=m}^{n} f(i) + \sum_{i=m}^{n} g(i) = \sum_{i=m}^{n} (f(i) + g(i))$$

Instead of adding two sums, you can sum their added contents. This just means that if you're going to sum up a bunch of stuff, it doesn't matter how you do it; that is,

```
sum(f(i) for i in S) + sum(g(i) for i in S)
```

is exactly the same as `sum(f(i) + g(i) for i in S)`.[1] This is just an instance of *associativity*. If you want to subtract two sums, you can use the same trick. If you want, you can pretend you're moving the constant factor –1 into the second sum.

A Tale of Two Tournaments

There are plenty of sums that you might find useful in your work, and a good mathematics reference will probably give you the solution to most of them. There are, however, two sums, or combinatorial problems, that cover the majority of the cases you'll meet in this book—or, indeed, most basic algorithm work.

I've been explaining these two ideas repeatedly over the years, using many different examples and metaphors, but I think one rather memorable (and I hope understandable) way of presenting them is as two forms of *tournaments*.

■ **Note**   There is, actually, a technical meaning of the word *tournament* in graph theory (a complete graph, where each edge is assigned a direction). That's not what I'm talking about here, although the concepts are related.

There are many types of tournaments, but let's consider two quite common ones, with rather catchy names. These are the *round-robin tournament* and the *knockout tournament*.

In a round-robin tournament (or, specifically, a *single* round-robin tournament), each contestant meets each of the others in turn. The question then becomes, how many matches or fixtures do we need, if we have, for example, n knights jousting? (Substitute your favorite competitive activity here, if you want.) In a knockout tournament, the competitors are arranged in pairs, and only the winner from each pair goes on to the next round. Here there are more questions to ask: For n knights, how many rounds do we need, and how many matches will there be, in total?

Shaking Hands

The round-robin tournament problem is exactly equivalent to another well-known puzzler: If you have n algorists meeting at a conference and they all shake hands, how many handshakes do you get? Or, equivalently, how many edges are there in a complete graph with n nodes (see Figure 3-1)? It's the same count you get in any kind of "all against all" situations. For example, if you have n locations on a map and want to find the two that are closest to each other, the simple (brute-force) approach would be to compare all points with all others. To find the running time to this algorithm, you need to solve the round-robin problem. (A more efficient solution to this *closest pair* problem is presented in Chapter 6.)

---

[1] As long as the functions don't have any side effects, that is, but behave like mathematical functions.

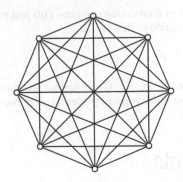

Figure 3-1. A complete graph, illustrating a round-robin tournament, or the handshake problem

You may very well have surmised that there will be a quadratic number of matches. "All against all" sounds an awful lot like "all times all," or n^2. Although it is true that the result is quadratic, the exact form of n^2 isn't entirely correct. Think about it—for one thing, only a knight with a death wish would ever joust against himself (or herself). And if Sir Galahad has crossed swords with Sir Lancelot, there is no need for Sir Lancelot to return the favor, because they surely have both fought *each other*, so a single match will do. A simple "*n* times *n*" solution ignores both of these factors, assuming that each knight gets a separate match against *each of the knights* (including themselves). The fix is simple: Let each knight get a match against all the *others*, yielding $n(n-1)$, and then, because we now have counted each match twice (once for each participating knight), we divide by two, getting the final answer, $n(n-1)/2$, which is indeed $\Theta(n^2)$.

Now we've counted these matches (or handshakes or map point comparisons) in one relatively straightforward way—and the answer may have seemed obvious. Well, what lies ahead may not exactly be rocket science either, but rest assured, there is a point to all of this . . . for now we count them all in a *different* way, which must yield the same result.

This other way of counting is this: The first knight jousts with $n-1$ others. Among the remaining, the second knight jousts with $n-2$. This continues down to the next to last, who fights the last match, against the last knight (who then fights zero matches against the zero remaining knights). This gives us the sum $n-1 + n-2 + ... + 1 + 0$, or `sum(i for i in range(n))`. We've counted each match only once, so the sum must yield the same count as before:

$$\sum_{i=0}^{n-1} i = \frac{n(n-1)}{2}$$

I could certainly just have given you that equation up front. I hope the extra packaging makes it slightly more meaningful to you. Feel free to come up with other ways of explaining this equation (or the others throughout this book), of course. For example, the insight often attributed to Gauss, in the story that opened this chapter, is that the sum of 1 through 100 can be calculated "from the outside," pairing 1 with 100, 2 with 99, and so forth, yielding 50 pairs that all sum to 101. If you generalize this to the case of summing from 0 to $n-1$, you get the same formula as before. And can you see how all this relates to the lower-left half, below the diagonal, of an adjacency matrix?

■ **Tip** An *arithmetic series* is a sum where the difference between any two consecutive numbers is a constant. Assuming this constant is positive, the sum will always be quadratic. In fact, the sum of i^k, where $i = 1 \ldots n$, for some positive constant k, will always be $\Theta(n^{k+1})$. The handshake sum is just a special case.

The Hare and the Tortoise

Let's say our knights are 100 in number and that the tournament staff are still a bit tired from last year's round robin. That's quite understandable, as there would have been 4,950 matches. They decide to introduce the (more efficient) knockout system and want to know how many matches they'll need. The solution can be a bit tricky to find ... or *blindingly* obvious, depending on how you look at it. Let's look at it from the slightly tricky angle first. In the first round, all the knights are paired, so we have $n/2$ matches. Only half of them go on to the second round, so there we have $n/4$ matches. We keep on halving until the last match, giving us the sum $n/2 + n/4 + n/8 + ... + 1$, or, equivalently, $1 + 2 + 4 + ... + n/2$. As you'll see later, this sum has numerous applications, but what is the answer?

Now comes the blindingly obvious part: In each match, one knight is knocked out. All except the winner are knocked out (and they're knocked out only once), so we need $n-1$ matches to leave only one man (or woman) standing. The tournament structure is illustrated as a rooted tree in Figure 3-2, where each leaf is a knight and each internal node represents a match. In other words:

$$\sum_{i=0}^{h-1} 2^i = n - 1$$

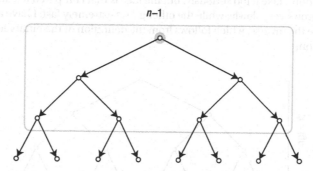

Figure 3-2. *A perfectly balanced rooted, binary tree with n leaves and n-1 internal nodes (root highlighted). The tree may be undirected, but the edges can be thought of as implicitly pointing downward, as shown*

The upper limit, $h-1$, is the number of rounds, or h the height of the binary tree, so $2^h = n$. Couched in this concrete setting, the result may not seem all that strange, but it sort of is, really. In a way, it forms the basis for the myth that there are more people alive than all those who have ever died. Even though the myth is wrong, it's not that far-fetched! The growth of the human population is roughly exponential and currently doubles about every 50 years. Let's say we had a fixed doubling time throughout history; this is not really true,[2] but play along. Or, to simplify things even further, assume that each generation is twice as populous as the one before.[3] Then, if the current generation consists of n individuals, the sum of *all generations past* will, as we have seen, be only $n-1$ (and, of course, some of them would still be alive).

---

[2]http://prb.org/Articles/2002/HowManyPeoplehaveEverLivedonEarth.aspx.
[3]If this were true, the human population would have consisted of one man and one woman about 32 generations ago ... but, as I said, play along.

WHY BINARY WORKS

We've just seen that when summing up the powers of two, you always get one less than the *next* power of two. For example, $1 + 2 + 4 = 8 - 1$, or $1 + 2 + 4 + 8 = 16 - 1$, and so forth. This is, from one perspective, exactly why binary counting works. A binary number is a string of zeros and ones, each of which determines whether a given power of two should be included in a sum (starting with $2^0 = 1$ on the far right). So, for example, 11010 would be $2 + 8 + 16 = 26$. Summing the first h of these powers would be equivalent to a number like 1111, with h ones. This is as far as we get with these h digits, but luckily, if these sum to $n-1$, the next power will be exactly n. For example, 1111 is 15, and 10000 is 16. (Exercise 3-3 asks you to show that this property lets you represent any positive integer as a binary number.)

Here's the first lesson about doubling, then: A perfectly balanced binary tree (that is, a rooted tree where all internal nodes have two children and all leaves have the same depth) has $n-1$ internal nodes. There are, however, a couple more lessons in store for you on this subject. For example, I still haven't touched upon the hare and tortoise hinted at in the section heading.

The hare and the tortoise are meant to represent the width and height of the tree, respectively. There are several problems with this image, so don't take it too seriously, but the idea is that compared to each other (actually, as a *function* of each other), one grows very slowly, while the other grows extremely fast. I have already stated that $n = 2^h$, but we might just as easily use the inverse, which follows from the definition of the binary logarithm: $h = \lg n$; see Figure 3-3 for an illustration.

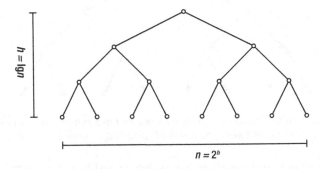

Figure 3-3. *The height and width (number of leaves) of a perfectly balanced binary tree*

Exactly how enormous the difference between these two is can be hard to fathom. One strategy would be to simply accept that they're extremely different—meaning that logarithmic-time algorithms are super-sweet, while exponential-time algorithms are totally bogus—and then try to pick up examples of these differences wherever you can. Let me give you a couple of examples to get started. First let's do a game I like to call "think of a particle." I think of one of the particles in the visible universe, and you try to guess which one, using only yes/no questions. OK? Shoot!

This game might seem like sheer insanity, but I assure you, that has more to do with the practicalities (such that keeping track of which particles have been ruled out) than with the number of alternatives. To simplify these practicalities a bit, let's do "think of a number" instead. There are many estimates for the number of particles we're talking about, but 10^{90} (that is, a one followed by 90 zeros) would probably be quite generous. You can even play this game yourself, with Python:

```
>>> from random import randrange
>>> n = 10**90
>>> p = randrange(10**90)
```

You now have an unknown particle (particle number p) that you can investigate with yes/no questions (no peeking!). For example, a rather unproductive question might be as follows:

```
>>> p == 52561927548332435090282755894003484804019842420331
False
```

If you've ever played "twenty questions," you've probably spotted the flaw here: I'm not getting enough "bang for the buck." The best I can do with a yes/no question is halving the number of remaining options. So, for example:

```
>>> p < n/2
True
```

Now we're getting somewhere! In fact, if you play your cards right (sorry for mixing metaphors—or, rather, games) and keep halving the remaining interval of candidates, you can actually find the answer in just under 300 questions. You can calculate this for yourself:

```
>>> from math import log
>>> log(n, 2) # base-two logarithm
298.97352853986263
```

If that seems mundane, let it sink in for a minute. By asking only yes/no questions, you can pinpoint *any particle in the observable universe in about five minutes!* This is a classic example of why logarithmic algorithms are so super-sweet. (Now try saying "logarithmic algorithm" ten times, fast.)

■ **Note**   This is an example of *bisection*, or *binary search*, one of the most important and well-known logarithmic algorithms. It is discussed further in the "Black Box" sidebar on the `bisect` module in Chapter 6.

Let's now turn to the bogus flip side of logarithms and ponder the equally weird exponentials. Any example for one is automatically an example for the other—if I asked you to start with a single particle and then double it repeatedly, you'd quickly fill up the observable universe. (It would take about 299 doublings, as we've seen.) This is just a slightly more extreme version of the old *wheat and chessboard* problem. If you place one grain of wheat on the first square of a chessboard, two on the second, four on the third, and so forth, how much wheat would you get?[4] The number of grains in the last square would be 2^{63} (we started at $2^0 = 1$) and according to the sum illustrated in Figure 3-2, this means the total would be $2^{64}-1 = 18{,}446{,}744{,}073{,}709{,}551{,}615$, or, for wheat, about $5 \cdot 10^{14}$kg. That's a *lot* of grain—hundreds of times the world's total yearly production! Now imagine that instead of grain, we're dealing with *time*. For a problem size n, your program uses $2n$ milliseconds. For $n = 64$, the program would then run for $584{,}542{,}046$ *years!* To finish today, that program would have had to run since long before there were any vertebrates around to write the code. Exponential growth can be scary.

By now, I hope you're starting to see how exponentials and logarithms are the inverses of one another. Before leaving this section, however, I'd like to touch upon another duality that arises when we're dealing with our hare and tortoise: The number of doublings from 1 to n is, of course, the same as the number of halvings from n to 1. This is painfully obvious, but I'll get back to it when we start working with recurrences in a bit, where this idea will be quite helpful. Take a look at Figure 3-4. The tree represents the doubling from 1 (the root node) to n (the n leaves), but I have also added some labels below the nodes, representing the halvings from n to 1. When working with recurrences,

---

[4]Reportedly, this is the reward that the creator of chess asked for and was granted ... although he was told to count each grain he received. I'm guessing he changed his mind.

these magnitudes will represent portions of the problem instance, and the related amount of work performed, for a set of recursive calls. When we try to figure out the total amount of work, we'll be using both the height of the tree and the amount of work performed at each level. We can see these values as a fixed number of tokens being passed down the tree. As the number of nodes doubles, the number of tokens per node is halved; the number of tokens per level remains n. (This is similar to the ice cream cones in the hint for Exercise 2-10.)

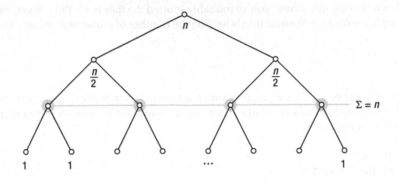

Figure 3-4. *Passing n tokens down through the levels of a binary tree*

■ **Tip**   A *geometric* (or *exponential*) *series* is a sum of k_i, where $i = 0...n$, for some constant k. If k is greater than 1, the sum will always be $\Theta(k^{n+1})$. The doubling sum is just a special case.

Subsets, Permutations, and Combinations

The number of binary strings of length k should be easy to compute, if you've read the previous section. You can, for example, think of the strings as directions for walking from the root to leaves in a perfectly balanced binary tree. The string length, k, will be the height of the tree, and the number of possible strings will equal the number of leaves, 2^k. Another, more direct way to see this is to consider the number of possibilities at each step: The first bit can be zero or one, and for each of these values, the second *also* has two possibilities, and so forth. It's like k nested for loops, each running two iterations; the total count is still 2^k.

┌───┐
│   **PSEUDOPOLYNOMIALITY**   │
└───┘

Nice word, huh? It's the name for certain algorithms with exponential running time that "look like" they have polynomial running times and that may even act like it in practice. The issue is that we can describe the running time as a function of many things, but we reserve the label "polynomial" for algorithms whose running time is a polynomial *in the size of the input*—the amount of storage required for a given instance, in some reasonable encoding. Let's consider the problem of primality checking or answering the question "Is this number a prime?" This problem has a polynomial solution, but it's not entirely obvious ... and the entirely obvious way to attack it actually yields a nonpolynomial solution.

Here's my stab at a relatively direct solution:

```
def is_prime(n):
    for i in range(2,n):
        if n % i == 0: return False
    return True
```

The algorithm here is to step through all positive integers smaller than *n*, starting at 2, checking whether they divide *n*. If one of them does, *n* is not a prime; otherwise, it is. This might *seem* like a polynomial algorithm, and indeed its running time is $\Theta(n)$. The problem is that *n* is not a legitimate problem size!

It can certainly be useful to describe the running time as linear in *n*, and we could even say that it is polynomial ... in *n*. But that does *not* give us the right to say that it is polynomial ... period. The size of a problem instance consisting of *n* is not *n*, but rather the number of bits needed to *encode n*, which, if *n* is a power of 2, is roughly lg *n* + 1. For an arbitrary positive integer, it's actually `floor(log(n,2))+1`.

Let's call this problem size (the number of bits) *k*. We then have roughly $n = 2^{k-1}$. Our precious $\Theta(n)$ running time, when rewritten as a function of the actual problem size, becomes $\Theta(2^k)$, which is clearly exponential.[5] There are other algorithms like this, whose running times are polynomial only when interpreted as a function of a numeric value in the input. (One example is a solution to the *knapsack* problem, discussed in Chapter 8.) These are all called *pseudopolynomial*.

The relation to subsets is quite direct: If each bit represents the presence or absence of an object from a size-*k* set, each bit string represents one of the 2^k possible subsets. Perhaps the most important consequence of this is that any algorithm that needs to check every subset of the input objects necessarily has an exponential running time complexity.

Although subsets are essential to know about for an algorist, permutations and combinations are perhaps a bit more marginal. You will probably run into them, though (and it wouldn't be Counting 101 without them), so here is a quick rundown of how to count them.

Permutations are orderings. If *n* people queue up for movie tickets, how many possible lines can we get? Each of these would be a permutation of the queuers. As mentioned in Chapter 2, the number of permutations of *n* items is the factorial of *n*, or *n*! (that includes the exclamation mark and is read "*n* factorial"). You can compute *n*! by multiplying *n* (the number of possible people in the first position) by *n*–1 (remaining options for the second position) and *n*–2 (third ...), and so forth, down to 1:

$$n! = n \cdot (n-1) \cdot (n-2) \cdot \ldots \cdot 2 \cdot 1$$

Not many algorithms have running times involving *n*! (although we'll revisit this count when discussing limits to sorting, in Chapter 6). One silly example with an expected running time of $\Theta(n \cdot n!)$ is the sorting algorithm *bogosort*, which consists of repeatedly shuffling the input sequence into a random order and checking whether the result is sorted.

Combinations are a close relative of both permutations and subsets. A combination of *k* elements, drawn from a set of *n*, is sometimes written *C*(*n*, *k*), or, for those of a mathematical bent:

$$\binom{n}{k}$$

---

[5]Do you see where the −1 in the exponent went? Remember, $2^{a+b} = 2^a \cdot 2^b$...

This is also called the *binomial coefficient* (or sometimes the *choose function*) and is read "*n* choose *k*." While the intuition behind the factorial formula is rather straightforward, how to compute the binomial coefficient isn't quite as obvious.[6]

Imagine (once again) you have *n* people lined up to see a movie, but there are only *k* places left in the theater. How many possible subsets of size *k* could possibly get in? That's exactly $C(n, k)$, of course, and the metaphor may do some work for us here. We already know that we have *n*! possible orderings of the entire line. What if we just count all these possibilities and let in the first *k*? The only problem then is that we've counted the subsets too many times. A certain group of *k* friends could stand at the head of the line in a lot of the permutations; in fact, we could allow these friends to stand in any of their *k*! possible permutations, and the remainder of the line could stand in any of their $(n-k)$! possible permutations without affecting who's getting in. Aaaand this gives us the answer!

$$\binom{n}{k} = \frac{n!}{k!(n-k)!}$$

This formula just counts all possible permutations of the line (*n*!) and divides by the number of times we count each "winning subset," as explained.

■ **Note**   A different perspective on calculating the binomial coefficient will be given in Chapter 8, on dynamic programming.

Note that we're selecting a *subset* of size *k* here, which means selection *without replacement*. If we just draw lots *k* times, we might draw the same person more than once, effectively "replacing" them in the pool of candidates. The number of possible results then would simply be *nk*. The fact that $C(n, k)$ counts the number of possible subsets of size *k* and 2^n counts the number of possible subsets in total gives us the following beautiful equation:

$$\sum_{k=0}^{n} \binom{n}{k} = 2^n$$

And that's it for these combinatorial objects. It's time for slightly more mind-bending prospect: solving equations that refer to themselves!

■ **Tip**   For most math, the interactive Python interpreter is quite handy as a calculator; the math module contains many useful mathematical functions. For symbolic manipulation like we've been doing in this chapter, though, it's not very helpful. There are symbolic math tools for Python, though, such as Sage (available from http://sagemath.org). If you just need a quick tool for solving a particularly nasty sum or recurrence (see the next section), you might want to check out Wolfram Alpha (http://wolframalpha.com). You just type in the sum or some other math problem, and out pops the answer.

---

[6]Another thing that's not immediately obvious is where the name "binomial coefficient" comes from. You might want to look it up. It's kind of neat.

Recursion and Recurrences

I'm going to assume that you have at least *some* experience with recursion, although I'll give you a brief intro in this section and even more detail in Chapter 4. If it's a completely foreign concept to you, it might be a good idea to look it up online or in some fundamental programming textbook.

The thing about recursion is that a function—directly or indirectly—calls itself. Here's a simple example of how to recursively sum a sequence:

```
def S(seq, i=0):
    if i == len(seq): return 0
    return S(seq, i+1) + seq[i]
```

Understanding how this function works and figuring out its running time are two closely related tasks. The functionality is pretty straightforward: The parameter i indicates where the sum is to start. If it's beyond the end of the sequence (the *base case*, which prevents infinite recursion), the function simply returns 0. Otherwise, it adds the value at position i to the sum of the remaining sequence. We have a constant amount of work in each execution of S, excluding the recursive call, and it's executed once for each item in the sequence, so it's pretty obvious that the running time is linear. Still, let's look into it:

```
def T(seq, i=0):
    if i == len(seq): return 1
    return T(seq, i+1) + 1
```

This new T function has virtually the same structure as S, but the values it's working with are different. Instead of returning a *solution to a subproblem*, like S does, it returns *the cost of finding that solution*. In this case, I've just counted the number of times the if statement is executed. In a more mathematical setting, you would count any relevant operations and use $\Theta(1)$ instead of 1, for example. Let's take these two functions out for a spin:

```
>>> seq = range(1,101)
>>> S(seq)
5050
```

What do you know, Gauss was right! Let's look at the running time:

```
>>> T(seq)
101
```

Looks about right. Here, the size n is 100, so this is $n+1$. It seems like this should hold in general:

```
>>> for n in range(100):
...     seq = range(n)
...     assert T(seq) == n+1
```

There are no errors, so the hypothesis does seem sort of plausible.

What we're going to work on now is how to find nonrecursive versions of functions such as T, giving us definite running time complexities for recursive algorithms.

Doing It by Hand

To describe the running time of recursive algorithms mathematically, we use recursive equations, called *recurrence relations*. If our recursive algorithm is like S in the previous section, then the recurrence relation is defined somewhat like T. Because we're working toward an asymptotic answer, we don't care about the constant parts, and we implicitly assume that $T(k) = \Theta(1)$, for some constant k. That means we can ignore the base cases when setting up our equation (unless they *don't* take a constant amount of time), and for S, our T can be defined as follows:

$$T(n) = T(n-1) + 1$$

This means that the time it takes to compute S(seq, i), which is $T(n)$, is equal to the time required for the recursive call S(seq, i+1), which is $T(n-1)$, plus the time required for the access seq[i], which is constant, or $\Theta(1)$. Put another way, we can reduce the problem to a smaller version of itself, from size n to $n-1$, in constant time and then solve the smaller subproblem. The total time is the sum of these two operations.

■ **Note**   As you can see, I use 1 rather than $\Theta(1)$ for the extra work (that is, time) outside the recursion. I could use the theta as well; as long as I describe the result asymptotically, it won't matter much. In this case, using $\Theta(1)$ might be risky, because I'll be building up a sum $(1 + 1 + 1 ...)$, and it would be easy to mistakenly simplify this sum to a constant if it contained asymptotic notation (that is, $\Theta(1) + \Theta(1) + \Theta(1) ...$).

Now, how do we *solve* an equation like this? The clue lies in our implementation of T as an executable function. Instead of having Python run it, we can simulate the recursion ourselves. The key to this whole approach is the following equation:

$$
\begin{aligned}
T(n) &= \boxed{T(n-1)} + 1 \\
&= \boxed{T(n-2)+1} + 1 \\
&= T(n-2) + 2
\end{aligned}
$$

The two subformulas I've put in boxes are identical, which is sort of the point. My rationale for claiming that the two boxes are the same lies in our original recurrence, for if ...

$$T(n) = T(n-1) + 1$$

... then:

$$\boxed{T(n-1)} = \boxed{T(n-2)+1}$$

I've simply replaced n with $n-1$ in the original equation (of course, $T((n-1)-1) = T(n-2)$), and *voilà*, we see that the boxes are equal. What we've done here is to use the definition of T with a smaller parameter, which is, essentially, what happens when a recursive call is evaluated. So, expanding the recursive call from $T(n-1)$, the first box, to $T(n-2) + 1$, the second box, is essentially simulating or "unraveling" one level of recursion. We still have the recursive call $T(n-2)$ to contend with, but we can deal with that in the same way!

$$
\begin{aligned}
T(n) &= T(n-1) + 1 \\
&= \boxed{T(n-2)} + 2 \\
&= \boxed{T(n-3)+1} + 2 \\
&= T(n-3) + 3
\end{aligned}
$$

The fact that $T(n-2) = T(n-3) + 1$ (the two boxed expressions) again follows from the original recurrence relation. It's at this point we should see a pattern: Each time we reduce the parameter by one, the sum of the work (or time) we've unraveled (outside the recursive call) goes *up* by one. If we unravel $T(n)$ recursively i steps, we get the following:

$$T(n) = T(n-i) + i$$

This is *exactly* the kind of expression we're looking for—one where the level of recursion is expressed as a variable i. Because all these unraveled expressions are equal (we've had equations every step of the way), we're free to set i to any value we want, as long as we don't go past the base case (for example, $T(1)$), where the original recurrence relation is no longer valid. What we do is go *right up to* the base case and try to make $T(n-i)$ into $T(1)$, because we know, or implicitly assume, that $T(1)$ is $\Theta(1)$, which would mean we had solved the entire thing. And we can easily do that by setting $i = n-1$:

$$
\begin{aligned}
T(n) &= T(n-(n-1)) + (n-1) \\
&= T(1) + n - 1 \\
&= \Theta(1) + n - 1 \\
&= \Theta(n)
\end{aligned}
$$

We have now, with perhaps more effort than was warranted, found that S has a linear running time, as we suspected. In the next section, I'll show you how to use this method for a couple of recurrences that aren't quite as straightforward.

■ **Caution**   This method, called the method of *repeated substitutions* (or sometimes the *iteration method*), is perfectly valid, if you're careful. However, it's quite easy to make an unwarranted assumption or two, *especially* in more complex recurrences. This means you should probably treat the result as a *hypothesis* and then check your answer using the techniques described in the section "Guessing and Checking" later in this chapter.

A Few Important Examples

The general form of the recurrences you'll normally encounter is $T(n) = a \cdot T(g(n)) + f(n)$, where a represents the number of recursive calls, $g(n)$ is the size of each subproblem to be solved recursively, and $f(n)$ is any extra work done in the function, in addition to the recursive calls.

■ **Tip**   It's certainly possible to formulate recursive algorithms that don't fit this schema, for example if the subproblem sizes are different. Such cases won't be dealt with in this book, but some pointers for more information are given in the section "If You're Curious ...," near the end of this chapter.

Table 3-1 summarizes some important recurrences—one or two recursive calls on problems of size $n-1$ or $n/2$, with either constant or linear additional work in each call. You've already seen recurrence number 1 in the previous section. In the following, I'll show you how to solve the last four using repeated substitutions, leaving the remaining three (2 to 4) for Exercises 3-7 to 3-9.

Table 3-1. *Some Basic Recurrences with Solutions, as Well as Some Sample Applications*

#	Recurrence	Solution	Example Applications
1	$T(n) = T(n-1) + 1$	$\Theta(n)$	Processing a sequence, for example, with reduce
2	$T(n) = T(n-1) + n$	$\Theta(n^2)$	Handshake problem
3	$T(n) = 2T(n-1) + 1$	$\Theta(2n)$	Towers of Hanoi
4	$T(n) = 2T(n-1) + n$	$\Theta(2n)$	
5	$T(n) = T(n/2) + 1$	$\Theta(\lg n)$	Binary search (see the "Black Box" sidebar on bisect in Chapter 6)
6	$T(n) = T(n/2) + n$	$\Theta(n)$	Randomized select, average case (see Chapter 6)
7	$T(n) = 2T(n/2) + 1$	$\Theta(n)$	Tree traversal (see Chapter 5)
8	$T(n) = 2T(n/2) + n$	$\Theta(n \lg n)$	Sorting by divide and conquer (see Chapter 6)

Before we start working with the last four recurrences (which are all examples of divide and conquer recurrences, explained more in detail later in this chapter and in Chapter 6), you might want to refresh your memory with Figure 3-5. It summarizes the results I've discussed so far about binary trees; sneakily enough, I've already given you all the tools you need, as you'll see in the following text.

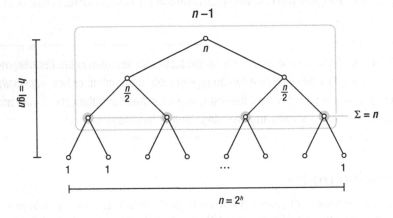

Figure 3-5. *A summary of some important properties of perfectly balanced binary trees*

■ **Note**   I've already mentioned the assumption that the base case has constant time ($T(k) = t_0$, $k \leq n_0$, for some constants t_0 and n_0). In recurrences where the argument to T is n/b, for some constant b, we run up against another technicality: The argument really should be an integer. We could achieve that by rounding (using floor and ceil all over the place), but it's common to simply ignore this detail (really assuming that n is a power of b). To remedy the sloppiness, you should check your answers with the method described in "Guessing and Checking" later in this chapter.

Look at recurrence 5. There's only one recursive call, on half the problem, and a constant amount of work in addition. If we see the full recursion as a tree (a *recursion tree*), this extra work ($f(n)$) is performed in each node, while the structure of the recursive calls is represented by the edges. The total amount of work ($T(n)$) is the sum of $f(n)$ over all the nodes (or those involved). In this case, the work in each node is constant, so we need to count only the number of nodes. Also, we have only *one* recursive call, so the full work is equivalent to a path from the root to a leaf. It should be obvious that $T(n)$ is logarithmic, but let's see how this looks if we try to unravel the recurrence, step-by-step:

$$T(n) = T(n/2) + 1$$
$$= \{T(n/4) + 1\} + 1$$
$$= \{T(n/8) + 1\} + 1 + 1$$

The curly braces enclose the part that is equivalent to the recursive call ($T(...)$) in the previous line. This stepwise unraveling (or repeated substitution) is just the first step of our solution method. The general approach is as follows:

1.   Unravel the recurrence until you see a pattern.

2.   Express the pattern (usually involving a sum), using a line number variable, i.

3.   Choose i so the recursion reaches its base case (and solve the sum).

The first step is what we have done already. Let's have a go at step 2:

$$T(n) = T(n/2^i) + \sum_{k=1}^{i} 1$$

I hope you agree that this general form captures the pattern emerging from our unraveling: For each unraveling (each line further down), we halve the problem size (that is, double the divisor) and add another unit of work (another 1). The sum at the end is a bit silly. We know we have i ones, so the sum is clearly just i. I've written it as a sum to show the general pattern of the method here.

To get to the base case of the recursion, we must get $T(n/2^i)$ to become, say, $T(1)$. That just means we have to halve our way from n to 1, which should be familiar by now: The recursion height is logarithmic, or $i = \lg n$. Insert that into the pattern, and you get that $T(n)$ is, indeed, $\Theta(\lg n)$.

The unraveling for recurrence 6 is quite similar, but here the sum is slightly more interesting:

$$T(n) = T(n/2) + n$$
$$= \{T(n/4) + n/2\} + n$$
$$= \{T(n/8) + n/4\} + n/2 + n$$

$$\vdots$$

$$= T(n/2^i) + \sum_{k=0}^{i-1} (n/2^k)$$

If you're having trouble seeing how I got to the general pattern, you might want to ponder it for a minute. Basically, I've just used the sigma notation to express the sum $n + n/2 + \ldots + n/(2^{i-1})$, which you can see emerging in the early unraveling steps. Before worrying about solving the sum, we once again set $i = \lg n$. Assuming that $T(1) = 1$, we get the following:

$$T(n) = 1 + \sum_{k=0}^{\lg n - 1} (n/2^k) = \sum_{k=0}^{\lg n} (n/2^k)$$

The last step there is just because $n/2^{\lg n} = 1$, so we can include the lonely 1 into the sum.

Now: Does this sum look familiar? Once again, take a look at Figure 3-5: If k is a *height*, then $n/2^k$ is the number of nodes at that height (we're halving our way from the leaves to the root). That means the sum is equal to the number of nodes, which is $\Theta(n)$.

Recurrences 7 and 8 introduce a wrinkle: multiple recursive calls. Recurrence 7 is similar to recurrence 5: Instead of counting the nodes on *one* path from root to leaves, we now follow *both* child edges from each node, so the count is equal to the number of nodes, or $\Theta(n)$. Can you see how recurrences 6 and 7 are just counting the same nodes in two different ways? I'll use our solution method on recurrence 8; the procedure for number 7 is very similar but worth checking:

$$
\begin{aligned}
T(n) &= 2T(n/2) + n \\
&= 2\{2T(n/4) + n/2\} + n \\
&= 2(2\{2T(n/8) + n/4\} + n/2) + n
\end{aligned}
$$

$$\vdots$$

$$= 2^i T(n/2^i) + n \cdot i$$

As you can see, the twos keep piling up in front, resulting in the factor of 2^i. The situation does seem a bit messy inside the parentheses, but luckily, the halvings and doublings even out perfectly: The $n/2$ is inside the first parentheses and is multiplied by 2; $n/4$ is multiplied by 4, and in general, $n/2^i$ is multiplied by 2^i, meaning that we're left with a sum of i repetitions of n, or simply $n \cdot i$. Once again, to get the base case, we choose $i = \lg n$:

$$T(n) = 2^{\lg n} T(n/2^{\lg n}) + n \cdot \lg n = n + n \lg n$$

In other words, the running time is $\Theta(n \lg n)$. Can even this result be seen in Figure 3-5? You bet! The work in the root node of the recursion tree is n; in each of the two recursive calls (the child nodes), this is halved. In other words, the work in each node is equal to the labels in Figure 3-5. We know that each row then sums to n, and we know there are $\lg n + 1$ rows of nodes, giving us a grand sum of $n \lg n + n$, or $\Theta(n \lg n)$.

Guessing and Checking

Both recursion and induction will be discussed in depth in Chapter 4. One of my main theses there is that they are like mirror images of one another; one perspective is that induction shows you why recursion works. In this section, I restrict the discussion to showing that our solutions to *recurrences* are correct (rather than discussing the recursive algorithms themselves), but it should still give you a glimpse of how these things are connected.

As I said earlier in this chapter, the process of unraveling a recurrence and "finding" a pattern is somewhat subject to unwarranted assumption. For example, we often assume that n is an integer power of two so that a recursion depth of exactly $\lg n$ is attainable. In most common cases, these assumptions work out just fine, but to be sure that a solution is correct, you should check it. The nice thing about being able to check the solution is that you can just conjure up a solution by guesswork or intuition and then (ideally) show that it's right.

■ **Note**   To keep things simple, I'll stick to the Big Oh in the following and work with upper limits. You can show the lower limits (and get Ω or Θ) in a similar manner.

Let's take our first recurrence, $T(n) = T(n-1) + 1$. We want to check whether it's correct that $T(n)$ is $O(n)$. As with experiments (discussed in Chapter 1), we can't really get where we want with asymptotic notation; we have to be more specific and insert some constants, so we try to verify that $T(n) \leq cn$, for some an arbitrary $c \geq 1$. Per our standard assumptions, we set $T(1) = 1$. So far, so good. But what about larger values for n?

This is where the induction comes in. The idea is quite simple: We start with $T(1)$, where we *know* our solution is correct, and then we try to show that it also applies to $T(2)$, $T(3)$, and so forth. We do this generically by proving an *induction step*, showing that if our solution is correct for $T(n-1)$, it will also be true for $T(n)$, for $n > 1$. This step would let us go from $T(1)$ to $T(2)$, from $T(2)$ to $T(3)$, and so forth, just like we want.

The key to proving an inductive step is the assumption (in this case) that we've got it right for $T(n-1)$. This is precisely what we use to get to $T(n)$, and it's called the *inductive hypothesis*. In our case, the inductive hypothesis is that $T(n-1) \leq c(n-1)$ (for some c), and we want to show that this carries over to $T(n)$:

$$
\begin{aligned}
T(n) &= \boxed{T(n-1)} + 1 \\
&\leq \boxed{c(n-1)} + 1 \qquad &&\text{We assume that } T(n-1) \leq c(n-1) \\
&= cn - c + 1 \\
&\leq cn &&\text{We know that } c \geq 1, so - c + 1 \leq 0
\end{aligned}
$$

I've highlighted the use of the induction hypotheses with boxes here: I replace $T(n-1)$ with $c(n-1)$, which (by the induction hypothesis) I know is a greater (or equally great) value. This makes the replacement safe, as long as I switch from an equality sign to "less than or equal" between the first and second lines. Some basic algebra later, and I've shown that the assumption $T(n-1) \leq c(n-1)$ leads to $T(n) \leq cn$, which (consequently) leads to $T(n+1) \leq c(n+1)$, and so forth. Starting at our base case, $T(1)$, we have now shown that $T(n)$ is, in general, $O(n)$.

The basic divide and conquer recurrences aren't much harder. Let's do recurrence 8 (from Table 3-1). This time, let's use something called *strong induction*. In the previous example, I only assumed something about the previous value ($n-1$, so-called weak *induction*); now, my induction hypothesis will be about *all smaller numbers*. More specifically, I'll assume that $T(k) \leq ck \lg k$ for all positive integers $k < n$ and show that this leads to $T(n) \leq cn \lg n$. The basic idea is still the same—our solution will still "rub off" from $T(1)$ to $T(2)$, and so forth—it's just that we get a little bit more to work with. In particular, we now hypothesize something about $T(n/2)$ as well, not just $T(n-1)$. Let's have a go:

$$
\begin{aligned}
T(n) &= 2T(n/2) + n \\
&\leq c((n/2)\lg(n/2)) + n \qquad &&\text{Assuming } T(k) \leq c(k \lg k) \text{ for } k = n/2 < n \\
&= c((n/2)(\lg n - \lg 2)) + n &&\lg(n/2) = \lg n - \lg 2 \\
&= c((n/2)\lg n - n/2) + n &&\lg 2 = 1 \\
&= n \lg n &&\text{Just set } c = 2
\end{aligned}
$$

As before, by assuming that we've already shown our result for smaller parameters, we show that it also holds for $T(n)$.

■ **Caution** Be wary of asymptotic notation in recurrences, especially for the recursive part. Consider the following (false) "proof" that $T(n) = 2T(n/2) + n$ means that $T(n)$ is $O(n)$, using the Big Oh directly in our induction hypothesis:

$$T(n) = 2 \cdot T(n/2) + n = 2 \cdot O(n/2) + n = O(n)$$

There are many things wrong with this, but the most glaring problem is, perhaps, that the induction hypothesis needs to be specific to individual values of the parameter ($k = 1, 2...$), but asymptotic notation necessarily applies to the entire function.

DOWN THE RABBIT HOLE (OR CHANGING OUR VARIABLE)

A word of warning: The material in this sidebar may be a bit challenging. If you already have your head full with recurrence concepts, it might be a good idea to revisit it at a later time.

In some (probably rare) cases, you may come across a recurrence that looks something like the following:

$$T(n) = aT(n^{1/b}) + f(n)$$

In other words, the subproblem sizes are b-roots of the original. *Now* what do you do? Actually, we can move into "another world" where the recurrence is easy! This other world must, of course, be some reflection of the real world, so we can get a solution to the original recurrence when we come back.

Our "rabbit hole" takes the form of what is called a *variable change*. It's actually a coordinated change, where we replace both T (to, say, S) and n (to m) so that our recurrence is really the same as before—we've just written it in a different way. What we want is to change $T(n^{1/b})$ into $S(m/b)$, which is easier to work with. Let's try a specific example, using a square root:

$$T(n) = 2T(n^{1/2}) + \lg n$$

How can we get $T(n^{1/2}) = S(m/2)$? A hunch might tell us that to get from powers to products, we need to involve logarithms. The trick here is to set $m = \lg n$, which in turn lets us insert $2m$ instead of n in the recurrence:

$$T(2m) = 2T((2^m)^{1/2}) + m = 2T(2^{m/2}) + m$$

By setting $S(m) = T(2^m)$, we can hide that power, and bingo! We're in Wonderland:

$$S(m) = 2S(m/2) + m$$

This should be easy to solve by now: $T(n) = S(m)$ is $\Theta(m \lg m) = \Theta(\lg n \cdot \lg \lg n)$.

In the first recurrence of this sidebar, the constants a and b may have other values, of course (and f may certainly be less cooperative), leaving us with $S(m) = aS(m/b) + g(m)$ (where $g(m) = f(2^m)$). You could hack away at this using repeated substitution, or you could use the cookie-cutter solutions given in the next section, because they are specifically suited to this sort of recurrence.

The Master Theorem: A Cookie-Cutter Solution

Recurrences corresponding to many of so-called divide and conquer algorithms (discussed in Chapter 6) have the following form (where $a \geq 1$ and $b > 1$):

$$T(n) = aT(n/b) + f(n)$$

The idea is that you have a recursive calls, each on a given percentage ($1/b$) of the dataset. In addition to the recursive calls, the algorithm does $f(n)$ units of work. Take a look at Figure 3-6, which illustrates such an algorithm. In our earlier trees, the number 2 was all-important, but now we have *two* important constants, a and b. The problem size allotted to each node is divided by b for each level we descend; this means that in order to reach a problem size of 1 (in the leaves), we need a height of $\log_b n$. Remember, this is the power to which b must be raised in order to get n.

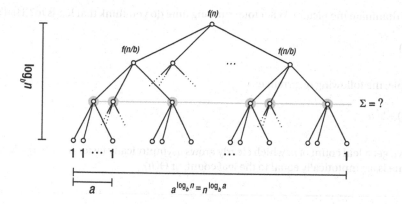

Figure 3-6. *A perfectly balanced, regular multiway (a-way) tree illustrating divide and conquer recurrences*

However, each internal node has a children, so the increase in the node count from level to level doesn't necessarily counteract the decrease in problem size. This means that the number of leaf nodes won't necessarily be n. Rather, the number of nodes increases by a factor a for each level, and with a height of $\log_b n$, we get a width of $a^{\log_b n}$. However, because of a rather convenient calculation rule for logarithms, we're allowed to switch a and n, yielding $n^{\log_b a}$ leaves. Exercise 3-10 asks you to show that this is correct.

The goal in this section is to build three cookie-cutter solutions, which together form the so-called master theorem. The solutions correspond to three possible scenarios: Either the majority of the work is performed (that is, most of the time is spent) in the *root node*, it is primarily performed in the *leaves*, or it is *evenly distributed* among the rows of the recursion tree. Let's consider the three scenarios one by one.

In the first scenario, most of the work is performed in the root, and by "most" I mean that it dominates the running time asymptotically, giving us a total running time of $\Theta(f(n))$. But how do we know that the root dominates? This happens if the work shrinks by (at least) a constant factor from level to level and if the root does more work (asymptotically) than the leaves. More formally:

$$af(n/b) \le cf(n),$$

for some $c < 1$ and large n, and

$$f(n) \in \Omega(n^{\log_b a + \varepsilon}),$$

for some constant $\varepsilon > 0$. This just means that $f(n)$ grows *strictly faster* than the number of leaves (which is why I've added the ε in the exponent of the leaf count formula). Take, for example, the following:

$$T(n) = 2T(n/3) + n.$$

Here, $a = 2$, $b = 3$ and $f(n) = n$. To find the leaf count, we need to calculate $\log_3 2$. We could do this by using the expression log 2/log 3 on a standard calculator, but in Python we can use the log function from the math module, and we find that log(2,3) is a bit less than 0.631. In other words, we want to know whether $f(n) = n$ is $\Omega(n^{0.631})$, which it clearly is, and this tells us that $T(n) = \Theta(f(n)) = \Theta(n)$. A shortcut here would be to see that b was greater than a, which could have told us immediately that n was the dominating part of the expression. Do you see why?

We can turn the root-leaf relationship on its head as well:

$$f(n) \in O(n^{\log_b a - \varepsilon})$$

Now the leaves dominate the picture. What total running time do you think that leads to? That's right:

$$T(n) \in \Theta(n^{\log_b a})$$

Take, for example, the following recurrence:

$$T(n) = 2T(n/2) + \lg n$$

Here $a = b$, so we get a leaf count of n, which clearly grows asymptotically faster than $f(n) = \lg n$. This means that the final running time is asymptotically equal to the leaf count, or $\Theta(n)$.

■ **Note**   To establish dominance for the root, we needed the extra requirement $af(n/b) \leq cf(n)$, for some $c < 1$. To establish leaf dominance, there is no similar requirement.

The last case is where the work in the root and the leaves has the same asymptotic growth:

$$f(n) \in \Theta(n^{\log_b a})$$

This then becomes the sum of every level of the tree (it neither increases nor decreases from root to leaves), which means that we can multiply it by the logarithmic height to get the total sum:

$$T(n) \in \Theta(n^{\log_b a} \lg n)$$

Take, for example, the following recurrence:

$$T(n) = 2T(n/4) + \sqrt{n}$$

The square root may seem intimidating, but it's just another power, namely, $n^{0.5}$. We have $a = 2$ and $b = 4$, giving us $\log_b a = \log_4 2 = 0.5$. What do you know—the work is $\Theta(n^{0.5})$ in both the root and the leaves, and therefore in every row of the tree, yielding the following total running time:

$$T(n) \in \Theta(n^{\log_b a} \lg n) = \Theta(\sqrt{n} \lg n).$$

Table 3-2 sums up the three cases of the master theorem, in the order they are customarily given: Case 1 is when the leaves dominate; case 2 is the "dead race," where all rows have the same (asymptotic) sum; and in case 3, the root dominates.

Table 3-2. *The Three Cases of the Master Theorem*

Case	Condition	Solution	Example
1	$f(n) \in O(n^{\log_b a - \varepsilon})$	$T(n) \in \Theta(n^{\log_b a})$	$T(n) = 2T(n/2) + \lg n$
2	$f(n) \in \Theta(n^{\log_b a})$	$T(n) \in \Theta(n^{\log_b a} \lg n)$	$T(n) = 2T(n/4) + \sqrt{n}$
3	$f(n) \in \Omega(n^{\log_b a + \varepsilon})$	$T(n) \in \Theta(f(n))$	$T(n) = 2T(n/3) + n$

So What Was All *That* About?

OK, there is a lot of math here but not a lot of coding so far. What's the point of all these formulas? Consider, for a moment, the Python programs in Listings 3-1 and 3-2.[7] (You can find a fully commented version of the mergesort function in Listing 6-6.) Let's say these were new algorithms, so you couldn't just search for their names on the Web, and your task was to determine which had the better asymptotic running time complexity.

Listing 3-1. Gnome Sort, An Example Sorting Algorithm

```python
def gnomesort(seq):
    i = 0
    while i < len(seq):
        if i == 0 or seq[i-1] <= seq[i]:
            i += 1
        else:
            seq[i], seq[i-1] = seq[i-1], seq[i]
            i -= 1
```

Listing 3-2. Merge Sort, Another Example Sorting Algorithm

```python
def mergesort(seq):
    mid = len(seq)//2
    lft, rgt = seq[:mid], seq[mid:]
    if len(lft) > 1: lft = mergesort(lft)
    if len(rgt) > 1: rgt = mergesort(rgt)
    res = []
    while lft and rgt:
        if lft[-1] >=rgt[-1]:
            res.append(lft.pop())
        else:
            res.append(rgt.pop())
    res.reverse()
    return (lft or rgt) + res
```

---

[7] Merge sort is a classic, first implemented by computer science legend John von Neumann on the EDVAC in 1945. You'll learn more about that and other similar algorithms in Chapter 6. Gnome sort was invented in 2000 by Hamid Sarbazi-Azad, under the name Stupid sort.

Gnome sort contains a single while loop and an index variable that goes from 0 to len(seq)-1, which might tempt us to conclude that it has a linear running time, but the statement i -= 1 in the last line would indicate otherwise. To figure out how long it runs, you need to understand something about how it works. Initially, it scans from a from the left (repeatedly incrementing i), looking for a position i where seq[i-1] is greater than seq[i], that is, two values that are in the wrong order. At this point, the else part kicks in.

The else clause swaps seq[i] and seq[i-1] and decrements i. This behavior will continue until, once again, seq[i-1] <= seq[i] (or we reach position 0) and order is restored. In other words, the algorithm alternately scans upward in the sequence for an out-of-place (that is, too small) element and moves that element down to a valid position by repeated swapping. What's the cost of all this? Let's ignore the average case and focus on the best and worst. The best case occurs when the sequence is sorted: gnomesort will just scan through a without finding anything out of place and then terminate, yielding a running time of $\Theta(n)$.

The worst case is a little less straightforward but not much. Note that once we find an element that is out of place, all elements before that point are already sorted, and moving the new element into a correct position won't scramble them. That means the number of sorted elements will increase by one each time we discover a misplaced element, and the next misplaced element will have to be further to the right. The worst possible cost of finding and moving a misplaced element into place is proportional to its position, so the worst running time could possibly get is $1 + 2 + \ldots + n{-}1$, which is $\Theta(n^2)$. This is a bit hypothetical at the moment—I've shown it can't get worse than this, but can it ever get this bad?

Indeed it can. Consider the case when the elements are sorted in descending order (that is, reversed with respect to what we want). Then every element is in the wrong place and will have to be moved all the way to the start, giving us the quadratic running time. So, in general, the running time of gnome sort is $\Omega(n)$ and $O(n^2)$, and these are tight bounds representing the best and worst cases, respectively.

Now, take a look at merge sort (Listing 3-2). It is a bit more complicated than gnome sort, so I'll postpone explaining how it manages to sort things until Chapter 6. Luckily, we can analyze its running time without understanding how it works! Just look at the overall structure. The input (seq) has a size of n. There are two recursive calls, each on a subproblem of $n/2$ (or as close as we can get with integer sizes). In addition, there is some work performed in a while loop and in res.reverse(); Exercise 3-11 asks you to show that this work is $\Theta(n)$. (Exercise 3-12 asks you what happens if you use pop(0) instead of pop().) This gives us the well-known recurrence number 8, $T(n) = 2T(n/2) + \Theta(n)$, which means that the running time of merge sort is $\Theta(n \lg n)$, regardless of the input. This means that if we're expecting the data to be almost sorted, we might prefer gnome sort, but in general we'd probably be much better off scrapping it in favor of merge sort.

■ **Note** Python's sorting algorithm, timsort, is a naturally adaptive version of merge sort. It manages to achieve the linear best-case running time while keeping the loglinear worst case. You can find some more details in the "Black Box" sidebar on timsort in Chapter 6.

Summary

The sum of the n first integers is quadratic, and the sum of the $\lg n$ first powers of two is linear. The first of these identities can be illustrated as a round-robin tournament, with all possible pairings of n elements; the second is related to a knockout tournament, with $\lg n$ rounds, where all but the winner must be knocked out. The number of permutations of n is $n!$, while the number of k-combinations (subsets of size k) from n, written $C(n, k)$, is $n!/(k!{\cdot}(n{-}k)!)$. This is also known as the *binomial coefficient*.

A function is recursive if it calls itself (directly or via other functions). A recurrence relation is an equation that relates a function to itself, in a recursive way (such as $T(n) = T(n/2) + 1$). These equations are often used to describe the running times of recursive algorithms, and to be able to solve them, we need to assume something about the base case of the recursion; normally, we assume that $T(k)$ is $\Theta(1)$, for some constant k. This chapter presents three main ways of solving recurrences: (1) repeatedly apply the original equation to unravel the recursive occurrences of T until you find a pattern; (2) guess a solution, and try to prove that it's correct using induction; and (3) for divide and conquer recurrences that fit one of the cases of the master theorem, simply use the corresponding solution.

If You're Curious ...

The topics of this chapter (and the previous, for that matter) are commonly classified as part of what's called *discrete mathematics*.[8] There are plenty of books on this topic, and most of the ones I've seen have been pretty cool. If you like that sort of thing, knock yourself out at the library or at a local or online bookstore. I'm sure you'll find plenty to keep you occupied for a long time.

One book I like that deals with counting and proofs (but not discrete math in general) is *Proofs That Really Count*, by Benjamin and Quinn. It's worth a look. If you want a solid reference that deals with sums, combinatorics, recurrences, and lots of other meaty stuff, specifically written for computer scientists, you should check out the classic *Concrete Mathematics*, by Graham, Knuth, and Patashnik. (Yeah, it's *that* Knuth, so you know it's good.) If you just need some place to look up the solution for a sum, you could try Wolfram Alpha (http://wolframalpha.com), as mentioned earlier, or get one of those pocket references full of formulas (again, probably available from your favorite bookstore).

If you want more details on recurrences, you could look up the standard methods in one of the algorithm textbooks I mentioned in Chapter 1, or you could research some of the more advanced methods, which let you deal with more recurrence types than those I've dealt with here. For example, *Concrete Mathematics* explains how to use so-called *generating functions*. If you look around online, you're also bound to find lots of interesting stuff on solving recurrences with *annihilators* or using the *Akra-Bazzi theorem*.

The sidebar on pseudopolynomiality earlier in this chapter used primality checking as an example. Many (older) textbooks claim that this is an unsolved problem (that is, that there are no known polynomial algorithms for solving it). Just so you know—that's not true anymore: In 2002, Agrawal, Kayal, and Saxena published their groundbreaking paper "PRIMES is in P," describing how to do polynomial primality checking. (Oddly enough, *factoring* numbers is still an unsolved problem.)

Exercises

3-1. Show that the properties described in the section "Working with Sums" are correct.

3-2. Use the rules from Chapter 2 to show that $n(n-1)/2$ is $\Theta(n^2)$.

3-3. The sum of the first k non-negative integer powers of 2 is $2^{k+1} - 1$. Show how this property lets you represent any positive integer as a binary number.

3-4. In the section "The Hare and the Tortoise," two methods of looking for a number are sketched. Turn these methods into number-guessing algorithms, and implement them as Python programs.

3-5. Show that $C(n, k) = C(n, n-k)$.

3-6. In the recursive function S early in the section "Recursion and Recurrences," assume that instead of using a position parameter, i, the function simply returned sec[0] + S(seq[1:]). What would the asymptotic running time be now?

3-7. Solve recurrence 2 in Table 3-1 using repeated substitution.

---

[8]If you're not sure about the difference between *discrete* and *discreet*, you might want to look it up.

3-8. Solve recurrence 3 in Table 3-1 using repeated substitution.

3-9. Solve recurrence 4 in Table 3-1 using repeated substitution.

3-10. Show that $x^{\log y} = y^{\log x}$, no matter the base of the logarithm.

3-11. Show that $f(n)$ is $\Theta(n)$ for the implementation of merge sort in Listing 3-2.

3-12. In merge sort in Listing 3-2, objects are popped from the end of each half of the sequence (with pop()). It might be more intuitive to pop from the beginning, with pop(0), to avoid having to reverse res afterward (I've seen this done in real life), but pop(0), just like insert(0), is a linear operation, as opposed to pop(), which is constant. What would such a switch mean for the overall running time?

References

Agrawal, M., Kayal, N., and Saxena, N. (2004). *PRIMES is in P*. The Annals of Mathematics, 160(2):781–793.

Akra, M. and Bazzi, L. (1998). *On the solution of linear recurrence equations*. Computational Optimization and Applications, 10(2):195–210.

Benjamin, A. T. and Quinn, J. (2003). *Proofs that Really Count: The Art of Combinatorial Proof*. The Mathematical Association of America.

Graham, R. L., Knuth, D. E., and Patashnik, O. (1994). *Concrete Mathematics: A Foundation for Computer Science*, second edition. Addison-Wesley Professional.

CHAPTER 4

■ ■ ■

Induction and Recursion ... and Reduction

You must never think of the whole street at once, understand? You must only concentrate on the next step, the next breath, the next stroke of the broom, and the next, and the next. Nothing else.

— Beppo Roadsweeper, in *Momo* by Michael Ende

In this chapter, I lay the foundations for your algorithm design skills. Algorithm design can be a hard thing to teach because there are no clear recipes to follow. There are some foundational principles, though, and one that pops up again and again is the principle of *abstraction*. I'm betting you're quite familiar with several kinds of abstraction already—most importantly, procedural (or functional) abstraction and object orientation. Both of these approaches let you isolate parts of your code and minimize the interactions between them so you can focus on a few concepts at a time.

The main ideas in this chapter—induction, recursion, and reduction—are also principles of abstraction. They're all about ignoring most of the problem, focusing on taking a *single step* toward a solution. The great thing is that this step is all you need; the rest follows automatically! The principles are often taught and used separately, but if you look a bit deeper, you see that they're very closely related: Induction and recursion are, in a sense, mirror images of one another, and both can be seen as examples of reduction. Here's a quick overview of what these terms actually mean:

- *Reduction* means transforming one problem to another. We normally reduce an unknown problem to one we know how to solve. The reduction may involve transforming both the input (so it works with the new problem) and the output (so it's valid for the original problem).

- *Induction*, or *mathematical induction*, is used to show that a statement is true for a large class of objects (often the natural numbers). We do this by first showing it to be true for a base case (such as the number 1) and then showing that it "carries over" from one object to the next; for example, if it's true for $n-1$, then it's true for n.

- *Recursion* is what happens when a function calls itself. Here we need to make sure the function works correctly for a (nonrecursive) base case and that it combines results from the recursive calls into a valid solution.

Both induction and recursion involve reducing (or decomposing) a problem to smaller *subproblems* and then taking one step beyond these, solving the full problem.

Note that although the perspective in this chapter may be a bit different from some current textbooks, it is by no means unique. In fact, much of the material was inspired by Udi Manber's wonderful paper "Using induction to design algorithms" from 1988 and his book from the following year, *Introduction to Algorithms: A Creative Approach*.

Oh, That's Easy!

Simply put, reducing a problem A to another problem B involves some form of transformation, after which a solution to B gives you (directly or with some massaging) a solution to A. Once you've learned a bunch of standard algorithms (you'll encounter many in this book), this is what you'll usually do when you come across a new problem. Can you change it in some way so that it can be solved with one of the methods you know? In many ways, this is the core process of *all* problem solving.

Let's take an example. You have a list of numbers, and you want to find the two (nonidentical) numbers that are closest to each other (that is, the two with the smallest absolute difference):

```
>>> from random import randrange
>>> seq = [randrange(10**10) for i in range(100)]
>>> dd = float("inf")
>>> for x in seq:
...     for y in seq:
...         if x == y: continue
...         d = abs(x-y)
...         if d < dd:
...             xx, yy, dd = x, y, d
...
>>> xx, yy
(15743, 15774)
```

Two nested loops, both over seq; it should be obvious that this is quadratic, which is generally not a good thing. Let's say you've worked with algorithms a bit, and you know that sequences can often be easier to deal with if they're *sorted*. You also know that sorting is, in general, loglinear, or $\Theta(n \lg n)$. See how this can help? The insight here is that the two closest numbers must be *next to each other* in the sorted sequence:

```
>>> seq.sort()
>>> dd = float("inf")
>>> for i in range(len(seq)-1):
...     x, y = seq[i], seq[i+1]
...     if x == y: continue
...     d = abs(x-y)
...     if d < dd:
...         xx, yy, dd = x, y, d
...
>>> xx, yy
(15743, 15774)
```

Faster algorithm, same solution. The new running time is loglinear, dominated by the sorting. Our original problem was "Find the two closest numbers in a sequence," and we reduced it to "Find the two closest numbers in a sorted sequence," by sorting seq. In this case, our reduction (the sorting) won't affect which answers we get. In general, we may need to transform the answer so it fits the original problem.

■ **Note** In a way, we just split the problem into two parts, sorting and scanning the sorted sequence. You could also say that the scanning is a way of reducing the original problem to the problem of sorting a sequence. It's all a matter of perspective.

Reducing A to B is a bit like saying "You want to solve A? Oh, that's easy, as long as you can solve B." See Figure 4-1 for an illustration of how reductions work.

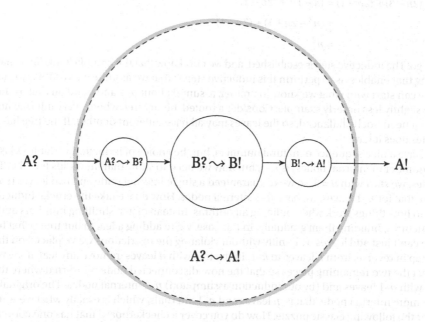

Figure 4-1. *Using a reduction from A to B to solve A with an algorithm for B. The algorithm for B (the central, inner circle) can transform the input B? to the output B!, while the reduction consists of the two transformations (the smaller circles) going from A? to B? and from B! to A!, together forming the main algorithm, which transforms the input A? to the output A!*

One, Two, Many

I've already used induction to solve some problems in Chapter 3, but let's recap and work through a couple of examples. When describing induction in the abstract, we say that we have a *proposition*, or statement, $P(n)$, and we want to show that it's true for any natural number n. For example, let's say we're investigating the sum of the first n odd numbers; $P(n)$ could then be the following statement:

$$1 + 3 + 5 + \cdots + (2n - 3) + (2n - 1) = n^2$$

This is eerily familiar—it's almost the same as the handshake sum we worked with in the previous chapter. You could easily get this new result by tweaking the handshake formula, but let's see how we'd prove it by induction instead. The idea in induction is to make our proof "sweep" over all the natural numbers, a bit like a row of dominoes falling. We start by establishing $P(1)$, which is quite obvious in this case, and then we need to show that each domino, if it falls, will topple the next. In other words, we must show that *if* the statement $P(n-1)$ is true, it follows that $P(n)$ is *also* true.

If we can show this implication, that is, $P(n-1) \Rightarrow P(n)$, the result will sweep across all values of n, starting with $P(1)$, using $P(1) \Rightarrow P(2)$ to establish $P(2)$, then move on to $P(3)$, $P(4)$, and so forth. In other words, the crucial thing is to establish the implication that lets us move one step further. We call it the *inductive step*. In our example, this means that we're assuming the following ($P(n-1)$):

$$1 + 3 + 5 + \cdots + (2n - 3) = (n - 1)^2$$

We can take this for granted, and we just splice it into the original formula and see whether we can deduce $P(n)$:

$$1 + 3 + 5 + \cdots + (2n - 3) + (2n - 1) = (n - 1)^2 + (2n - 1)$$
$$= (n^2 - 2n + 1) + (2n - 1)$$
$$= n^2$$

And there you go. The inductive step is established, and we now know that the formula holds for all natural numbers n.

The main thing that enables us to perform this inductive step is that we assume we've already established $P(n-1)$. This means that we can start with what we know (or, rather, assume) about n-1 and build on that to show something about n. Let's try a slightly less orderly example. Consider a rooted, binary tree where every internal node has two children (although it need not be balanced, so the leaves may all have different depths). If the tree has n leaves, how many internal nodes does it have?[1]

We no longer have a nice sequence of natural numbers, but the choice of induction variable (n) is pretty obvious. The solution (the number of internal nodes) is n-1, but now we need to show that this holds for all n. To avoid some boring technicalities, we start with $n = 3$, so we're guaranteed a single internal node and two leaves (so clearly $P(3)$ is true). Now, assume that for n-1 leaves, we have n-2 internal nodes. How do we take the crucial inductive step to n?

This is closer to how things work when building algorithms. Instead of just shuffling numbers and symbols, we're thinking about structures, building them gradually. In this case, we're adding a leaf to our tree. What happens? The problem is that we can't just add leaves willy-nilly without violating the restrictions we've placed on the trees. Instead, we can work the step in reverse, from n leaves to n-1. In the tree with n leaves, remove any leaf along with its (internal) parent, and connect the two remaining pieces so that the now-disconnected node is inserted where the parent was. This is a legal tree with n-1 leaves and (by our induction assumption) n-2 internal nodes. The original tree had one more leaf and one more internal node, that is, n leaves and n-1 internals, which is exactly what we wanted to show.

Now, consider the following classic puzzle. How do you cover a checkerboard that has one corner square missing, using L-shaped tiles, as illustrated in Figure 4-2? Is it even possible? Where would you start? You *could* try a brute-force solution, just starting with the first piece, placing it in every possible position (and with every possible orientation), and, for each of those, trying every possibility for the second, and so forth. That wouldn't exactly be efficient. How can we reduce the problem? Where's the reduction?[2]

Figure 4-2. *An incomplete checkerboard, to be covered by L-shaped tiles. The tiles may be rotated, but they may not overlap*

---

[1]This is actually Exercise 2-10, but you can still have a go at that, if you want. Try to solve it *without* using induction.
[2]Actually, the solution idea presented in the following will work for a checkerboard where an arbitrary square is missing. I recommend you verify that for yourself.

Placing a single tile and assuming that we can solve the rest or assuming that we've solved all but one and then placing the last one—that's certainly a reduction. We've transformed the problem from one to another, but the catch is that we have no solution for the *new* problem *either*, so it doesn't really help. To use induction (or recursion), the reduction must (generally) be between instances of *the same problem* of *different sizes*. For the moment, our problem is defined only for the specific board in Figure 4-2, but generalizing it to other sizes shouldn't be too problematic. Given this generalization, do you see any useful reductions?

The question is how we can carve up the board into smaller ones of the same shape. It's quadratic, so a natural starting point might be to split it into four smaller squares. The *only* thing standing between us and a complete solution at that point is that only *one* of the four board parts has the same shape as the original, with the missing corner. The other three are complete (quarter-size) checkerboards. That's easily remedied, however. Just place a single tile so that it covers one corner from each of these three subboards, and, as if by magic, we now have four subproblems, each equivalent to (but smaller than) the full problem!

To clarify the induction here, let's say you don't actually place the tile quite yet. You just note which three corners to leave open. By the *inductive hypothesis*, you can cover the three subboards (with the *base case* being four-square boards), and once you've finished, there will be three squares left to cover, in an L-shape.[3] The *inductive step* is then to place this piece, implicitly combining the four subsolutions. Now, because of induction, we haven't only solved the problem for the eight-by-eight case; the solution holds for *any* board of this kind, as long as its sides are (equal) powers of two.

■ **Note**   We haven't really used induction over all board sizes or all side lengths here. We have implicitly assumed that the side lengths are $2k$, for some positive integer k, and used induction over k. The result is perfectly valid, but it is important to note exactly what we've proven. The solution does *not* hold, for example, for odd-sided boards.

This design was really more of a proof than an actual algorithm. Turning it into an algorithm isn't all that hard, though. You first need to consider all subproblems consisting of four squares, making sure to have their open corners properly aligned. Then you combine these into subproblems consisting of 16 squares, still making sure the open corners are placed so that they can be joined with L-pieces. Although you can certainly set this up as an iterative program with a loop, it turns out to be quite a bit easier with recursion, as you'll see in the next section.

Mirror, Mirror

In his excellent web video show, Ze Frank once made the following remark: "'You know there's nothing to fear but fear itself.' Yeah, that's called recursion, and that would lead to infinite fear, so thank you."[4] Another common piece of advice is, "In order to understand recursion, one must first understand recursion."

Indeed. Recursion can be hard to wrap your head around—although infinite recursion is a rather pathological case.[5] In a way, recursion really makes sense only as a mirror image of induction (see Figure 4-3). In induction, we (conceptually) start with a base case and show how the inductive step can take us further, up to the full problem size, n. For weak induction,[6] we assume (the inductive hypothesis) that our solution works for $n-1$, and from that, we deduce that it works for n. Recursion usually seems more like breaking things down. You start with a full problem, of size n. You delegate the subproblem of size $n-1$ to a recursive call, wait for the result, and extend the subsolution you get to a full solution. I'm sure you can see how this is really just a matter of perspective. In a way, induction shows us why recursion works, and recursion gives us an easy way of (directly) implementing our inductive ideas.

---

[3]An important part of this inductive hypothesis is that we can solve the problem no matter which corner is missing.
[4]*the show with zefrank*, February 22, 2007.
[5]Ever tried to search for *recursion* with Google? You might want to try it. And pay attention to the search suggestion.
[6]As mentioned in Chapter 3, in *weak* induction the induction hypothesis applies to $n-1$, while in *strong* induction it applies to all positive integers $k < n$.

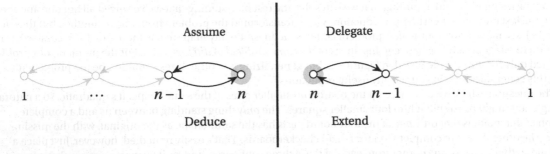

Figure 4-3. *Induction (on the left) and recursion (on the right), as mirror images of each other*

Take the checkerboard problem from the previous section, for example. The easiest way of formulating a solution to that (at least in my opinion) is recursive. You place an L-piece so that you get four equivalent subproblems, and then you solve them recursively. By induction, the solution will be correct.

IMPLEMENTING THE CHECKERBOARD COVERING

Although the checkerboard covering problem has a very easy recursive solution *conceptually*, implementing it can require a bit of thinking. The details of the implementation aren't crucial to the main point of the example, so feel free to skip this sidebar, if you want. One way of implementing a solution is shown here:

```
def cover(board, lab=1, top=0, left=0, side=None):
    if side is None: side = len(board)

    # Side length of subboard:
    s = side // 2

    # Offsets for outer/inner squares of subboards:
    offsets = (0, -1), (side-1, 0)

    for dy_outer, dy_inner in offsets:
        for dx_outer, dx_inner in offsets:
            # If the outer corner is not set...
            if not board[top+dy_outer][left+dx_outer]:
                # ... label the inner corner:
                board[top+s+dy_inner][left+s+dx_inner] = lab

    # Next label:
    lab += 1
    if s > 1:
        for dy in [0, s]:
            for dx in [0, s]:
                # Recursive calls, if s is at least 2:
                lab = cover(board, lab, top+dy, left+dx, s)

    # Return the next available label:
    return lab
```

Although the recursive algorithm is simple, there is some bookkeeping to do. Each call needs to know which subboard it's working on and the number (or label) of the current L-tile. The main work in the function is checking which of the four center squares to cover with the L-tile. We cover only the three that don't correspond to a missing (outer) corner. Finally, there are four recursive calls, one for each of the four subproblems. (The next available label is returned, so it can be used in the next recursive call.) Here's an example of how you might run the code:

```
>>> board = [[0]*8 for i in range(8)] # Eight by eight checkerboard
>>> board[7][7] = -1                   # Missing corner
>>> cover(board)
22
>>> for row in board:
...     print((" %2i"*8) % tuple(row))
  3  3  4  4  8  8  9  9
  3  2  2  4  8  7  7  9
  5  2  6  6 10 10  7 11
  5  5  6  1  1 10 11 11
 13 13 14  1 18 18 19 19
 13 12 14 14 18 17 17 19
 15 12 12 16 20 17 21 21
 15 15 16 16 20 20 21 -1
```

As you can see, all the numerical labels form L-shapes (except for -1, which represents the missing corner). The code can be a bit hard to understand, but imagine understanding it, not to mention *designing* it, without a basic knowledge of induction or recursion!

Induction and recursion go hand in hand in that it is often possible to directly implement an inductive idea recursively. However, there are several reasons why an iterative implementation may be superior. There is usually less overhead with using a loop than with recursion (so it can be faster), and in most languages (Python included), there is a limit to how deep the recursion can go (the maximum stack depth). Take the following example, which just traverses a sequence:

```
>>> def trav(seq, i=0):
...     if i==len(seq): return
...     trav(seq, i+1)
...
>>> trav(range(100))
>>>
```

It works, but try running it on range(1000). You'll get a RuntimeError complaining that you've exceeded the maximum recursion depth.

■ **Note** Many so-called functional programming languages implement something called *tail recursion optimization*. Functions like the previous (where the only recursive call is the last statement of a function) are modified so that they don't exhaust the stack. Typically, the recursive calls are rewritten to loops internally.

Luckily, any recursive function can be rewritten into an iterative one, and vice versa. In some cases, recursion is very natural, though, and you may need to fake it in your iterative program, using a stack of your own (as in nonrecursive *depth-first search*, explained in Chapter 5).

Let's look at a couple of basic algorithms where the algorithmic idea can be easily understood by thinking recursively but where the implementation lends itself well to iteration.[7] Consider the problem of sorting (a favorite in teaching computer science). As before, ask yourself, where's the reduction? There are many ways of reducing this problem (in Chapter 6 we'll be reducing it by half), but consider the case where we reduce the problem by *one element*. Either we can assume (inductively) that the first $n-1$ elements are already sorted and insert element n in the right place, or we can find the largest element, place it at position n, and then sort the remaining elements recursively. The former gives us *insertion sort*, while the latter gives *selection sort*.

■ **Note** These algorithms aren't all that useful, but they're commonly taught because they serve as excellent examples. Also, they're classics, so any algorist should know how they work.

Take a look at the recursive insertion sort in Listing 4-1. It neatly encapsulates the algorithmic idea. To get the sequence sorted up to position i, first sort it recursively up to position $i-1$ (correct by the induction hypothesis) and then swap element seq[i] down until it reaches its correct position among the already sorted elements. The base case is when $i = 0$; a single element is trivially sorted. If you wanted, you could add a default case, where i is set to len(seq)-1. As explained, even though this implementation lets us encapsulate the induction hypothesis in a recursive call, it has practical limitations (for example, in the length of the sequence it'll work on).

Listing 4-1. Recursive Insertion Sort

```
def ins_sort_rec(seq, i):
    if i==0: return                              # Base case -- do nothing
    ins_sort_rec(seq, i-1)                        # Sort 0..i-1
    j = i                                         # Start "walking" down
    while j > 0 and seq[j-1] > seq[j]:            # Look for OK spot
        seq[j-1], seq[j] = seq[j], seq[j-1]       # Keep moving seq[j] down
        j -= 1                                    # Decrement j
```

Listing 4-2 shows the iterative version more commonly known as *insertion sort*. Instead of recursing backward, it iterates forward, from the first element. If you think about it, that's exactly what the recursive version does too. Although it seems to start at the end, the recursive calls go all the way back to the first element before the while loop is ever executed. After that recursive call returns, the while loop is executed on the *second* element, and so on, so the behaviors of the two versions are identical.

Listing 4-2. Insertion Sort

```
def ins_sort(seq):
    for i in range(1,len(seq)):                   # 0..i-1 sorted so far
        j = i                                     # Start "walking" down
        while j > 0 and seq[j-1] > seq[j]:        # Look for OK spot
            seq[j-1], seq[j] = seq[j], seq[j-1]   # Keep moving seq[j] down
            j -= 1                                # Decrement j
```

Listings 4-3 and 4-4 contain a recursive and an iterative version of selection sort, respectively.

---

[7]These algorithms aren't all that useful, but they're commonly taught, because they serve as excellent examples. Also, they're classics, so any algorist should know how they work.

Listing 4-3. Recursive Selection Sort

```
def sel_sort_rec(seq, i):
    if i==0: return                              # Base case -- do nothing
    max_j = i                                    # Idx. of largest value so far
    for j in range(i):                           # Look for a larger value
        if seq[j] > seq[max_j]: max_j = j        # Found one? Update max_j
    seq[i], seq[max_j] = seq[max_j], seq[i]      # Switch largest into place
    sel_sort_rec(seq, i-1)                       # Sort 0..i-1
```

Listing 4-4. Selection Sort

```
def sel_sort(seq):
    for i in range(len(seq)-1,0,-1):             # n..i+1 sorted so far
        max_j = i                                # Idx. of largest value so far
        for j in range(i):                       # Look for a larger value
            if seq[j] > seq[max_j]: max_j = j    # Found one? Update max_j
        seq[i], seq[max_j] = seq[max_j], seq[i]  # Switch largest into place
```

Once again, you can see that the two are quite similar. The recursive implementation explicitly represents the inductive hypothesis (as a recursive call), while the iterative version explicitly represents repeatedly performing the inductive step. Both work by finding the largest element (the for loop looking for max_j) and swapping that to the end of the sequence prefix under consideration. Note that you could just as well run all the four sorting algorithms in this section from the beginning, rather than from the end (sort all objects *to the right* in insertion sort or look for the *smallest* element in selection sort).

BUT WHERE IS THE REDUCTION?

Finding a useful reduction is often a crucial step in solving an algorithmic problem. If you don't know where to b egin, ask yourself, where is the reduction?

However, it may not be entirely clear how the ideas in this section jibe with the picture of a reduction presented in Figure 4-1. As explained, a reduction transforms instances from problem A to instances of problem B and then transforms the output of B to valid output for A. But in induction and reduction, we've only reduced the problem size. Where *is* the reduction, really?

Oh, it's there—it's just that we're reducing from A to A. There is some transformation going on, though. The reduction makes sure the instances we're reducing *to* are *smaller* than the original (which is what makes the induction work), and when transforming the output, we increase the size again.

These are two major variations of reductions: reducing to a different problem and reducing to a shrunken version of the same. If you think of the subproblems as vertices and the reductions as edges, you get the *subproblem graph* discussed in Chapter 2, a concept I'll revisit several times. (It's especially important in Chapter 8.)

Designing with Induction (and Recursion)

In this section, I'll walk you through the design of algorithmic solutions to three problems. The problem I'm building up to, topological sorting, is one that occurs quite a bit in practice and that you may very well need to implement yourself one day, if your software manages any kind of dependencies. The first two problems are perhaps less useful, but great fun, and they're good illustrations of induction (and recursion).

Finding a Maximum Permutation

Eight persons with very particular tastes have bought tickets to the movies. Some of them are happy with their seats, but most of them are not, and after standing in line in Chapter 3, they're getting a bit grumpy. Let's say each of them has a favorite seat, and you want to find a way to let them switch seats to make as many people as possible happy with the result (ignoring other audience members, who may eventually get a bit tired by the antics of our moviegoers). However, because they are all rather grumpy, all of them refuse to move to another seat if they can't get their favorite.

This is a form of *matching problem*. You'll encounter a few other of those in Chapter 10. We can model the problem (instance) as a graph, like the one in Figure 4-4. The edges point from where people are currently sitting to where they *want* to sit. (This graph is a bit unusual in that the nodes don't have unique labels; each person, or seat, is represented twice.)

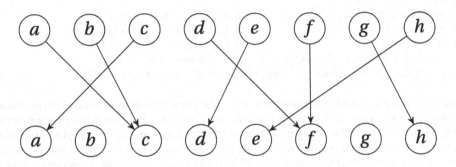

Figure 4-4. *A mapping from the set {a ... h} to itself*

■ **Note**   This is an example of what's called a *bipartite* graph, which means that the nodes can be partitioned into two sets, where all the edges are *between* the sets (and none of them *inside* either). In other words, you could color the nodes using only two colors so that no neighbors had the same color.

Before we try to design an algorithm, we need to formalize the problem. Truly understanding the problem is always a crucial first step in solving it. In this case, we want to let as many people as possible get the seat they're "pointing to." The others will need to remain seated. Another way of viewing this is that we're looking for a subset of the people (or of the pointing fingers) that forms a *one-to-one* mapping, or *permutation*. This means that no one in the set points outside it, and each seat (in the set) is pointed to exactly once. That way, everyone in the permutation is free to permute—or switch seats—according to their wishes. We want to find a permutation that is *as large as possible* (to reduce the number of people that fall outside it and have their wishes denied).

Once again, our first step is to ask, where is the reduction? How can we reduce the problem to a smaller one? What subproblem can we delegate (recursively) or assume (inductively) to be solved already? Let's go with simple (weak) induction and see whether we can shrink the problem from n to $n-1$. Here, n is the number of people (or seats), that is, $n = 8$ for Figure 4-4. The inductive assumption follows from our general approach. We simply assume that we can solve the problem (that is, find a maximum subset that forms a permutation) for $n-1$ people. The *only thing* that requires any creative problem solving is safely removing a single person so that the remaining subproblem is one that we can build on (that is, one that is part of a total solution).

If each person points to a different seat, the entire set forms a permutation, which must certainly be as big as it can be—no need to remove anyone because we're already done. The base case is also trivial. For $n = 1$, there is nowhere to move. So, let's say that $n > 1$ and that at least two persons are pointing to the same seat (the only way the permutation can be broken). Take a and b in Figure 4-4, for example. They're both pointing to c, and we can safely say that *one of them* must be eliminated. However, which one we choose is crucial. Say, for example, we choose to remove *a* (both the person and the seat). We then notice that *c* is pointing to *a*, which means that *c* must also be eliminated. Finally, *b* points to *c* and must be eliminated as well—meaning that we could have simply eliminated *b* to begin with, keeping *a* and *c* (who just want to trade seats with each other).

When looking for inductive steps like this, it can often be a good idea to look for something that stands out. What, for example, about a seat that no one wants to sit in (that is, a node in the lower row in Figure 4-4 that has no in-edges)? In a valid solution (a permutation), at most one person (element) can be placed in (mapped to) any given seat (position). That means there's no room for empty seats, because at least two people will then be trying to sit in the same seat. In other words, it is not only OK to remove an empty seat (and the corresponding person); it's actually *necessary*. For example, in Figure 4-4, the nodes marked *b* cannot be part of *any* permutation, certainly not one of maximum size. Therefore, we can eliminate *b*, and what remains is a smaller instance (with $n = 7$) of the same problem , and, by the magic of induction, we're done!

Or are we? We always need to make certain we've covered every eventuality. Can we be sure that there will always be an empty seat to eliminate, if needed? Indeed we can. Without empty seats, the *n* persons must collectively point to all the *n* seats, meaning that they all point to *different* seats, so we already have a permutation.

It's time to translate the inductive/recursive algorithm idea into an actual implementation. An early decision is always how to represent the objects in the problem instances. In this case, we might think in terms of a graph or perhaps a function that maps between the objects. However, in essence, a mapping like this is just a position (0...$n-1$) associated with each element (also 0...$n-1$), and we can implement this using a simple list. For example, the example in Figure 4-4 (if $a = 0$, $b = 1$, ...) can be represented as follows:

```
>>> M = [2, 2, 0, 5, 3, 5, 7, 4]
>>> M[2] # c is mapped to a
0
```

■ **Tip**   When possible, try to use a representation that is as *specific* to your problem as possible. More general representations can lead to more bookkeeping and complicated code; if you use a representation that implicitly embodies some of the constraints of the problem, both finding and implementing a solution can be much easier.

We can now implement the recursive algorithm idea directly if we want, with some brute-force code for finding the element to eliminate. It won't be very efficient, but an inefficient implementation can sometimes be an instructive place to start. See Listing 4-5 for a relatively direct implementation.

Listing 4-5. A Naïve Implementation of the Recursive Algorithm Idea for Finding a Maximum Permutation

```
def naive_max_perm(M, A=None):
    if A is None:                       # The elt. set not supplied?
        A = set(range(len(M)))          # A = {0, 1, ... , n-1}
    if len(A) == 1: return A            # Base case -- single-elt. A
    B = set(M[i] for i in A)            # The "pointed to" elements
    C = A - B                           # "Not pointed to" elements
    if C:                               # Any useless elements?
        A.remove(C.pop())               # Remove one of them
        return naive_max_perm(M, A)     # Solve remaining problem
    return A                            # All useful -- return all
```

The function naive_max_perm receives a set of remaining people (A) and creates a set of seats that are pointed to (B). If it finds an element in A that is not in B, it removes the element and solves the remaining problem recursively. Let's use the implementation on our example, M.[8]

```
>>> naive_max_perm(M)
{0, 2, 5}
```

So, *a*, *c*, and *f* can take part in the permutation. The others will have to sit in nonfavorite seats.

The implementation isn't too bad. The handy set type lets us manipulate sets with ready-made high-level operations, rather than having to implement them ourselves. There are some problems, though. For one thing, we might want an iterative solution. This is easily remedied—the recursion can quite simply be replaced by a loop (like we did for insertion sort and selection sort). A worse problem, though, is that the algorithm is quadratic! (Exercise 4-10 asks you to show this.)

The most wasteful operation is the repeated creation of the set B. If we could just keep track of which chairs are no longer pointed to, we could eliminate this operation entirely. One way of doing this would be to keep a *count* for each element. We could decrement the count for chair *x* when a person pointing to *x* is eliminated, and if *x* ever got a count of zero, both person and chair *x* would be out of the game.

■ **Tip** This idea of *reference counting* can be useful in general. It is, for example, a basic component in many systems for garbage collection (a form of memory management that automatically deallocates objects that are no longer useful). You'll see this technique again in the discussion of topological sorting.

There may be more than one element to be eliminated at any one time, but we can just put any new ones we come across into a "to-do" list and deal with them later. If we needed to make sure the elements were eliminated in the order in which we discover that they're no longer useful, we would need to use a *first-in, first-out* queue such as the deque class (discussed in Chapter 5).[9] We don't really care, so we could use a set, for example, but just appending to and popping from a list will probably give us quite a bit less overhead. But feel free to experiment, of course. You can find an implementation of the iterative, linear-time version of the algorithm in Listing 4-6.

Listing 4-6. Finding a Maximum Permutation

```
def max_perm(M):
    n = len(M)                          # How many elements?
    A = set(range(n))                   # A = {0, 1, ... , n-1}
    count = [0]*n                       # C[i] == 0 for i in A
    for i in M:                         # All that are "pointed to"
        count[i] += 1                   # Increment "point count"
    Q = [i for i in A if count[i] == 0] # Useless elements
    while Q:                            # While useless elts. left...
        i = Q.pop()                     # Get one
        A.remove(i)                     # Remove it
        j = M[i]                        # Who's it pointing to?
        count[j] -= 1                   # Not anymore...
        if count[j] == 0:               # Is j useless now?
            Q.append(j)                 # Then deal w/it next
    return A                            # Return useful elts.
```

[8]If you're using Python 2.6 or older, the result would be set([0, 2, 5]).
[9]Inserting into or removing from the start of a list is a linear-time operation, remember? Generally not a good idea.

■ **Tip** In recent versions of Python, the `collections` module contains the `Counter` class, which can count (hashable) objects for you. With it, the `for` loop in Listing 4-7 could have been replaced with the assignment `count = Counter(M)`. This might have some extra overhead, but it would have the same asymptotic running time.

Listing 4-7. A Naïve Solution to the Celebrity Problem

```
def naive_celeb(G):
    n = len(G)
    for u in range(n):              # For every candidate...
        for v in range(n):         # For everyone else...
            if u == v: continue    # Same person? Skip.
            if G[u][v]: break      # Candidate knows other
            if not G[v][u]: break  # Other doesn't know candidate
        else:
            return u               # No breaks? Celebrity!
    return None                    # Couldn't find anyone
```

Some simple experiments (see Chapter 2 for tips) should convince you that even for rather small problem instances, `max_perm` is quite a bit faster than `naive_max_perm`. They're both pretty fast, though, and if all you're doing is solving a single, moderately sized instance, you might be just as satisfied with the more direct of the two. The inductive thinking would still have been useful in providing you with a solution that could actually find the answer. You could, of course, have tried every possibility, but *that* would have resulted in a totally useless algorithm. If, however, you had to solve some really large instances of this problem or even if you had to solve many moderate instances, the extra thinking involved in coming up with a linear-time algorithm would probably pay off.

COUNTING SORT & FAM

If the elements you're working with in some problem are hashable or, even better, integers that you can use directly as indices (like in the permutation example), *counting* should be a tool you keep close at hand. One of the most well-known (and really, really pretty) examples of what counting can do is *counting sort*. As you'll see in Chapter 6, there is a (loglinear) limit to how fast you can sort (in the worst case), if all you know about your values is whether they're greater/less than each other.

In many cases, this is a reality you have to accept, for example, if you're sorting objects with custom comparison methods. And loglinear is much better than the quadratic sorting algorithms we've seen so far. However, if you can *count* your elements, you can do better. You can sort in linear time! And what's more, the counting sort algorithm is really simple. (And did I mention how pretty it is?)

```
from collections import defaultdict

def counting_sort(A, key=lambda x: x):
    B, C = [], defaultdict(list)      # Output and "counts"
    for x in A:
        C[key(x)].append(x)           # "Count" key(x)
    for k in range(min(C), max(C)+1): # For every key in the range
        B.extend(C[k])                # Add values in sorted order
    return B
```

By default, I'm just sorting objects based on their values. By supplying a key function, you can sort by anything you'd like. Note that the keys must be integers in a limited range. If this range is 0...k–1, the running time is then $\Theta(n + k)$. (Although the common implementation simply *counts* the elements and then figures out where to put them in B, Python makes it easy to just build value lists for each key and then concatenate them.) If several values have the same key, they'll end up in the original order with respect to each other. Sorting algorithms with this property are called *stable*.

Counting-sort does need more space than an in-place algorithm like Quicksort, for example, so if your data set and value range is large, you might get a slowdown from a lack of memory. This can partly be handled by handling the value range more efficiently. We can do this by sorting numbers on *individual digits* (or strings on individual characters or bit vectors on fixed-size chunks). If you first sort on the *least* significant digit, because of stability, sorting on the *second least* significant digit won't destroy the internal ordering from the first run. (This is a bit like sorting column by column in a spreadsheet.) This means that for *d* digits, you can sort *n* numbers in $\Theta(dn)$ time. This algorithm is called *radix sort*, and Exercise 4-11 asks you to implement it.

Another somewhat similar linear-time sorting algorithm is *bucket sort*. It assumes that your values are evenly (uniformly) distributed in an interval, for example, real numbers in the interval [0,1), and uses *n buckets*, or subintervals, that you can put your values into directly. In a way, you're hashing each value into its proper slot, and the average (expected) size of each bucket is $\Theta(1)$. Because the buckets are in order, you can go through them and have your sorting in $\Theta(n)$ time, in the average case, for random data. (Exercise 4-12 asks you to implement bucket sort.)

The Celebrity Problem

In the celebrity problem, you're looking for a celebrity in a crowd. It's a bit far-fetched, though it could perhaps be used in analyses of social networks such as Facebook and Twitter. The idea is as follows: The celebrity knows no one, but everyone knows the celebrity.[10] A more down-to-earth version of the same problem would be examining a set of dependencies and trying to find a place to start. For example, you might have threads in a multithreaded application waiting for each other, with even some cyclical dependencies (so-called deadlocks), and you're looking for one thread that isn't waiting for any of the others but that all of the others are dependent on. (A much more realistic way of handling dependencies—topological sorting—is dealt with in the next section.)

No matter how we dress the problem up, its core can be represented in terms of graphs. We're looking for one node with incoming edges from *all other nodes*, but with *no outgoing* edges. Having gotten a handle on the structures we're dealing with, we can implement a brute-force solution, just to see whether it helps us understand anything (see Listing 4-7).

The naive_celeb function tackles the problem head on. Go through all the people, checking whether each person is a celebrity. This check goes through all the *others*, making sure they all know the candidate person and that the candidate person does not know any of them. This version is clearly quadratic, but it's possible to get the running time down to linear.

The key, as before, lies in finding a reduction—reducing the problem from *n* persons to *n*–1 as cheaply as possible. The naive_celeb implementation does, in fact, reduce the problem step by step. In iteration *k* of the outer loop, we know that none of 0...k-1 can be the celebrity, so we need to solve the problem only for the remainder, which is exactly what the remaining iterations do. This reduction is clearly correct, as is the algorithm. What's new in this situation is that we have to try to improve the *efficiency* of the reduction. To get a linear algorithm, we need to perform the reduction in *constant time*. If we can do that, the problem is as good as solved. As you can see, this inductive way of thinking can really help pinpoint where we need to employ our creative problem-solving skills.

---

[10]There are proverbs where this celebrity is replaced with a clown, a fool, or a monkey. Somewhat fitting, perhaps.

Once we've zeroed in on what we need to do, the problem isn't all that hard. To reduce the problem from *n* to *n*–1, we must find a *noncelebrity*, someone who either knows someone or is unknown by someone else. And if we check G[u][v] for *any* nodes u and v, we can eliminate either u or v! If G[u][v] is true, we eliminate u; otherwise, we eliminate v. If we're guaranteed that there *is* a celebrity, this is all we need. Otherwise, we can still eliminate all but one candidate, but we need to finish by checking whether they are, in fact, a celebrity, like we did in naive_celeb. You can find an implementation of the algorithm based on this reduction in Listing 4-8. (You could implement the algorithm idea even more directly using sets; do you see how?)

Listing 4-8. A Solution to the Celebrity Problem

```
def celeb(G):
    n = len(G)
    u, v = 0, 1                     # The first two
    for c in range(2,n+1):         # Others to check
        if G[u][v]: u = c          # u knows v? Replace u
        else:       v = c          # Otherwise, replace v
    if u == n:      c = v          # u was replaced last; use v
    else:           c = u          # Otherwise, u is a candidate
    for v in range(n):             # For everyone else...
        if c == v: continue        # Same person? Skip.
        if G[c][v]: break          # Candidate knows other
        if not G[v][c]: break      # Other doesn't know candidate
    else:
        return c                   # No breaks? Celebrity!
    return None                    # Couldn't find anyone
```

To try these celebrity-finding functions, you can just whip up a random graph.[11] Let's switch each edge on or off with equal probability:

```
>>> from random import randrange
>>> n = 100
>>> G = [[randrange(2) for i in range(n)] for i in range(n)]
```

Now make sure there is a celebrity in there and run the two functions:

```
>>> c = randrange(n)
>>> for i in range(n):
...     G[i][c] = True
...     G[c][i] = False
...
>>> naive_celeb(G)
57
>>> celeb(G)
57
```

Note that though one is quadratic and one is linear, the time to build the graph (whether random or from some other source) is quadratic here. That could be avoided (for a *sparse* graph, where the average number of edges is less than $\Theta(n)$), with some other graph representation; see Chapter 2 for suggestions.

[11]There is, in fact, a rich theory about random graphs. A web search should turn up lots of material.

Topological Sorting

In almost any project, the tasks to be undertaken will have dependencies that partially restrict their ordering. For example, unless you have a very avant-garde fashion sense, you need to put on your socks before your boots, but whether you put on your hat before your shorts is of less importance. Such dependencies are (as mentioned in Chapter 2) easily represented as a directed acyclic graph (DAG), and finding an ordering that respect the dependencies (so that all the edges point forward in the ordering) is called *topological sorting*.

Figure 4-5 illustrates the concept. In this case, there is a unique valid ordering, but consider what would happen if you removed the edge *ab*, for example—then *a* could be placed anywhere in the order, as long as it was before *f*.

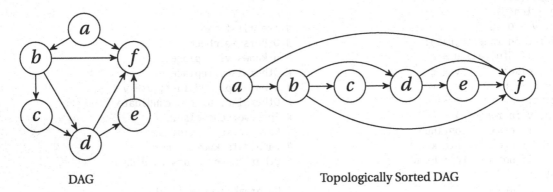

DAG   Topologically Sorted DAG

Figure 4-5. *A directed acyclic graph (DAG) and its nodes in topologically sorted order*

The problem of topological sorting occurs in many circumstances in any moderately complex computer system. Things need to be done, and they depend on other things ... where to start? A rather obvious example is installing software. Most modern operating systems have at least one system for automatically installing software components (such as applications or libraries), and these systems can automatically detect when some dependency is missing and then download and install it. For this to work, the components must be installed in a topologically sorted order.[12]

There are also algorithms (such as the one for finding shortest paths in DAGs and, in a sense, most algorithms based on dynamic programming) that are based on a DAG being sorted topologically as an initial step. However, while standard sorting algorithms are easy to encapsulate in standard libraries and the like, abstracting away graph algorithms so they work with any kind of dependency structure is a bit harder ... so the odds aren't too bad that you'll need to implement it at some point.

■ **Tip**   If you're using a Unix system of some sort, you can play around with topological sorting of graphs described in plain-text files, using the `tsort` command.

We already have a good representation of the structures in our problem (a DAG). The next step is to look for some useful reduction. As before, our first intuition should probably be to remove a node and solve the problem (or assume that it is already solved) for the remaining *n*–1. This reasonably obvious reduction can be implemented in a manner similar to insertion sort, as shown in Listing 4-9. (I'm assuming adjacency sets or adjacency dicts or the like here; see Chapter 2 for details.)

---

[12]The description "detect when some dependency is missing, download and install it" is, in fact, almost a literal description of *another* algorithm topological sorting, which is discussed in Chapter 5.

Listing 4-9. A Naïve Algorithm for Topological Sorting

```
def naive_topsort(G, S=None):
    if S is None: S = set(G)              # Default: All nodes
    if len(S) == 1: return list(S)        # Base case, single node
    v = S.pop()                           # Reduction: Remove a node
    seq = naive_topsort(G, S)             # Recursion (assumption), n-1
    min_i = 0
    for i, u in enumerate(seq):
        if v in G[u]: min_i = i+1         # After all dependencies
    seq.insert(min_i, v)
    return seq
```

Although I hope it's clear (by induction) that `naive_topsort` is *correct*, it is also clearly quadratic (by recurrence 2 from Table 3-1). The problem is that it chooses an *arbitrary* node at each step, which means that it has to look where the node fits after the recursive call (which gives the linear work). We can turn this around and work more like selection sort. Find the right node to remove before the recursive call. This new idea, however, leaves us with two questions. First, which node should we remove? And second, how can we find it efficiently?[13]

We're working with a sequence (or at least we're working *toward* a sequence), which should perhaps give us an idea. We can do something similar to what we do in selection sort and pick out the element that should be placed first (or last ... it doesn't really matter; see Exercise 4-19). Here, we can't just place it first—we need to really remove it from the graph, so the rest is still a DAG (an equivalent but smaller problem). Luckily, we can do this without changing the graph representation directly, as you'll see in a minute.

How would you find a node that can be put first? There could be more than one valid choice, but it doesn't matter which one you take. I hope this reminds you of the maximum permutation problem. Once again, we want to find the nodes that have no in-edges. A node without in-edges can safely be placed first because it doesn't depend on any others. If we (conceptually) remove all its out-edges, the remaining graph, with $n-1$ nodes, will also be a DAG that can be sorted in the same way.

■ **Tip**   If a problem reminds you of a problem or an algorithm you already know, that's probably a good sign. In fact, building a mental archive of problems and algorithms is one of the things that can make you a skilled algorist. If you're faced with a problem and you have no immediate associations, you could systematically consider any relevant (or semirelevant) techniques you know and look for reduction potential.

Just like in the maximum permutation problem, we can find the nodes without in-edges by *counting*. By maintaining our counts from one step to the next, we need not start fresh each time, which reduces the linear step cost to a constant one (yielding a linear running time in total, as in recurrence 1 in Table 3-1). Listing 4-10 shows an iterative implementation of this counting-based topological sorting. (Can you see how the iterative structure still embodies the recursive idea?) The only assumption about the graph representation is that we can iterate over the nodes and their neighbors.

---

[13]Without effective selection, we're not gaining anything. For example, the algorithms I've compared with, insertion and selection sort, are both quadratic, because selecting the largest or smallest element among unsorted elements isn't any easier than inserting it among sorted ones.

Listing 4-10. Topological Sorted of a Directed, Acyclic Graph

```
def topsort(G):
    count = dict((u, 0) for u in G)      # The in-degree for each node
    for u in G:
        for v in G[u]:
            count[v] += 1                # Count every in-edge
    Q = [u for u in G if count[u] == 0]  # Valid initial nodes
    S = []                               # The result
    while Q:                             # While we have start nodes...
        u = Q.pop()                      # Pick one
        S.append(u)                      # Use it as first of the rest
        for v in G[u]:
            count[v] -= 1                # "Uncount" its out-edges
            if count[v] == 0:            # New valid start nodes?
                Q.append(v)              # Deal with them next
    return S
```

BLACK BOX: TOPOLOGICAL SORTING AND PYTHON'S MRO

The kind of structural ordering we've been working with in this section is actually an integral part of Python object-oriented inheritance semantics. For single inheritance (each class is derived from a single superclass), picking the right attribute or method to use is easy. Simply walk upward in the "chain of inheritance," first checking the instance, then the class, then the superclass, and so forth. The first class that has what we're looking for is used.

However, if you can have more than one superclass, things get a bit tricky. Consider the following example:

```
>>> class X: pass
>>> class Y: pass
>>> class A(X,Y): pass
>>> class B(Y,X): pass
```

If you were to derive a new class C from A and B, you'd be in trouble. You wouldn't know whether to look for methods in X or Y.

In general, the inheritance relationship forms a DAG (you can't inherit in a cycle), and in order to figure out where to look for methods, most languages create a *linearization* of the classes, which is simply a topological sorting of the DAG. Recent versions of Python use a method resolution order (or MRO) called C3 (see the references for more information), which in addition to linearizing the classes in a way that makes as much sense as possible also prohibits problematic cases such as the one in the earlier example.

PAGE 3			
DEPARTMENT	COURSE	DESCRIPTION	PREREQS
COMPUTER SCIENCE	CPSC 432	INTERMEDIATE COMPILER DESIGN, WITH A FOCUS ON DEPENDENCY RESOLUTION.	CPSC 432

Dependencies. The prereqs for CPSC 357, the class on package management, are CPSC 432, CPSC 357, and glibc2.5 or later (http://xkcd.com/754)

Stronger Assumptions

The default induction hypothesis when designing algorithm is "We can solve smaller instances with this," but sometimes that isn't enough to actually perform the induction step or to perform it efficiently. Choosing the order of the subproblems can be important (such as in topological sorting), but sometimes we must actually make a *stronger* assumption to piggyback some extra information on our induction. Although a stronger assumption might seem to make the proof harder,[14] it actually just gives us *more to work with* when deducing the step from n–1 (or n/2, or some other size) to n.

Consider the idea of *balance factors*. These are used in some types of balanced trees (discussed in Chapter 6) and are a measure of how balanced (or unbalanced) a tree or subtree is. For simplicity, we assume that each internal node has two children. (In an actual implementation, some of the leaves might simply be None or the like.) A balance factor is defined for each internal node and is set to the difference between the heights of the left and right subtrees, where height is the greatest distance from the node (downward) to a leaf. For example, the left child of the root in Figure 4-6 has a balance factor of –2 because its left subtree is a leaf (with a height of 0), while its right child has a height of 2.

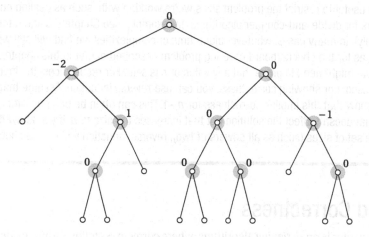

Figure 4-6. *Balance factors for a binary tree. The balance factors are defined only for internal nodes (highlighted) but could trivially be set to zero for leaves*

---

[14]In general, you should, of course, be careful about making unwarranted assumptions. In the words of Alec Mackenzie (as quoted by Brian Tracy), "Errant assumptions lie at the root of every failure." Or, as most people would put it, "Assumption is the mother of all f@#k-ups." Assumptions in induction are *proven*, though, step by step, from the base case.

Calculating balance factors isn't a very challenging algorithm design problem, but it does illustrate a point. Consider the obvious (divide-and-conquer) reduction. To find the balance factor for the root, solve the problem recursively for each subtree and then extend/combine the partial solutions to a complete solution. Easy peasy. Except ... it won't work. The inductive assumption that we can solve smaller subproblems won't help us here because the solution (that is, the balance factor) for our subproblems doesn't contain enough information to make the inductive step! The balance factor isn't defined in terms of its children's balance factors—it's defined in terms of their *heights*. We can easily solve this by just strengthening our assumption. We assume that we can find the balance factors and the *heights* of any tree with $k < n$ nodes. We can now use the heights in the inductive step, finding both the balance factor (left height minus right height) and the height (max of left and right height, plus one) for size n in our inductive step. Problem solved! Exercise 4-20 asks you to work out the details here.

■ **Note**   Recursive algorithms over trees are intimately linked with *depth-first search*, discussed in Chapter 5.

Thinking formally about strengthening the inductive hypothesis can sometimes be a bit confusing. Instead, you can just think about what extra information you need to "piggyback" on your inductive step in order to build a larger solution. For example, when working with topological sorting earlier, it was clear that piggybacking (and maintaining) the in-degrees while we were stepping through the partial solutions made it possible to perform the inductive step more efficiently.

For more examples of strengthening induction hypotheses, see the *closest point* problem in Chapter 6 and the *interval containment* problem in Exercise 4-21.

REVERSE INDUCTION AND POWERS OF TWO

Sometimes it can be useful to restrict the problem sizes we're working with, such as dealing only with powers of two. This often occurs for divide-and-conquer algorithms, for example (see Chapters 3 and 6 for recurrences and examples, respectively). In many cases, whatever algorithms or complexities we find will still work for any value of n, but sometimes, as for the checkerboard covering problem described earlier in this chapter, this just isn't the case. To be certain, we might need to prove that any value of n is safe. For recurrences, the induction method in Chapter 3 can be used. For showing correctness, you can use *reverse* induction. Assume that the algorithm is correct for n and show that this implies correctness for $n-1$. This can often be done by simply introducing a "dummy" element that doesn't affect the solution but that increases the size to n. If you know the algorithm is correct for an infinite set of sizes (such as all powers of two), reverse induction will let you show that it's true for *all* sizes.

Invariants and Correctness

The main focus of this chapter is on *designing* algorithms, where correctness follows from the design process. Perhaps a more common perspective on induction in computer science is *correctness proofs*. It's basically the same thing that I've been discussing in this chapter but with a slightly different angle of approach. You're presented with a finished algorithm, and you need to show that it works. For a recursive algorithm, the ideas I've already shown you can be used rather directly. For a loop, you can also think recursively, but there is a concept that applies more directly to induction proofs for iteration: *loop invariants*. A loop invariant is something that is true after each iteration of a loop, given some preconditions; it's called an *invariant* because it doesn't vary—it's true from beginning to end.

Usually, the final solution is the special case that the invariant attains after the final iteration, so if the invariant always holds (given the preconditions of the algorithm) and you can show that the loop terminates, you've shown that the algorithm is correct. Let's try this approach with insertion sort (Listing 4-2). The invariant for the loop is that the elements $0...i$ are sorted (as hinted at by the first comment in the code). If we want to use this invariant to prove correctness, we need to do the following:

1. Use induction to show that it is, in fact, true after each iteration.

2. Show that we'll get the correct answer if the algorithm terminates.

3. Show that the algorithm terminates.

The induction in step 1 involves showing a base case (that is, *before* the first iteration) and an inductive step (that a single run of the loop preserves the invariant). The second step involves using the invariant at the point of termination. The third step is usually easy to prove (perhaps by showing that you eventually "run out" of something).[15]

Steps 2 and 3 should be obvious for insertion sort. The for loop will terminate after n iterations, with $i = n-1$. The invariant then says that elements $0...n-1$ are sorted, which means that the problem is solved. The base case ($i = 0$) is trivial, so all that remains is the inductive step—to show that the loop preserves the invariant, which it does, by inserting the next element in the correct spot among the sorted values (without disrupting the sorting).

Relaxation and Gradual Improvement

The term *relaxation* is taken from mathematics, where it has several meanings. The term has been picked up by algorists and is used to describe the crucial step in several algorithms, particularly shortest-path algorithms based on dynamic programming (discussed in Chapters 8 and 9), where we gradually improve our approximations to the optimum. The idea of incrementally improving a solution in this way is also central to algorithms finding maximum flow (Chapter 10). I won't go into how these algorithms work just yet, but let's look at a simple example of something that might be called *relaxation*.

You are in an airport, and you can reach several other airports by plane. From each of those airports, you can take the train to several towns and cities. Let's say that you have a dict or list of flight times, A, so that A[u] is the time it will take you to get to airport u. Similarly, B[u][v] will give you the time it takes to get from airport u to town v by train. (B can be a list of lists or a dict of dicts, for example; see Chapter 2.) Consider the following randomized way of estimating the time it will take you to get to each town, C[v]:

```
>>> for v in range(n):
...     C[v] = float('inf')
>>> for i in range(N):
...     u, v = randrange(n), randrange(n)
...     C[v] = min(C[v], A[u] + B[u][v]) # Relax
```

The idea here is to repeatedly see whether we can improve our estimate for C[v] by choosing another route. First go to u by plane, and then you take the train to v. If that gives us a better total time, we update C. As long as N is really large, we will eventually get the right answer for every town.

For relaxation-based algorithms that actually *guarantee* correct solutions, we need to do better than this. For the airplane + train problem, this is fairly easy (see Exercise 4-22). For more complex problems, you may need rather subtle approaches. For example, you can show that the value of your solution increases by an integer in every iteration; if the algorithm terminates only when you hit the optimal (integer) value, it must be correct. (This is similar to the case for maximum flow algorithms.) Or perhaps you need to show how correct estimates spread across elements of the problem instance, such as nodes in a graph. If this seems a bit general at the moment, don't worry—I'll get plenty specific when we encounter algorithms that use the technique.

---

[15]Even though showing termination is usually easy, the general problem is, in fact, *not (algorithmically) solvable*. See the discussion of the *halting problem* in Chapter 11 for details.

■ **Tip** Designing algorithms with relaxation can be like a game. Each relaxation is one "move," and you try to get the optimal solution with as few moves as possible. You can always get there by just relaxing all over the place, but the key lies in performing your moves in the right order. This idea will be explored further when we deal with shortest paths in DAGs (Chapter 8), Bellman-Ford, and Dijkstra's algorithm (Chapter 9).

Reduction + Contraposition = Hardness Proof

This section is really just a bit of foreshadowing of what you'll encounter in Chapter 11. You see, although reductions are used to *solve* problems, the only context in which most textbooks discuss them is *problem complexity*, where they're used to show that you (probably) *can't* solve a given problem. The idea is really quite simple, yet I've seen it trip up many (perhaps even most) of my students.

The hardness proofs are based on the fact that we only allow easy (that is, fast) reductions.[16] Let's say you're able to reduce problem A to B (so a solution to B gives you one for A as well; take a look at Figure 4-1 if you need to refresh your memory on how this works). We then know that if B is *easy*, A must be easy *as well*. That follows directly from the fact that we can use B, along with an easy reduction, to solve A.

For example, let A be finding the *longest* path between two nodes in a DAG, and let B be finding the *shortest* path between two nodes in a DAG. You can then reduce A to B by simply viewing all edges as negative. Now, if you learn of some efficient algorithm to find *shortest* paths in DAGs that permits negative edge weights (which you will, in Chapter 8), you automatically also have an efficient algorithm for finding for *longest* paths with *positive* edge weights.[17] The reason for this is that, with asymptotic notation (which is implicitly used here), you could say that "fast + fast = fast." In other words, fast reduction + fast solution to B = fast solution to A.

Now let's apply our friend *contraposition*. We've established "If B is easy, then A is easy." The contrapositive is "If A is hard, then B is hard."[18] This should still be quite easy to understand, intuitively. If we know that A is hard, no matter how we approach it, we know B can't be easy—because if it *were* easy, it would supply us with an easy solution to A, and A wouldn't be hard after all (a contradiction).

I hope the section has made sense so far. Now there's just one last step to the reasoning. If I come across a new, unknown problem X, and I already know that the problem Y is hard, how can I use a reduction to show that X is hard?

There are basically two alternatives, so the odds should be about 50-50. Oddly enough, it seems that more than half the people I ask get this wrong before they think about it a bit. The answer is, reduce Y to X. (Did you get it right?) If you know Y is hard and you reduce it to X, then X must be hard, because otherwise it could be used to solve Y easily—a contradiction.

Reducing in the other direction doesn't really get you anywhere. For example, fixing a smashed computer is hard, but if you want to know whether fixing your (unsmashed) computer is easy or hard, smashing it isn't going to prove anything.

So, to sum up the reasoning here:

- If you can (easily) reduce A to B, then B is at least as hard as A.

- If you want to show that X is hard and you know that Y is hard, reduce Y to X.

---

[16]The most important case in Chapter 11 is be when "easy" means polynomial. The logic applies in other cases too.

[17]Only in DAGs, though. Finding longest paths in general graphs is an unsolved problem, as discussed in Chapter 11.

[18]As you may recall, the contrapositive of "If X, then Y" is "If not Y, then not X," and these statements are equivalent. For example, "I think, therefore I am" is equivalent to "I am not, therefore I think not." However, it is *not* equivalent to "I am, therefore I think."

One of the reasons this is so confusing for many people is that we normally think of reductions as transforming a problem to something *easier*. Even the name "reduction" connotes this. However, if we're solving A by reducing it to B, it only *seems* like B is easier, because it's something we already know how to solve. After the reduction, A is *just as easy*—because we can solve it through B (with the addition of an easy, fast reduction). In other words, as long as your reduction isn't doing any heavy lifting, you can *never* reduce to something easier, because the act of reduction automatically evens things out. Reduce A to B, and B is automatically *at least as hard* as A.

Let's leave it at that for now. I'll get into the details in Chapter 11.

Problem Solving Advice

Here is some advice for solving algorithmic problems and designing algorithms, summing up some of the main ideas of this chapter:

- **Make sure you really understand the problem.** What is the input? The output? What's the precise relationship between the two? Try to represent the problem instances as familiar structures, such as sequences or graphs. A direct, brute-force solution can sometimes help clarify exactly what the problem is.

- **Look for a reduction.** Can you transform the input so it works as input for another problem that you can solve? Can you transform the resulting output so that you can use it? Can you reduce an instance of size n to an instance of size $k < n$ and extend the recursive solution (inductive hypothesis) back to n?

  Together, these two form a powerful approach to algorithm design. I'm going to add a third item here, as well. It's not so much a third step as something to keep in mind while working through the first two:

- **Are there extra assumptions you can exploit?** Integers in a fixed value range can be sorted more efficiently than arbitrary values. Finding the shortest path in a DAG is easier than in an arbitrary graph, and using only non-negative edge weights is often easier than arbitrary edge weights.

At the moment, you should be able to start using the first two pieces of advice in constructing your algorithms. The first (understanding and representing the problem) may seem obvious, but a deep understanding of the structure of the problem can make it much easier to find a solution. Consider special cases or simplifications to see whether they give you ideas. Wishful thinking can be useful here, dropping parts of the problem specification, so you can think of one or a few aspects at a time. ("What if we ignored the edge weights? What if all the numbers were 0 or 1? What if all the strings were of equal length? What if every node had exactly k neighbors?")

The second item (looking for a reduction) has been discussed a lot in this chapter, especially reducing to (or decomposing into) subproblems. This is crucial when designing your own spanking new algorithms, but ordinarily, it is much more likely that you'll find an algorithm that *almost* fits. Look for patterns in or aspects of the problem that you recognize, and scan your mental archives for algorithms that might be relevant. Instead of constructing an algorithm that will solve the problem, can you construct an algorithm that will transform the instances so an existing algorithm can solve them? Working systematically with the problems and algorithms you know can be more productive than waiting for inspiration.

The third item is more of a general observation. Algorithms that are tailored to a specific problem are usually more efficient than more general algorithms. Even if you know a general solution, perhaps you can tweak it to use the extra constraints of this particular problem? If you've constructed a brute-force solution in an effort to understand the problem, perhaps you can develop that into a more efficient solution by using these quirks of the problem? Think of modifying insertion sort so it becomes bucket sort,[19] for example, because you know something about the distribution of the values.

---

[19]Discussed in the sidebar "Counting Sort & Fam," earlier in this chapter.

Summary

This chapter is about designing algorithms by somehow reducing a problem to something you know how to solve. If you reduce to a different problem entirely, you can perhaps solve it with an existing algorithm. If you reduce it to one or more subproblems (smaller instances of the same problem), you can solve it inductively, and the inductive design gives you a new algorithm. Most examples in this chapter have been based on weak induction or extending solutions to subproblems of size $n-1$. In later chapters, especially Chapter 6, you will see more use of strong induction, where the subproblems can be of any size $k < n$.

This sort of size reduction and induction is closely related to recursion. Induction is what you use to show that recursion is correct, and recursion is a very direct way of implementing most inductive algorithm ideas. However, rewriting the algorithm to be iterative can avoid the overhead and limitations of recursive functions in most nonfunctional programming languages. If an algorithm is iterative to begin with, you can still think of it recursively, by viewing the subproblem solved so far as if it were calculated by a recursive call. Another approach would be to define a loop invariant, which is true after every iteration and which you prove using induction. If you show that the algorithm terminates, you can use the invariant to show correctness.

Of the examples in this chapter, the most important one is probably topological sorting: ordering the nodes of a DAG so that all edges point forward (that is, so that all dependencies are respected). This is important for finding a valid order of performing tasks that depend on each other, for example, or for ordering subproblems in more complex algorithms. The algorithm presented here repeatedly removes nodes without in-edges, appending them to the ordering and maintaining in-degrees for all nodes to keep the solution efficient. Chapter 5 describes another algorithm for this problem.

In some algorithms, the inductive idea isn't linked only to subproblem sizes. They are based on gradual improvement of some estimate, using an approach called *relaxation*. This is used in many algorithms for finding shortest paths in weighted graphs, for example. To prove that these are correct, you may need to uncover patterns in how the estimates improve or how correct estimates spread across elements of your problem instances.

While reductions have been used in this chapter to show that a problem is *easy*, that is, to find a solution for it, you can also use reductions to show that one problem is *at least as hard* as another. If you reduce problem A to problem B, and the reduction itself is easy, then B must be at least as hard as A (or we get a contradiction). This idea is explored in more detail in Chapter 11.

If You're Curious ...

As I said in the introduction, this chapter is to a large extent inspired by Udi Manber's paper "Using induction to design algorithms." Information on both that paper and his later book on the same subject can be found in the "References" section. I highly recommend that you at least take a look at the paper, which you can probably find online. You will also encounter several examples and applications of these principles throughout the rest of the book.

If you really want to understand how recursion can be used for virtually anything, you might want to play around with a functional language, such as Haskell (see http://haskell.org) or Clojure (see http://clojure.org). Just going through some basic tutorials on functional programming could deepen your understanding of recursion, and, thereby, induction, greatly, especially if you're a bit new to this way of thinking. You could even check out the books by Rabhi and Lapalme on algorithms in Haskell and by Okasaki on data structures in functional languages in general.

Although I've focused exclusively on the inductive properties of recursion here, there are other ways of showing how recursion works. For example, there exists a so-called fixpoint theory of recursion that can be used to determine what a recursive function really does. It's rather heavy stuff, and I wouldn't recommend it as a place to *start*, but if you want to know more about it, you could check out the book by Zohar Manna or (for a slightly easier but also less thorough description) the one by Michael Soltys.

If you'd like more problem-solving advice, Pólya's *How to Solve It* is a classic, which keeps being reprinted. Worth a look. You might also want to get *The Algorithm Design Manual* by Steven Skiena. It's a reasonably comprehensive reference of basic algorithms, along with a discussion of design principles. He even has a quite useful checklist for solving algorithmic problems.

Exercises

4-1. A graph that you can draw in the plane without any edges crossing each other is called *planar*. Such a drawing will have a number of *regions*, areas bounded by the edges of the graph, as well as the (infinitely large) area *around* the graph. If the graph has V, E, and F nodes, edges, and regions, respectively, Euler's formula for connected planar graphs says that $V - E + F = 2$. Prove that this is correct using induction.

4-2. Consider a plate of chocolate, consisting of n squares in a rectangular arrangement. You want to break it into individual squares, and the only operation you'll use is breaking one of the current rectangles (there will be more, once you start breaking) into two pieces. What is the most efficient way of doing this?

4-3. Let's say you're going to invite some people to a party. You're considering n friends, but you know that they will have a good time only if each of them knows at least k others at the party. (Assume that if A knows B, then B automatically knows A.) Solve your problem by designing an algorithm for finding the largest possible subset of your friends where everyone knows at least k of the others, if such a subset exists.

Bonus question: If your friends know d others in the group *on average* and at least *one* person knows at least *one* other, show that you can always find a (nonempty) solution for $k \le d/2$.

4-4. A node is called *central* if the greatest (unweighted) distance from that node to any other in the same graph is minimum. That is, if you sort the nodes by their greatest distance to any other node, the central nodes will be at the beginning. Explain why an unrooted tree has either one or two central nodes, and describe an algorithm for finding them.

4-5. Remember the knights in Chapter 3? After their first tournament, which was a round-robin tournament, where each knight jousted one of the other, the staff want to create a ranking. They realize it might not be possible to create a *unique* ranking or even a proper topological sorting (because there may be cycles of knights defeating each other), but they have decided on the following solution: order the knights in a sequence $K_1, K_2, \ldots, Kn$, where K_1 defeated K_2, K_2 defeated K_3, and so forth (K_{i-1} defeated K_i, for $i=2\ldots n$). Prove that it is always possible to construct such a sequence by designing an algorithm that builds it.

4-6. George Pólya (the author of *How to Solve It*; see the "References" section) came up with the following entertaining (and intentionally fallacious) "proof" that all horses have the same color. If you have only a single horse, then there's clearly only one color (the base case). Now we want to prove that n horses have the same color, under the inductive hypothesis that all sets of $n-1$ horses do. Consider the sets $\{1, 2, \ldots, n-1\}$ and $\{2, 3, \ldots, n\}$. These are both of size $n-1$, so in each set, there is only one color. However, because the sets overlap, the same must be true for $\{1, 2, \ldots n\}$. Where's the error in this argument?

4-7. In the example early in the section "One, Two, Many," where we wanted to show how many internal nodes a binary tree with n leaves had, instead of "building up" from $n-1$ to n, we started with n nodes and deleted one leaf and one internal node. Why was that OK?

4-8. Use the standard rules from Chapter 2 and the recurrences from Chapter 3 and show that the running times of the four sorting algorithms in Listings 4-1 through 4-4 are all quadratic.

4-9. In finding a maximum permutation recursively (such as in Listing 4-5), how can we be sure that the permutation we end up with contains at least one person? Shouldn't it be possible, in theory, to remove everyone?

4-10. Show that the naïve algorithm for finding the maximum permutation (Listing 4-5) is quadratic.

4-11. Implement radix sort.

4-12. Implement bucket sort.

4-13. For numbers (or strings or sequences) with a fixed number of digits (or characters or elements), d, radix sort has a running time of $\Theta(dn)$. Let's say you are sorting number whose digit counts vary greatly. A standard radix sort would require you to set d to the maximum of these, padding the rest with initial zeros. If, for example, a single number had a lot more digits than all the others, this wouldn't be very efficient. How could you modify the algorithm to have a running time of $\Theta(\sum d_i)$, where d_i is the digit count of the ith number?

4-14. How could you sort n numbers in the value range $1...n^2$ in $\Theta(n)$ time?

4-15. When finding in-degrees in the maximum permutation problem, why could the count array simply be set to `[M.count(i) for i in range(n)]`?

4-16. The section "Designing with Induction (and Recursion)" describes solutions to three problems. Compare the naïve and final versions of the algorithms experimentally.

4-17. Explain why `naive_topsort` is correct; why is it correct to insert the last node directly after its dependencies?

4-18. Write a function for generating random DAGs. Write an automatic test that checks that `topsort` gives a valid orderings, using your DAG generator.

4-19. Redesign `topsort` so it selects the *last* node in each iteration, rather than the *first*.

4-20. Implement the algorithm for finding balance factors in a binary tree.

4-21. An *interval* can be represented, for example, as a pair of numbers, such as (3.2, 4.9). Let's say you have a list of such intervals (where no intervals are identical), and you want know which intervals that fall inside other intervals. An interval (u,v) falls inside (x,y) when $x \le u$ and $v \le y$. How would you do this efficiently?

4-22. How would you improve the relaxation-based algorithm for the airplane + train problem in the section "Relaxation and Gradual Improvement" so that you are guaranteed an answer in polynomial time?

4-23. Consider three problems, *foo*, *bar*, and *baz*. You know that *bar* is hard and that *baz* is easy. How would you go about showing that *foo* was hard? How would you show that it was easy?

References

Manber, U. (1988). Using induction to design algorithms. *Communications of the ACM*, 31(11):1300–1313.

Manber, U. (1989). *Introduction to Algorithms: A Creative Approach*. Addison-Wesley.

Manna, Z. (1974). *Mathematical Theory of Computation*. McGraw-Hill Book Company.

Okasaki, C. (1999). *Purely Functional Data Structures*. Cambridge University Press.

Pólya, G. (2009). *How To Solve It: A New Aspect of Mathematical Method*. Ishi Press.

Rabhi, F. A. and Lapalme, G. (1999). *Algorithms: A Functional Approach*. Addison-Wesley.

Simionato, M. (2006). The Python 2.3 method resolution order. `http://python.org/download/releases/2.3/mro`.

Skiena, S. S. (2008). *The Algorithm Design Manual*, second edition. Springer.

Soltys, M. (2010). *An Introduction to the Analysis of Algorithms*. World Scientific.

CHAPTER 5

■ ■ ■

Traversal: The Skeleton Key of Algorithmics

You are in a narrow hallway. This continues for several metres and ends in a doorway. Halfway along the passage you can see an archway where some steps lead downwards. Will you go forwards to the door (turn to 5), or creep down the steps (turn to 344)?

— Steve Jackson, *Citadel of Chaos*

Graphs are a powerful mental (and mathematical) model of structure in general; if you can formulate a problem as one dealing with graphs, even if it doesn't *look* like a graph problem, you are probably one step closer to solving it. It just so happens that there is a highly useful mental model for graph *algorithms* as well—a skeleton key, if you will.[1] That skeleton key is *traversal*: discovering, and later visiting, all the nodes in a graph. And it's not just about *obvious* graphs. Consider, for example, how painting applications such as GIMP or Adobe Photoshop can fill a region with a single color, so-called flood fill. That's an application of what you'll learn here (see Exercise 5-4). Or perhaps you want to serialize some complex data structure and need to make sure you examine all its constituent objects? That's traversal. Listing all files and directories in a part of the file system? Manage dependencies between software packages? More traversal.

But traversal isn't only useful directly; it's a crucial component and underlying principle in many *other* algorithms, such as those in Chapters 9 and 10. For example, in Chapter 10, we'll try to match *n* people with *n* jobs, where each person has skills that match only some of the jobs. The algorithm works by tentatively assigning people to jobs but then reassigning them if someone else needs to take over. This reassignment can then trigger *another* reassignment, possibly resulting in a cascade. As you'll see, this cascade involves moving back and forth between people and jobs, in a sort of zig-zag pattern, starting with an idle person and ending with an available job. What's going on here? You guessed it: traversal.

I'll cover the idea from several angles and, in several versions, trying to tie the various strands together where possible. This means covering two of the most well-known basic traversal strategies, *depth-first search* and *breadth-first search*, building up to a slightly more complex traversal-based algorithm for finding so-called strongly connected components.

Traversal is useful in that it lets us build a layer abstraction on top of some basic induction. Consider the problem of finding the connected components of a graph (see Figure 5-1 for an example). As you may recall from Chapter 2, a graph is connected if there is a path from each node to each of the others and if the connected components are the maximal subgraphs that are (individually) connected. One way of finding a connected component would be to start at some place in the graph and gradually grow a larger connected subgraph until we can't get any further. How can we be sure that we have then reconstructed an entire component?

---

[1]I've "stolen" the subtitle for this chapter from Dudley Ernest Littlewood's *The Skeleton Key of Mathematics*.

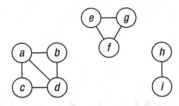

Figure 5-1. *An undirected graph with three connected components*

Let's look at the following related problem. Show that you can order the nodes in a connected graph, $v_1, v_2, \ldots, v_n$, so that for any $i = 1 \ldots n$, the subgraph over $v_1, \ldots, v_i$ is connected. If we can show this and we can figure out how to do the ordering, we can go through all the nodes in a connected component and know when they're all used up.

How do we do this? Thinking inductively, we need to get from i–1 to i. We know that the subgraph over the i–1 first nodes is connected. What next? Well, because there are paths between any pair of nodes, consider a node u in the first i–1 nodes and a node v in the remainder. On the path from u to v, consider the last node that is *in* the component we've built so far, as well as the first node *outside* it. Let's call them x and y. Clearly there must be an edge between them, so adding y to the nodes of our growing component keeps it connected, and we've shown what we set out to show.

I hope you can see how easy the resulting procedure actually is. It's just a matter of adding nodes that are connected to the component, and we discover such nodes by following an edge. An interesting point is that as long as we keep connecting new nodes to our component in this way, we're building a *tree*. This tree is called a *traversal tree* and is a spanning tree of the component we're traversing. (For a directed graph, it would span only the nodes we could reach, of course.)

To implement this procedure, we need to keep track of these "fringe" or "frontier" nodes that are just one edge away. If we start with a single node, the frontier will simply be its neighbors. As we start exploring, the neighbors of newly visited nodes will form the new fringe, while those nodes we visit now fall inside it. In other words, we need to maintain the fringe as a collection of some sort, where we can remove the nodes we visit and add their neighbors, unless they're already on the list or we've already visited them. It becomes a sort of to-do list of nodes we want to visit but haven't gotten around to yet. You can think of the ones we *have* visited as being checked off.

For those of you who have played old-school role-playing games such as Dungeons & Dragons (or, indeed, many of today's video games), Figure 5-2 might help clarify these ideas. It shows a typical dungeon map.[2] Think of the rooms (and corridors) as nodes and the doors between them as edges. There are some multiple edges (doors) here, but that's really not a problem. I've also added a "you are here" marker to the map, along with some tracks indicating how you got there.

---

[2]If you're not a gamer, feel free to imagine this as your office building, dream home, or whatever strikes your fancy.

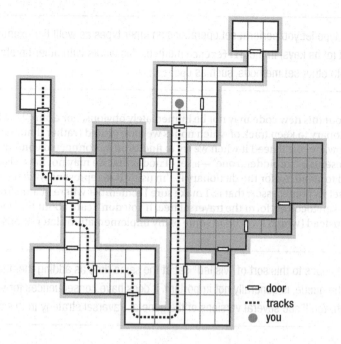

Figure 5-2. *A partial traversal of a typical role-playing dungeon. Think of the rooms as nodes and the doors as edges. The traversal tree is defined by your tracks; the fringe (the traversal queue) consists of the neighboring rooms, the light ones without footprints. The remaining (darkened) rooms haven't been discovered yet*

Notice that there are three kinds of rooms: the ones you've actually visited (those with tracks through them), those you know about because you've seen their doors, and those you don't know about yet (darkened). The unknown rooms are (of course) separated from the visited rooms by a frontier of known but unvisited rooms, just like in any kind of traversal. Listing 5-1 gives a simple implementation of this general traversal strategy (with the comments referring to graphs rather than dungeons).[3]

Listing 5-1. Walking Through a Connected Component of a Graph Represented Using Adjacency Sets

```
def walk(G, s, S=set()):              # Walk the graph from node s
    P, Q = dict(), set()              # Predecessors + "to do" queue
    P[s] = None                       # s has no predecessor
    Q.add(s)                          # We plan on starting with s
    while Q:                          # Still nodes to visit
        u = Q.pop()                   # Pick one, arbitrarily
        for v in G[u].difference(P, S): # New nodes?
            Q.add(v)                  # We plan to visit them!
            P[v] = u                  # Remember where we came from
    return P                          # The traversal tree
```

---

[3]I'll be using dicts with adjacency sets as the default representation in the following, although many of the algorithms will work nicely with other representations from Chapter 2 as well. Usually, rewriting an algorithm to use a different representation isn't too hard either.

■ **Tip** Objects of the `set` type let you perform set operations on other types as well! For example, in Listing 5-1, I use the dict P as if it were a set (of its keys) in the `difference` method. This works with other iterables too, such as `list` or `deque`, for example, and with other set methods, such as `update`.

A couple of things about this new code may not be immediately obvious. For example, what is the S parameter, and why am I using a dictionary to keep track of which nodes we have visited (rather than, say, a set)? The S parameter isn't all that useful right now, but we'll need it when we try to find *strongly* connected components (near the end of the chapter). Basically, it represents a "forbidden zone"—a set of nodes that we may not have visited during our traversal but that we have been told to avoid. As for the dictionary P, I'm using it to represent *predecessors*. Each time we add a new node to the queue, I set its predecessor; that is, I make sure I remember where I came from when I found it. These predecessors will, when taken together, form the traversal tree. If you don't care about the tree, you're certainly free to use a set of visited nodes instead (which I will do in some of my implementations later in this chapter).

■ **Note** Whether you add nodes to this sort of "visited" set at the same time as adding them to the queue or later, when you pop them from the queue, is generally not important. It does have consequences for where you need to add an "if visited ..." check, though. You'll see several versions of the general traversal strategy in this chapter.

The `walk` function will traverse a single connected component (assuming the graph is undirected). To find *all* the components, you need to wrap it in a loop over the nodes, like in Listing 5-2.

Listing 5-2. Finding Connected Components

```
def components(G):                       # The connected components
    comp = []
    seen = set()                         # Nodes we've already seen
    for u in G:                          # Try every starting point
        if u in seen: continue           # Seen? Ignore it
        C = walk(G, u)                   # Traverse component
        seen.update(C)                   # Add keys of C to seen
        comp.append(C)                   # Collect the components
    return comp
```

The `walk` function returns a predecessor map (traversal tree) for the nodes it has visited, and I collect those in the `comp` list (of connected components). I use the `seen` set to make sure I don't traverse from a node in one of the earlier, already visited components. Note that even though the operation `seen.update(C)` is linear in the size of C, the call to `walk` has already done the same amount of work, so asymptotically, it doesn't cost us anything. All in all, finding the components like this is $\Theta(E + V)$ because every edge and node has to be explored.[4]

The `walk` function doesn't really do all that much. Still, in many ways, this simple piece of code is the backbone of this chapter and (as the chapter title says) a skeleton key to understanding many of the other algorithms you're going to learn. It might be worth studying it a bit. Try to perform the algorithm manually on a graph of your choice (such as the one in Figure 5-1). Do you see how it is guaranteed to explore an entire connected component? It's important

---

[4]This is the running time of all the traversal algorithms in this chapter, except (sometimes) IDDFS.

to note that the order in which the nodes are returned from Q.pop *does not matter*. The entire component will be explored, regardless. That very order, though, is the crucial element that defines the behavior of the walk, and by tweaking it, we can get several useful algorithms right out of the box.

For a couple of other graphs to traverse, see Figures 5-3 and 5-4. (For more about these examples, see the nearby sidebar.)

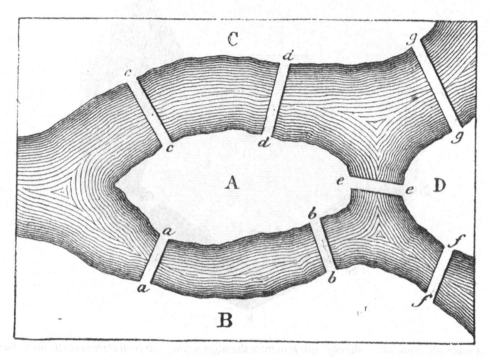

Figure 5-3. *The bridges of Königsberg (today, Kaliningrad) in 1759. The illustration is taken from Récréations Mathématiques, vol 1 (Lucas, 1891, p. 22)*

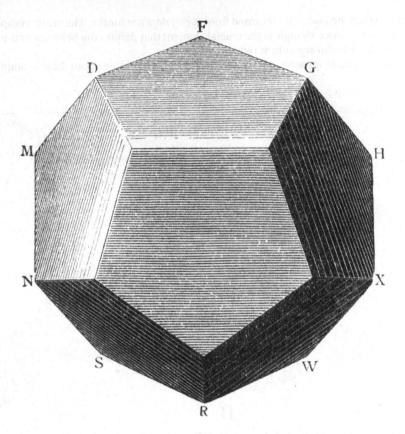

Figure 5-4. *A dodecahedron, where the objective is to trace the edges so you visit each vertex exactly once. The illustration is taken from Récréations Mathématiques, vol 2 (Lucas, 1896, p. 205)*

ISLAND-HOPPING IN KALININGRAD

Heard of the seven bridges of Königsberg (now known as Kaliningrad)? In 1736, the Swiss mathematician Leonhard Euler came across a puzzle dealing with these, which many of the inhabitants had tried to solve for quite some time. The question was, could you start anywhere in town, cross all seven bridges once, and get back where you started? (You can find the layout of the bridges in Figure 5-3.) To solve the puzzle, Euler decided to abstract away the particulars and . . . invented graph theory. Seems like a good place to start, no?

As you may notice, the structure of the banks and islands in Figure 5-3 is that of a multigraph; for example, there are two edges between A and B and between A and C. That doesn't really affect the problem. (We could easily invent some imaginary islands in the middle of some of these edges to get an ordinary graph.)

What Euler ended up proving is that it's possible to visit every edge of a (multi)graph exactly once and end up where you started if and only if the graph is connected and each node has an even degree. The resulting *closed walk* (roughly, a path where you can visit nodes more than once) is called an *Euler tour*, or *Euler circuit*, and such graphs are *Eulerian*. (You can easily see that the Königsberg isn't Eulerian; all its vertices are of odd degree.)

It's not so hard to see that connectedness and even-degree nodes are *necessary* conditions (disconnectedness is clearly a barrier, and an odd-degree node will necessarily stop your tour at some point). It's a little less obvious that they are *sufficient* conditions. We can prove this by induction (big surprise, eh?), but we need to be a bit careful about our induction parameter. If we start removing nodes or edges, the reduced problem may no longer be Eulerian, and our induction hypothesis won't apply. Let's not worry about connectivity. If the reduced graph isn't connected, we can apply the hypothesis to each connected component. But what about the even degrees?

We're allowed to visit the nodes as often as we want, so what we'll be removing (or "using up") is a set of edges. If we remove an even number of edges from each node we visit, out hypothesis will apply. One way of doing this would be to remove the edges of some closed walk (not necessarily visiting all nodes, of course). The question is whether such a closed walk will always exist in an Eulerian graph. If we just start walking from some node, u, every node we enter will go from even degree to odd degree, so we can safely leave it again. As long as we never visit an edge twice, we will eventually get back to u.

Now, let the induction hypothesis be that any connected graph with even-degree nodes and fewer than E edges has a closed walk containing each edge exactly once. We start with E edges and remove the edges of an arbitrary closed walk. We now have one or more Eulerian components, each of which is covered by our hypothesis. The last step is to combine the Euler tours in these components. Our original graph was connected, so the closed walk we removed will necessarily connect the components. The final solution consists of this combined walk, with a "detour" for the Euler tour of each component.

In other words, deciding whether a graph is Eulerian is pretty easy, and finding an Euler tour isn't that hard either (see Exercise 5-2). The Eulerian tour does, however, have a more problematic relative: the Hamilton cycle.

The Hamilton cycle is named after Sir William Rowan Hamilton, an Irish mathematician (among other things), who proposed it as a game (called *The Icosian Game*), where the objective is to visit each of the vertices of a dodecahedron (a 12-sided Platonic solid, or d12) exactly once and return to your origin (see Figure 5-4). More generally, a Hamilton cycle is a subgraph containing all the nodes of the full graph (exactly once, as it is a proper cycle). As I'm sure you can see, Königsberg is Hamiltonian (that is, it has a Hamilton cycle). Showing that the dodecahedron is Hamiltonian is a bit harder. In fact, the problem of finding Hamilton paths in general graphs is a hard problem—one for which no efficient algorithm is known (more on this in Chapter 11). Sort of odd, considering how similar the problems are, don't you think?

A Walk in the Park

It's late autumn in 1887, and a French telegraphic engineer is wandering through a well-kept garden maze, watching the leaves beginning to turn. As he walks through the passages and intersections of the maze, he recognizes some of the greenery and realizes that he has been moving in a circle. Being an inventive sort, he starts to ponder how he could have avoided this blunder and how he might best find his way out. He remembers being told, as a child, that if he kept turning left at every intersection, he would eventually find his way out, but he can easily see that such a simple strategy won't work. If his left turns take him back where he started before he gets to the exit, he's trapped in an infinite cycle. No, he'll need to find another way. As he finally fumbles his way out of the maze, he has a flash of insight. He rushes home to his notebooks, ready to start sketching out his solution.

OK, this might not be how it actually happened. I admit it, I made it all up, even the year.[5] What *is* true, though, is that a French telegraphic engineer named Trémaux in the late 1880s invented an algorithm for traversing mazes. I'll get to that in a second, but first let's explore the "keep turning left" strategy (also known as the *left-hand rule*) and see how it works—and when it doesn't.

---

[5]Hey, even the story of Newton and the apple is apocryphal.

No Cycles Allowed

Consider the maze in Figure 5-5. As you can see, there are no cycles in it; its underlying structure is that of a tree, as illustrated by the figure on the right. Here the "keep one hand on the wall" strategy will work nicely.[6] One way of seeing why it works is to observe that the maze really has only one inner wall (or, to put it another way, if you put wallpaper inside it, you could use one continuous strip). Look at the outer square. As long as you're not allowed to create cycles, any obstacles you draw have to be connected to it in exactly one place, and this doesn't create any problems for the left-hand rule. Following this traversal strategy, you'll discover all nodes and walk every passage twice (once in either direction).

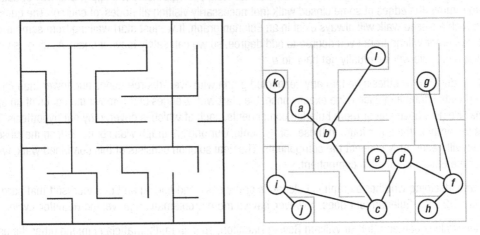

Figure 5-5. *A tree, drawn as a maze and as a more conventional graph diagram, superimposed on the maze*

The left-hand rule is designed to be executed by an individual actually walking a maze, using only local information. To get a firm grip on what is really going on, we could drop this perspective and formulate the same strategy *recursively*.[7] Once you're familiar with recursive thinking, such formulations can make it easier to see that an algorithm is correct, and this is one of the easiest recursive algorithms out there. For a basic implementation (which assumes one of our standard graph representations for the tree), see Listing 5-3.

Listing 5-3. Recursive Tree-Traversal

```
def tree_walk(T, r):          # Traverse T from root r
    for u in T[r]:            # For each child. . .
        tree_walk(T, u)       # ... traverse its subtree
```

In terms of the maze metaphor, if you're standing at an intersection and you can go left or right, you first traverse the part of the maze to the left and then the one to the right. And that's it. It should be obvious (perhaps with the aid of a little induction) that this strategy will traverse the entire maze. Note that only the act of walking *forward* through each passage is explicitly described here. When you walk the subtree rooted at node *u*, you walk forward to *u* and start working on the new passages out from there. Eventually, you will return to the root, *r*. Going backward like this, over your own tracks, is called *backtracking* and is implicit in the recursive algorithm. Each time a recursive call returns, you automatically backtrack to the node where the call originated. (Do you see how this backtracking behavior is consistent with the left-hand rule?)

---

[6]Tracing your tour from *a*, you should end up with the node sequence *a, b, c, d, e, f, g, h, d, c, i, j, i, k, i, c, b, l, b, a*.

[7]This recursive version would be harder to use if you were actually faced with a real-life maze, of course.

Imagine that someone poked a hole through one of the walls in the maze so that the corresponding graph suddenly had a cycle. Perhaps they busted through the wall just north of the dead end at node *e*. If you started your walk at *e*, walking north, you could keep left all you wanted, but you'd never traverse the entire maze—you'd keep walking in circles.[8] This is a problem we face when traversing general graphs.[9] The general idea in Listing 5-1 gives us a way out of this problem, but before I get into that, let's see what our French telegraphic engineer came up with.

How to Stop Walking in Circles

Édouard Lucas describes Tremaux's algorithm for traversing mazes in the first volume of his *Récréations Mathématiques* in 1891. Lucas writes, in his introduction:[10]

> *To completely traverse all the passages of a labyrinth twice, from any initial point, simply follow the rules posed by Trémaux, marking each entry to or exit from an intersection. These rules may be summarized as follows: When possible, avoid passing an intersection you have already visited, and avoid taking passages you have already traversed. Is this not a prudent approach, which also applies in everyday life?*

Later in the book, he goes on to describe the method in much more detail, but it is really quite simple, and the previous quote covers the main idea nicely. Instead of marking each entry or exit (say, with a piece of chalk), let's just say you have muddy boots, so you can see our own tracks (like in Figure 5-2). Trémaux would then tell you to start walking in any direction, backtracking whenever you came to a dead end or an intersection you had already walked through (to avoid cycles). You can't traverse a passage more than twice (once forward and once backward), so if you're *backtracking* into an intersection, you walk forward into one of the unexplored passages, if there are any. If there *aren't* any, you keep backtracking (into some other passage with a single set of footprints).[11]

And that's the algorithm. One interesting observation to make is that although you can choose several passages for *forward* traversal, there will always be only *one* available for backtracking. Do you see why that is? The only way there could be *two* (or more) would be if you had set off in another direction from an intersection and then come back to it without backtracking. In this case, though, the rules state that you should *not* enter the intersection but backtrack immediately. (This is also the reason why you'll never end up traversing a passage twice in the same direction.)

The reason I've used the "muddy boots" description here is to make the backtracking really clear; it's exactly like the one in the recursive tree traversal (which, again, was equivalent to the left-hand rule). In fact, if formulated recursively, Trémaux's algorithm is just like the tree walk, with the addition of a bit of memory. We know which nodes we have already visited and pretend there's a wall preventing us from entering them, in effect simulating a tree structure (which becomes our traversal tree).

See Listing 5-4 for a recursive version of Trémaux's algorithm. In this formulation, it is commonly known as *depth-first search*, and it is one of the most fundamental (and fundamentally important) traversal algorithms.[12]

---

[8]And just like that, a spelunker can turn troglodyte.

[9]People seem to end up walking in circles when wandering in the wild as well. And research by the U.S. Army suggests that people prefer going south, for some reason (as long as they have their bearings). Neither strategy is particularly helpful if you're aiming for a complete traversal, of course.

[10]My translation.

[11]You can perform the same procedure even if your boots aren't muddy. Just make sure to clearly mark entries and exits (say, with a piece of chalk). In this case, it's important to make two marks when you come to an old intersection and immediately start backtracking.

[12]In fact, in some contexts, the term *backtracking* is used as a synonym for recursive traversal, or depth-first search.

Listing 5-4. Recursive Depth-First Search

```
def rec_dfs(G, s, S=None):
    if S is None: S = set()          # Initialize the history
    S.add(s)                         # We've visited s
    for u in G[s]:                   # Explore neighbors
        if u in S: continue          # Already visited: Skip
        rec_dfs(G, u, S)             # New: Explore recursively
```

■ **Note**   As opposed to the walk function in Listing 5-1, it would be wrong to use the `difference` method on G[s] in the loop here because S might change in the recursive call and you could easily end up visiting some nodes multiple times.

Go Deep!

Depth-first search (DFS) gets some of its most important properties from its recursive structure. Once we start working with one node, we make sure we traverse all other nodes we can reach from it before moving on. However, as mentioned in Chapter 4, recursive functions can always be rewritten as iterative ones, possibly simulating the call stack with a stack of our own. Such an iterative formulation of DFS can be useful, both to avoid filling up the call stack and because it might make certain of the algorithm's properties clearer. Luckily, to simulate recursive traversal, all we need to do is use a stack rather than a set in an algorithm quite like walk in Listing 5-1. Listing 5-5 shows this iterative DFS.

Listing 5-5. Iterative Depth-First Search

```
def iter_dfs(G, s):
    S, Q = set(), []                 # Visited-set and queue
    Q.append(s)                      # We plan on visiting s
    while Q:                         # Planned nodes left?
        u = Q.pop()                  # Get one
        if u in S: continue          # Already visited? Skip it
        S.add(u)                     # We've visited it now
        Q.extend(G[u])               # Schedule all neighbors
        yield u                      # Report u as visited
```

Beyond the use of a stack (a *last-in, first-out*, or LIFO, queue, in this case implemented by a list, using append and pop), there are a couple of tweaks here. For example, in my original walk function, the queue was a set, so we'd never risk having the same node scheduled for more than one visit. Once we start using other queue structures, this is no longer the case. I've solved this by checking a node for membership in S (that is, whether we've already visited the node) before adding its neighbors.

To make the traversal a bit more useful, I've also added a yield statement, which will let you iterate over the graph nodes in DFS order. For example, if you had the graph from Figure 2-3 in the variable G, you could try the following:

```
>>> list(iter_dfs(G, 0))
[0, 5, 7, 6, 2, 3, 4, 1]
```

One thing worth noting is that I just ran DFS on a *directed graph*, while I've discussed only how it would work on *undirected graphs*. Actually, both DFS and the other traversal algorithms work just as well for directed graphs. However, if you use DFS on a directed graph, you can't expect it to explore an entire connected component. For example, for the graph in Figure 2-3, traversing from any other start node than *a* would mean that *a* would never be seen because it has no in-edges.

■ **Tip** For finding connected components in a directed graph, you can easily construct the underlying undirected graph as a first step. Or you could simply go through the graph and add all the reverse edges. This can be useful for other algorithms as well. Sometimes, you may not even construct the undirected graph; simply considering each edge in both directions when using the directed graph may be sufficient.

You can think of this in terms of Trémaux's algorithm as well. You'd still be allowed to traverse each (directed) passage both ways, but you'd be allowed to go *forward* only along the edge direction, and you'd have to *backtrack against* the edge direction.

In fact, the structure of the iter_dfs function is pretty close to how we might implement the general traversal algorithm hinted at earlier—one where only the queue need be replaced. Let's beef up walk to the more mature traverse (Listing 5-6).

Listing 5-6. A General Graph Traversal Function

```
def traverse(G, s, qtype=set):
    S, Q = set(), qtype()
    Q.add(s)
    while Q:
        u = Q.pop()
        if u in S: continue
        S.add(u)
        for v in G[u]:
            Q.add(v)
        yield u
```

The default queue type here is set, making it similar to the original (arbitrary) walk. You could easily define a stack type (with the proper add and pop methods of our general queue protocol), perhaps like this:

```
class stack(list):
    add = list.append
```

The previous depth-first test could then be repeated as follows:

```
>>> list(traverse(G, 0, stack))
[0, 5, 7, 6, 2, 3, 4, 1]
```

Of course, it's also quite OK to implement special-purpose versions of the various traversal algorithms, even though they can be expressed in much the same form.

Depth-First Timestamps and Topological Sorting (Again)

As mentioned earlier, remembering and avoiding previously visited nodes is what keeps us from going in circles (or, rather, cycles), and a traversal without cycles naturally forms a tree. Such traversal trees have different names based on how they were constructed; for DFS, they are aptly named *depth-first trees* (or DFS trees). As with any traversal tree, the structure of a DFS tree is determined by the order in which the nodes are visited. The thing that is particular to DFS trees is that all descendants of a node u are processed in the time interval from when u is discovered to when we backtrack through it.

To make use of this property, we need to know when the algorithm is backtracking, which can be a bit hard in the iterative version. Although you could extend the iterative DFS from Listing 5-5 to keep track of backtracking (see Exercise 5-7), I'll be extending the recursive version (Listing 5-4) here. See Listing 5-7 for a version that adds timestamps to each node: one for when it is discovered (discover time, or d) and one for when we backtrack through it (finish time, or f).

Listing 5-7. Depth-First Search with Timestamps

```
def dfs(G, s, d, f, S=None, t=0):
    if S is None: S = set()          # Initialize the history
    d[s] = t; t += 1                 # Set discover time
    S.add(s)                         # We've visited s
    for u in G[s]:                   # Explore neighbors
        if u in S: continue          # Already visited. Skip
        t = dfs(G, u, d, f, S, t)    # Recurse; update timestamp
    f[s] = t; t += 1                 # Set finish time
    return t                         # Return timestamp
```

The parameters d and f should be mappings (dictionaries, for example). The DFS property then states that (1) every node is discovered *before* its descendants in the DFS tree, and (2) every node is finished *after* its descendants in the DFS. This follows rather directly from the recursive formulation of the algorithm, but you could easily do an induction proof to convince yourself that it's true.

One immediate consequence of this property is that we can use DFS for topological sorting, already discussed in Chapter 4. If we perform DFS on a DAG, we could simply sort the nodes based on their descending finish times, and they'd be topologically sorted. Each node u would then precede all its descendants in the DFS tree, which would be any nodes reachable from u, that is, nodes that depend on u. It is in cases like this that it pays to know how an algorithm works. Instead of first calling our timestamping DFS and then sorting afterward, we could simply perform the topological sorting *during* a custom DFS, by appending nodes when backtracking, as shown in Listing 5-8.[13]

Listing 5-8. Topological Sorting Based on Depth-First Search

```
def dfs_topsort(G):
    S, res = set(), []               # History and result
    def recurse(u):                  # Traversal subroutine
        if u in S: return            # Ignore visited nodes
        S.add(u)                     # Otherwise: Add to history
        for v in G[u]:
            recurse(v)               # Recurse through neighbors
        res.append(u)                # Finished with u: Append it
```

---

[13]The dfs_topsort function can also be used to sort the nodes of a *general* graph by decreasing finish times, as needed when looking for strongly connected components, discussed later in this chapter.

```
for u in G:                          # Cover entire graph
    recurse(u)
res.reverse()                        # It's all backward so far
return res
```

There are a few things that are worth noting in this new topological sorting algorithm. For one thing, I'm explicitly including a for loop over all the nodes to make sure the entire graph is traversed. (Exercise 5-8 asks you to show that this will work.) The check for whether a node is already in the history set (S) is now placed right inside recurse, so we don't need to put it in both of the for loops. Also, because recurse is an internal function, with access to the surrounding scope (in particular, S and res), the only parameter needed is the node we're traversing from. Finally, remember that we want the nodes to be sorted in *reverse*, based on their finish times. That's why the res list is reversed before it's returned.

This topsort performs some processing on each node as it backtracks over them (it appends them to the result list). The order in which DFS backtracks over nodes (that is, the order of their finish times) is called *postorder*, while the order in which it visits them in the first place is called *preorder*. Processing at these times is called *preorder* or *postorder* processing. (Exercise 5-9 asks you to add general hooks for this sort of processing in DFS.)

NODE COLORS AND EDGE TYPES

In describing traversal, I have distinguished between three kinds of nodes: those we don't know about, those in our queue, and those we've visited (and whose neighbors are now in the queue). Some books (such as *Introduction to Algorithms*, by Cormen et al., mentioned in Chapter 1) introduce a form of node coloring, which is especially important in DFS. Each node is considered white to begin with; they're gray in the interval between their discover time and their finish time, and they're black thereafter. You don't really need this classification in order to *implement* DFS, but it can be useful in understanding it (or, at least, it might be useful to know about it if you're going to read a text that uses the coloring).

In terms of Trémaux's algorithm, gray intersections would be ones we've seen but have since avoided; black intersections would be the ones we've been forced to enter a second time (while backtracking).

These colors can also be used to classify the edges in the DFS tree. If an edge *uv* is explored and the node *v* is white, the edge is a *tree edge*—that is, it's part of the traversal tree. If *v* is gray, it's a so-called *back edge*, one that goes back to an ancestor in the DFS tree. Finally, if *v* is black, the edge is either what is called a *forward edge* or a *cross edge*. A forward edge is an edge to a descendant in the traversal tree, while a cross edge is any other edge (that is, not a tree, back or forward edge).

Note that you can classify the edges without actually using any explicit color labeling. Let the time span of a node be the interval from its discover time to its finish time. A descendant will then have a time span contained in its ancestor's, while nodes unrelated by ancestry will have nonoverlapping intervals. Thus, you can use the timestamps to figure out whether something is, say, a back or forward edge. Even with color labeling, you'd need to consult the timestamps to differentiate between forward and cross edges.

You probably won't need this classification much, although it does have one important use. If you find a back edge, the graph contains a cycle, but if you don't, it doesn't. (Exercise 5-10 asks you to show this.) In other words, you can use DFS to check whether a graph is a DAG (or, for undirected graphs, a tree). Exercise 5-11 asks you to consider how other traversal algorithms would work for this purpose.

Infinite Mazes and Shortest (Unweighted) Paths

Until now, the overeager behavior of DFS hasn't been a problem. We let it loose in a maze (graph), and it veers off in some direction, as far as it can, before it starts backtracking. This can be problematic, though, if the maze is extremely large. Maybe what we're looking for, such as an exit, is close to where we started; if DFS sets off in a different direction, it may not return for *ages*. And if the maze is infinite, it will *never* get back, even though a different traversal might have found the exit in a matter of minutes. Infinite mazes may sound far-fetched, but they're actually a close analogy to an important type of traversal problem—that of looking for a solution in a state-space.

But getting lost by being over-eager, like DFS, isn't only a problem in huge graphs. If we're looking for the *shortest paths* (disregarding edge weights, for now) from our start node to all the others, DFS will, most likely, give us the wrong answer. Take a look at the example in Figure 5-6. What happens is that DFS, in its eagerness, keeps going until it reaches *c* via a *detour*, as it were. If we want to find the shortest paths to all other nodes (as illustrated in the figure on the right), we need to be more conservative. To avoid taking a detour and reaching a node "from behind," we need to advance our traversal "fringe" one step at a time. First visit all nodes one step away and then all those two steps away, and so forth.

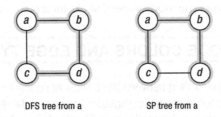

DFS tree from a   SP tree from a

Figure 5-6. *Two traversals of a size four cycle. The depth-first tree (highlighted, left) will not necessarily contain minimal paths, as opposed to the shortest path tree (highlighted, right)*

In keeping with the maze metaphor, let's briefly take a look at another maze exploration algorithm, described by Øystein (aka Oystein) Ore in 1959. Just like Trémaux, Ore asks you to make marks at passage entries and exits. Let's say you start at intersection *a*. First, you visit all intersections one passage away, each time backtracking to your starting point. If any of the passages you followed were dead ends, you mark them as closed once you return. Any passages leading you to an intersection where you've already been are also marked as closed (at both ends).

At this point, you'd like to start exploring all intersections *two* steps (that is, passages) away. Mark and go through one of the open passages from *a*; it should now have two marks on it. Let's say you end up in intersection *b*. Now, traverse (and mark) all open passages from *b*, making sure to close them if they lead to dead ends or intersections you've already seen. After you're done, backtrack to *a*. Once you've returned to *a*, you continue the process with the other open passages, until they've all received two marks. (These two marks mean that you've traversed intersections two steps away through the passages.)

Let's jump to step n.[14] You've visited all intersections $n-1$ steps away, so all open passages from *a* now have $n-1$ marks on them. Open passages at any intersections next to *a*, such as the *b* you visited earlier, will have $n-2$ marks on them, and so forth. To visit all intersections at a distance of n from your starting point, you simply move to all neighbors of *a* (such as *b*), adding marks to the passages as you do so, and visit all intersections at a distance $n-1$ out from them following the same procedure (which will work, by inductive hypothesis).

Once again, using only local information like this might make the bookkeeping a bit tedious (and the explanation a bit confusing). However, just like Trémaux's algorithm had a very close relative in the recursive DFS, Ore's method can be formulated in a way that might suit our computer science brains better. The result is something called *iterative deepening depth-first search*, or IDDFS,[15] and it simply consists of running a depth-constrained DFS with an iteratively incremented depth limit.

---

[14]In other words, let's think inductively.
[15]IDDFS isn't *completely* equivalent to Ore's method because it doesn't mark edges as closed in the same way. Adding that kind of marking is certainly possible and would be a form of *pruning*, discussed later in this chapter.

Listing 5-9 gives a fairly straightforward implementation of IDDFS. It keeps a global set called `yielded`, consisting of the nodes that have been discovered for the first time and therefore yielded. The inner function, `recurse`, is basically a recursive DFS with a depth limit, d. If the limit is zero, no further edges are explored recursively. Otherwise, the recursive calls receive a limit of d-1. The main for loop in the `iddfs` function goes through every depth limit from 0 (just visit, and yield, the start node) to `len(G)-1` (the maximum possible depth). If all nodes have been discovered before such a depth is reached, though, the loop is broken.

Listing 5-9. Iterative Deepening Depth-First Search

```
def iddfs(G, s):
    yielded = set()                          # Visited for the first time
    def recurse(G, s, d, S=None):            # Depth-limited DFS
        if s not in yielded:
            yield s
            yielded.add(s)
        if d == 0: return                    # Max depth zero: Backtrack
        if S is None: S = set()
        S.add(s)
        for u in G[s]:
            if u in S: continue
            for v in recurse(G, u, d-1, S):  # Recurse with depth-1
                yield v
    n = len(G)
    for d in range(n):                       # Try all depths 0..V-1
        if len(yielded) == n: break          # All nodes seen?
        for u in recurse(G, s, d):
            yield u
```

■ **Note** If we were exploring an unbounded graph (such as an infinite state space), looking for a particular node (or a kind of node), we might just keep trying larger depth limits until we found the node we wanted.

It's not entirely obvious what the running time of IDDFS is. Unlike DFS, it will usually traverse many of the edges and nodes multiple times, so a linear running time is far from guaranteed. For example, if your graph is a path and you start IDDFS from one end, the running time will be *quadratic*. However, this example is rather pathological; if the traversal tree branches out a bit, most of its nodes will be at the bottom level (as in the knockout tournament in Chapter 3), so for many graphs the running time will be linear or close to linear.

Try running `iddfs` on a simple graph, and you'll see that the nodes will be yielded in order from the closest to the furthest from the start node. All with a distance of k are returned, then all with a distance of $k + 1$, and so forth. If we wanted to find the actual distances, we could easily perform some extra bookkeeping in the `iddfs` function and yield the distance along with the node. Another way would be to maintain a distance table (similar to the discover and finish times we worked with earlier, for DFS). In fact, we could have one dictionary for distances and one for the parents in the traversal tree. That way, we could retrieve the actual shortest paths, as well as the distances. Let's focus on the paths for now, and instead of modifying `iddfs` to include the extra information, we'll build it into *another* traversal algorithm: *breadth-first search* (BFS).

Traversing with BFS is, in fact, quite a bit easier than with IDDFS. You just use the general traversal framework (Listing 5-6) with a *first-in first-out* queue. This is, in fact, the only salient difference from DFS: we've replaced LIFO with FIFO (see Listing 5-10). The consequence is that nodes discovered early will be visited early, and we'll be exploring the graph level by level, just like in IDDFS. The advantage, though, is that we needn't visit any nodes or edges multiple times, so we're back to guaranteed linear performance.[16]

Listing 5-10. Breadth-First Search

```
def bfs(G, s):
    P, Q = {s: None}, deque([s])          # Parents and FIFO queue
    while Q:
        u = Q.popleft()                    # Constant-time for deque
        for v in G[u]:
            if v in P: continue            # Already has parent
            P[v] = u                       # Reached from u: u is parent
            Q.append(v)
    return P
```

As you can see, the bfs function is similar to iter_dfs, from Listing 5-5. I've replaced the list with a deque, and I keep track of which nodes have already received a parent in the traversal tree (that is, they're in P), rather than remembering which nodes we have visited (S). To extract a path to a node u, you can simply "walk backward" in P:

```
>>> path = [u]
>>> while P[u] is not None:
...     path.append(P[u])
...     u = P[u]
...
>>> path.reverse()
```

You are, of course, free to use this kind of parent dictionary in DFS as well, or to use yield to iterate over the nodes in BFS, for that matter. Exercise 5-13 asks you to modify the code to find the distances (rather than the paths).

■ **Tip**   One way of visualizing BFS and DFS is as browsing the Web. DFS is what you get if you keep following links and then use the Back button once you're done with a page. The backtracking is a bit like an "undo." BFS is more like opening every link in a new window (or tab) behind those you already have and then closing the windows as you finish with each page.

There is really only one situation where IDDFS would be preferable over BFS: when searching a huge tree (or some state space "shaped" like a tree). Because there are no cycles, we don't need to remember which nodes we've visited, which means that IDDFS needs only store the path back to the starting node.[17] BFS, on the other hand, must keep the entire fringe in memory (as its queue), and as long as there is some branching, this fringe will grow exponentially with the distance to the root. In other words, in these cases IDDFS can save a significant amount of memory, with little or no asymptotic slowdown.

---

[16]On the other hand, we'll be jumping from node to node in a manner that could not possibly be implemented in a real-life maze.
[17]To have any memory savings, you'd have to remove the S set. Because you'd be traversing a tree, that wouldn't cause any trouble (that is, traversal cycles).

BLACK BOX: DEQUE

As mentioned briefly several times already, Python lists make nice stacks (LIFO queues) but poor (FIFO) queues. Appending to them takes constant time (at least when averaged over many such appends), but popping from (or inserting at) the front takes linear time. What we want for algorithms such as BFS is a *double-ended queue*, or *deque*. Such queues are often implemented as linked lists (where appending/prepending and popping at either end are constant-time operations), or so-called circular buffers—arrays where we keep track of the position of both the first element (the head) and the last element (the tail). If either the head or the tail moves beyond its end of the array, we just let it "flow around" to the other side, and we use the mod (%) operator to calculate the actual indices (hence the term *circular*). If we fill the array completely, we can just reallocate the contents to a bigger one, like with dynamic arrays (see the "Black Box" sidebar on list in Chapter 2).

Luckily, Python has a deque class in the collections module in the standard library. In addition to methods such as append, extend, and pop, which are performed on the *right* side, it has *left* equivalents, called appendleft, extendleft, and popleft. Internally, the deque is implemented as a doubly linked list of *blocks*, each of which is an array of individual elements. Although asymptotically equivalent to using a linked list of individual elements, this reduces overhead and makes it more efficient in practice. For example, the expression d[k] would require traversing the first k elements of the deque d if it were a plain list. If each block contains b elements, you would only have to traverse k//b blocks.

Strongly Connected Components

While traversal algorithms such as DFS, IDDFS, and BFS are useful in their own right, earlier I alluded to the role of traversal as an underlying structure in *other* algorithms. You'll see this in many coming chapters, but I'll end this one with a classical example—a rather knotty problem that can be solved elegantly with some understanding of basic traversal.

The problem is that of finding *strongly connected components* (SCCs), sometimes known simply as *strong components*. SCCs are a directed analog for connected components, which I showed you how to find at the beginning of this chapter. A connected component is a maximal subgraph where all nodes can reach each other if you ignore edge directions (or if the graph is undirected). To get *strongly* connected components, though, you need to follow the edge directions; so, SCCs are the maximal subgraphs where there is a directed path from any node to any other. Finding SCCs and similar structures is an important part of the data flow analysis in modern optimizing compilers, for example.

Consider the graph in Figure 5-7. It is quite similar to the one we started with (Figure 5-1); although there are some additional edges, the SCCs of this new graph consist of the same nodes as the connected components of the undirected original. As you can see, inside the (highlighted) strong components, any node can reach any other, but this property breaks down if you try to add other nodes to any of them.

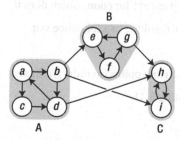

Figure 5-7. A directed graph with three SCCs (highlighted): A, B, and C

Imagine performing a DFS on this graph (possibly traversing from several starting points to ensure you cover the entire graph). Now consider the finish times of the nodes in, say, the strong components A and B. As you can see, there is an edge from A to B, but there is no way to get from B to A. This has consequences for the finish times. You can be certain that A will be finished later than B. That is, the last finish time in A will be later than the last finish time in B. Take a look at Figure 5-7, and it should be obvious why this is so. If you start in B, you can never get into A, so B will finish completely before you even *start* (let alone *finish*) your traversal of A. If, however, you start in A, you know that you'll never get stuck in there (every node can reach every other), so before finishing the traversal, you *will* eventually migrate to B, and you'll have to finish that (and, in this case, C) completely before you backtrack to A.

In fact, in general, if there is an edge from any strong component X to another strong component Y, the last finish time in X will be later than the latest in Y. The reasoning is the same as for our example (see Exercise 5-16). I based my conclusion on the fact that you couldn't get from B to A, though—and this is, in fact, how it works for SCCs in general, because SCCs form a DAG! Therefore, if there's an edge from X to Y, there will never be any path from Y to X.

Consider the highlighted components in Figure 5-7. If you contract them to single "supernodes" (keeping edges where there were edges originally), you end up with a graph—let's call it the SCC graph—which looks like this:

This is clearly a DAG, but why will such an SCC graph *always* be acyclic? Just assume that there is a cycle in the SCC graph. That would mean that you could get from one SCC to another and back again. Do you see a problem with that? Yeah, exactly: every node in the first SCC could reach every node in the second, and vice versa; in fact, all SCCs on such a cycle would combine to form a *single SCC*, which is a contradiction of our initial assumption that they were separate.

Now, let's say you flipped all the edges in the graph. This won't affect which nodes belong together in SCCs (see Exercise 5-15), but it *will* affect the SCC graph. In our example, you could no longer get out of A. And if you had traversed A and started a new round in B, you couldn't escape from that, leaving only C. And ... wait a minute ... I just found the strong components there, didn't I? To apply this idea in general, we always need to start in the SCC without any in-edges in the original graph (that is, with no out-edges after they're flipped). Basically, we're looking for the first SCC in a topological sorting of the SCC graph. (And then we'll move on to the second, and so on.) Looking back at our initial DFS reasoning, that's where we'd be if we started our traversal with the node that has the *latest finish time*. In fact, if we choose our starting points for the final traversal by decreasing finish times, we're guaranteed to fully explore one SCC at the time because we'll be blocked from moving to the next one by the reverse edges.

This line of reasoning can be a bit tough to follow, but the main idea isn't all that hard. If there's an edge from A to B, A will have a later (final) finish time than B. If we choose starting points for our (second) traversal based on decreasing finish times, this means that we'll visit A before B. Now, if we *reverse* all the edges, we can still explore all of A, but we can't move on to B, and this lets us explore a single SCC at a time.

What follows is an outline of the algorithm. Note that instead of "manually" using DFS and sorting the nodes in reverse by finish time, I simply use the `dfs_topsort` function, which does that job for me.[18]

1. Run `dfs_topsort` on the graph, resulting in a sequence `seq`.

2. Reverse all edges.

3. Run a full traversal, selecting starting points (in order) from `seq`.

For an implementation of this, see Listing 5-11.

---

[18]This might seem like cheating because I'm using topological sorting on a non-DAG. The idea is just to get the nodes sorted by decreasing finish time, though, and that's exactly what `dfs_topsort` does—in linear time.

Listing 5-11. Kosaraju's Algorithm for Finding Strongly Connected Components

```
def tr(G):                                # Transpose (rev. edges of) G
    GT = {}
    for u in G: GT[u] = set()             # Get all the nodes in there
    for u in G:
        for v in G[u]:
            GT[v].add(u)                  # Add all reverse edges
    return GT

def scc(G):
    GT = tr(G)                            # Get the transposed graph
    sccs, seen = [], set()
    for u in dfs_topsort(G):              # DFS starting points
        if u in seen: continue           # Ignore covered nodes
        C = walk(GT, u, seen)            # Don't go "backward" (seen)
        seen.update(C)                    # We've now seen C
        sccs.append(C)                    # Another SCC found
    return sccs
```

If you try running scc on the graph in Figure 5-7, you should get the three sets {a, b, c, d}; {e, f, g}; and {i, h}.[19] Note that when calling walk, I have now supplied the S parameter to make it avoid the *previous* SCCs. Because all edges are pointing backward, it would be all too easy to start traversing into these unless that was expressly prohibited.

■ **Note**   It might seem tempting to drop the call to tr(G), to *not* reverse all edges and instead reverse the sequence returned by dfs_topsort (that is, to select starting points sorted by ascending rather than descending finish time). That would not work, however (as Exercise 5-17 asks you to show).

GOALS AND PRUNING

The traversal algorithms discussed in this chapter will visit every node they can reach. Sometimes, however, you're looking for a specific node (or a kind of node), and you'd like to ignore as much of the graph as you can. This kind of search is called *goal-directed*, and the act of ignoring potential subtrees of the traversal is called *pruning*. For example, if you knew that the node you were looking for was within *k* steps of the starting node, running a traversal with a depth limit of *k* would be a form of pruning. Searching by bisection or in search trees (discussed in Chapter 6) also involves pruning. Rather than traversing the entire search tree, you only visit the subtrees that might contain the value you are looking for. The trees are constructed so that you can usually discard most subtrees at each step, leading to highly efficient algorithms.

Knowledge of where you're going can also let you choose the most promising direction first (so-called *best-first search*). An example of this is the A* algorithm, discussed in Chapter 9. If you're searching a space of possible solutions, you can also evaluate how *promising* a given direction is (that is, how good is the best solution we could find by following this edge?). By ignoring edges that wouldn't help you improve on the best you've found so far, you can speed things up considerably. This approach is called *branch and bound* and is discussed in Chapter 11.

---

[19]Actually, walk will return a traversal tree for each strong component.

Summary

In this chapter, I've shown you the basics of moving around in graphs, be they directed or not. This idea of traversal forms the basis—directly or conceptually—for many of the algorithms you'll learn later in this book and for other algorithms that you'll probably encounter later. I've used examples of maze traversal algorithms (such as Trémaux's and Ore's), although they were mainly meant as starting points for more computer-friendly approaches. The general procedure for traversing a graph involves maintaining a conceptual to-do list (a queue) of nodes you've discovered, where you check off those that you have actually visited. The list initially contains only the start node, and in each step you visit (and check off) one of the nodes, while adding its neighbors to the list. The ordering (schedule) of items on the list determines, to a large extent, what kind of traversal you are doing: using a LIFO queue (stack) gives depth-first search (DFS), while using a FIFO queue gives breadth-first search (BFS), for example. DFS, which is equivalent to a relatively direct recursive traversal, lets you find discover and finish times for each node, and the interval between these for a descendant will fall inside that of an ancestor. BFS has the useful property that it can be used to find the shortest (unweighted) paths from one node to another. A variation of DFS, called *iterative deepening DFS*, also has this property, but it is more useful for searching in large trees, such as the state spaces discussed in Chapter 11.

If a graph consists of several connected components, you will need to restart your traversal once for each component. You can do this by iterating over all the nodes, skipping those that have already been visited, and starting a traversal from the others. In a directed graph, this approach may be necessary even if the graph is connected because the edge directions may prevent you from reaching all nodes otherwise. To find the *strongly* connected components of a directed graph—the parts of the graph where all nodes can reach each other—a slightly more involved procedure is needed. The algorithm discussed here, Kosaraju's algorithm, involves first finding the finish times for all nodes and then running a traversal in the *transposed* graph (the graph with all edges reversed), using descending finish times to select starting points.

If You're Curious ...

If you like traversal, don't worry. We'll be doing more of that soon enough. You can also find details on DFS, BFS, and the SCC algorithm discussed in, for example, the book by Cormen et al. (see "References," Chapter 1). If you're interested in finding strong components, there are references for Tarjan's and Gabow's (or, rather, the Cheriyan-Mehlhorn/Gabow) algorithms in the "References" section of this chapter.

Exercises

5-1. In the `components` function in Listing 5-2, the set of seen nodes is updated with an entire component at a time. Another option would be to add the nodes one by one inside `walk`. How would that be different (or, perhaps, not so different)?

5-2. If you're faced with a graph where each node has an even degree, how would you go about finding an Euler tour?

5-3. If every node in a directed graph has the same in-degree as out-degree, you could find a *directed* Euler tour. Why is that? How would you go about it, and how is this related to Trémaux's algorithm?

5-4. One basic operation in image processing is the so-called *flood fill*, where a region in an image is filled with a single color. In painting applications (such as GIMP or Adobe Photoshop), this is typically done with a paint bucket tool. How would you implement this sort of filling?

5-5. In Greek mythology, when Ariadne helped Theseus overcome the Minotaur and escape the labyrinth, she gave him a ball of fleece thread so he could find his way out again. But what if Theseus forgot to fasten the thread outside on his way in and remembered the ball only once he was thoroughly lost—what could he use it for then?

5-6. In recursive DFS, backtracking occurs when you return from one of the recursive calls. But where has the backtracking gone in the iterative version?

5-7. Write a nonrecursive version of DFS that can deal determine finish times.

5-8. In dfs_topsort (Listing 5-8), a recursive DFS is started from every node (although it terminates immediately if the node has already been visited). How can we be sure that we will get a valid topological sorting, even though the order of the start nodes is completely arbitrary?

5-9. Write a version of DFS where you have hooks (overridable functions) that let the user perform custom processing in pre- and postorder.

5-10. Show that if (and only if) DFS finds no back edges, the graph being traversed is acyclic.

5-11. What challenges would you face if you wanted to use other traversal algorithms than DFS to look for cycles in directed graphs? Why don't you face these challenges in undirected graphs?

5-12. If you run DFS in an undirected graph, you won't have any forward or cross edges. Why is that?

5-13. Write a version of BFS that finds the distances from the start node to each of the others, rather than the actual paths.

5-14. As mentioned in Chapter 4, a graph is called *bipartite* if you can partition the nodes into two sets so that no neighbors are in the same set. Another way of thinking about this is that you're coloring each node either black or white (for example) so that no neighbors get the same color. Show how you'd find such a bipartition (or two-coloring), if one exists, for any undirected graph.

5-15. If you reverse all the edges of a directed graph, the strongly connected components remain the same. Why is that?

5-16. Let X and Y be two strongly connected components of the same graph, *G*. Assume that there is at least one edge from X to Y. If you run DFS on *G* (restarting as needed, until all nodes have been visited), the latest finish time in X will always be later than the latest in Y. Why is that?

5-17. In Kosaraju's algorithm, we find starting nodes for the final traversal by descending finish times from an initial DFS, and we perform the traversal in the transposed graph
(that is, with all edges reversed). Why couldn't we just use *ascending* finish times in the *original* graph?

References

Cheriyan, J. and Mehlhorn, K. (1996). Algorithms for dense graphs and networks on the random access computer. *Algorithmica*, 15(6):521-549.

Littlewood, D. E. (1949). *The Skeleton Key of Mathematics: A Simple Account of Complex Algebraic Theories.* Hutchinson & Company, Limited.

Lucas, É. (1891). *Récréations Mathématiques*, volume 1, second edition. Gauthier-Villars et fils, Imprimeurs-Libraires. Available online at http://archive.org.

Lucas, É. (1896). *Récréations Mathématiques*, volume 2, second edition. Gauthier-Villars et fils, Imprimeurs-Libraires. Available online at http://archive.org.

Ore, O. (1959). An excursion into labyrinths. *Mathematics Teacher*, 52:367-370.

Tarjan, R. (1972). Depth-first search and linear graph algorithms. *SIAM Journal on Computing*, 1(2): 146-160.

CHAPTER 6

■ ■ ■

Divide, Combine, and Conquer

Divide and rule, a sound motto;
Unite and lead, a better one.

— Johann Wolfgang von Goethe, *Gedichte*

This chapter is the first of three dealing with well-known *design strategies*. The strategy dealt with in this chapter, *divide and conquer* (or simply D&C), is based on decomposing your problem in a way that improves performance. You divide the problem instance, solve subproblems recursively, combine the results, and thereby conquer the problem—a pattern that is reflected in the chapter title.[1]

Tree-Shaped Problems: All About the Balance

I have mentioned the idea of a subproblem graph before: We view subproblems as nodes and dependencies (or reductions) as edges. The simplest structure such a subproblem graph can have is a tree. Each subproblem may depend on one or more others, but we're free to solve these other subproblems independently of each other. (When we remove this independence, we end up with the kind of overlap and entanglements dealt with in Chapter 8.) This straightforward structure means that as long as we can find the proper reduction, we can implement the recursive formulation of our algorithm directly.

You already have all the puzzle pieces needed to understand the idea of divide-and-conquer algorithms. Three ideas that I've already discussed cover the essentials:

- Divide-and-conquer recurrences, in Chapter 3

- Strong induction, in Chapter 4

- Recursive traversal, in Chapter 5

The recurrences tell you something about the performance involved, the induction gives you a tool for understanding how the algorithms work, and the recursive traversal (DFS in trees) is a raw skeleton for the algorithms.

Implementing the recursive formulation of our induction step directly is nothing new. I showed you how some simple sorting algorithms could be implemented that way in Chapter 4, for example. The one crucial addition in the design method of divide and conquer is *balance*. This is where strong induction comes in: Instead of recursively implementing the step from $n-1$ to n, we want to go from $n/2$ to n. That is, we take solutions of size $n/2$ and build a solution of size n. Instead of (inductively) assuming that we can solve subproblems of size $n-1$, we assume that we can deal with all subproblems of sizes smaller than n.

---

[1]Note that some authors use the *conquer* term for the base case of the recursion, yielding the slightly different ordering: divide, conquer, and combine.

What does this have to do with balance, you ask? Think of the weak induction case. We're basically dividing our problem in two parts: one of size n-1 and one of size 1. Let's say the cost of the inductive step is linear (a quite common case). Then this gives us the recurrence $T(n) = T(n\text{-}1) + T(1) + n$. The two recursive calls are wildly unbalanced, and we end up, basically, with our handshake recurrence, with a resulting quadratic running time. What if we managed to distribute the work more evenly among our two recursive calls? That is, could we reduce the problem to two subproblems of similar size? In that case, the recurrence turns into $T(n) = 2T(n/2) + n$. This should also be quite familiar: It's the canonical divide-and-conquer recurrence, and it yields a loglinear ($\Theta(n \lg n)$) running time—a *huge* improvement.

Figures 6-1 and 6-2 illustrate the difference between the two approaches, in the form of recursion trees. Note that the number of nodes is identical—the main effect comes from the distribution of *work* over those nodes. This may seem like a conjuror's trick; where does the work go? The important realization is that for the simple, unbalanced stepwise approach (Figure 6-1), many of the nodes are assigned a high workload, while for the balanced divide-and-conquer approach (Figure 6-2), most nodes have very *little* work to do. For example, in the unbalanced recursion, there will always be roughly a quarter of the calls that each has a cost of at least $n/2$, while in the balanced recursion, there will be only three, *no matter the value of n.* That's a pretty significant difference.

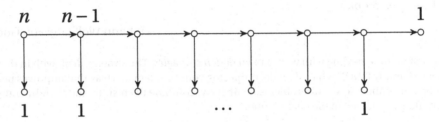

Figure 6-1. *An unbalanced decomposition, with linear division/combination cost and quadratic running time in total*

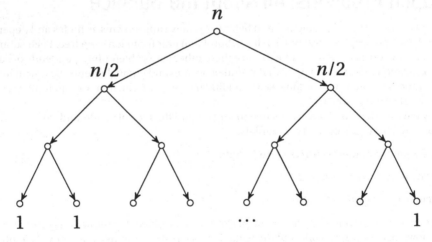

Figure 6-2. *Divide and conquer: a balanced decomposition, with linear division/combination cost and loglinear running time in total*

Let's try to recognize this pattern in an actual problem. The *skyline problem*[2] is a rather simple example. You are given a sorted sequence of triples (L,H,R), where L is the left x-coordinate of a building, H is its height, and R is its right x-coordinate. In other words, each triple represents the (rectangular) silhouette of a building, from a given vantage point. Your task is to construct a skyline from these individual building silhouettes.

---

[2]Described by Udi Manber in his *Introduction to Algorithms* (see "References" in Chapter 4).

Figures 6-3 and 6-4 illustrate the problem. In Figure 6-4, a building is being added to an existing skyline. If the skyline is stored as a list of triples indicating the horizontal line segments, adding a new building can be done in linear time by (1) looking for the left coordinate of the building in the skyline sequence and (2) elevating all that are lower than this building, until (3) you find the right coordinate of the building. If the left and right coordinates of the new building are in the middle of some horizontal segments, they'll need to be split in two. For simplicity, we can assume that we start with a zero-height segment covering the entire skyline.

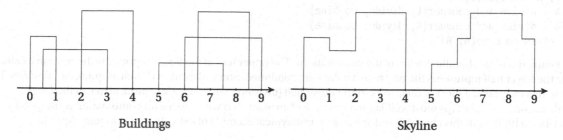

Buildings   Skyline

Figure 6-3. *A set of building silhouettes and the resulting skyline*

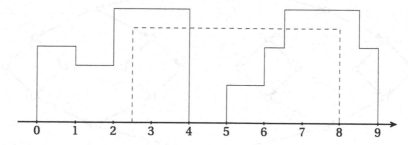

Figure 6-4. *Adding a building (dashed) to a skyline (solid)*

The details of this merging aren't all that important here. The point is that we can add a building to the skyline in linear time. Using simple (weak) induction, we now have our algorithm: We start with a single building and keep adding new ones until we're done. And, of course, this algorithm has a quadratic running time. To improve this, we want to switch to strong induction—divide and conquer. We can do this by noting that merging two skylines is no harder than merging one building with a skyline: We just traverse the two in "lockstep," and wherever one has a higher value than the other, we use the maximum, splitting horizontal line segments where needed. Using this insight, we have our second, improved algorithm: To create a skyline for all the buildings, first (recursively) create *two* skylines, based on half the buildings each, and then merge them. This algorithm, as I'm sure you can see, has a loglinear running time. Exercise 6-1 asks you to actually implement this algorithm.

The Canonical D&C Algorithm

The recursive skyline algorithm hinted at in the previous section exemplifies the prototypical way a divide-and-conquer algorithm works. The input is a set (perhaps a sequence) of elements; the elements are partitioned, in at most linear time, into two sets of roughly equal size, the algorithm is run recursively on each half, and the results are combined, also in at most linear time. It's certainly possible to modify this standard form (you'll see an important variation in the next section), but this schema encapsulates the core idea.

Listing 6-1 sketches out a general divide-and-conquer function. Chances are you'll be implementing a custom version for each algorithm, rather than using a general function such as this, but it does illustrate how these algorithms work. I'm assuming here that it's OK to simply return S in the base case; that depends on how the combine function works, of course.[3]

Listing 6-1. A General Implementation of the Divide-and-Conquer Scheme

```
def divide_and_conquer(S, divide, combine):
    if len(S) == 1: return S
    L, R = divide(S)
    A = divide_and_conquer(L, divide, combine)
    B = divide_and_conquer(R, divide, combine)
    return combine(A, B)
```

Figure 6-5 is another illustration of the same pattern. The upper half of the figure represents the recursive calls, while the lower half represents the way return values are combined. Some algorithms (such as quicksort, described later in this chapter) do most of their work in the *upper* half (division), while some are more active in the *lower* (combination). The perhaps most well-known example of an algorithm with a focus on combination is merge sort (described a bit later in this chapter), which is also a prototypical example of a divide-and-conquer algorithm.

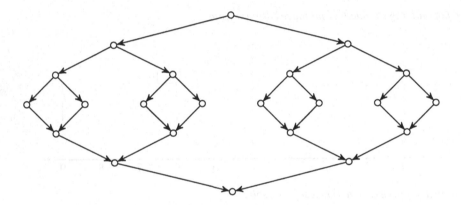

Figure 6-5. *Dividing, recursing, and combining in a divide-and-conquer algorithm*

Searching by Halves

Before working through some more examples that fit the general pattern, let's look at a *related* pattern, which discards one of the recursive calls. You've already seen this in my earlier mentions of binary search (bisection): It divides the problem into two equal halves and then recurses on only *one* of those halves. The core principle here is still balance. Consider what would happen in a totally unbalanced search. If you recall the "think of a particle" game from Chapter 3, the unbalanced solution would be equivalent to asking "Is *this* your particle?" for each particle in the universe. The difference is still encapsulated by Figures 6-1 and 6-2, except the work in each node (for this problem) is constant, and we only actually perform the work along a path from the root to a leaf.

Binary search may not seem all that interesting. It's efficient, sure, but searching through a sorted sequence ... isn't that sort of a limited area of application? Well, no, not really. First, that operation in itself can be important as a component in other algorithms. Second, and perhaps as importantly, binary search can be a more general approach to looking for things. For example, the idea can be used for numerical optimization, such as with Newton's method, or in debugging your code. Although "debugging by bisection" can be efficient enough when done manually ("Does the code crash before it reaches this print statement?"), it is also used in some revision control systems (RCSs), such as Mercurial and Git.

---

[3]For example, in the skyline problem, you would probably want to split the base case element (*L,H,R*) into two pairs, (*L,H*) and (*R,H*), so the combine function can build a sequence of points.

It works like this: You use an RCS to keep track of changes in your code. It stores many different versions, and you can "travel back in time," as it were, and examine old code at any time. Now, say you encounter a new bug, and you understandably enough want to find it. How can your RCS help? First, you write a test for your test suite—one that will detect the bug if it's there. (That's always a good first step when debugging.) You make sure to set up the test so that the RCS can access it. Then you ask the RCS to look for the place in your history where the bug appeared. How does it do that? Big surprise: by binary search. Let's say you know the bug appeared between revisions 349 and 574. The RCS will first revert your code to revision 461 (in the middle between the two) and run your test. Is the bug there? If so, you know it appeared between 349 and 461. If not, it appeared between 462 and 574. Lather, rinse, repeat.

This isn't just a neat example of what bisection can be used for; it also illustrates a couple of other points nicely. First, it shows that you can't always use stock implementations of known algorithms, even if you're not really modifying them. In a case such as this, chances are that the implementors behind your RCS had to implement the binary search themselves. Second, it's a good example of a case where reducing the number of basic operations can be crucial—more so than just implementing things efficiently. Compiling your code and running the test suite is likely to be slow anyway, so you'd like to do this as few times as possible.

BLACK BOX: BISECT

Binary search can be applied in many settings, but the straight "search for a value on a sorted sequence" version is available in the standard library, in the bisect module. It contains the bisect function, which works as expected:

```
>>> from bisect import bisect
>>> a = [0, 2, 3, 5, 6, 8, 8, 9]
>>> bisect(a, 5)
4
```

Well, it's *sort of* what you'd expect ... it doesn't return the position of the 5 that's already there. Rather, it reports the position to insert the new 5, making sure it's placed *after* all existing items with the same value. In fact, bisect is another name for bisect_right, and there's also a bisect_left:

```
>>> from bisect import bisect_left
>>> bisect_left(a, 5)
3
```

The bisect module is implemented in C, for speed, but in earlier versions (prior to Python 2.4) it was actually a plain Python module, and the code for bisect_right was as follows (with my comments):

```
def bisect_right(a, x, lo=0, hi=None):
    if hi is None:                       # Searching to the end
        hi = len(a)
    while lo < hi:                       # More than one possibility
        mid = (lo+hi)//2                 # Bisect (find midpoint)
        if x < a[mid]: hi = mid          # Value < middle? Go left
        else: lo = mid+1                 # Otherwise: go right
    return lo
```

As you can see, the implementation is iterative, but it's entirely equivalent to the recursive version.

There is also another pair of useful functions in this module: insort (alias for insort_right) and insort_left. These functions find the right position, like their bisect counterparts, and then actually insert the element. While the insertion is still a linear operation, at least the search is logarithmic (and the actual insertion code is pretty efficiently implemented).

Sadly, the various functions of the `bisect` library don't support the `key` argument, used in `list.sort`, for example. You can achieve similar functionality with the so-called decorate, sort, undecorate (or, in this case, decorate, search, undecorate) pattern, or DSU for short:

```
>>> seq = "I aim to misbehave".split()
>>> dec = sorted((len(x), x) for x in seq)
>>> keys = [k for (k, v) in dec]
>>> vals = [v for (k, v) in dec]
>>> vals[bisect_left(keys, 3)]
'aim'
```

Or, you could do it more compactly:

```
>>> seq = "I aim to misbehave".split()
>>> dec = sorted((len(x), x) for x in seq)
>>> dec[bisect_left(dec, (3, ""))][1]
'aim'
```

As you can see, this involves creating a new, decorated list, which is a linear operation. Clearly, if we do this before every search, there'd be no point in using `bisect`. If, however, we can keep the decorated list between searches, the pattern can be useful. If the sequence isn't sorted to begin with, we can perform the DSU as part of the sorting, as in the previous example.

Traversing Search Trees ... with Pruning

Binary search is the bee's knees. It's one of the simplest algorithms out there, but it really packs a punch. There is one catch, though: To use it, your values must be sorted. Now, if we could keep them in a linked list, that wouldn't be a problem. For any object we wanted to insert, we'd just find the position with bisection (logarithmic) and then insert it (constant). The problem is—that won't work. Binary search needs to be able to check the middle value in constant time, which we can't do with a linked list. And, of course, using an array (such as Python's lists) won't help. It'll help with the bisection, but it ruins the insertion.

If we want a modifiable structure that's efficient for search, we need some kind of middle ground. We need a structure that is similar to a linked list (so we can insert elements in constant time) but that still lets us perform a binary search. You may already have figured the whole thing out, based on the section title, but bear with me. The first thing we need when searching is to access the middle item in constant time. So, let's say we keep a direct link to that. From there, we can go left or right, and we'll need to access the middle element of either the left half or the right half. So ... we can just keep direct links from the first item to these two, one "left" reference and one "right" reference.

In other words, we can just represent the structure of the binary search as an explicit tree structure! Such a tree would be easily modifiable, and we could traverse it from root to leaf in logarithmic time. So, searching is really our old friend traversal—but with pruning. We wouldn't want to traverse the entire tree (resulting in a so-called linear scan). Unless we're building the tree from a sorted sequence of values, the "middle element of the left half" terminology may not be all that helpful. Instead, we can think of what we need to implement our pruning. When we look at the root, we need to be able to prune one of the subtrees. (If we found the value we wanted in an internal node and the tree didn't contain duplicates, we wouldn't continue in *either* subtree, of course.)

The *one thing* we need is the so-called search tree property: For a subtree rooted at *r*, all the values in the *left* subtree are *smaller than* (or equal to) the value of *r*, while those in the *right* subtree are *greater*. In other words, the value at a subtree root *bisects the subtree*. An example tree with this property is shown in Figure 6-6, where the node labels indicate the values we're searching. A tree structure like this could be useful in implementing a *set*; that is, we could check whether a given value was present. To implement a *mapping*, however, each node would contain both a key, which we searched for, and a value, which was what we wanted.

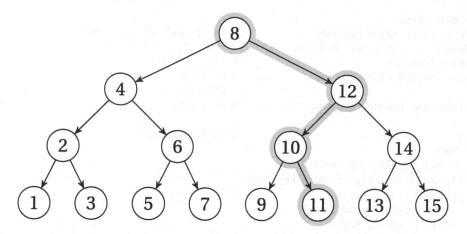

Figure 6-6. *A (perfectly balanced) binary search tree, with the search path for 11 highlighted*

Usually, you don't build a tree in bulk (although that can be useful at times); the main motivation for using trees is that they're dynamic, and you can add nodes one by one. To add a node, you search for where it *should* have been and then add it as a new leaf there. For example, the tree in Figure 6-6 might have been built by initially adding 8 and then 12, 14, 4, and 6, for example. A different ordering might have given a different tree.

Listing 6-2 gives you a simple implementation of a binary search tree, along with a wrapper that makes it look a bit like a dict. You could use it like this, for example:

```
>>> tree = Tree()
>>> tree["a"] = 42
>>> tree["a"]
42
>>> "b" in tree
False
```

As you can see, I've implemented insertion and search as free-standing functions, rather than methods. That's so that they'll work also on None nodes. (You don't have to do it like that, of course.)

Listing 6-2. Insertion into and Search in a Binary Search Tree

```
class Node:
    lft = None
    rgt = None
    def __init__(self, key, val):
        self.key = key
        self.val = val

def insert(node, key, val):
    if node is None: return Node(key, val)     # Empty leaf: add node here
    if node.key == key: node.val = val         # Found key: replace val
    elif key < node.key:                       # Less than the key?
        node.lft = insert(node.lft, key, val)  # Go left
    else:                                       # Otherwise...
        node.rgt = insert(node.rgt, key, val)  # Go right
    return node
```

```
def search(node, key):
    if node is None: raise KeyError        # Empty leaf: it's not here
    if node.key == key: return node.val    # Found key: return val
    elif key < node.key:                   # Less than the key?
        return search(node.lft, key)       # Go left
    else:                                  # Otherwise...
        return search(node.rgt, key)       # Go right

class Tree:                                # Simple wrapper
    root = None
    def __setitem__(self, key, val):
        self.root = insert(self.root, key, val)
    def __getitem__(self, key):
        return search(self.root, key)
    def __contains__(self, key):
        try: search(self.root, key)
        except KeyError: return False
        return True
```

■ **Note** The implementation in Listing 6-2 does not permit the tree to contain duplicate keys. If you insert a new value with an existing key, the old value is simply overwritten. This could easily be changed because the tree structure itself does not preclude duplicates.

SORTED ARRAYS, TREES, AND DICTS: CHOICES, CHOICES

Bisection (on sorted arrays), binary search trees, and dicts (that is, hash tables) all implement the same basic functionality: They let you search efficiently. There are some important differences, though. Bisection is fast, with little overhead, but works only on sorted arrays (such as Python lists). And sorted arrays are hard to maintain; adding elements takes linear time. Search trees have more overhead but are dynamic and let you insert and remove elements. In many cases, though, the clear winner will be the hash table, in the form of dict. Its average asymptotic running time is constant (as opposed to the logarithmic running time of bisection and search trees), and it is close to that in practice, with little overhead.

Hashing requires you to be able to compute a hash value for your objects. In practice, you can almost always do this, but in theory, bisection and search trees are a bit more flexible here—they need only to compare objects and figure out which one is smaller.[4] This focus on ordering also means that search trees will let you access your values in sorted order—either all of them or just a portion. Trees can also be extended to work in multiple dimensions (to search for points inside a hyperrectangular region) or to even stranger forms of search criteria, where hashing may be hard to achieve. There are more common cases, too, when hashing isn't immediately applicable. For example, if you want the entry that is closest to your lookup key, a search tree would be the way to go.

---

[4]Actually, more flexible may not be entirely correct. There are many objects (such as complex numbers) that can be hashed but that cannot be compared for size.

Selection

I'll round off this section on "searching by half" with an algorithm you may not end up using a lot in practice but that takes the idea of bisection in an interesting direction. Besides, it sets the stages for quicksort (next section), which is one of the classics.

The problem is to find the kth largest number in an unsorted sequence, in *linear time*. The most important case is, perhaps, to find the median—the element that *would have been* in the middle position (that is, $(n+1)//2$), had the sequence been sorted.[5] Interestingly, as a side effect of how the algorithm works, it will also allow us to identify which objects are *smaller* than the object we seek. That means we'll be able to find the k smallest (and, simultaneously, the $n-k$ largest) elements with a running time of $\Theta(n)$, meaning that the value of k doesn't matter!

This may be stranger than it seems at first glance. The running time constraint rules out sorting (unless we can count occurrences and use counting sort, as discussed in Chapter 4). Any other *obvious* algorithm for finding the k smallest objects would use some data structure to keep track of them. For example, you could use an approach similar to insertion sort: Keep the k smallest objects found so far either at the beginning of the sequence or in a separate sequence.

If you kept track of which one of them was largest, checking each *large* object in the main sequence would be fast (just a constant-time check). If you needed to add an object, though, and you already had k, you'd have to remove one. You'd remove the largest, of course, but then you'd have to find out which one was now largest. You could keep them sorted (that is, stay close to insertion sort), but the running time would be $\Theta(nk)$ anyway.

One step up from this (asymptotically) would be to use a *heap*, essentially transforming our "partial insertion sort" into a "partial heap sort," making sure that there are never more than k elements in the heap. (See the "Black Box" sidebar about binary heaps, heapq, and heapsort for more information.) This would give you a running time of $\Theta(n \lg k)$, and for a reasonably small k, this is almost identical to $\Theta(n)$, and it lets you iterate over the main sequence without jumping around in memory, so in practice it might be the solution of choice.

■ **Tip**   If you're looking for the k smallest (or largest) objects in an iterable in Python, you would probably use the nsmallest (or nlargest) function from the heapq module if your k is small, relative to the total number of objects. If the k is large, you should probably sort the sequence (either using the sort method or using the sorted function) and pick out the k first objects. Time your results to see what works best—or just choose the version that makes your code as clear as possible.

So, how can we take the next step, asymptotically, and remove dependence on k altogether? It turns out that guaranteeing a linear worst case is a bit knotty, so let's focus on the average case. Now, if I tell you to try applying the idea of divide and conquer, what would you do? A first clue might be that we're aiming for a linear running time; what "divide by half" recurrence does that? It's the one with a single recursive call (which is equivalent to the knockout tournament sum): $T(n) = T(n/2) + n$. In other words, we divide the problem in half (or, for now, in half on average) by performing linear work, just like the more canonical divide-and-conquer approach, but we manage to eliminate one half, taking us closer to binary search. What we need to figure out, in order to design this algorithm, is how to partition the data in linear time so that we end up with all our objects in one half.

As always, systematically going through the tools at our disposal, and framing the problem as clearly as we can, makes it much easier to figure out a solution. We've arrived at a point where what we need is to partition a sequence into two halves, one consisting of *small* values and one of *large* values. And we don't have to guarantee that the halves are equal—only that they'll be equal *on average*. A simple way of doing this is to choose one of the values as a so-called *pivot* and use it to divide the others: All those *smaller* than (or equal to) the pivot end up in the left half, while those

---

[5]In statistics, the median is also defined for sequences of even length. It is then the average of the two middle elements. That's not an issue we worry about here.

larger end up on the right. Listing 6-3 gives you a possible implementation of partition and select. Note that this version of partition is primarily meant to be readable; Exercise 6-11 asks you to see whether you can remove some overhead. The way select is written here, it returns the *k*th smallest element; if you'd rather have all the *k* smallest elements, you can simply rewrite it to return lo instead of pi.

Listing 6-3. A Straightforward Implementation of Partition and Select

```
def partition(seq):
    pi, seq = seq[0], seq[1:]              # Pick and remove the pivot
    lo = [x for x in seq if x <= pi]       # All the small elements
    hi = [x for x in seq if x > pi]        # All the large ones
    return lo, pi, hi                      # pi is "in the right place"

def select(seq, k):
    lo, pi, hi = partition(seq)            # [<= pi], pi, [>pi]
    m = len(lo)
    if m == k: return pi                   # We found the kth smallest
    elif m < k:                            # Too far to the left
        return select(hi, k-m-1)           # Remember to adjust k
    else:                                  # Too far to the right
        return select(lo, k)               # Just use original k here
```

SELECTING IN LINEAR TIME, GUARANTEED!

The selection algorithm implemented in this section is known as *randomized select* (although the randomized version usually chooses the pivot more randomly than here; see Exercise 6-13). It lets you do selection (for example, find the median) in linear *expected* time, but if the pivot choices are poor at each step, you end up with the handshake recurrence (linear work, but reducing size by only 1) and thereby quadratic running time. While such an extreme result is unlikely in practice (though, again, see Exercise 6-13), you *can* in fact avoid it also in the worst case.

It turns out guaranteeing that the pivot is even a small percentage into the sequence (that is, not at either end, or a constant number of steps from it) is enough for the running time to be linear. In 1973, a group of algorists (Blum, Floyd, Pratt, Rivest, and Tarjan) came up with a version of the algorithm that gives exactly this kind of guarantee.

The algorithm is a bit involved, but the core idea is simple enough: First divide the sequence into groups of five, or some other small constant. Find the median in each, using, for example, a simple sorting algorithm. So far, we've used only linear time. Now, find the median *among these medians*, using the linear selection algorithm recursively. This will work, because the number of medians is smaller than the size of the original sequence—still a bit mind-bending. The resulting value is a pivot that is guaranteed to be good enough to avoid the degenerate recursion—use it as a pivot in your selection.

In other words, the algorithm is used recursively in two ways: first, on the sequence of medians, to find a good pivot, and second, on the original sequence, using this pivot.

While the algorithm is important to know about for theoretical reasons because it means selection can be done in guaranteed linear time, you'll probably never actually use it in practice.

Sorting by Halves

Finally, we've arrived at the topic most commonly associated with the divide-and-conquer strategy: sorting. I'm not going to delve into this too deeply, because Python already has one of the best sorting algorithms ever devised (see the "Black Box" sidebar about timsort, later in this section), and its implementation is highly efficient. In fact, list.sort is so efficient, you'd probably consider it as a first choice in place of other, asymptotically slightly better algorithms (for example, for selection). Still, the sorting algorithms in this section are among the most well-known algorithms, so you should understand how they work. Also, they are a great example of the way divide and conquer is used to design algorithms.

Let's first consider one of the celebrities of algorithm design: C. A. R. Hoare's *quicksort*. It's closely related to the selection algorithm from the previous section, which is also due to Hoare (and sometimes called *quickselect*). The extension is simple: If quickselect represents traversal with pruning—finding a path in the recursion tree down to the *k*th smallest element—then quicksort represents a full traversal, which means finding a solution for *every k*. Which is the smallest element? The second smallest? And so forth. By putting them all in their place, the sequence is sorted. Listing 6-4 shows a version of quicksort.

Listing 6-4. Quicksort

```
def quicksort(seq):
    if len(seq) <= 1: return seq          # Base case
    lo, pi, hi = partition(seq)           # pi is in its place
    return quicksort(lo) + [pi] + quicksort(hi) # Sort lo and hi separately
```

As you can see, the algorithm is simple, as long as you have partition in place. (Exercises 6-11 and 6-12 ask you to rewrite quicksort and partition to yield an in-place sorting algorithm.) First, it splits the sequence into those we know must be to the left of pi and those that must be to the right. These two halves are then sorted recursively (correct by inductive assumption). Concatenating the halves, with the pivot in the middle, is guaranteed to result in a sorted sequence. Because we're not guaranteed that partition will balance the recursion properly, we know only that quicksort is loglinear in the *average* case—in the worst case it's quadratic.[6]

Quicksort is an example of a divide-and-conquer algorithm that does its main work *before* the recursive calls, in *dividing* its data (using partition). The combination part is trivial. We can do it the other way around, though: trivially split our data down the middle, guaranteeing a balanced recursion (and a nice worst-case running time), and then make an effort at combining, or *merging* the results. This is exactly what *merge sort* does. Just like our skyline algorithm from the beginning of this chapter goes from inserting a single building to merging two skylines, merge sort goes from inserting a single element in a sorted sequence (insertion sort) to merging two sorted sequences.

You've already seen the code for merge sort in Chapter 3 (Listing 3-2), but I'll repeat it here, with some comments (Listing 6-5).

Listing 6-5. Merge Sort

```
def mergesort(seq):
    mid = len(seq)//2                     # Midpoint for division
    lft, rgt = seq[:mid], seq[mid:]
    if len(lft) > 1: lft = mergesort(lft) # Sort by halves
    if len(rgt) > 1: rgt = mergesort(rgt)
    res = []
```

---

[6]In theory, we could use the guaranteed linear version of select to find the median and use that as a pivot. That's not something likely to happen in practice, though.

```
    while lft and rgt:                    # Neither half is empty
        if lft[-1] >=rgt[-1]:             # lft has greatest last value
            res.append(lft.pop())         # Append it
        else:                             # rgt has greatest last value
            res.append(rgt.pop())         # Append it
    res.reverse()                         # Result is backward
    return (lft or rgt) + res             # Also add the remainder
```

Understanding how this works should be a bit easier now than it was in Chapter 3. Note the merging part has been written to show what's going on here. If you were to actually use merge sort (or a similar algorithm) in Python, you would probably use heapq.merge to do the merging.

BLACK BOX: TIMSORT

The algorithm hiding in list.sort is one invented (and implemented) by Tim Peters, one of the big names in the Python community.[7] The algorithm, aptly named *timsort*, replaces an earlier algorithm that had lots of tweaks to handle special cases such as segments of ascending and descending values, and the like. In timsort, these cases are handled by the general mechanism, so the performance is still there (and in some cases, it's much improved), but the algorithm is cleaner and simpler. The algorithm is still a bit too involved to explain in detail here; I'll try to give you a quick overview. For more details, take a look at the source.[8]

Timsort is a close relative to merge sort. It's an *in-place* algorithm, in that it merges segments and leaves the result in the original array (although it uses some auxiliary memory during the merging). Instead of simply sorting the array half-and-half and then merging those, though, it starts at the beginning, looking for segments that are *already sorted* (possibly in reverse), called *runs*. In random arrays, there won't be many, but in many kinds of real data, there may be a lot—giving the algorithm a clear edge over a plain merge sort and a *linear* running time in the best case (and that covers a lot of cases beyond simply getting a sequence that's already sorted).

As timsort iterates over the sequence, identifying runs and pushing their bounds onto a stack, it uses some heuristics to decide which runs are to be merged when. The idea is to avoid the kind of merge imbalance that would give you a quadratic running time while still exploiting the structure in the data (that is, the runs). First, any really short runs are artificially extended and sorted (using a stable insertion sort). Second, the following invariants are maintained for the three topmost runs on the stack, A, B, and C (with A on top): len(A) > len(B) + len(C) and len(B) > len(C). If the first invariant is violated, the smaller of A and C is merged with B, and the result replaces the merged runs in the stack. The second invariant may still not hold, and the merging continues until both invariants hold.

The algorithm uses some other tricks as well, to get as much speed as possible. If you're interested, I recommend you check out the source.[9] If you'd rather not read C code, you could also take a look at the pure Python version of timsort, available as part of the PyPy project.[10] Their implementation has excellent comments and is clearly written. (The PyPy project is discussed in Appendix A.)

---

[7]Timsort is, in fact, also used in Java SE 7, for sorting arrays.

[8]See, for example, the file listsort.txt in the source code (or online, http://svn.python.org/projects/python/trunk/Objects/listsort.txt).

[9]You can find the actual C code at http://svn.python.org/projects/python/trunk/Objects/listobject.c.

[10]See https://bitbucket.org/pypy/pypy/src/default/rpython/rlib/listsort.py.

How Fast Can We Sort?

One important result about sorting is that divide-and-conquer algorithms such as merge sort are *optimal*; for arbitrary values (where we can figure out which is bigger) it's impossible, in the worst case, to do any better than $\Omega(n \lg n)$. An important case where this holds is when we sort arbitrary real numbers.[11]

■ **Note**   Counting sort and its relatives (discussed in Chapter 4) seem to break this rule. Note that there we can't sort arbitrary values—we need to be able to count occurrences, which means that the objects must be hashable, and we need to be able to iterate over the value range in linear time.

How do we know this? The reasoning is actually quite simple. First insight: Because the values are arbitrary and we're assuming that we can figure out only whether one of them is greater than another, each object comparison boils down to a yes/no question. Second insight: The number of orderings of n elements is $n!$, and we're looking for exactly one of them. Where does that get us? We're back to "think of a particle," or, in this case, "think of a permutation." This means that the best we can do is to use $\Omega(\lg n!)$ yes/no questions (the comparisons) to get the right permutation (that is, to sort the numbers). And it just so happens that $\lg n!$ is asymptotically equivalent to $n \lg n$.[12] In other words, the running time in the worst case is $\Omega(\lg n!) = \Omega(n \lg n)$.

How, you say, do we arrive at this equivalence? The easiest way is to just use *Stirling's approximation*, which says that $n!$ is $\Theta(n^n)$. Take the logarithm and Bob's your uncle.[13] Now, we derived the bound for the *worst* case; using information theory (which I won't go into here), it is, in fact, possible to show that this bound holds also in the *average* case. In other words, in a very real sense, unless we know something substantial about the value range or distribution of our data, loglinear is the best we can do.

Three More Examples

Before wrapping up this chapter with a slightly advanced (and optional) section, here are three examples for the road. The first two deal with computational geometry (where the divide-and-conquer strategy is frequently useful), while the last one is a relatively simple problem (with some interesting twists) on a sequence of numbers. I have only sketched the solutions, because the point is mainly to illustrate the design principle.

Closest Pair

The problem: You have a set of points in the plane, and you want to find the two that are closest to each other. The first idea that springs to mind is, perhaps, to use brute force: For each point, check all the others, or, at least, the ones we haven't looked at yet. This is, by the handshake sum, a quadratic algorithm, of course. Using divide and conquer, we can get that down to loglinear.

This is a rather nifty problem, so if you're into puzzle-solving, you might want to try to solve it for yourself before reading my explanation. The fact that you should use divide and conquer (and that the resulting algorithm is loglinear) is a strong hint, but the solution is by no means obvious.

---

[11]Real numbers usually aren't all that arbitrary, of course. As long as your numbers use a fixed number of bits, you can use radix sort (mentioned in Chapter 4) and sort the values in linear time.

[12]I think that's so cool, I wanted to add an exclamation mark after the sentence ... but I guess that might have been a bit confusing, given the subject matter.

[13]Actually, the approximation isn't asymptotic in nature. If you want the details, you'll find them in any good mathematics reference.

The structure of the algorithm follows almost directly from the (merge sort-like) loglinear divide-and-conquer schema: We'll divide the points into two subsets, recursively find the closest pair in each, and then—in linear time—merge the results. By the power of induction/recursion (and the divide-and-conquer schema), we have now reduce the problem to this merging operation. But we can peel away even a bit more before we engage our creativity: The result of the merge must be either (1) the closest pair from the left side, (2) the closest pair on the right side, or (3) a pair consisting of *one point from either side*. In other words, what we need to do is find the closest pair "straddling" the division line. While doing this, we also have an upper limit to the distance involved (the minimum of the closest pairs from the left and right sides).

Having drilled down to the essence of the problem, let's look at how bad things can get. Let's say, for the moment, that we have sorted all points in the middle region (of width $2d$) by their y-coordinate. We then want to go through them in order, considering other points to see whether we find any points closer than d (the smallest distance found so far). For each point, how many other "neighbors" must we consider?

This is where the crucial insight of the solution enters the picture: on either side of the midline, we know that all points are at least a distance of d apart. Because what we're looking for is a pair at *most* a distance apart, straddling the midline, we need to consider only a vertical slice of height d (and width $2d$) at any one time. And how many points can fit inside this region?

Figure 6-7 illustrates the situation. We have no lower bounds on the distances between left and right, so in the worst case, we may have coinciding points on the middle line (highlighted). Beyond that, it's quite easy to show that at most four points with a minimum distance of d can fit inside a $d \times d$ square, which we have on either side; see Exercise 6-15. This means that we need to consider at most eight points in total in such a slice, which means our current point at most needs to be compared to its next seven neighbors. (Actually, it's sufficient to consider the *five* next neighbors; see Exercise 6-16.)

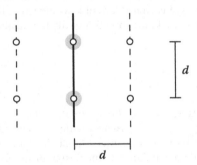

Figure 6-7. *Worst case: eight points in a vertical slice of the middle region. The size of the slice is $d \times 2d$, and each of the two middle (highlighted) points represents a pair of coincident points*

We're *almost* done; the only remaining problems are sorting by x- and y-coordinates. We need the x-sorting to be able to divide the problem in equal halves at each step, and we need the y-sorting to do the linear traversal while merging. We can keep two arrays, one for each sorting order. We'll be doing the recursive division on the x array, so that's pretty straightforward. The handling of y isn't quite so direct but still quite simple: When dividing the data set by x, we partition the y array based on x-coordinates. When combining the data, we *merge* them, just like in merge sort, thus keeping the sorting while using only linear time.

■ **Note**   For the algorithm to work, we much return the *entire subset of points*, sorted, from each recursive calls. The filtering of points too far from the midline must be done on a copy.

You can see this as a way of strengthening the induction hypothesis (as discussed in Chapter 4) in order to get the desired running time: Instead of only assuming we can find the closest points in smaller point sets, we *also* assume that we can get the points back *sorted*.

Convex Hull

Here's another geometric problem: Imagine pounding *n* nails into a board and strapping a rubber band around them; the shape of the rubber band is a so-called convex hull for the points represented by the nails. It's the smallest convex[14] region containing the points, that is, a convex polygon with lines between the "outermost" of the points. See Figure 6-8 for an example.

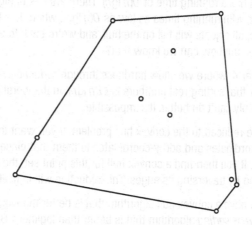

Figure 6-8. *A set of points and their convex hull*

By now, I'm sure you're suspecting how we'll be solving this: Divide the point set into two equal halves along the *x*-axis and solve them recursively. The only part remaining is the linear-time combination of the two solutions. Figure 6-9 hints at what we need: We must find the upper and lower *common tangents*. (That they're tangents basically means that the angles they form with the preceding and following line segments should curve inward.)

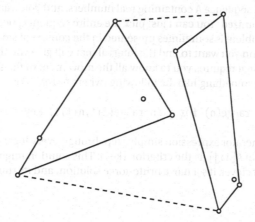

Figure 6-9. *Combining two smaller convex hull by finding upper and lower common tangents (dashed)*

---

[14]A region is convex if you can draw a line between any two points inside it, and the line stays inside the region.

Without going into implementation details, assume that you can check whether a line is an upper tangent for either half. (The lower part works in a similar manner.) You can then start with the *rightmost* point of the *left* half and the *leftmost* point of the *right* half. As long as the line between your points is not an upper tangent for the left part, you move to the next point along the subhull, counterclockwise. Then you do the same for the right half. You may have to do this more than once. Once the top is fixed, you repeat the procedure for the lower tangent. Finally, you remove the line segments that now fall between the tangents, and you're done.

HOW FAST CAN WE FIND A CONVEX HULL?

The divide-and-conquer solution has a running time of $O(n \lg n)$. There are lots of algorithms for finding convex hulls, some asymptotically faster, with running times as low as $O(n \lg h)$, where h is the number of points on the hull. In the worst case, of course, all objects will fall on the hull, and we're back to $\Theta(n \lg n)$. In fact, this is the best time possible, in the worst case—but how can we know that?

We can use the idea from Chapter 4, where we show hardness through *reduction*. We already know from the discussion earlier in this chapter that sorting real numbers is $\Omega(n \lg n)$, in the worst case. This is independent of what algorithm you use; you simply can't do better. It's impossible.

Now, observe that sorting can be reduced to the convex hull problem. If you want to sort n real numbers, you simply use the numbers as *x*-coordinates and add *y*-coordinates to them that place them on a gentle curve. For example, you could have $y = x^2$. If you then find a convex hull for this point set, the values will lie in sorted order on it, and you can find the sorting by traversing its edges. This reduction will in itself take only linear time.

Imagine, for a moment, that you have a convex hull algorithm that is better than loglinear. By using the linear reduction, you subsequently have a *sorting* algorithm that is better than loglinear. But that's impossible! In other words, because there exists a simple (here, linear) reduction from sorting to finding a convex hull, the latter problem is at least as hard as the former. So ... loglinear is the best we can do.

Greatest Slice

Here's the last example: You have a sequence A containing real numbers, and you want to find a slice (or segment) A[i:j] so that sum(A[i:j]) is maximized. You can't just pick the entire sequence, because there may be negative numbers in there as well.[15] This problem is sometimes presented in the context of stock trading—the sequence contains changes in stock prices, and you want to find the interval that will give you the greatest profit. Of course, this presentation is a bit flawed, because it requires you to know all the movement of the stock beforehand.

An obvious solution would be something like the following (where n=len(A)):

```
result = max((A[i:j] for i in range(n) for j in range(i+1,n+1)), key=sum)
```

The two for clauses in the generator expression simply step through every legal start and end point, and we then take the maximum, using the sum of A[i:j] as the criterion (key). This solution might score "cleverness" points for its concision, but it's not really that clever. It's a naïve brute-force solution, and its running time is *cubic* (that is, $\Theta(n^3)$)! In other words, it's *really* bad.

---

[15]I'm still assuming that we want a *nonempty* interval. If it turns out to have a negative sum, you could always use an empty interval instead.

It might not be immediately apparent how we can avoid the two explicit for loops, but let's start by trying to avoid the one hiding in sum. One way to do this would be to consider all intervals of length k in one iteration, then move to $k+1$, and so on. This would still give us a quadratic number of intervals to check, but we could use a trick to make the scan cost linear: We calculate the sum for the first interval as normal, but each time the interval is shifted one position to the right, we simply subtract the element that now falls outside it, and we add the new element:

```
best = A[0]
for size in range(1,n+1):
    cur = sum(A[:size])
    for i in range(n-size):
        cur += A[i+size] - A[i]
        best = max(best, cur)
```

That's not a lot better, but at least now we're down to a *quadratic* running time. There's no reason to quit here, though.

Let's see what a little divide and conquer can buy us. When you know what to look for, the algorithm—or at least a rough outline—almost writes itself: Divide the sequence in two, find the greatest slice in either half (recursively), and then see whether there's a greater one straddling the middle (as in the closest point example). In other words, the only thing that requires creative problem solving is finding the greatest slice straddling the middle. We can reduce that even further—that slice will necessarily consist of the greatest slice extending from the middle to the left and the greatest slice extending from the middle to the right. We can find these separately, in linear time, by simply traversing and summing from the middle in either direction.

Thus, we have our loglinear solution to the problem. Before leaving it entirely, though, I'll point out that there *is*, in fact, a *linear* solution as well; see Exercise 6-18.

REALLY DIVIDING THE WORK: MULTIPROCESSING

The purpose of the divide-and-conquer design method is to balance the workload so that each recursive call takes as little time as possible. You could go even further, though, and ship the work out to *separate processors* (or cores). If you have a huge number of processors to use, you could then, in theory, do nifty things such as finding the maximum or sum of a sequence in logarithmic time. (Do you see how?)

In a more realistic scenario, you might not have an unlimited supply of processors at your disposal, but if you'd like to exploit the power of those you have, the multiprocessing module can be your friend. Parallel programming is commonly done using parallel (operating system) *threads*. Although Python has a threading mechanism, it does not support true parallel execution. What you *can* do, though, is use parallel *processes*, which in modern operating systems are really efficient. The multiprocessing module gives you an interface that makes handling parallel processes look quite a bit like threading.

Tree Balance ... and Balancing[*]

If we insert random values into a binary search tree, it's going to end up pretty balanced on average. If we're unlucky, though, we *could* end up with a totally unbalanced tree, basically a linked list, like the one in Figure 6-1. Most real-world uses of search trees include some form of *balancing*, that is, a set of operations that reorganize the tree, to make sure it is balanced (but without destroying its search tree property, of course).

---

[*]This section is a bit hard and is not essential in order to understand the rest of the book. Feel free to skim it or even skip it entirely. You might want to read the "Black Box" sidebar on binary heaps, heapq, and heapsort, though, later in the section.

There's a ton of different tree structures and balancing methods, but they're generally based on two fundamental operations:

- **Node splitting (and merging).** Nodes are allowed to have more than two children (and more than one key), and under certain circumstances, a node can become *overfull*. It is then split into two nodes (potentially making its *parent* overfull).

- **Node rotations.** Here we still use binary trees, but we switch edges. If *x* is the parent of *y*, we now make *y* the parent of *x*. For this to work, *x* must take over one of the children of *y*.

This might seem a bit confusing in the abstract, but I'll go into a bit more detail, and I'm sure you'll see how it all works. Let's first consider a structure called the *2-3-tree*. In a plain binary tree, each node can have up to two children, and they each have a single key. In a 2-3-tree, though, we allow a node to have one *or two* keys and up to *three* children. Anything in the *left* subtree now has to be smaller than the *smallest* of the keys, and anything in the *right* subtree is greater than the *greatest* of the keys—and anything in the middle subtree must fall between the two. Figure 6-10 shows an example of the two node types of a 2-3-tree.

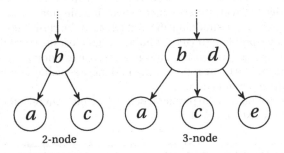

Figure 6-10. *The node types in a 2-3-tree*

■ **Note**   The 2-3-tree is a special case of the B-tree, which forms the basis of almost all database systems, and disk-based trees used in such diverse areas as geographic information systems and image retrieval. The important extension is that B-trees can have thousands of keys (and subtrees), and each node is usually stored as a contiguous block on disk. The main motivation for the large blocks is to minimize the number of disk accesses.

Searching a 2-3-node is pretty straightforward—just a recursive traversal with pruning, like in a plain binary search tree. Insertion requires a bit of extra attention, though. As in a binary search tree, you first search for the proper leaf where the new value can be inserted. In a binary search tree, though, that will always be a None reference (that is, an empty child), where you can "append" the new node as a child of an existing one. In a 2-3-tree, though, you'll always try to add the new value to an *existing leaf*. (The first value added to the tree will necessarily need to create a new node, though; that's the same for any tree.) If there's room in the node (that is, it's a 2-node), you simply add the value. If not, you have three keys to consider (the two already there and your new one).

The solution is to *split* the node, moving the *middle* of the three values up to the parent. (If you're splitting the root, you'll have to make a new root.) If the *parent* is now overfull, you'll need to split *that*, and so forth. The important result of this splitting behavior is that all leaves end up on the same level, meaning that the tree is fully balanced.

Now, while the idea of node splitting is relatively easy to understand, let's stick to our even simpler binary trees for now. You see, it's possible to use the *idea* of the 2-3-tree while not really *implementing* it as a 2-3-tree. We can simulate the whole thing using only binary nodes! There are two upsides to this: First, the structure is simpler and more consistent, and second, you get to learn about rotations (an important technique in general) without having to worry about a whole new balancing scheme!

The "simulation" I'm going to show you is called the AA-tree, after its creator, Arne Andersson.[16] Among the many rotation-based balancing schemes, the AA-tree really stands out in its simplicity (though there's still quite a bit to wrap your head around, if you're new to this kind of thing). The AA-tree is a binary tree, so we need to have a look at how to simulate the 3-nodes we'll be using to get balance. You can see how this works in Figure 6-11.

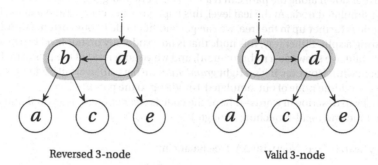

Reversed 3-node   Valid 3-node

Figure 6-11. *Two simulated 3-nodes (highlighted) in an AA-tree. Note that the one on the left is reversed and must be repaired*

This figure shows you several things at once. First, you get an idea of how a 3-node is simulated: You simply link up two nodes to act as a single *pseudonode* (as highlighted). Second, the figure illustrates the idea of *level*. Each node is assigned a level (a number), with the level of all leaves being 1. When we pretend that two nodes form a 3-node, we simply give them the same level, as shown by the vertical placement in the figure. Third, the edge "inside" a 3-node (called a *horizontal* edge) can *point only to the right*. That means that the leftmost subfigure illustrates an *illegal* node, which must be repaired, using a *right rotation*: Make c the left child of d and d the right child of b, and finally, make d's old parent the parent of b instead. Presto! You've got the rightmost subfigure (which is valid). In other words, the edge to the middle child and the horizontal edge switch places. This operation is called *skew*.

There is one other form of illegal situation that can occur and that must be fixed with rotations: an overfull pseudonode (that is, a 4-node). This is shown in Figure 6-12. Here we have three nodes chained on the same level (c, e, and f). We want to simulate a split, where the middle key (e) would be moved up to the parent (a), as in a 2-3-tree. In this case, that's as simple as rotating c and e, using a *left rotation*. This is basically just the opposite of what we did in Figure 6-11. In other words, we move the child pointer of c down from e to d, and we move the child pointer of e up from d to c. Finally, we move the child pointer of a from c to e. To later remember that a and e now form a new 3-node, we increment the level of e (see Figure 6-12). This operation is called (naturally enough) *split*.

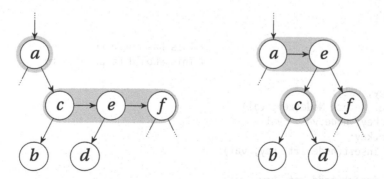

Figure 6-12. *An overfull pseudonode, and the result of the repairing left rotation (swapping the edges (e,d) and (c,e)), as well as making e the new child of a*

---

[16]The AA-tree is, in a way, a version of the BB-tree, or the *binary B-tree*, which was introduced by Rudolph Bayer in 1971 as a binary representation of the 2-3-tree.

You insert a node into an AA-tree just like you would in a standard, unbalanced binary tree; the only difference is that you perform some cleanup afterward (using skew and split). The full code can be found in Listing 6-6. As you can see, the cleanup (one call to skew and one to split) is performed as part of the backtracking in the recursion—so nodes are repaired on the path back up to the root. How does that work, really?

The operations further down along the path can really do only one thing that will affect us: They can put another node into "our" current simulated node. At the leaf level, this happens whenever we add a node, because they all have level 1. If the current node is further up in the tree, we can get another node in our current (simulated) node if one has been moved up during a split. Either way, this node that is now suddenly on our level can be either a *left* child or a *right* child. If it's a *left* child, we skew (do a right rotation), and we've gotten rid of the problem. If it's a *right* child, it's not a problem to begin with. However, if it's a right *grandchild*, we have an overfull node, so we do a split (a left rotation) and promote the middle node of our simulated 4-node up to the parent's level.

This is all pretty tricky to describe in words—I hope the code is clear enough that you'll understand what's going on. (It might take some time and head-scratching, though.)

Listing 6-6. The Binary Search Tree, Now with AA-Tree Balancing

```
class Node:
    lft = None
    rgt = None
    lvl = 1                              # We've added a level...
    def __init__(self, key, val):
        self.key = key
        self.val = val

def skew(node):                          # Basically a right rotation
    if None in [node, node.lft]: return node    # No need for a skew
    if node.lft.lvl != node.lvl: return node    # Still no need
    lft = node.lft                       # The 3 steps of the rotation
    node.lft = lft.rgt
    lft.rgt = node
    return lft                           # Switch pointer from parent

def split(node):                         # Left rotation & level incr.
    if None in [node, node.rgt, node.rgt.rgt]: return node
    if node.rgt.rgt.lvl != node.lvl: return node
    rgt = node.rgt
    node.rgt = rgt.lft
    rgt.lft = node
    rgt.lvl += 1                         # This has moved up
    return rgt                           # This should be pointed to

def insert(node, key, val):
    if node is None: return Node(key, val)
    if node.key == key: node.val = val
    elif key < node.key:
        node.lft = insert(node.lft, key, val)
    else:
        node.rgt = insert(node.rgt, key, val)
    node = skew(node)                    # In case it's backward
    node = split(node)                   # In case it's overfull
    return node
```

Can we be sure that the AA-tree will be balanced? Indeed we can, because it faithfully simulates the 2-3-tree (with the level property representing actual tree levels in the 2-3-tree). The fact that there's an extra edge inside the simulated 3-nodes can no more than double any search path, so the asymptotic search time is still logarithmic.

BLACK BOX: BINARY HEAPS, HEAPQ, AND HEAPSORT

A *priority queue* is a generalization of the LIFO and FIFO queues discussed in Chapter 5. Instead of basing the order only on when an item is added, each item receives a *priority*, and you always retrieve the remaining item with the lowest priority. (You could also use maximum priority, but you normally can't have both in the same structure.) This kind of functionality is important as a component of several algorithms, such as Prim's, for finding minimum spanning trees (Chapter 7), or Dijkstra's, for finding shortest paths (Chapter 9). There are many ways of implementing a priority queue, but probably the most common data structure used for this purpose is the *binary heap*. (There are other kinds of heaps, but the unqualified term *heap* normally refers to binary heaps.)

Binary heaps are *complete* binary trees. That means they are as balanced as they can get, with each level of the tree filled up, except (possibly) the lowest level, which is filled as far as possible from the left. Arguably the most important aspect of their structure, though, is the so-called *heap property*: The value of every parent is smaller than those of both children. (This holds for a *minimum heap*; for a *maximum heap*, each parent is greater.) As a consequence, the root has the smallest value in the heap. The property is similar to that of search trees but not *quite* the same, and it turns out that the heap property is much easier to maintain without sacrificing the balance of the tree. You never modify the structure of the tree by splitting or rotating nodes in a heap. You only ever need to swap parent and child nodes to restore the heap property. For example, to "repair" the root of a subtree (which is too big), you simply swap it with its smallest child and repair that subtree recursively (as needed).

The heapq module contains an efficient heap implementation that represents its heaps in lists, using a common "encoding": If a is a heap, the children of a[i] are found in a[2*i+1] and a[2*i+2]. This means that the root (the smallest element) is always found in a[0]. You can build a heap from scratch, using the heappush and heappop functions. You might also start out with a list that contains lots of values, and you'd like to make it into a heap. In that case, you can use the heapify function.[17] It basically repairs every subtree root, starting at the bottom right, moving left and up. (In fact, by skipping the leaves, it needs only work on the left half of the array.) The resulting running time is linear (see Exercise 6-9). If your list is sorted, it's already a valid heap, so you can just leave it alone.

Here's an example of building a heap piece by piece:

```
>>> from heapq import heappush, heappop
>>> from random import randrange
>>> Q = []
>>> for i in range(10):
...         heappush(Q, randrange(100))
...
>>> Q
[15, 20, 56, 21, 62, 87, 67, 74, 50, 74]
>>> [heappop(Q) for i in range(10)]
[15, 20, 21, 50, 56, 62, 67, 74, 74, 87]
```

[17]It is quite common to call this operation *build-heap* and to reserve the name *heapify* for the operation that repairs a single node. Thus, *build-heap* runs *heapify* on all nodes but the leaves.

Just like `bisect`, the `heapq` module is implemented in C, but it *used* to be a plain Python module. For example, here is the code (from Python 2.3) for the function that moves an object down until it's smaller than both of its children (again, with my comments):

```
def sift_up(heap, startpos, pos):
    newitem = heap[pos]                    # The item we're sifting up
    while pos > startpos:                  # Don't go beyond the root
        parentpos = (pos - 1) >>1          # The same as (pos - 1) // 2
        parent = heap[parentpos]           # Who's your daddy?
        if parent <= newitem: break        # Valid parent found
        heap[pos] = parent                 # Otherwise: copy parent down
        pos = parentpos                    # Next candidate position
    heap[pos] = newitem                    # Place the item in its spot
```

Note that the original function was called `_siftdown` because it's sifting the value *down* in the list. I prefer to think of it as sifting it *up* in the implicit tree structure of the heap, though. Note also that, just like `bisect_right`, the implementation uses a loop rather than recursion.

In addition to `heappop`, there is `heapreplace`, which will pop the smallest item and insert a new element at the same time, which is a bit more efficient than a `heappop` followed by a `heappush`. The `heappop` operation returns the root (the first element). To maintain the shape of the heap, the last item is moved to the root position, and from there it is swapped downward (in each step, with its smallest child) until it is smaller than both its children. The `heappush` operation is just the reverse: The new element is appended to the list and is repeatedly swapped with its parent until it is greater than its parent. Both of these operations are logarithmic (also in the worst case, because the heap is guaranteed to be balanced).

Finally, the module has (since version 2.6) the utility functions `merge`, `nlargest`, and `nsmallest` for merging sorted inputs and finding the *n* largest and smallest items in an iterable, respectively. The latter two functions, unlike the others in the module, take the same kind of `key` argument as `list.sort`. You can simulate this in the other functions with the DSU pattern, as mentioned in the sidebar on `bisect`.

Although you would probably never use them that way in Python, the heap operations can also form a simple, efficient, and asymptotically optimal sorting algorithm called *heapsort*. It is normally implemented using a max-heap and works by first performing `heapify` on a sequence, then repeatedly popping off the root (as in `heappop`), and finally placing it in the now empty last slot. Gradually, as the heap shrinks, the original array is filled from the right with the largest element, the second largest, and so forth. In other words, heap sort is basically selection sort where a heap is used to implement the selection. Because the initialization is linear and each of the *n* selections is logarithmic, the running time is loglinear, that is, optimal.

Summary

The algorithm design strategy of divide and conquer involves a decomposition of a problem into roughly equal-sized subproblems, solving the subproblems (often by recursion), and combining the results. The main reason this is useful it that the workload is balanced, typically taking you from a quadratic to a loglinear running time. Important examples of this behavior include merge sort and quicksort, as well as algorithms for finding the closest pair or the convex hull of a point set. In some cases (such as when searching a sorted sequence or selecting the median element), all but one of the subproblems can be pruned, resulting in a traversal from root to leaf in the subproblem graph, yielding even more efficient algorithms.

The subproblem structure can also be represented explicitly, as it is in binary search trees. Each node in a search tree is greater than the descendants in its left subtree but less than those in its right subtree. This means that a binary search can be implemented as a traversal from the root. Simply inserting random values haphazardly will, on average, yield a tree that is balanced enough (resulting in logarithmic search times), but it is also possible to *balance* the tree, using node splitting or rotations, to guarantee logarithmic running times in the worst case.

If You're Curious ...

If you like bisection, you should look up *interpolation search*, which for uniformly distributed data has an average-case running time of $O(\lg \lg n)$. For implementing sets (that is, efficient membership checking) other than sorted sequences, search trees and hash tables, you could have a look at *Bloom filters*. If you like search trees and related structures, there are lots of them out there. You could find tons of different balancing mechanisms (*red black trees*, *AVL-trees*, *splay trees*), some of them randomized (*treaps*), and some of them only abstractly representing trees (*skip lists*). There are also whole families of specialized tree structures for indexing multidimensional coordinates (so-called spatial access methods) and distances (*metric access methods*). Other trees structures to check out are *interval trees*, *quadtrees*, and *octtrees*.

Exercises

6-1. Write a Python program that implements the solution to the skyline problem.

6-2. Binary search divides the sequence into two approximately equal parts in each recursive step. Consider *ternary* search, which divides the sequence into *three* parts. What would its asymptotic complexity be? What can you say about the number of comparisons in binary and ternary search?

6-3. What is the point of multiway search trees, as opposed to binary search trees?

6-4. How could you extract all keys from a binary search tree in sorted order, in linear time?

6-5. How would you delete a node from a binary search tree?

6-6. Let's say you insert n random values into an initially empty binary search tree. What would, on average, be the depth of the leftmost (that is, smallest) node?

6-7. In a min-heap, when moving a large node downward, you always switch places with the *smallest* child. Why is that important?

6-8. How (or why) does the heap encoding work?

6-9. Why is the operation of building a heap linear?

6-10. Why wouldn't you just use a balanced binary search tree instead of a heap?

6-11. Write a version of partition that partitions the elements in place (that is, moving them around in the original sequence). Can you make it faster than the one in Listing 6-3?

6-12. Rewrite quicksort to sort elements in place, using the in-place partition from Exercise 6-11.

6-13. Let's say you rewrote select to choose the pivot using, for example, `random.choice`. What difference would that make? (Note that the same strategy can be used to create a *randomized quicksort*.)

6-14. Implement a version of quicksort that uses a key function, just like `list.sort`.

6-15. Show that a square of side d can hold at most four points that are all at least a distance of d apart.

6-16. In the divide-and-conquer solution to the closest pair problem, you can get away with examining at most the next seven points in the mid-region points, sorted by y-coordinate. Show how you could quite easily reduce this number to five.

6-17. The *element uniqueness* problem is to determine whether all elements of a sequence are unique. This problem has a proven loglinear lower bound in the worst case for real numbers. Show that this means the closest pair problem *also* has a loglinear lower bound in the worst case.

6-18. How could you solve the greatest slice problem in linear time?

References

Andersson, A. (1993). Balanced search trees made simple. In *Proceedings of the Workshop on Algorithms and Data Structures* (WADS), pages 60-71.

Bayer, R. (1971). Binary B-trees for virtual memory. In *Proceedings of the ACM SIGFIDET Workshop on Data Description, Access and Control*, pages 219-235.

Blum, M., Floyd, R. W., Pratt, V., Rivest, R. L., and Tarjan, R. E. (1973). Time bounds for selection. *Journal of Computer and System Sciences*, 7(4):448-461.

de Berg, M., Cheong, O., van Kreveld, M., and Overmars, M. (2008). *Computational Geometry: Algorithms and Applications*, third edition. Springer.

CHAPTER 7

■ ■ ■

Greed Is Good? Prove It!

It's not a question of enough, pal.

— Gordon Gekko, *Wall Street*

So-called greedy algorithms are short-sighted, in that they make each choice in isolation, doing what looks good right here, right now. In many ways, *eager* or *impatient* might be better names for them because other algorithms also usually try to find an answer that is as good as possible; it's just that the greedy ones take what they can get at this moment, not worrying about the future. Designing and implementing a greedy algorithm is usually easy, and when they work, they tend to be highly efficient. The main problem is showing that they *do* work—if, indeed, they do. That's the reason for the "Prove It!" part of the chapter title.

This chapter deals with greedy algorithms that give correct (optimal) answers; I'll revisit the design strategy in Chapter 11, where I'll relax this requirement to "almost correct (optimal)."

Staying Safe, Step by Step

The common setting for greedy algorithms is a series of choices (just like, as you'll see, for dynamic programming). The greed involves making each choice with local information, doing what looks most promising without regard for context or future consequences, and then, once the choice has been made, never looking back. If this is to lead to a solution, we must make sure that each choice is *safe*—that it doesn't destroy our future prospects. You'll see many examples of how we can ensure this kind of safety (or, rather, how we can prove that an algorithm is safe), but let's start out by looking at the "step by step" part.

The kind of problems solved with greedy algorithms typically build a solution gradually. It has a set of "solution pieces" that can be combined into partial, and eventually complete, solutions. These pieces can fit together in complex ways; there may be many ways of combining them, and some pieces may no longer fit once we've used certain others. You can think of this as a jigsaw puzzle with many possible solutions (see Figure 7-1). The jigsaw picture is blank, and the puzzle pieces are rather regular, so they can be used in several locations and combinations.

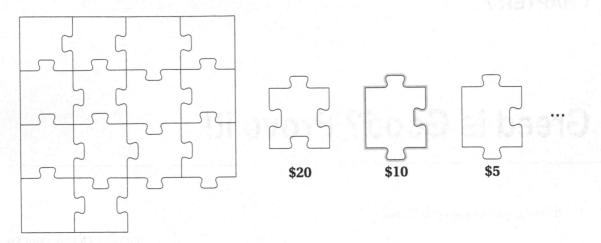

Figure 7-1. *A partial solution, and some greedily ordered pieces (considered from left to right), with the next greedy choice highlighted*

Now add a *value* to each puzzle piece. This is an amount you'll be awarded for fitting that particular piece into the complete solution. The goal is then to find a way to lay the jigsaw that gets you the highest total value—that is, we have an optimization problem. Solving a combinatorial optimization problem like this is, in general, not at all a simple task. You might need to consider every possible way of placing the pieces, yielding an exponential (possibly factorial) running time.

Let's say you're filling in the puzzle row by row, from the top, so you always know where the next piece must go. The greedy approach in this setting is as easy as it gets, at least for selecting the pieces to use. Just sort the pieces by decreasing value and consider them one by one. If a piece won't fit, you discard it. If it fits, you use it, without regard for future pieces.

Even without looking at the issue of correctness (or optimality), it's clear that this kind of algorithm needs a couple of things to be able to run at all:

- A set of candidate elements, or *pieces*, with some *value* attached

- A way of checking whether a partial solution is valid, or *feasible*

So, partial solutions are built as collections of solution pieces. We check each piece in turn, starting with the most valuable one, and add each piece that leads to a larger, still valid solution. There are certainly subtleties that could be added to this (for example, the total value needn't be a sum of element values, and we might want to know when we're done, without having to exhaust the set of elements), but this'll do as a prototypical description.

A simple example of this kind of problem is that of making change—trying to add up to a given sum with as few coins and bills as possible. For example, let's say someone owes you $43.68 and gives you a hundred-dollar bill. What do you do? The reason this problem is a nice example is that we all instinctively know the right thing to do here[1]: We start with the biggest denominations possible and work our way down. Each bill or coin is a puzzle piece, and we're trying to cover the number $56.32 exactly. Instead of sorting a set of bills and coins, we can think of sorting *stacks* of them, because we have many of each. We sort these stacks in descending order and start handing out the largest denominations, like in the following code (working with cents, to avoid floating-point issues):

```
>>> denom = [10000, 5000, 2000, 1000, 500, 200, 100, 50, 25, 10, 5, 1]
>>> owed = 5632
>>> payed = []
>>> for d in denom:
```

---

[1]No, it's not to run away and buy comic books.

```
...        while owed >=d:
...            owed -= d
...            payed.append(d)
...
>>> sum(payed)
5632
>>> payed
[5000, 500, 100, 25, 5, 1, 1]
```

Most people probably have little doubt that this works; it seems like the obvious thing to do. And, indeed, it works, but the solution is in some ways very brittle. Even changing the list of available denominations in minor ways will destroy it (see Exercise 7-1). Figuring out which currencies the greedy algorithm will work with isn't straightforward (although there is an algorithm for it), and the general problem itself is unsolved. In fact, it's closely related to the knapsack problem, which is discussed in the next section.

Let's turn to a different kind of problem, related to the matching we worked with in Chapter 4. The movie is over (with many arguing that the TV show was clearly superior), and the group decides to go out for some tango, and once again, they face a matching problem. Each pair of people has a certain compatibility, which they've represented as a number, and they want the sum of these over all the pairs to be as high as possible. Dance pairs of the same gender are not uncommon in tango, so we needn't restrict ourselves to the bipartite case—and what we end up with is the *maximum-weight matching problem*. In this case (or the bipartite case, for that matter), greed won't work in general. However, by some freak coincidence, *all the compatibility numbers* happen to be *distinct powers of two*. Now, what happens?[2]

Let's first consider what a greedy algorithm would look like here and then see why it yields an optimal result. We'll be building a solution piece by piece—let the pieces be all the possible pairs and a partial solution be a set of pairs. Such a partial solution is valid only if everyone participates in at most one of its pairs. The algorithm will then be roughly as follows:

1. List potential pairs, sorted by decreasing compatibility.
2. Pick the first unused pair from the list.
3. Is anyone in the pair already occupied? If so, discard it; otherwise, use it.
4. Are there any more pairs on the list? If so, go to 2.

As you'll see later, this is rather similar to Kruskal's algorithm for minimum spanning trees (although *that* works regardless of the edge weights). It also is a rather prototypical greedy algorithm. Its correctness is another matter. Using distinct powers of two is sort of cheating because it would make virtually any greedy algorithm work; that is, you'd get an optimal result as long as you could get a valid solution at all (see Exercise 7-3). Even though it's cheating, it illustrates the central idea here: making the greedy choice is *safe*. Using the most compatible of the remaining couples will *always* be at least as good as any other choice.[3]

In the following sections, I'll show you some well-known problems that can be solved using greedy algorithms. For each algorithm, you'll see how it works and why greed is correct. Near the end of the chapter, I'll sum up some general approaches to proving correctness that you can use for other problems.

[2]The idea for this version of the problem comes from Michael Soltys (see references in Chapter 4).
[3]To be on the safe side, just let me emphasize that this greedy solution would *not* work in general, with an arbitrary set of weights. The distinct powers of two are key here.

EAGER SUITORS AND STABLE MARRIAGES

There is, in fact, one classical matching problem that can be solved (sort of) greedily: *the stable marriage problem*. The idea is that each person in a group has preferences about whom he or she would like to marry. We'd like to see everyone married, and we'd like the marriages to be *stable*, meaning that there is no man who prefers a woman outside his marriage who also prefers him. (To keep things simple, we disregard same-sex marriages and polygamy here.)

There's a simple algorithm for solving this problem, designed by David Gale and Lloyd Shapley. The formulation is quite gender-conservative but will certainly also work if the gender roles are reversed. The algorithm runs for a number of *rounds*, until there are no unengaged men left. Each round consists of two steps:

1. Each unengaged man proposes to his favorite of the women he has not yet asked.

2. Each woman is (provisionally) engaged to her favorite suitor and rejects the rest.

This can be viewed as greedy in that we consider only the available favorites (both of the men and women) right now. You might object that it's only *sort of* greedy in that we don't lock in and go straight for marriage; the women are allowed to break their engagement if a more interesting suitor comes along. Even so, once a man has been rejected, he has been rejected for good, which means that we're guaranteed progress and a quadratic worst-case running time.

To show that this is an optimal and correct algorithm, we need to know that everyone gets married and that the marriages are stable. Once a woman is engaged, she stays engaged (although she may replace her fiancé). There is no way we can get stuck with an unmarried pair, because at some point the man would have proposed to the woman, and she would have (provisionally) accepted his proposal.

How do we know the marriages are stable? Let's say Scarlett and Stuart are both married but not to each other. Is it possible they secretly prefer each other to their current spouses? No. If this were so, Stuart would already have proposed to her. If she accepted that proposal, she must later have found someone she liked better; if she rejected it, she would already have a preferable mate.

Although this problem may seem silly and trivial, it is not. For example, it is used for admission to some colleges and to allocate medical students to hospital jobs. There are, in fact, entire books (such as those by Donald Knuth and by Dan Gusfield and Robert W. Irwing) devoted to the problem and its variations.

All the Girls. *You know that I'll never leave you. Not as long as she's with someone.* (`http://xkcd.com/770`)

The Knapsack Problem

This problem is, in a way, a generalization of the change-making problem, discussed earlier. In that problem, we used the coin denominations to determine whether a partial/full solution was valid (don't give too much/give the exact amount), and the number of coins measured the quality of the eventual solution. The knapsack problem is framed in different terms: We have a set of items that we want to take with us, each with a certain *weight* and *value*; however, our knapsack has a maximum capacity (an upper bound on the total weight), and we want to maximize the total value we get.

The knapsack problem covers many applications. Whenever you are to select a valuable set of objects (memory blocks, text fragments, projects, people), where each object has an individual value (possibly be linked to money, probability, recency, competence, relevance, or user preferences), but you are constrained by some resource (be it time, memory, screen real-estate, weight, volume or something else entirely), you may very well be solving a version of the knapsack problem. There are also special cases and closely related problems, such as the *subset sum* problem, discussed in Chapter 11, and the problem of making change, as discussed earlier. This wide applicability is also its weakness—what makes it such a hard problem to solve. As a rule, the more expressive a problem is, the harder it is to find an efficient algorithm for it. Luckily, there are special cases that we *can* solve in various ways, as you'll see in the following sections.

Fractional Knapsack

This is the simplest of the knapsack problems. Here we're not required to include or exclude entire objects; we might be stuffing our backpack with tofu, whiskey, and gold dust, for example (making for a somewhat odd picnic). We needn't allow arbitrary fractions, though. We could, for example, use a resolution of grams or ounces. (We could be even more flexible; see Exercise 7-6.) How would you approach this problem?

The important thing here is to find the *value-to-weight* ratio. For example, most people would agree that gold dust has the most value per gram (though it might depend on what you'd use it for); let's say the whiskey falls between the two (although I'm sure there are those who'd dispute that). In that case, to get the most out of our backpack, we'd stuff it full with gold dust—or at least with the gold dust we have. If we run out, we start adding the whiskey. If there's still room left over when we're out of whiskey, we top it all off with tofu (and start dreading the unpacking of this mess).

This is a prime example of a greedy algorithm. We go straight for the good (or, at least, expensive) stuff. If we use a discrete weight measure, this can, perhaps, be even easier to see; that is, we don't need to worry about ratios. We basically have a set of individual grams of gold dust, whiskey, and tofu, and we sort them according to their value. Then, we (conceptually) pack the grams one by one.

Integer Knapsack

Let's say we abandon the fractions, and now need to include entire objects—a situation more likely to occur in real life, whether you're programming or packing your bag. Then the problem is suddenly a *lot* harder to solve. For now, let's say we're still dealing with *categories* of objects, so we can add an integer amount (that is, number of objects) from each category. Each category then has a fixed weight and value that holds for all objects. For example, all gold bars weigh the same and have the same value; the same holds for bottles of whiskey (we stick to a single brand) and packages of tofu. Now, what do we do?

There are two important cases of the integer knapsack problem—the bounded and unbounded cases. The bounded case assumes we have a fixed number of objects in each category,[4] and the unbounded case lets us use as many as we want. Sadly, greed won't work in either case. In fact, these are both unsolved problems, in the sense that no polynomial algorithms are known to solve them in general. There *is* hope, however. As you'll see in the next chapter, we can use dynamic programming to solve the problems in *pseudopolynomial* time, which may be good

---

[4]If we view each object individually, this is often called *0-1 knapsack* because we can take 0 or 1 of each object.

enough in many important cases. Also, for the *unbounded* case, it turns out that the greedy approach ain't half bad! Or, rather, it's at least *half good*, meaning we'll never get less than half the optimum value. And with a slight modification, you can get as good results for the bounded version, too. This concept of greedy approximation is discussed in more detail in Chapter 11.

■ **Note** This is mainly an initial "taste" of the knapsack problem. I'll deal more thoroughly with a solution to the integer knapsack problem in Chapter 8.

Huffman's Algorithm

Huffman's algorithm is another one of the classics of greed. Let's say you're working with some emergency central where people call for help. You're trying to put together some simple yes/no questions that can be posed in order to help the callers diagnose an acute medical problem and decide on the appropriate course of action. You have a list of the conditions that should be covered, along with a set of diagnostic criteria, severity, and frequency of occurrence. Your first thought is to build a balanced binary tree, constructing a question in each node that will split the list (or sublist) of possible conditions in half. This seems too simplistic, though; the list is long and includes many noncritical conditions. Somehow, you need to take severity and frequency of occurrence into account.

It's usually a good idea to simplify any problem at first, so you decide to focus on frequency. You realize that the balanced binary tree is based on the assumption of *uniform probability*—dividing the list in half won't do if some items are more probable. If, for example, there's an even chance that the patient is unconscious, *that's* the thing to ask about—even if "Does the patient have a rash?" might actually split the list in the middle. In other words, you want a *weighted* balancing: You want the expected number of questions to be as low as possible. You want to minimize the *expected depth* of your (pruned) traversal from root to leaf.

You find that this idea can be used to account for the severity as well. You'd want to prioritize the most dangerous conditions so they can be identified quickly ("Is the patient breathing?"), at the cost of making patients with less critical ailments wait through a couple of extra questions. You do this, with the help of some health professionals, by giving each condition a *cost* or *weight*, combining the frequency (probability) and the health risk involved. Your goal for the tree structure is still the same. How can you minimize the sum of $depth(u) \times weight(u)$ over all leaves u?

This problem certainly has other applications as well. In fact, the original (and most common) application is *compression*—representing a text more compactly—through *variable-length codes*. Each character in your text has a frequency of occurrence, and you want to exploit this information to give the characters encodings of different lengths so as to minimize the expected length of any text. Equivalently, for any character, you want to minimize the expected length of its encoding.

Do you see how this is similar to the previous problem? Consider the version where you focused only on the probability of a given medical condition. Now, instead of minimizing the number of yes/no questions needed to identify some medical affliction, we want to minimize the number of bits needed to identify a character. Both the yes/no answers and the bits uniquely identify paths to leaves in a binary tree (for example, zero = *no* = *left* and one = *yes* = *right*).[5] For example, consider the characters *a* through *f*. One way of encoding them is given by Figure 7-2 (just ignore the numbers in the nodes for now). For example, the code for *g* (given by the highlighted path) would be 101. Because all characters are in the leaves, there would be no ambiguity when decoding a text that had been compressed with this scheme (see Exercise 7-7). This property, that no valid code is a prefix of another, gives rise to the term *prefix code*.

---

[5]Not only is it unimportant whether zero means *left* or *right*, it is also unimportant which subtrees are on the left and which are on the right. Shuffling them won't matter to the optimality of the solution.

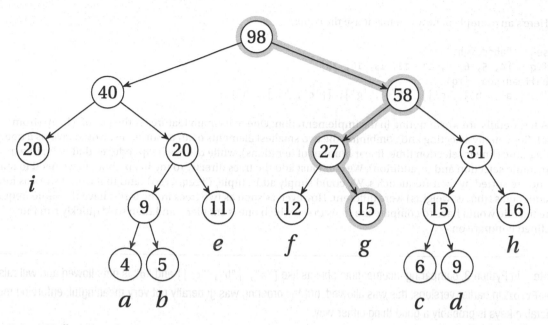

Figure 7-2. *A Huffman tree for a–i, with frequencies/weights 4, 5, 6, 9, 11, 12, 15, 16, and 20, and the path represented by the code 101 (right, left, right) highlighted*

The Algorithm

Let's start by designing a greedy algorithm to solve this problem, before showing that it's correct (which is, of course, the crucial step). The most obvious greedy strategy would, perhaps, be to add the characters (leaves) one by one, starting with the one with the greatest frequency. But where would we add them? Another way to go (which you'll see again in Kruskal's algorithm, in a bit) is to let a partial solution consist of *several* tree fragments and then repeatedly *combine* them. When we combine two trees, we add a new, shared root and give it a weight equal to the sum of its children, that is, the previous roots. This is exactly what the numbers inside the nodes in Figure 7-2 mean.

Listing 7-1 shows one way of implementing Huffman's algorithm. It maintains a partial solution as a forest, with each tree represented as nested lists. For as long as there are at least two separate trees in the forest, the two lightest trees (the ones with lowest weights in their roots) are picked out, combined, and placed back in, with a new root weight.

Listing 7-1. Huffman's Algorithm

```
from heapq import heapify, heappush, heappop
from itertools import count

def huffman(seq, frq):
    num = count()
    trees = list(zip(frq, num, seq))          # num ensures valid ordering
    heapify(trees)                            # A min-heap based on frq
    while len(trees) > 1:                      # Until all are combined
        fa, _, a = heappop(trees)             # Get the two smallest trees
        fb, _, b = heappop(trees)
        n = next(num)
        heappush(trees, (fa+fb, n, [a, b]))   # Combine and re-add them
    return trees[0][-1]
```

Here's an example of how you might use the code:

```
>>> seq = "abcdefghi"
>>> frq = [4, 5, 6, 9, 11, 12, 15, 16, 20]
>>> huffman(seq, frq)
[['i', [['a', 'b'], 'e']], [['f', 'g'], [['c', 'd'], 'h']]]
```

A few details are worth noting in the implementation. One of its main features is the use of a heap (from heapq). Repeatedly selecting and combining the two smallest elements of an unsorted list would give us a quadratic running time (linear selection time, linear number of iterations), while using a heap reduces that to loglinear (logarithmic selection and re-addition). We can't just add the trees directly to the heap, though; we need to make sure they're sorted by their frequencies. We could simply add a tuple, (freq, tree), and that would work as long as all frequencies (that is, weights) were different. However, as soon as two trees in the forest have the same frequency, the heap code would have to compare the trees to see which one is smaller—and then we'd quickly run into undefined comparisons.

■ **Note**   In Python 3, comparing incompatible objects like ["a", ["b", "c"]] and "d" is not allowed and will raise a TypeError. In earlier versions, this was allowed, but the ordering was generally not very meaningful; enforcing more predictable keys is probably a good thing either way.

A solution is to add a field between the two, one that is guaranteed to differ for all objects. In this case, I simply use a counter, resulting in (freq, num, tree), where frequency ties are broken using the arbitrary num, avoiding direct comparison of the (possibly incomparable) trees.[6]

As you can see, the resulting tree structure is equivalent to the one shown in Figure 7-2.

To compress and decompress a text using this technique, you need some pre- and post-processing, of course. First, you need to count characters to get the frequencies (for example, using the Counter class from the collections module). Then, once you have your Huffman tree, you must find the codes for all the characters. You could do this with a simple recursive traversal, as shown in Listing 7-2.

Listing 7-2. Extracting Huffman Codes from a Huffman Tree

```
def codes(tree, prefix=""):
    if len(tree) == 1:
        yield (tree, prefix)               # A leaf with its code
        return
    for bit, child in zip("01", tree):     # Left (0) and right (1)
        for pair in codes(child, prefix + bit): # Get codes recursively
            yield pair
```

The codes function yields (char, code) pairs suitable for use in the dict constructor, for example. To use such a dict to compress a code, you'd just iterate over the text and look up each character. To *decompress* the text, you'd rather use the Huffman tree directly, traversing it using the bits in the input for directions (that is, determining whether you should go left or right); I'll leave the details as an exercise for the reader.

---

[6]If a future version of the heapq library lets you use a key function, such as in list.sort, you'd no longer need this tuple wrapping at all, of course.

The First Greedy Choice

I'm sure you can see that the Huffman codes will let you faithfully encode a text and then decode it again—but how can it be that it is *optimal* (within the class of codes we're considering)? That is, why is the expected depth of any leaf minimized using this simple, greedy procedure?

As we usually do, we now turn to induction: We need to show that we're safe all the way from start to finish—that the greedy choice won't get us in trouble. We can often split this proof into two parts, what is often called (*i*) *the greedy choice property* and (*ii*) *optimal substructure* (see, for example, Cormen et al. in the "References" section of Chapter 1). The greedy choice property means that the greedy choice gives us a new partial solution that is part of an optimal one. The optimal substructure, which is *very* closely related to the material of Chapter 8, means that the *rest* of the problem, after we've made our choice, can *also* be solved just like the original—if we can find an optimal solution to the subproblem, we can combine it with our greedy choice to get a solution to the entire problem. In other words, an optimal solution is built from optimal subsolutions.

To show the greedy choice property for Huffman's algorithm, we can use an *exchange argument* (see, for example, Kleinberg and Tardos in the "References" section of Chapter 1). This is a general technique used to show that our solution is at least as good as an optimal one (and therefore optimal)—or in this case, that there *exists* a solution with our greedy choice that is at least this good. The "at least as good" part is proven by taking a hypothetical (totally unknown) optimal solution and then gradually changing it into our solution (or, in this case, one containing the bits we're interested in) *without making it worse*.

The greedy choice for Huffman's algorithm involves placing the two lightest elements as sibling leaves on the lowest level of the tree. (Note that we're worried about only the *first* greedy choice; the optimal substructure will deal with the rest of the induction.) We need to show that this is safe—that there exists an optimal solution where the two lightest elements are, indeed, bottom-level sibling leaves. Start the exchange argument by positing another optimal tree where these two elements are *not* lowest-level siblings. Let a and b be the lowest-frequency elements, and assume that this hypothetical, optimal tree has c and d as sibling leaves at maximum depth. We assume that a is lighter (has a lower weight/frequency) than b and that c is lighter than d.[7] Under the circumstances, we also know that a is lighter than c and b is lighter than d. For simplicity, let's assume that the frequences of a and d are different because otherwise the proof is simple (see Exercise 7-8).

What happens if we swap a and c? And then swap b and d? For one thing, we now have a and b as bottom-level siblings, which we wanted, but what has happened to the expected leaf depth? You could fiddle around with the full expressions for weighted sums here, but the simple idea is: We've moved some heavy nodes *up* in the tree and moved some light nodes *down*. This means that some short paths are now given a higher weight in the sum, while some long paths have been given a lower weight. All in all, the total cost cannot have increased. (Indeed, if the depths and weights are all different, our tree will be *better*, and we have a proof by contradiction because our hypothetical alternative optimum cannot exist—the greedy way is the best there is.)

Going the Rest of the Way

Now, that was the first half of the proof. We know that making the first greedy choice was OK (the greedy choice property), but we need to know that it's OK to *keep* using greedy choices (optimal substructure). We need to get a handle on what the remaining subproblem *is* first, though. Preferably, we'd like it to have the same structure as the original, so the machinery of induction can do its job properly. In other words, we'd like to reduce things to a new, smaller set of elements for which we can build an optimal tree and then show how we can build on that.

The idea is to view the first two combined leaves as a new element, ignoring the fact that it's a tree. We worry only about its root. The subproblem then becomes finding an optimal tree for this new set of elements—which we can assume is all right, by induction. The only remaining question is whether this tree is optimal once we expand this node back to a three-node subtree, by once again including its leaf children; this is the crucial part that will give us the induction step.

---

[7] They might also have *equal* weights/frequencies; that doesn't affect the argument.

Let's say our two leaves are, once again, a and b, with frequencies $f(a)$ and $f(b)$. We lump them together as a single node with a frequency $f(a) + f(b)$ and construct an optimal tree. Let's assume that this combined node ends up at depth D. Then its contribution to the total tree cost is $D \times (f(a) + f(b))$. If we now expand the two children, their parent node no longer contributes to the cost, but the total contribution of the leaves (which are now at depth $D + 1$) will be $(D + 1) \times (f(a) + f(b))$. In other words, the full solution has a cost that exceeds the optimal subsolution by $f(a) + f(b)$. Can we be sure that this is optimal?

Yes, we can, and we can prove it by contradiction, assuming that it is *not* optimal. We conjure up another, better tree—and assume that it, too, has a and b as bottom-level siblings. (We know, by the arguments in the previous section, that an optimal tree like this exists.) Once again, we can collapse a and b, and we end up with a solution to our subproblem that is *better* than the one we had ... but the one we had was optimal by assumption! In other words, we cannot find a global solution that is better than one that contains an optimal subsolution.

Optimal Merging

Although Huffman's algorithm is normally used to construct optimal prefix codes, there are other ways of interpreting the properties of the Huffman tree. As explained initially, one could view it as a decision tree, where the expected traversal depth is minimized. We can use the weights of the internal nodes in our interpretation too, though, yielding a rather different application.

We can view the Huffman tree as a sort of fine-tuned divide-and-conquer tree, where we don't do a flat balancing like in Chapter 6, but where the balance has been designed to take the leaf weights into account. We can then interpret the leaf weights as subproblem sizes, and if we assume that the cost of combining (merging) subproblems is linear (as is often the case in divide and conquer), the sum of all the internal node weights represents the total work performed.

A practical example of this is merging sorted files, for example. Merging two files of sizes n and m takes time linear in $n+m$. (This is similar to the problem of joining in relational database or of merging sequences in algorithms such as timsort.) In other words, if you imagine the leaves in Figure 7-2 to be files and their weights to be file sizes, the internal nodes represent the cost of the total merging. If we can minimize the sum of the internal nodes (or, equivalently, the sum of all the nodes), we will have found the optimal merging schedule. (Exercise 7-9 asks you to show that this really matters.)

We now need to show that a Huffman tree does, indeed, minimize the node weights. Luckily, we can piggyback this proof on the previous discussion. We know that in a Huffman tree, the sum of depth times weight over all leaves is minimized. Now, consider how each leaf contributes to the sum over all nodes: The leaf weight occurs as a summand once in each of its ancestor nodes—which means that the sum is exactly the same! That is, `sum(weight(node) for node in nodes)` is the same as `sum(depth(leaf)*weight(leaf) for leaf in leaves)`. In other words, Huffman's algorithm is exactly what we need for our optimal merging.

■ **Tip**   The Python standard library has several modules dealing with compression, including `zlib`, `gzip`, `bz2`, `zipfile`, and `tar`. The `zipfile` module deals with ZIP files, which use compression that is based on, among other things, Huffman codes.[8]

---

[8]By the way, did you know that the ZIP code of Huffman, Texas, is 77336?

Minimum Spanning Trees

Now let's take a look at the perhaps most well-known example of a greedy problem: finding minimum spanning trees. The problem is an old one—it's been around at least since the early 20th century. It was first solved by the Czech mathematician Otakar Borůvka in 1926, in an effort to construct a cheap electrical network for Moravia. His algorithm has been rediscovered many times since then, and it still forms the basis of some of the fastest known algorithms known today. The algorithms I'll discuss in this section (Prim's and Kruskal's) are in some way a bit simpler but have the same asymptotic running time complexity ($O(m \lg n)$, for n nodes and m edges).[9] If you're interested in the history of this problem, including the repeated rediscoveries of the classic algorithms, take a look at the paper "On the History of the Minimum Spanning Tree Problem," by Graham and Hell. (For example, you'll see that Prim and Kruskal aren't the only ones to lay claim to their eponymous algorithms.)

We're basically looking for the cheapest way of connecting all the nodes of a weighted graph, given that we can use only a subset of its edges to do the job. The cost of a solution is simply the weight sum for the edges we use.[10] This could be useful in building an electrical grid, constructing the core of a road or railroad network, laying out a circuit, or even performing some forms of clustering (where we'd only *almost* connect all the nodes). A minimum spanning tree can also be used as a foundation for an approximate solution to the traveling salesrep problem introduced in Chapter 1 (see Chapter 11 for a discussion on this).

A spanning tree T of a connected, undirected graph G has the same node set as G and a subset of the edges. If we associate an edge weight function with G so edge e has weight $w(e)$, then the weight of the spanning tree, $w(T)$, is the sum of $w(e)$ for every edge e in T. In the *minimum spanning tree problem*, we want to find a spanning tree over G that has minimum weight. (Note that there may be more than one.) Note also that if G is disconnected, it will have *no* spanning trees, so in the following, it is generally assumed that the graphs we're working with are connected.

In Chapter 5, you saw how to build spanning trees using traversal; building minimum spanning trees can also be built in an incremental step like this, and that's where the greed comes in: We *gradually* build the tree by adding one edge at the time. At each step, we choose the *cheapest* (or *lightest*) edge among those permitted by our building procedure. This choice is *locally optimal* (that is, greedy) and *irrevocable*. The main task for this problem, or any other greedy problem, becomes showing that these *locally* optimal choices lead to a *globally* optimal solution.

The Shortest Edge

Consider Figure 7-3. Let the edge weights correspond to the Euclidean distances between the nodes as they're drawn (that is, the actual edge lengths). If you were to construct a spanning tree for this graph, where would you start? Could you be certain that some edge had to be part of it? Or at least that a certain edge would be safe to include? Certainly (e,i) looks promising. It's tiny! In fact, it's the shortest of all the edges—the one with the lowest weight. But is that enough?

---

[9]You can, in fact, combine Borůvka's algorithm with Prim's to get a faster algorithm.
[10]Do you see why the result cannot contain any cycles, as long as we assume positive edge weights?

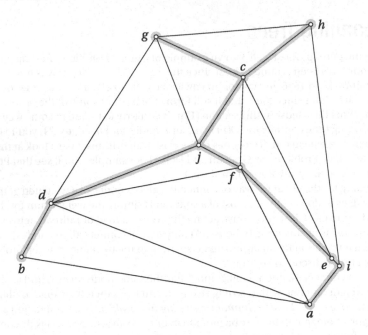

Figure 7-3. *A Euclidean graph and its minimum spanning tree (highlighted)*

As it turns out, it is. Consider any spanning tree *without* the minimum-weight edge (e,i). The spanning tree would have to include both e and i (by definition), so it would also include a single path from e to i. If we now were to add (e,i) to the mix, we'd get a *cycle*, and in order to get back to a proper spanning tree, we'd have to remove one of the edges of this cycle—it doesn't matter which. Because (e,i) is the smallest, removing *any other* edge would yield a smaller tree than we started out with. Right? In other words, any tree *not* including the shortest edge can be made smaller, so the minimum spanning tree *must* include the shortest edge. (As you'll see, this is the basic idea behind Kruskal's algorithm.)

What if we consider all the edges incident at a single node—can we draw any conclusions then? Take a look at b, for example. By the definition of spanning trees, we must connect b to the rest somehow, which means we must include *either* (b,d) *or* (b,a). Again, it seems tempting to choose the shortest of the two. And once again, the greedy choice turns out to be very sensible. Once again, we prove that the alternative is inferior using a proof by contradiction: Assume that it was better to use (b,a). We'd build our minimum spanning tree with (b,a) included. Then, just for fun, we'd add (b,d), creating a cycle. But, hey—if we remove (b,a), we have *another* spanning tree, and because we've switched one edge for a shorter one, this new tree must be *smaller*. In other words, we have a contradiction, and the one without (b,d) couldn't have been minimal in the first place. And *this* is the basic idea behind Prim's algorithm, which we'll look at after Kruskal's.

In fact, both of these ideas are special cases of a more general principle involving *cuts*. A cut is simply a partitioning of the graph nodes into two sets, and in this context we're interested in the edges that pass between these two node sets. We say that these edges *cross* the cut. For example, imagine drawing a vertical line in Figure 7-3, right between d and g; this would give a cut that is crossed by five edges. By now I'm sure you're catching on: We can be *certain* that it will be safe to include the shortest edge across the cut, in this case (d,j). The argument is once again exactly the same: We build an alternative tree, which will necessarily include at least one other edge across the cut (in order to keep the graph connected). If we then add (d,j), at least one of the other, longer edges across the cut would be part of the same cycle as (d,j), meaning that it would be safe to remove the other edge, giving a smaller spanning tree.

You can see how the two first ideas are special cases of this "shortest edge across a cut" principle: Choosing the shortest edge in the graph will be safe because it will be shortest in every cut in which it participates, and choosing the shortest edge incident to any node will be safe because it's the shortest edge over the cut that separates that node from the rest of the graph. In the following, I expand on these ideas, turning them into two full-fledged greedy algorithms for finding minimum spanning trees. The first (Kruskal's) is close to the prototypical greedy algorithm, while the next (Prim's) uses the principles of traversal, with the greedy choice added on top.

What About the Rest?

Showing that the first greedy choice is OK isn't enough. We need to show that the remaining problem is a smaller instance of the same problem—that our reduction is safe to use inductively. In other words, we need to establish optimal substructure. This isn't too hard (Exercise 7-12), but there's another approach that's perhaps even simpler here: We prove the invariant that our solution is part (a subgraph) of a minimum spanning tree. We keep adding edges as long as the solution isn't a spanning tree (that is, as long as there are edges left that won't form a cycle), so if this invariant is true, the algorithm must terminate with a full, minimum spanning tree.

So, is the invariant true? Initially, our partial solution is empty, which is clearly a partial, minimum spanning tree. Now, assume inductively that we've built some partial, minimum spanning tree T and that we add a safe edge (that is, one that doesn't create a cycle and that is the shortest one across some cut). Clearly, the new structure is still a forest (because we meticulously avoid creating cycles). Also, the reasoning in the previous section still applies: Among the spanning trees containing T, the one(s) including this safe edge will be smaller than those that don't. Because (by assumption), at least one of the trees containing T is a minimum spanning tree, at least one of those containing T and the safe edge will *also* be a minimum spanning tree.

Kruskal's Algorithm

This algorithm is close to the general greedy approach outlined at the beginning of this chapter: Sort the edges and start picking. Because we're looking for *short* edges, we sort them by increasing length (or weight). The only wrinkle is how to detect edges that would lead to an invalid solution. The only way to invalidate our solution would be to add a cycle, but how can we check for that? A straightforward solution would be to use traversal; every time we consider an edge (u,v), we traverse our tree from u to see whether there is a path to v. If there is, we discard it. This seems a bit wasteful, though; in the worst case, the traversal check would take linear time in the size of our partial solution.

What else could we do? We *could* maintain a set of the nodes in our tree so far, and then for a prospective edge (u,v), we'd see whether both were in the solution. This would mean that sorting the edges is what dominates; checking each edge could be done in constant time. There's just one crucial flaw in this plan: It won't work. It *would* work if we could guarantee that the partial solution was *connected* at every step (which is what we'll be doing in Prim's algorithm), but we can't. So even if two nodes are part of our solution so far, they may be in different trees, and connecting them would be perfectly valid. What we need to know is that they aren't in the *same* tree.

Let's try to solve this by making each node in the solution know which component (tree) it belongs to. We can let one of the nodes in a component act as a *representative*, and then all the nodes in that component could point to that representative. This leaves the problem of *combining* components. If all nodes of the merged component had to point to the same representative, this combination (or union) would be a linear operation. Can we do better? We could *try*; for example, we could let each node point to *some* other node, and we'd follow that chain until we reached the representative (which would point to itself). Joining would then just be a matter of having one representative point to the other (constant time). There are no immediate guarantees on how long the chain of references would be, but it's a first step, at least.

This is what I've done in Listing 7-3, using the map C to implement the "pointing." As you can see, each node is initially the representative of its own component, and then I repeatedly connect components with new edges, in sorted order. Note that the way I've implemented this, I'm expecting an undirected graph where each edge is represented just once (that is, using one of its directions, chosen arbitrarily).[11] As always, I'm assuming that every node is a key in the graph, though, possibly with an empty weight map (that is, G[u] = {} if u has no out-edges).

---

[11]Going back and forth between this representation and one where you have edges both ways isn't really hard, but I'll leave the details as an exercise for the reader.

Listing 7-3. A Naïve Implementation of Kruskal's Algorithm

```
def naive_find(C, u):                         # Find component rep.
    while C[u] != u:                          # Rep. would point to itself
        u = C[u]
    return u

def naive_union(C, u, v):
    u = naive_find(C, u)                       # Find both reps
    v = naive_find(C, v)
    C[u] = v                                   # Make one refer to the other

def naive_kruskal(G):
    E = [(G[u][v],u,v) for u in G for v in G[u]]
    T = set()                                  # Empty partial solution
    C = {u:u for u in G}                       # Component reps
    for _, u, v in sorted(E):                  # Edges, sorted by weight
        if naive_find(C, u) != naive_find(C, v):
            T.add((u, v))                      # Different reps? Use it!
            naive_union(C, u, v)               # Combine components
    return T
```

The naïve Kruskal works, but it's not all that great. (What, the name gave it away?) In the worst case, the chain of references we need to follow in naive_find could be linear. A rather obvious idea might be to always have the *smaller* of the two components in naive_union point to the *larger*, giving us some balance. Or we could think even more in terms of a balanced tree and give each node a *rank*, or *height*. If we always made the lowest-ranking representative point to the highest-ranking one, we'd get a total running time of $O(m \lg n)$ for the calls to naive_find and naive_union (see Exercise 7-16).

This would actually be fine because the sorting operation to begin with is $\Theta(m \lg n)$ anyway.[12] There is one other trick that is commonly used in this algorithm, though, called *path compression*. It entails "pulling the pointers along" when doing a find, making sure all the nodes we examine on our way now point directly to the representative. The more nodes point directly at the representative, the faster things should go in later finds, right? Sadly, the reasoning behind exactly how and why this helps is far too knotty for me to go into here (although I'd recommend Sect. 21.4 in *Introduction to Algorithms* by Cormen et al., if you're interested). The end result, though, is that the worst-case total running time of the unions and finds is $O(m\alpha(n))$, where $\alpha(n)$ is *almost* a constant. In fact, you can assume that $\alpha(n) \leq 4$, for any even remotely plausible value for n. For an improved implementation of find and union, see Listing 7-4.

Listing 7-4. Kruskal's Algorithm

```
def find(C, u):
    if C[u] != u:
        C[u] = find(C, C[u])                   # Path compression
    return C[u]

def union(C, R, u, v):a
    u, v = find(C, u), find(C, v)
    if R[u] > R[v]:                            # Union by rank
        C[v] = u
```

---

[12]We're sorting m edges, but we also know that m is $O(n^2)$, and (because the graph is connected), m is $\Omega(n)$. Because $\Theta(\lg n^2) = \Theta(2 \cdot \lg n) = \Theta(\lg n)$, we get the result.

```
    else:
        C[u] = v
    if R[u] == R[v]:                              # A tie: Move v up a level
        R[v] += 1

def kruskal(G):
    E = [(G[u][v],u,v) for u in G for v in G[u]]
    T = set()
    C, R = {u:u for u in G}, {u:0 for u in G}     # Comp. reps and ranks
    for _, u, v in sorted(E):
        if find(C, u) != find(C, v):
            T.add((u, v))
            union(C, R, u, v)
    return T
```

All in all, the running time of Kruskal's algorithm is $\Theta(m \lg n)$, which comes from the sorting.

Note that you might want to represent your spanning trees differently (that is, not as sets of edges). The algorithm should be easy to modify in this respect—or you could just build the structure you want based on the edge set T.

■ **Note**   The subproblem structure used in Kruskal's algorithm is an example of a *matroid*, where the feasible partial solutions are simply sets—in this case, cycle-free edge sets. For matroids, greed works. Here are the rules: All subsets of feasible sets must also be feasible, and larger sets must have elements that can extend smaller ones.

Prim's Algorithm

Kruskal's algorithm is simple on the conceptual level—it's a direct translation of the greedy approach to the spanning tree problem. As you just saw, though, there is some complexity in the validity checking. In this respect, Prim's algorithm is a bit simpler.[13] The main idea in Prim's algorithm is to traverse the graph from a starting node, always adding the shortest edge connected to the tree. This is safe because the edge will be the shortest one crossing the cut around our partial solution, as explained earlier.

This means that Prim's algorithm is just another traversal algorithm, which should be a familiar concept if you've read Chapter 5. As discussed in that chapter, the main difference between traversal algorithms is the ordering of our "to-do" list—among the unvisited nodes we've discovered, which one do we grow our traversal tree to next? In breadth-first search, we used a simple queue (that is, a deque); in Prim's algorithm, we simply replace this queue with a *priority queue*, implemented with a heap, using the heapq library (discussed in a "Black Box" sidebar in Chapter 6).

There is one important issue here, though: Most likely, we will discover new edges pointing to nodes that are *already in our queue*. If the new edge we discovered was *shorter* than the previous one, we should *adjust the priority* based on this new edge. This, however, can be quite a hassle. We'd need to find the given node inside the heap, change the priority, and then restructure the heap so that it would still be correct. You could do that by having a mapping from each node to its position in the heap, but then you'd have to update that mapping when performing heap operations, and you could no longer use the heapq library.

---

[13]Actually, the difference is deceptive. Prim's algorithm is based on traversal and heaps—concepts we've already dealt with—while Kruskal's algorithm introduced a new disjoint set mechanism. In other words, the difference in simplicity is mostly a matter of perspective and abstraction.

It turns out there's another way, though. A really pretty solution, which will also work with other priority-based traversals (such as Dijkstra's algorithm and A*, discussed in Chapter 9), is to simply add the nodes *multiple times*. Each time you find an edge to a node, you add the node to the heap (or other priority queue) with the appropriate weight, and you *don't care if it's already in there*. Why could this possibly work?

- We're using a priority queue, so if a node has been added multiple times, by the time we remove one of its entries, it will be the one with the lowest weight (at that time), which is the one we want.

- We make sure we don't add the same node to our traversal tree more than once. This can be ensured by a constant-time membership check. Therefore, all but one of the queue entries for any given node will be discarded.

- The multiple additions won't affect asymptotic running time (see Exercise 7-17).

There are important consequences for the actual running time as well. The (much) simpler code isn't only easier to understand and maintain; it also has a lot less overhead. And because we can use the super-fast heapq library, the net consequence is most likely a large performance gain. (If you'd like to try the more complex version, which is used in many algorithm books, you're welcome, of course.)

■ **Note** Re-adding a node with a lower weight is equivalent to a relaxation, as discussed in Chapter 4. As you'll see, I also add the predecessor node to the queue, making any explicit relaxation unnecessary. When implementing Dijkstra's algorithm in Chapter 9, however, I use a separate `relax` function. These two approaches are interchangeable (so you could have Prim's *with* `relax` and Dijkstra's *without* it).

You can see my version of Prim's algorithm in Listing 7-5. Because heapq doesn't (yet) support sorting keys, as `list.sort` and friends do, I'm using (weight, node) pairs in the heap, discarding the weights when the nodes are popped off. Beyond the use of a heap, the code is similar to the implementation of breadth-first search in Listing 5-10. That means that a lot of the understanding here should come for free.

Listing 7-5. Prim's Algorithm

```
from heapq import heappop, heappush

def prim(G, s):
    P, Q = {}, [(0, None, s)]
    while Q:
        _, p, u = heappop(Q)
        if u in P: continue
        P[u] = p
        for v, w in G[u].items():
            heappush(Q, (w, u, v))
    return P
```

Note that unlike kruskal, in Listing 7-4, the prim function in Listing 7-5 assumes that the graph G is an undirected graph where *both* directions are explicitly represented, so we can easily traverse each edge in both directions.[14]

---

[14]As I mentioned when discussing Kruskal's algorithm, adding and removing such redundant reverse edges is quite easy, if you need to do so.

As with Kruskal's algorithm, you may want to represent the resulting spanning tree differently from what I do here. Rewriting that part should be pretty easy.

■ **Note**   The subproblem structure used in Prim's algorithm is an example of a *greedoid*, which is a simplification and generalization of matroids where we no longer require all subsets of feasible sets to be feasible. Sadly, having a greedoid is not in itself a guarantee that greed will work—though it is a step in the right direction.

A SLIGHTLY DIFFERENT PERSPECTIVE

In their historical overview of minimum spanning tree algorithms, Ronald L. Graham and Pavol Hell outline three algorithms that they consider especially important and that have played a central role in the history of the problem. The first two are the algorithms that are commonly attributed to Kruskal and Prim (although the second one was originally formulated by Vojtěch Jarník in 1930), while the third is the one initially described by Borůvka. Graham and Hell succinctly explain the algorithms as follows. A partial solution is a spanning forest, consisting of a set of *fragments* (components, trees). Initially, each node is a fragment. In each iteration, edges are added, joining fragments, until we have a spanning tree.

Algorithm 1: Add a shortest edge that joins two different fragments.

Algorithm 2: Add a shortest edge that joins the fragment containing the root to another fragment.

Algorithm 3: For every fragment, add the shortest edge that joins it to another fragment.

For algorithm 2, the root is chosen arbitrarily at the beginning. For algorithm 3, it is assumed that all edge weights are different to ensure that no cycles can occur. As you can see, all three algorithms are based on the same fundamental fact—that the shortest edge over a cut is safe. Also, in order to implement them efficiently, you need to be able to find shortest edges, detect whether two nodes belong to the same fragment, and so forth (as explained for algorithms 1 and 2 in the main text). Still, these brief explanations can be useful as a memory aid or to get the bird's-eye perspective on what's going on.

Greed Works. But When?

Although induction is generally used to show that a greedy algorithm is correct, there are some extra "tricks" that can be employed. I've already used some in this chapter, but here I'll try to give you an overview, using some simple problems involving time intervals. It turns out there are many problems of this type that can be solved by greedy algorithms. I'm not including code for these; the implementations are pretty straightforward (although it might be a useful exercise to actually implement them).

Keeping Up with the Best

This is what Kleinberg and Tardos (in *Algorithm Design*) call *staying ahead*. The idea is to show that as you build your solution, one step at a time, the greedy algorithm will always have gotten *at least as far* as a hypothetical optimal algorithm would have. Once you reach the finish line, you've shown that greed is optimal. This technique can be useful in solving a common example of greed: *resource scheduling*.

The problem involves selecting a set of *compatible intervals*. Normally, we think of these intervals as time intervals (see Figure 7-4). Compatibility simply means that none of them should overlap, so this could be used to model requests for using a resource, such as a lecture hall, for certain time periods. Another example would be to let *you* be the "resource" and to let the intervals be various activities you'd like to participate in. Either way, our optimization task is to choose as many mutually compatible (nonoverlapping) intervals as possible. For simplicity, we can assume that no start or end points are identical. Handling identical values is not significantly harder.

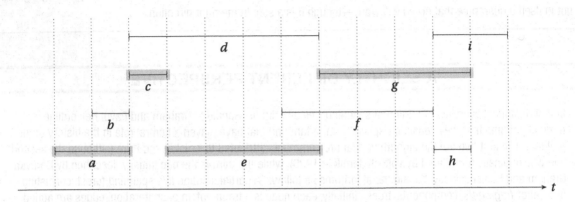

Figure 7-4. *A set of random intervals where at most four mutually compatible intervals (for example, a, c, e and g) can be found*

There are two obvious candidates for greedy selection here: If we go from left to right on the timeline, we might want to start with either the interval that *starts* first or the one that *ends* first, eliminating any other overlapping intervals. I hope it is clear that the first alternative can't work (Exercise 7-18), which leaves us to show that the other one *does* work.

The algorithm is (roughly) as follows:

1. Include the interval with the lowest finish time in the solution.

2. Remove all of the remaining intervals that overlap with the one from step 1.

3. Any remaining intervals? Go to step 1.

Running this algorithm on the interval set in Figure 7-4 results in the highlighted set of intervals (*a, c, e* and *g*). The resulting solution is clearly valid; that is, there aren't any overlapping intervals in it. This will be the case in general; we need show only that it's optimal, that is, that we have as many intervals as possible. Let's try to apply the idea of staying ahead.

Let's say our intervals are, in the order in which they were added, $i_1 \ldots i_k$, and that the hypothetical, optimal solution gives the intervals $j_1 \ldots j_m$. We want to show that $k = m$. Assume that the optimal intervals are sorted by finishing (and starting) times.[15] To show that our algorithm stays ahead of the optimal one, we need to show that for any $r \leq k$, the finish time of i_r is at least as early as that of j_r, and we can prove this by induction.

For $r = 1$, it is obviously correct: The greedy algorithm chooses i_1, which is the element with the minimum finish time. Now, let $r > 1$ and assume that our hypothesis holds for $r - 1$. The question then becomes whether it is possible for the greedy algorithm to "fall behind" at this step. That is, is it possible that the finish time for i_r could now be greater than that of j_r? The answer is clearly no, because the greedy algorithm could just as well have chosen j_r (which is compatible with j_{r-1}, and therefore also with i_{r-1}, which finishes at least as early).

---

[15]Because the intervals don't overlap, sorting by starting and finishing times is equivalent.

So, the greedy algorithm keeps up with the best, all the way to the end. However, this "keeping up" dealt only with finishing times, not the number of intervals. We need to show that keeping up will yield an optimal solution, and we can do so by contradiction: If the greedy algorithm is *not* optimal, then $m > k$. For every r, including $r = k$, we know that i_r finishes at least as early as j_r. Because $m > k$, there must be an interval j_{r+1} that we didn't use. This must start after j_r, and therefore after i_r, which means that we *could* have—and, indeed, *would* have—included it. In other words, we have a contradiction.

No Worse Than Perfect

This is a technique I used in showing the greedy choice property for Huffman's algorithm. It involves showing that you can transform a hypothetical optimal solution to the greedy one, without reducing the quality. Kleinberg and Tardos call this an *exchange argument*. Let's put a twist on the interval problem. Instead of having fixed starting and ending times, we now have a *duration* and a *deadline*, and you're free to schedule the intervals—let's call them *tasks*—as you want, as long as they don't overlap. You also have a given starting time, of course.

However, any task that goes past its deadline incurs a penalty equal to its delay, and you want to minimize the maximum of these delays. On the surface, this might seem like a rather complex scheduling problem (and, indeed, many scheduling problems are really hard to solve). Surprisingly, though, you can find the optimum schedule through a super-simple greedy strategy: Always perform the most urgent task. As is often the case for greedy algorithms, the correctness proof is a bit tougher than the algorithm itself.

The greedy solution has no gaps in it. As soon as we're done with one task, we start the next. There will also be at least one optimal solution without gaps—if we have an optimal solution *with* gaps, we can always close these up, resulting in earlier finish times for the later tasks. Also, the greedy solution will have no *inversions* (jobs scheduled before other jobs with earlier deadlines). We can show that all solutions without gaps or inversions have the same maximum delay. Two such solutions can differ only in the order of tasks with identical deadlines, and these must be scheduled consecutively. Among the tasks in such a consecutive block, the maximum delay depends only on the last task, and this delay doesn't depend on the order of the tasks.

The only thing that remains to be proven is that there exists an optimal solution without gaps or inversions, because it would be equivalent to the greedy solution. This proof has three parts:

- If the optimal solution has an inversion, there are two consecutive tasks where the first has a later deadline than the second.

- Switching these two removes one inversion.

- Removing this inversion will not increase the maximum delay.

The first point should be obvious enough. Between two inverted tasks, there must be some point where the deadlines start decreasing, giving us the two consecutive, inverted tasks. As for the second point, swapping the tasks clearly removes one inversion, and no new inversions are created. The third point requires a little care. Swapping tasks i and j (so j now comes first) can potentially increase the lateness of only i; all other tasks are safe. In the new schedule, i finishes where j finished before. Because (by assumption) the deadline of i was *later* than that of j, the delay cannot possibly have increased. Thus, the third part of the proof is done.

It should be clear that these parts together show that the greedy schedule minimizes the maximum delay.

Staying Safe

This is where we started: To make sure a greedy algorithm is correct, we must make sure each greedy step along the way is safe. One way of doing this is the two-part approach of showing (1) the greedy choice property, that is, that a greedy choice is compatible with optimality, and (2) optimal substructure, that is, that the remaining subproblem is a smaller instance that must also be solved optimally. The greedy choice property, for example, can be shown using an exchange argument (as was done for the Huffman algorithm).

Another possibility is to treat safety as an invariant. Or, in the words of Michael Soltys (see the "References" section of Chapter 4), we need to show that if we have a *promising* partial solution, a greedy choice will yield a new, bigger solution that is *also* promising. A partial solution is promising if it can be extended to an optimal solution. This is the approach I took in the section "What about the rest?" earlier in this chapter; there, a solution was promising if it was contained in (and, thus, could be extended to) a minimum spanning tree. Showing that "the current partial solution is promising" is an invariant of the greedy algorithm, as you keep making greedy choices, is really all you need.

Let's consider a final problem involving time intervals. The problem is simple enough, and so is the algorithm, but the correctness proof is rather involved.[16] It can serve as an example of the effort that may be required to show that a relatively simple greedy algorithm is correct.

This time, we once again have a set of tasks with deadlines, as well as a starting time (such as the present). This time, though, these are *hard* deadlines—if we can't get a task done before its deadline, we can't take it on at all. In addition, each task has a given *profit* associated with it. As before, we can perform only one task at a time, and we can't split them into pieces, so we're looking for a set of jobs that we can actually do, and that gives us as large a total profit as possible. However, to keep things simple, this time all tasks take *the same amount of time*—one time step. If d is the latest deadline, as measured in time steps from the starting point, we can start with an empty schedule of d empty slots and then fill those slots with tasks.

The solution to this problem is, in a way, *doubly* greedy. First, we consider the tasks by decreasing profit, starting with the most profitable task; that's the first greedy part. Then comes the second part: We place each task in the latest possible free slot that it can occupy, based on its deadline. If there is no free, valid slot, we discard the task. Once we're done, if we haven't filled all the slots, we're certainly free to perform tasks earlier, so as to remove the gaps—it won't affect the profit or allow us to perform any more tasks. To get a feel for this solution, you might want to actually implement it (Exercise 7-20).

The solution sounds intuitively appealing; we give the profitable tasks precedence, and we make sure they use a minimum of our precious "early time," by pushing them as far toward their deadline as possible. But, once again, we won't rely on intuition. We'll use a bit of induction, showing that as we add tasks in this greedy fashion, our schedule stays promising.

■ **Caution**   The following presentation does not involve any deep math or rocket science and is more of an informal explanation than a full, technical proof. Still, it *is* a bit involved and might hurt your brain. If you don't feel up to it, feel free to skip ahead to the chapter summary.

As is invariably the case, the initial, empty solution is promising. In moving beyond the base case, it's important to remember that the schedule is really promising only if it can be extended to an optimal schedule *using the remaining tasks*, as this is the only way we're allowed to extend it. Now, assume we have a promising partial schedule P. Some of its slots are filled in, and some are not. The fact that P is promising means that it can be extended to an optimal schedule—let's call it S. Also, let's say T is the next task under consideration.

We now have four cases to consider:

- T won't fit in P, because there is no room before the deadline. In this case, T can't affect anything, so P is still promising once T is discarded.

- T will fit in P, and it ends up in the same position as in S. In this case, we're actually extending toward S, so P is still promising.

---

[16]Versions of this problem can be found in Soltys' book (see "References" in Chapter 4) and that of Cormen et al. (see "References" in Chapter 1). My proof closely follows Soltys's, while Cormen et al. choose to prove that the problem forms a matroid, which means that a greedy algorithm will work on it.

- T will fit, but it ends up somewhere else. This might seem somewhat troubling.

- T will fit, but S doesn't contain it. Even more troubling, perhaps.

Clearly we need to address the last two cases, because they seem to be building *away* from the optimal schedule S. The thing is, there may be more than one optimal schedule—we just need to show that we can still reach *one of them* after T has been added.

First, let's consider the case where we greedily add T, and it's not in the same place as it would have been in S. Then we can build a schedule that's *almost* like S, except that T has swapped places with another task T'. Let's call this other schedule S'. By construction, T is placed *as late as possible* in S', which means it must be placed *earlier* in S. Conversely, T' must be placed *later* in S and therefore *earlier* in S'. This means that we cannot have broken the deadline of T' when constructing S', so it's a valid solution. Also, because S and S' consist of the same tasks, the profits must be identical.

The only case that remains is if T is *not* scheduled in the optimal schedule S. Again, let S' be *almost* like S. The only difference is that we've scheduled T with our algorithm, effectively "overwriting" some other task T' in S. We haven't broken any deadlines, so S' is valid. We also know that we can get from P to S' (by *almost* following the steps needed to get to S, just using T instead of T').

The last question then becomes, does S' have the same profit as S? We can prove that it does, by contradiction. Assume that T' has a greater profit than T, which is the only way in which S could have a higher profit. If this were the case, the greedy algorithm would have considered T' before T. As there is at least one free slot before the deadline of T', the greedy algorithm would have scheduled it, necessarily in a different position than T, and therefore in a different position than in S. But we assumed that we could extend P to S, and if it has a task in a different position, we have a contradiction.

■ **Note**   This is an example of a proof technique called *proof by cases*, where we add some conditions to the situation and make sure to prove what we want for all cases that these conditions can create.

Summary

Greedy algorithms are characterized by how they make decisions. In building a solution, step-by-step, each added element is the one that looks best *at the moment it's added*, without concern for what went before or what will happen later. Such algorithms can often be quite simple to design and implement, but showing that they are correct (that is, optimal) is often challenging. In general, you need to show that making a greedy choice is *safe*—that if the solution you had was promising, that is, it could be extended to an optimal one, then the one after the greedy choice is *also* promising. The general principles, as always, is that of induction, though there are a couple of more specialized ideas that can be useful. For example, if you can show that a hypothetical optimal solution can be modified to become the greedy solution *without loss of quality*, then the greedy solution is optimal. Or, if you can show that during the solution building process, the greedy partial solutions in some sense *keep up with* a hypothetical optimal sequence of solutions, all the way to the final solution, you can (with a little care) use that to show optimality.

Important greedy problems and algorithms discussed in this chapter include the knapsack problem (selecting a weight-bounded subset of items with maximum value), where the fractional version can be solved greedily; Huffman trees, which can be used to create optimal prefix codes and are built greedily by combining the smallest trees in the partial solution; and minimum spanning trees, which can be built using Kruskal's algorithm (keep adding the smallest valid edge) or Prim's algorithm (keep connecting the node that is closest to your tree).

If You're Curious …

There is a deep theory about greedy algorithms that I haven't really touched upon in this chapter, dealing with such beasts as matroids, greedoids, and so-called matroid embeddings. Although the greedoid stuff is a bit hard and the matroid embedding stuff can get really confusing fast, matroids aren't really that complicated, and they present an elegant perspective on *some* greedy problems. (Greedoids are more general, and matroid embeddings are the most general of the three, actually covering *all* greedy problems.) For more information on matroids, you could have a look at the book by Cormen et al. (see the "References" section of Chapter 1).

If you're interested in why the change-making problem is hard in general, you should have a look at the material in Chapter 11. As noted earlier, though, for a lot of currency systems, the greedy algorithm works just fine. David Pearson has designed an algorithm for checking *whether this is the case*, for any given currency; if you're interested, you should have a look at his paper (see "References").

If you find you need to build minimum *directed* spanning trees, branching out from some starting node, you can't use Prim's algorithm. A discussion of an algorithm that *will* work for finding these so-called min-cost arborescences can be found in the book by Kleinberg and Tardos (see the "References" section of Chapter 1).

Exercises

7-1. Give an example of a set of denominations that will break the greedy algorithm for giving change.

7-2. Assume that you have coins whose denominations are powers of some integer $k > 1$.
Why can you be certain that the greedy algorithm for making change would work in this case?

7-3. If the weights in some selection problem are unique powers of two, a greedy algorithm will generally maximize the weight sum. Why?

7-4. In the stable marriage problem, we say that a marriage between two people, say, Jack and Jill, is *feasible* if there exists a stable pairing where Jack and Jill are married. Show that the Gale-Shapley algorithm will match each man with his highest-ranking feasible wife.

7-5. Jill is Jack's best feasible wife. Show that Jack is Jill's *worst* feasible husband.

7-6. Let's say the various things you want to pack into your knapsack are *partly* divisible. That is, you can divide them at certain evenly spaced points (such as a candy bar divided into squares). The different items have different spacings between their breaking points. Could a greedy algorithm still work?

7-7. Show that the codes you get from a Huffman code are free of ambiguity. That is, when decoding a Huffman-coded text, you can always be certain of where the symbol boundaries go and which symbols go where.

7-8. In the proof for the greedy choice property of Huffman trees, it was assumed that the frequencies of a and d were different. What happens if they're not?

7-9. Show that a bad merging schedule can give a worse running time, asymptotically, than a good one and that this really depends on the frequencies.

7-10. Under what circumstances can a (connected) graph have multiple minimum spanning trees?

7-11. How would you build a *maximum* spanning tree (that is, one with maximum edge-weight sum)?

7-12. Show that the minimum spanning tree problem has optimal substructure.

7-13. What will Kruskal's algorithm find if the graph isn't connected? How could you modify Prim's algorithm to do the same?

7-14. What happens if you run Prim's algorithm on a *directed* graph?

7-15. For n points in the plane, no algorithm can find a minimum spanning tree (using Euclidean distance) faster than loglinear in the worst case. How come?

7-16. Show that m calls to either *union* or *find* would have a running time of $O(m \lg n)$ if you used union by rank.

7-17. Show that when using a binary heap as priority queue during a traversal, adding nodes once for each time they're encountered won't affect the asymptotic running time.

7-18. In selecting the largest nonoverlapping subset of a set of intervals, going left to right, why can't we use a greedy algorithm based on *starting* times?

7-19. What would the running time be of the algorithm finding the largest set of nonoverlapping intervals?

7-20. Implement the greedy solution for the scheduling problem where each task has a cost and a hard deadline and where all tasks take the same amount of time to perform.

References

Gale, D. and Shapley, L. S. (1962). College admissions and the stability of marriage. *The American Mathematical Monthly*, 69(1):9-15.

Graham, R. L. and Hell, P. (1985). On the history of the minimum spanning tree problem. *IEEE Annals on the History of Computing*, 7(1).

Gusfield, D. and Irving, R. W. (1989). *The Stable Marriage Problem: Structure and Algorithms*. The MIT Press.

Helman, P., Moret, B. M. E., and Shapiro, H. D. (1993). An exact characterization of greedy structures. *SIAM Journal on Discrete Mathematics*, 6(2):274-283.

Knuth, D. E. (1996). *Stable Marriage and Its Relation to Other Combinatorial Problems: An Introduction to the Mathematical Analysis of Algorithms*. American Mathematical Society.

Korte, B. H., Lovász, L., and Schrader, R. (1991). *Greedoids*. Springer-Verlag.

Nešetřil, J., Milková, E., and Nešetřilová, H. (2001). Otakar Borůvka on minimum spanning tree problem: Translation of both the 1926 papers, comments, history. Discrete Mathematics, 233(1-3):3-36.

Pearson, D. (2005). A polynomial-time algorithm for the change-making problem. *Operations Research Letters*, 33(3):231-234.

CHAPTER 8

███

Tangled Dependencies and Memoization

Twice, adv. Once too often.

— Ambrose Bierce, *The Devil's Dictionary*

Many of you may know the year 1957 as the birth year of programming languages.[1] For algorists, a possibly even more significant event took place this year: Richard Bellman published his groundbreaking book *Dynamic Programming*. Although Bellman's book is mostly mathematical in nature, not really aimed at programmers at all (perhaps understandable, given the timing), the core ideas behind his techniques have laid the foundation for a host of very powerful algorithms, and they form a solid design method that any algorithm designer needs to master.

The term *dynamic programming* (or simply DP) can be a bit confusing to newcomers. Both of the words are used in a different way than most might expect. *Programming* here refers to making a set of choices (as in "linear programming") and thus has more in common with the way the term is used in, say, television, than in writing computer programs. *Dynamic* simply means that things change over time—in this case, that each choice depends on the previous one. In other words, this "dynamicism" has little to do with the program you'll write and is just a description of the problem class. In Bellman's own words, "I thought dynamic programming was a good name. It was something not even a Congressman could object to. So I used it as an umbrella for my activities."[2]

The core technique of DP, when applied to algorithm design, is caching. You decompose your problem recursively/inductively just like before—but you allow overlap between the subproblems. This means that a plain recursive solution could easily reach each base case an exponential number of times; however, by caching these results, this exponential waste can be trimmed away, and the result is usually both an impressively efficient algorithm *and* a greater insight into the problem.

Commonly, DP algorithms turn the recursive formulation upside down, making it iterative and filling out some data structure (such as a multidimensional array) step by step. Another option—one I think is particularly suited to high-level languages such as Python—is to implement the recursive formulation directly but to cache the return values. If a call is made more than once with the same arguments, the result is simply returned directly from the cache. This is known as *memoization*.

---

[1] This was the year the first FORTRAN compiler was released by John Backus's group. Many consider this the first *complete* compiler, although the first compiler ever was written in 1942, by Grace Hopper.
[2] See *Richard Bellman on the Birth of Dynamic Programming* in the references.

■ **Note** Although I think memoization makes the underlying principles of DP clear, I do consistently rewrite the memoized versions to iterative programs throughout the chapter. While memoization is a great first step, one that gives you increased insight as well as a prototype solution, there are factors (such as limited stack depth and function call overhead) that may make an iterative solution preferable in some cases.

The basic ideas of DP are quite simple, but they can take a bit getting used to. According to Eric V. Denardo, another authority on the subject, "Most beginners find all of them strange and alien." I'll be trying my best to stick to the core ideas and not get lost in formalism. Also, by placing the main emphasis on recursive decomposition and memoization, rather than iterative DP, I hope the link to all the work we've done so far in the book should be pretty clear.

Before diving into the chapter, here's a little puzzle: Say you have a sequence of numbers, and you want to find its *longest increasing* (or, rather *nondecreasing*) subsequence—or one of them, if there are more. A subsequence consists of a subset of the elements in their original order. So, for example, in the sequence [3, 1, 0, 2, 4], one solution would be [1, 2, 4]. In Listing 8-1 you can see a reasonably compact solution to this problem. It uses efficient, built-in functions such as `combinations` from `itertools` and `sorted` to do its job, so the overhead should be pretty low. The algorithm, however, is a plain brute-force solution: Generate every subsequence and check them individually to see whether they're already sorted. In the worst case, the running time here is clearly exponential.

Writing a brute-force solution can be useful in understanding the problem and perhaps even in getting some ideas for better algorithms; I wouldn't be surprised if you could find several ways of improving `naive_lis`. However, a substantial improvement can be a bit challenging. Can you, for example, find a quadratic algorithm (somewhat challenging)? What about a loglinear one (pretty hard)? I'll show you how in a minute.

Listing 8-1. A Naïve Solution to the Longest Increasing Subsequence Problem

```
from itertools import combinations

def naive_lis(seq):
    for length in range(len(seq), 0, -1):      # n, n-1, ... , 1
        for sub in combinations(seq, length):  # Subsequences of given length
            if list(sub) == sorted(sub):       # An increasing subsequence?
                return sub                     # Return it!
```

Don't Repeat Yourself

You may have heard of the DRY principle: Don't repeat yourself. It's mainly used about your *code*, meaning that you should avoid writing the same (or almost the same) piece of code more than once, relying instead of various forms of abstraction to avoid cut-and-paste coding. It is certainly one of the most important basic principles of programming, but it's not what I'm talking about here. The basic idea of this chapter is to avoid having your *algorithm* repeat itself. The principle is so simple, and even quite easy to implement (at least in Python), but the mojo here is really deep, as you'll see as we progress.

But let's start with a couple of classics: Fibonacci numbers and Pascal's triangle. You may well have run into these before, but the reason that "everyone" uses them is that they can be pretty instructive. And fear not—I'll put a Pythonic twist on the solutions here, which I hope will be new to most of you.

The Fibonacci series of numbers is defined recursively as starting with two ones, with every subsequent number being the sum of the two previous. This is easily implemented as a Python function[3]:

```
>>> def fib(i):
...     if i < 2: return 1
...     return fib(i-1) + fib(i-2)
```

Let's try it out:

```
>>> fib(10)
89
```

Seems correct. Let's be a bit bolder:

```
>>> fib(100)
```

Uh-oh. It seems to hang. Something is clearly wrong. I'm going to give you a solution that is absolutely overkill for this particular problem but that you can actually use for all the problems in this chapter. It's the neat little memo function in Listing 8-2. This implementation uses nested scopes to give the wrapped function memory—if you'd like, you could easily use a class with cache and func attributes instead.

■ **Note** There is actually an equivalent decorator in the functools module of the Python standard library, called lru_cache (available since Python 3.2, or in the package functools32 for Python 2.7[4]). If you set its maxsize argument to None, it will work as a full memoizing decorator. It also provides a cache_clear method, which you could call between uses of your algorithm.

Listing 8-2. A Memoizing Decorator

```
from functools import wraps

def memo(func):
    cache = {}                          # Stored subproblem solutions
    @wraps(func)                        # Make wrap look like func
    def wrap(*args):                    # The memoized wrapper
        if args not in cache:           # Not already computed?
            cache[args] = func(*args)   # Compute & cache the solution
        return cache[args]              # Return the cached solution
    return wrap                         # Return the wrapper
```

Before getting into what memo actually does, let's just try to use it:

```
>>> fib = memo(fib)
>>> fib(100)
573147844013817084101
```

---

[3]Some definitions start with zero and one. If you want that, just use return i instead of return 1. The only difference is to shift the sequence indices by one.
[4]https://pypi.python.org/pypi/functools32/3.2.3

Hey, it worked! But ... why?

The idea of a *memoized* function[5] is that it caches its return values. If you call it a second time with the same parameters, it will simply return the cached value. You can certainly put this sort of caching logic inside your function, but the memo function is a more reusable solution. It's even designed to be used as a *decorator*[6]:

```
>>> @memo
... def fib(i):
...     if i < 2: return 1
...     return fib(i-1) + fib(i-2)
...
>>> fib(100)
573147844013817084101
```

As you can see, simply tagging fib with @memo can somehow reduce the running time *drastically*. And I still haven't really explained how or why.

The thing is, the recursive formulation of the Fibonacci sequence has two subproblems, and it sort of *looks* like a divide-and-conquer thing. The main difference is that the subproblems have *tangled dependencies*. Or, to put it in another way, we're faced with *overlapping subproblems*. This is perhaps even clearer in this rather silly relative of the Fibonacci numbers: a recursive formulation of the powers of two:

```
>>> def two_pow(i):
...     if i == 0: return 1
...     return two_pow(i-1) + two_pow(i-1)
...
>>> two_pow(10)
1024
>>> two_pow(100)
```

Still horrible. Try adding @memo, and you'll get the answer instantly. *Or,* you could try to make the following change, which is actually *equivalent*:

```
>>> def two_pow(i):
...     if i == 0: return 1
...     return 2*two_pow(i-1)
...
>>> print(two_pow(10))
1024
>>> print(two_pow(100))
1267650600228229401496703205376
```

I've reduced the number of recursive calls from two to one, going from an exponential running time to a linear one (corresponding to recurrences 3 and 1, respectively, from Table 3-1). The magic part is that this is equivalent to what the memoized version does. The first recursive call would be performed as normal, going all the way to the bottom (i == 0). Any call after that, though, would go straight to the cache, giving only a constant amount of extra work. Figure 8-1 illustrates the difference. As you can see, when there are overlapping subproblems (that is, nodes with the same number) on multiple levels, the redundant computation quickly becomes exponential.

---

[5]That is *memo-ized*, not *memorized*.

[6]The use of the wraps decorator from the functools module doesn't affect the functionality. It just lets the decorated function (such as fib) retain its properties (such as its name) after wrapping. See the Python docs for details.

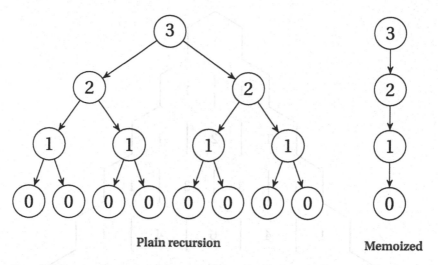

Plain recursion   **Memoized**

Figure 8-1. *Recursion trees showing the impact of memoization. Node labels are subproblem parameters*

Let's solve a slightly more useful problem[7]: calculating binomial coefficients (see Chapter 3). The combinatorial meaning of $C(n,k)$ is the number of k-sized subsets you can get from a set of size n. The first step, as almost always, is to look for some form of reduction or recursive decomposition. In this case, we can use an idea that you'll see several times when working with dynamic programming[8]: We decompose the problem by *conditioning on whether some element is included*. That is, we get one recursive call if an element *is* included and another if it *isn't*. (Do you see how two_pow could be interpreted in this way? See Exercise 8-2.)

For this to work, we often think of the elements in order so that a single evaluation of $C(n,k)$ would only worry about whether element number n should be included. If it *is* included, we have to count the k-1-sized subsets of the remaining n-1 elements, which is simply $C(n-1,k-1)$. If it is *not* included, we have to look for subsets of size k, or $C(n-1,k)$. In other words:

$$\binom{n}{k} = \binom{n-1}{k-1} + \binom{n-1}{k}$$

In addition, we have the following base cases: $C(n,0) = 1$ for the single empty subset, and $C(0,k) = 0$, $k > 0$, for nonempty subsets of an empty set.

This recursive formulation corresponds to what is often called *Pascal's triangle* (after one if its discoverers, Blaise Pascal), although it was first published in 1303 by the great Chinese mathematician Zhu Shijie, who claimed it was discovered early in the second millennium CE. Figure 8-2 shows how the binomial coefficients can be placed in a triangular pattern so that each number is the sum of the two above it. This means that the *row* (counting from zero) corresponds to n, and the *column* (the number of the cell, counting from zero at the left in its row) corresponds to k. For example, the value 6 corresponds to $C(4,2)$ and can be calculated as $C(3,1) + C(3,2) = 3 + 3 = 6$.

---

[7]This is still just an example for illustrating the basic principles.
[8]For example, this "In or not?" approach is used in solving the knapsack problem, later in this chapter.

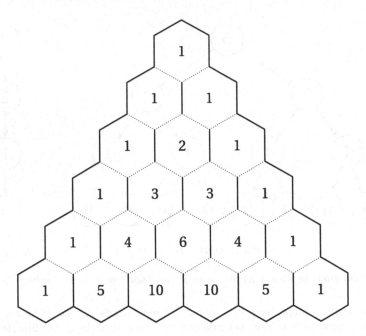

Figure 8-2. Pascal's triangle

Another way of interpreting the pattern (as hinted at by the figure) is *path counting*. How many paths are there, if you go only downward, past the dotted lines, from the top cell to each of the others? This leads us to the same recurrence—we can come either from the cell above to the left or from the one above to the right. The number of paths is therefore the sum of the two. This means that the numbers are proportional to the *probability* of passing each of them if you make each left/right choice randomly on your way down. This is exactly what happens in games like the Japanese game Pachinko or in Plinko on *The Price Is Right*. There, a ball is dropped at the top and falls down between pins placed in some regular grid (such as the intersections of the hexagonal grid in Figure 8-2). I'll get back to this path counting in the next section—it's actually more important than it might seem at the moment.

The code for $C(n,k)$ is trivial:

```
>>> @memo
>>> def C(n,k):
...     if k == 0: return 1
...     if n == 0: return 0
...     return C(n-1,k-1) + C(n-1,k)
>>> C(4,2)
6
>>> C(10,7)
120
>>> C(100,50)
100891344545564193334812497256
```

You should try it both with and without the @memo, though, to convince yourself of the enormous difference between the two versions. Usually, we associate caching with some constant-factor speedup, but this is another ballpark entirely. For most of the problems we'll consider, the memoization will mean the difference between exponential and polynomial running time.

■ **Note**   Some of the memoized algorithms in this chapter (notably the one for the knapsack problem, as well as the ones in this section) are *pseudopolynomial* because we get a polynomial running time as a function of one of the *numbers* in the input, not only its *size*. Remember, the ranges of these numbers are exponential in their encoding size (that is, the number of bits used to encode them).

In most presentations of dynamic programming, memoized functions are, in fact, not used. The recursive decomposition is an important step of the algorithm design, but it is usually treated as just a mathematical tool, whereas the actual implementation is "upside down"—an iterative version. As you can see, with a simple aid such as the @memo decorator, memoized solutions can be really straightforward, and I don't think you should shy away from them. They'll help you get rid of nasty exponential explosions, without getting in the way of your pretty, recursive design.

However, as discussed before (in Chapter 4), you may at times want to rewrite your code to make it iterative. This can make it faster, and you avoid exhausting the stack if the recursion depth gets excessive. There's another reason, too: The iterative versions are often based on a specially constructed cache, rather than the generic "dict keyed by parameter tuples" used in my @memo. This means that you can sometimes use more efficient structures, such as the multidimensional arrays of NumPy, perhaps combined with Cython (see Appendix A), or even just nested lists. This custom cache design makes it possible to do use DP in more low-level languages, where general, abstract solutions such as our @memo decorator are often not feasible. Note that even though these two techniques often go hand in hand, you are certainly free to use an iterative solution with a more generic cache or a recursive one with a tailored structure for your subproblem solutions.

Let's reverse our algorithm, filling out Pascal's triangle directly. To keep things simple, I'll use a defaultdict as the cache; feel free to use nested lists, for example. (See also Exercise 8-4.)

```
>>> from collections import defaultdict
>>> n, k = 10, 7
>>> C = defaultdict(int)
>>> for row in range(n+1):
...     C[row,0] = 1
...     for col in range(1,k+1):
...         C[row,col] = C[row-1,col-1] + C[row-1,col]
...
>>> C[n,k]
120
```

Basically the same thing is going on. The main difference is that we need to figure out which cells in the cache need to be filled out, and we need to find a safe order to do it in so that when we're about to calculate C[row,col], the cells C[row-1,col-1] and C[row-1,col] are already calculated. With the memoized function, we needn't worry about either issue: It will calculate whatever it needs recursively.

■ **Tip**   One useful way to visualize dynamic programming algorithms with one or two subproblem parameters (such as *n* and *k*, here) is to use a (real or imagined) spreadsheet. For example, try calculating binomial coefficients in a spreadsheet by filling the first column with ones and filling in the rest of the first row with zeros. Put the formula =A1+B1 into cell B2, and copy it to the remaining cells.

Shortest Paths in Directed Acyclic Graphs

At the core of dynamic programming lies the idea of sequential decision problems. Each choice you make leads to a new situation, and you need to find the best sequence of choices that gets you to the situation you want. This is similar to how greedy algorithms work—it's just that they rely on which choice looks best *right now*, while in general, you have to be less myopic and take future effects into consideration.

The prototypical sequential decision problem is finding your way from one node to another in a directed, acyclic graph. We represent the possible states of our decision process as individual nodes. The out-edges represent the possible choices we can make in each state. The edges have weights, and finding an optimal set of choices is equivalent to finding a shortest path. Figure 8-3 gives an example of a DAG where the shortest path from node *a* to node *f* has been highlighted. How should we go about finding this path?

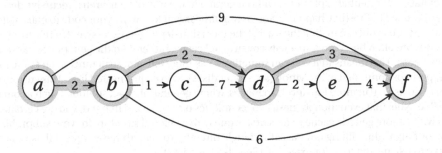

Figure 8-3. *A topologically sorted DAG. Edges are labeled with weights, and the shortest path from a to f has been highlighted*

It should be clear how this is a sequential decision process. You start in node *a*, and you have a choice between following the edge to *b* or the edge to *f*. On the one hand, the edge to *b* looks promising because it's so cheap, while the one to *f* is tempting because it goes straight for the goal. We can't go with simple strategies like this, however. For example, the graph has been constructed so that following the shortest edge from each node we visit, we'll follow the *longest* path.

As in previous chapters, we need to think inductively. Let's assume that we already *know* the answer for all the nodes we can move to. Let's say the distance from a node v to our end node is $d(v)$. Let the edge weight of edge (u,v) be $w(u,v)$. Then, if we're in node u, we already (by inductive hypothesis) know $d(v)$ for each neighbor v, so we just have to follow the edge to the neighbor v that minimizes the expression $w(u,v) + d(v)$. In other words, we minimize the sum of the first step and the shortest path from there.

Of course, we don't really *know* the value of $d(v)$ for all our neighbors, but as for any inductive design, that'll take care of itself through the magic of recursion. The only problem is the overlapping subproblems. For example, in Figure 8-3, finding the distance from *b* to *f* requires finding the shortest path from, for example, *d* to *f*. But so does finding the shortest path from *c* to *f*. We have exactly the same situation as for the Fibonacci numbers, two_pow, or Pascal's triangle. Some subproblems will be solved an exponential number of times if we implement the recursive solution directly. And just as for those problems, the magic of memoization removes all the redundancy, and we end up with a *linear-time algorithm* (that is, for n nodes and m edges, the running time is $\Theta(n + m)$).

A direct implementation (using something like a dict of dicts representation of the edge weight function) can be found in Listing 8-3. If you remove @memo from the code, you end up with an exponential algorithm (which may still work well for relatively small graphs with few edges).

Listing 8-3. Recursive, Memoized DAG Shortest Path

```
def rec_dag_sp(W, s, t):                    # Shortest path from s to t
    @memo                                   # Memoize f
    def d(u):                               # Distance from u to t
        if u == t: return 0                 # We're there!
        return min(W[u][v]+d(v) for v in W[u]) # Best of every first step
    return d(s)                             # Apply f to actual start node
```

In my opinion, the implementation in Listing 8-3 is quite elegant. It directly expresses the inductive idea of the algorithm, while abstracting away the memoization. However, this is not the classical way of expressing this algorithm. What is customarily done here, as in so many other DP algorithms, is to turn the algorithm "upside down" and make it iterative.

The iterative version of the DAG shortest path algorithm works by propagating partial solutions step by step, using the relaxation idea introduced in Chapter 4.[9] Because of the way we represent graphs (that is, we usually access nodes by out-edges, rather than in-edges), it can be useful to reverse the inductive design: Instead of thinking about where we want to *go*, we think about where we want to *come from*. Then we want to make sure that once we reach a node *v*, we have already propagated correct answers from all *v*'s predecessors. That is, we have already relaxed its in-edges. This raises the question—how can we be sure we've done that?

The way to know is to sort the nodes topologically, as they are in Figure 8-3. The neat thing about the *recursive* version (in Listing 8-3) is that no separate topological sorting is needed. The recursion implicitly performs a DFS and does all updates in topologically sorted order *automatically*. For our iterative solution, though, we need to perform a separate topological sorting. If you want to get away from the recursion entirely, you can use `topsort` from Listing 4-10; if you don't mind, you could use `dfs_topsort` from Listing 5-7 (although then you're already quite close to the memoized recursive solution). The function `dag_sp` in Listing 8-4 shows you this more common, iterative solution.

Listing 8-4. DAG Shortest Path

```
def dag_sp(W, s, t):                        # Shortest path from s to t
    d = {u:float('inf') for u in W}         # Distance estimates
    d[s] = 0                                # Start node: Zero distance
    for u in topsort(W):                    # In top-sorted order...
        if u == t: break                    # Have we arrived?
        for v in W[u]:                      # For each out-edge ...
            d[v] = min(d[v], d[u] + W[u][v]) # Relax the edge
    return d[t]                             # Distance to t (from s)
```

The idea of the iterative algorithm is that as long as we have relaxed each edge *out* from each of your possible *predecessors* (that is, those earlier in topologically sorted order), we must necessarily have relaxed all the *in*-edges to *you*. Using this, we can show inductively that each node receives a correct distance estimate at the time we get to it in the outer for loop. This means that once we get to the target node, we will have found the correct distance.

Finding the actual path corresponding to this distance isn't all that hard either (see Exercise 8-5). You could even build the entire shortest path tree from the start node, just like the traversal trees in Chapter 5. (You'd have to remove the break statement, though, and keep going till the end.) Note that some nodes, including those earlier than the start node in topologically sorted order, may not be reached at all and will keep their infinite distances.

---

[9]This approach is also closely related to Prim's and Dijkstra's algorithms, as well as the Bellman-Ford algorithm (see Chapters 7 and 9).

■ **Note**   In most of this chapter, I focus on finding the optimal *value* of a solution, without the extra bookkeeping needed to reconstruct the solution that gives rise to that value. This approach makes the presentation simpler but may not be what you want in practice. Some of the exercises ask you to extend algorithms to find the actual solutions; you can find an example of how to do this at the end of the section about the knapsack problem.

VARIETIES OF DAG SHORTEST PATH

Although the basic algorithm is the same, there are many ways of finding the shortest path in a DAG and, by extension, solving most DP problems. You could do it recursively, with memoization, or you could do it iteratively, with relaxation. For the recursion, you could start at the first node, try various "next steps," and then recurse on the remainder, or if your graph representation permits, you could look at the last node and try "previous steps" and recurse on the initial part. The former is usually much more natural, while the latter corresponds more closely to what happens in the iterative version.

Now, if you use the iterative version, you also have two choices: You can relax the edges *out of* each node (in topologically sorted order), or you can relax all edges *into* each node. The latter more obviously yields a correct result but requires access to nodes by following edges backward. This isn't as far-fetched as it seems when you're working with an *implicit* DAG in some non-graph problem. (For example, in the longest increasing subsequence problem, discussed later in this chapter, looking at all backward "edges" can be a useful perspective.)

Outward relaxation, called *reaching*, is exactly equivalent when you relax all edges. As explained, once you get to a node, all its in-edges will have been relaxed anyway. *However*, with reaching, you can do something that's hard in the recursive version (or relaxing in-edges): pruning. If, for example, you're interested only in finding all nodes that are within a distance r, you can skip any node that has distance estimate greater than r. You will still need to visit every node, but you can potentially ignore lots of edges during the relaxation. This won't affect the asymptotic running time, though (Exercise 8-6).

Note that finding the *shortest* paths in a DAG is surprisingly similar to, for example, finding the *longest* path, or even counting the *number of paths* between two nodes in a DAG. The latter problem is just what we did with Pascal's triangle earlier; the same approach would work for an arbitrary DAG. These things aren't quite as easy for general graphs, though. Finding shortest paths in a general graph is a bit harder (in fact, Chapter 9 is devoted to this topic), while finding the *longest* path is an *unsolved problem* (see Chapter 11 for more on this).

Longest Increasing Subsequence

Although finding the shortest path in a DAG is the canonical DP problem, a lot—perhaps the majority—of the DP problems you'll come across won't have anything to do with (explicit) graphs. In these cases, you'll have to sniff out the DAG or sequential decision process yourself. Or perhaps it'll be easier to think of it in terms of recursive decomposition and ignore the whole DAG structure. In this section, I'll follow both approaches with the problem introduced at the beginning of this chapter: finding the longest nondecreasing subsequence. (The problem is normally called "longest increasing subsequence," but I'll allow multiple identical values in the result here.)

Let's go straight for the induction, and we can think more in graph terms later. To do the induction (or recursive decomposition), we need to define our subproblems—one of the main challenges of many DP problems. In many sequence-related problems, it can be useful to think in terms of prefixes—that we've figured out all we need to know about a prefix and that the inductive step is to figure things out for another element. In this case, that might mean that we'd found the longest increasing subsequence for each prefix, but that's not informative enough. We need to strengthen our induction hypothesis so we can actually implement the inductive step. Let's try, instead, to find the longest increasing subsequence that *ends* at each given position.

If we've already know how to find this for the first k positions, how can we find it for position $k + 1$? Once we've gotten this far, the answer is pretty straightforward: We just look at the previous positions and look at those whose elements are smaller than the current one. Among those, we choose the one that is at the end of the longest subsequence. Direct recursive implementation will give us exponential running time, but once again, memoization gets rid of the exponential redundancy, as shown in Listing 8-5. Once again, I've focused on finding the *length* of the solution; extending the code to find the actual subsequence isn't all that hard (Exercise 8-10).

Listing 8-5. A Memoized Recursive Solution to the Longest Increasing Subsequence Problem

```
def rec_lis(seq):                        # Longest increasing subseq.
    @memo
    def L(cur):                          # Longest ending at seq[cur]
        res = 1                          # Length is at least 1
        for pre in range(cur):           # Potential predecessors
            if seq[pre] <= seq[cur]:     # A valid (smaller) predec.
                res = max(res, 1 + L(pre))  # Can we improve the solution?
        return res
    return max(L(i) for i in range(len(seq)))  # The longest of them all
```

Let's make an iterative version as well. In this case, the difference is really rather slight—quite reminiscent of the mirror illustration in Figure 4-3. Because of how recursion works, rec_lis will solve the problem for each position in order (0, 1, 2 …). All we need to do in the iterative version is to switch out the recursive call with a lookup and wrap the whole thing in a loop. See Listing 8-6 for an implementation.

Listing 8-6. A Basic Iterative Solution to the Longest Increasing Subsequence Problem

```
def basic_lis(seq):
    L = [1] * len(seq)
    for cur, val in enumerate(seq):
        for pre in range(cur):
            if seq[pre] <= val:
                L[cur] = max(L[cur], 1 + L[pre])
    return max(L)
```

I hope you see the resemblance to the recursive version. In this case, the iterative version might be just as easy to understand as the recursive one.

Now, think of this as a DAG: Each sequence element is a node, and there is an implicit edge from each element to each following element that is larger—that is, to any element that is a permissible successor in an increasing subsequence (see Figure 8-4). *Voilà!* We're now solving the DAG longest path problem. That's actually pretty clear in the basic_lis function. We don't have the edges explicitly represented, so it has to look at each previous element to see whether it's a valid predecessor, but if it is, it simply relaxes the in-edge (that's what the line with the max expression does, really). Can we improve the solution at the current position by using this "previous step" in the decision process (that is, this in-edge or this valid predecessor)?[10]

---

[10]Actually, for the longest increasing subsequence problem, we're looking for the longest *of all the paths*, rather just the longest between any two given points.

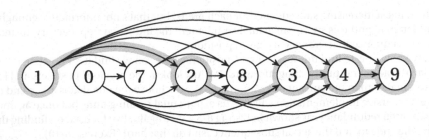

Figure 8-4. *A number sequence and the implicit DAG where each path is an increasing subsequence. One of the longest increasing subsequences has been highlighted*

As you can see, there is more than one way to view most DP problems. Sometimes you want to focus on the recursive decomposition and induction; sometimes you'd rather try to sniff out some DAG structure; sometimes, yet again, it can pay to look at what's right there in front of you. In this case, that would be the sequence. The algorithm is still quadratic, and as you may have noticed, I called it *basic_lis* ... that's because I have another trick up my sleeve.

The main time sink in the algorithm is looking over the previous elements to find the best among those that are valid predecessors. You'll find that this is the case in some DP algorithms—that the inner loop is devoted to a linear search. If this is the case, it might be worth trying to replace it with a *binary* search. It's not at all obvious how that would be possible in this case, but simply knowing what we're looking for—what we're trying to do—can sometimes be of help. We're trying to do some form of bookkeeping that will let us perform a bisection when looking for the optimal predecessor.

A crucial insight is that if more than one predecessor terminate subsequences of length *m*, it doesn't matter which one of them we use—they'll all give us an optimal answer. Say, we want to keep only *one* of them around; which one should we keep? The only safe choice would be to keep the smallest of them, because that wouldn't wrongly preclude any later elements from building on it. So let's say, inductively, that at a certain point we have a sequence end of endpoints, where end[idx] is the smallest among the endpoints we've seen for increasing subsequences of length idx+1 (we're indexing from 0). Because we're iterating over the sequence, these will all have occurred earlier than our current value, val. All we need now is an inductive step for extending end, finding out how to add val to it. If we can do that, at the end of the algorithm len(end) will give us the final answer—the length of the longest increasing subsequence.

The end sequence will necessarily be nondecreasing (Exercise 8-8). We want to find the largest idx such that end[idx-1] <= val. This would give us the longest sequence that val could contribute to, so adding val at end[idx] will either improve the current result (if we need to append it) or reduce the current end-point value at that position. After this addition, the end sequence still has the properties it had before, so the induction is safe. And the good thing is—we can find idx using the (super-fast) bisect function![11] You can find the final code in Listing 8-7. If you wanted, you could get rid of some of the calls to bisect (Exercise 8-9). If you want to extract the actual sequence, and not just the length, you'll need to add some extra bookkeeping (Exercise 8-10).

Listing 8-7. Longest Increasing Subsequence

```python
from bisect import bisect

def lis(seq):                          # Longest increasing subseq.
    end = []                           # End-values for all lengths
    for val in seq:                    # Try every value, in order
        idx = bisect(end, val)         # Can we build on an end val?
        if idx == len(end): end.append(val)   # Longest seq. extended
        else: end[idx] = val           # Prev. endpoint reduced
    return len(end)                    # The longest we found
```

---

[11]This devilishly clever little algorithm was first was first described by Michael L. Fredman in 1975.

That's it for the longest increasing subsequence problem. Before we dive into some well-known examples of dynamic programming, here's a recap of what we've seen so far. When solving problems using DP, you still use recursive decomposition or inductive thinking. You still need to show that an optimal or correct global solution depends on optimal or correct solutions to your subproblems (optimal substructure, or the principle of optimality). The main difference from, say, divide and conquer is just that you're allowed to have overlapping subproblems. In fact, that overlap is the *raison d'être* of DP. You might even say that you should *look for* a decomposition *with overlap*, because eliminating that overlap (with memoization) is what will give you an efficient solution. In addition to the perspective of "recursive decomposition with overlap," you can often see DP problems as sequential decision problems or as looking for special (for example, shortest or longest) paths in a DAG. These perspectives are all equivalent, but they can fit various problems differently.

Sequence Comparison

Comparing sequences for similarity is a crucial problem in much of molecular biology and bioinformatics, where the sequences involved are generally DNA, RNA, or protein sequences. It is used, among other things, to construct phylogenetic (that is, evolutionary) trees—which species have descended from which? It can also be used to find genes that are shared by people who have a given illness or who are receptive to a specific drug. Different kinds of sequence or string comparison is also relevant for many kinds of information retrieval. For example, you may search for "The Color Out of Space" and expect to find "The Colour Out of Space"—and for that to happen, the search technology you're using needs to somehow know that the two sequences are sufficiently similar.

There are several ways of comparing sequences, many of which are more similar than one might think. For example, consider the problem of finding the *longest common subsequence* (LCS) between two sequences and finding the *edit distance* between them. The LCS problem is similar to the longest increasing subsequence problem—except that we're no longer looking for *increasing* subsequence. We're looking for subsequences that also occur in a *second* sequence. (For example, the LCS of *Starwalker*[12] and *Starbuck* is *Stark*.) The edit distance (also known as Levenshtein distance) is the minimum number of editing operations (insertions, deletions, or replacements) needed to turn one sequence into another. (For example, the edit distance between *enterprise* and *deuteroprism* is 4.) If we disallow replacements, the two are actually equivalent. The longest common subsequence is the part that *stays the same* when editing one sequence into the other with as few edits as possible. Every other character in either sequence must be inserted or deleted. Thus, if the length of the sequences are m and n and the length of the longest common subsequence is k, the edit distance without replacements is $m+n-2k$.

I'll focus on LCS here, leaving edit distance for an exercise (Exercise 8-11). Also, as before, I'll restrict myself to the cost of the solution (that is, the length of the LCS). Adding some extra bookkeeping to let you find the underlying structure follows the standard pattern (Exercise 8-12). For some related sequence comparison problems, see the "If You're Curious ..." section near the end of this chapter.

Although dreaming up a polynomial algorithm to find the longest common subsequence can be really tough if you haven't been exposed to any of the techniques in this book, it's surprisingly simple using the tools I've been discussing in this chapter. As for all DP problems, the key is to design a set of subproblems that we can relate to each other (that is, a recursive decomposition with tangled dependencies). It can often help to think of the set of subproblems as being *parametrized* by a set of indexes or the like. These will then be our induction variables.[13] In this case, we can work with *prefixes* of the sequences (just like we worked with prefixes of a single sequence in the longest increasing subsequence problem). Any pair of prefixes (identified by their lengths) gives rise to a subproblem, and we want to relate them in a subproblem graph (that is, a dependency DAG).

---

[12]Using *Skywalker* here gives the slightly less interesting LCS *Sar*.
[13]Normally, of course, induction works on only *one* integer variable, such as problem size. The technique can easily be extended to multiple variables, though, where the induction hypothesis applies wherever at least *one* of the variables is smaller.

Let's say our sequences are a and b. As with inductive thinking in general, we start with two arbitrary prefixes, identified by their lengths i and j. What we need to do is relate the solution to this problem to some other problems, where at least one of the prefixes is smaller. Intuitively, we'd like to temporarily chop off some elements from the end of either sequence, solve the resulting problem by our inductive hypothesis, and stick the elements back on. If we stick with weak induction (reduction by one) along either sequence, we get three cases: Chop the last element from a, from b, or from both. If we remove an element from just one sequence, it's excluded from the LCS. If we drop the last from *both*, however, what happens depends on whether the two elements are *equal* or not. If they are, we can use them to extend the LCS by one! (If not, they're of no use to us.)

This, in fact, gives us the entire algorithm (except for a couple of details). We can express the length of the LCS of a and b as a function of prefix lengths i and j as follows:

$$L(i,j) = \begin{cases} 0 & \text{if } i = 0 \text{ or } j = 0 \\ 1 + L(i-1, j-1) & \text{if } a_i = b_j \\ \max\{L(i-1, j), L(i, j-1)\} & \text{otherwise} \end{cases}$$

In other words, if either prefix is empty, the LCS is empty. If the last elements are equal, that element is the last element of the LCS, and we find the length of the rest (that is, the earlier part) recursively. If the last elements *aren't* equal, we have only two options: Chop on element off either a or b. Because we can choose freely, we take the best of the two results. Listing 8-8 gives a simple memoized implementation of this recursive solution.

Listing 8-8. A Memoized Recursive Solution to the LCS Problem

```
def rec_lcs(a,b):                          # Longest common subsequence
    @memo                                  # L is memoized
    def L(i,j):                            # Prefixes a[:i] and b[:j]
        if min(i,j) < 0: return 0          # One prefix is empty
        if a[i] == b[j]: return 1 + L(i-1,j-1)  # Match! Move diagonally
        return max(L(i-1,j), L(i,j-1))     # Chop off either a[i] or b[j]
    return L(len(a)-1,len(b)-1)            # Run L on entire sequences
```

This recursive decomposition can easily be seen as a dynamic decision process (do we chop off an element from the first sequence, from the second, or from both?), which can be represented as a DAG (see Figure 8-5). We start in the node represented by the full sequences, and we try to find the longest path back to the node representing two empty prefixes. It's important to be clear about what the "longest path" is here, though—that is, what the edge weights are. The *only time* we can extend the LCS (which is our goal) is when we chop off two identical elements, represented by the DAG edges that are diagonal when the nodes are placed in a grid, as in Figure 8-5. These edges, then, have a weight of one, while the other edges have a weight of zero.

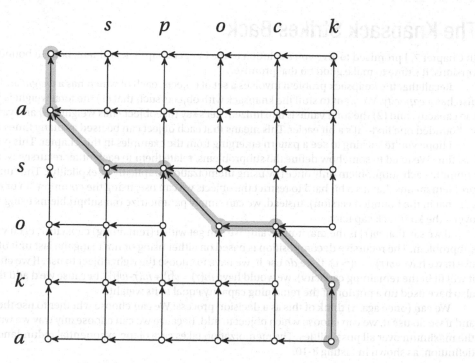

Figure 8-5. *The underlying DAG of the LCS problem, where horizontal and vertical edges have zero cost. The longest path (that is, the one with the most diagonals) from corner to corner, where the diagonals represent the LCS, is highlighted*

For the usual reasons, you may want to reverse the solution and make it iterative. Listing 8-9 gives you a version that saves memory by keeping only the current and the previous row of the DP matrix. (You could save a bit more, though; see Exercise 8-13.) Note that cur[i-1] corresponds to L(i-1,j) in the recursive version, while pre[i] and pre[i-1] correspond to L(i,j-1) and L(i-1,j-1), respectively.

Listing 8-9. An Iterative Solution to the Longest Common Subsequence (LCS)

```
def lcs(a,b):
    n, m = len(a), len(b)
    pre, cur = [0]*(n+1), [0]*(n+1)        # Previous/current row
    for j in range(1,m+1):                 # Iterate over b
        pre, cur = cur, pre                # Keep prev., overwrite cur.
        for i in range(1,n+1):             # Iterate over a
            if a[i-1] == b[j-1]:           # Last elts. of pref. equal?
                cur[i] = pre[i-1] + 1      # L(i,j) = L(i-1,j-1) + 1
            else:                          # Otherwise...
                cur[i] = max(pre[i], cur[i-1])  # max(L(i,j-1),L(i-1,j))
    return cur[n]                          # L(n,m)
```

The Knapsack Strikes Back

In Chapter 7, I promised to give you a solution to the integer knapsack problem, both in bounded and unbounded versions. It's time to make good on that promise.

Recall that the knapsack problem involves a set of objects, each of which has a *weight* and a *value*. Our knapsack also has a *capacity*. We want to stuff the knapsack with objects such that (1) the total weight is less than or equal to the capacity, and (2) the total value is maximized. Let's say that object i has weight $w[i]$ and value $v[i]$. Let's do the unbounded one first—it's a bit easier. This means that each object can be used as many times as you want.

I hope you're starting to see a pattern emerging from the examples in this chapter. This problem fits the pattern just fine: We need to somehow define the subproblems, relate them to each other recursively, and then make sure we compute each subproblem only once (by using memoization, implicitly or explicitly). The "unboundedness" of the problem means that it's a bit hard to restrict the objects we can use, using the common "in or out" idea (although we'll use that in the bounded version). Instead, we can simply parametrize our subproblems using—that is, use induction over—the knapsack capacity.

If we say that $m(r)$ is the maximum value we can get with a (remaining) capacity r, each value of r gives us a subproblem. The recursive decomposition is based on either using or not using the last unit of the capacity. If we *don't* use it, we have $m(r) = m(r-1)$. If we *do* use it, we have to choose the right object to use. If we choose object i (provided it will fit in the remaining capacity), we would have $m(r) = v[i] + m(r-w[i])$, because we'd add the value of i, but we'd also have used up a portion of the remaining capacity equal to its weight.

We can (once again) think of this as a decision process: We can choose whether to use the last capacity unit, and if we do use it, we can choose which object to add. Because we can choose any way we want, we simply take the maximum over all possibilities. The memoization takes care of the exponential redundancy in this recursive definition, as shown in Listing 8-10.

Listing 8-10. A Memoized Recursive Solution to the Unbounded Integer Knapsack Problem

```
def rec_unbounded_knapsack(w, v, c):    # Weights, values and capacity
    @memo                               # m is memoized
    def m(r):                           # Max val. w/remaining cap. r
        if r == 0: return 0             # No capacity? No value
        val = m(r-1)                    # Ignore the last cap. unit?
        for i, wi in enumerate(w):      # Try every object
            if wi > r: continue         # Too heavy? Ignore it
            val = max(val, v[i] + m(r-wi))  # Add value, remove weight
        return val                      # Max over all last objects
    return m(c)                         # Full capacity available
```

The running time here depends on the capacity and the number of objects. Each memoized call m(r) is computed only once, which means that for a capacity c, we have $\Theta(c)$ calls. Each call goes through all the n objects, so the resulting running time is $\Theta(cn)$. (This will, perhaps, be easier to see in the equivalent iterative version, coming up next. See also Exercise 8-14 for a way of improving the constant factor in the running time.) Note that this is *not* a polynomial running time because c can grow exponentially with the actual problem size (the number of bits). As mentioned earlier, this sort of running time is called *pseudopolynomial*, and for reasonably sized capacities, the solution is actually quite efficient.

Listing 8-11 shows an iterative version of the algorithm. As you can see, the two implementations are virtually identical, except that the recursion is replaced with a for loop, and the cache is now a list.[14]

---

[14]You could preallocate the list, with m = [0]*(c+1), if you prefer, and then use m[r] = val instead of the append.

Listing 8-11. An Iterative Solution to the Unbounded Integer Knapsack Problem

```
def unbounded_knapsack(w, v, c):
    m = [0]
    for r in range(1,c+1):
        val = m[r-1]
        for i, wi in enumerate(w):
            if wi > r: continue
            val = max(val, v[i] + m[r-wi])
        m.append(val)
    return m[c]
```

Now let's get to the perhaps more well-known knapsack version—the 0-1 knapsack problem. Here, each object can be used at most once. (You could easily extend this to more than once, either by adjusting the algorithm a bit or by just including the same object more than once in the problem instance.) This is a problem that occurs a lot in practical situations, as discussed in Chapter 7. If you've ever played a computer game with an inventory system, I'm sure you know how frustrating it can be. You've just slain some mighty monster and find a bunch of loot. You try to pick it up but see that you're overencumbered. What now? Which objects should you keep, and which should you leave behind?

This version of the problem is quite similar to the unbounded one. The main difference is that we now add another parameter to the subproblems: In addition to restricting the capacity, we add the "in or out" idea and restrict how many of the objects we're allowed to use. Or, rather, we specify which object (in order) is "currently under consideration," and we use strong induction, assuming that all subproblems where we either consider an earlier object, have a lower capacity, or both, can be solved recursively.

Now we need to relate these subproblems to each other and build a solution from subsolutions. Let $m(k,r)$ be the maximum value we can have with the first k objects and a remaining capacity r. Then, clearly, if $k = 0$ or $r = 0$, we will have $m(k,r) = 0$. For other cases, we once again have to look at what our decision is. For this problem, the decision is simpler than in the unbounded one; we need consider only whether we want to include the last object, $i = k$-1. If we *don't*, we will have $m(k,r) = m(k$-$1,r)$. In effect, we're just "inheriting" the optimum from the case where we hadn't considered i yet. Note that if $w[i] > r$, we have no choice but to drop the object.

If the object is small enough, though, we can include it, meaning that $m(k,r) = v[i] + m(k$-$1,r$-$w[i])$, which is quite similar to the unbounded case, except for the extra parameter (k).[15] Because we can choose freely whether to include the object, we try both alternatives and use the maximum of the two resulting values. Again, the memoization removes the exponential redundancy, and we end up with code like the one in Listing 8-12.

Listing 8-12. A Memoized Recursive Solution to the 0-1 Knapsack Problem

```
def rec_knapsack(w, v, c):                     # Weights, values and capacity
    @memo                                       # m is memoized
    def m(k, r):                                # Max val., k objs and cap r
        if k == 0 or r == 0: return 0           # No objects/no capacity
        i = k-1                                  # Object under consideration
        drop = m(k-1, r)                         # What if we drop the object?
        if w[i] > r: return drop                # Too heavy: Must drop it
        return max(drop, v[i] + m(k-1, r-w[i])) # Include it? Max of in/out
    return m(len(w), c)                          # All objects, all capacity
```

In a problem such as LCS, simply finding the value of a solution can be useful. For LCS, the length of the longest common subsequence gives us an idea of how similar two sequences are. In many cases, though, you'd like to find the actual solution giving rise to the optimal cost. The iterative knapsack version in Listing 8-13 constructs an extra table, called P because it works a bit like the predecessor tables used in traversal (Chapter 5) and shortest path

---

[15]The object index $i = k$-1 is just a convenience. We might just as well write $m(k,r) = v[k$-$1] + m(k$-$1,r$-$w[k$-$1])$.

algorithms (Chapter 9). Both versions of the 0-1 knapsack solutions have the same (pseudopolynomial) running time as the unbounded ones, that is, $\Theta(cn)$.

Listing 8-13. An Iterative Solution to the 0-1 Knapsack Problem

```
def knapsack(w, v, c):                         # Returns solution matrices
    n = len(w)                                 # Number of available items
    m = [[0]*(c+1) for i in range(n+1)]        # Empty max-value matrix
    P = [[False]*(c+1) for i in range(n+1)]    # Empty keep/drop matrix
    for k in range(1,n+1):                      # We can use k first objects
        i = k-1                                # Object under consideration
        for r in range(1,c+1):                 # Every positive capacity
            m[k][r] = drop = m[k-1][r]         # By default: drop the object
            if w[i] > r: continue              # Too heavy? Ignore it
            keep = v[i] + m[k-1][r-w[i]]       # Value of keeping it
            m[k][r] = max(drop, keep)          # Best of dropping and keeping
            P[k][r] = keep > drop              # Did we keep it?
    return m, P                                # Return full results
```

Now that the knapsack function returns more information, we can use it to extract the set of objects actually included in the optimal solution. For example, you could do something like this:

```
>>> m, P = knapsack(w, v, c)
>>> k, r, items = len(w), c, set()
>>> while k > 0 and r > 0:
...     i = k-1
...     if P[k][r]:
...         items.add(i)
...         r -= w[i]
...     k -= 1
```

In other words, by simply keeping some information about the choices made (in this case, keeping or dropping the element under consideration), we can gradually trace ourselves back from the final state to the initial conditions. In this case, I start with the last object and check P[k][r] to see whether it was included. If it was, I subtract its weight from r; if it wasn't, I leave r alone (as we still have the full capacity available). In either case, I decrement k because we're done looking at the last element and now want to have a look at the next-to-last element (with the updated capacity). You might want to convince yourself that this backtracking operation has a linear running time.

The same basic idea can be used in all the examples in this chapter. In addition to the core algorithms presented (which generally compute only the optimal *value*), you can keep track of what choice was made at each step and then backtrack once the optimum has been found.

Binary Sequence Partitioning

Before concluding this chapter, let's take a look at another typical kind of DP problem, where some sequence is recursively partitioned in some manner. You could think of this as adding parentheses to the sequence, so that we go from, for example, ABCDE to ((AB)((CD)E)). This has several applications, such as the following:

- *Matrix chain multiplication*: We have a sequence of matrices, and we want to multiply them all together into a single matrix. We can't swap them around (matrix multiplication isn't commutative), but we can place the parentheses where we want, and this can affect the number of operations needed. Our goal is to find the parenthesization (phew!) that gives the lowest number of operations.

- *Parsing arbitrary context-free languages:*[16] The grammar for any context-free language can be rewritten to *Chomsky normal form*, where each production rule produces either a terminal, the empty string, or a pair *AB* of nonterminals *A* and *B*. Parsing a string then is basically equivalent to setting the parentheses just like in the matrix example. Each parenthesized group then represents a nonterminal.

- *Optimal search trees*: This is a tougher version of the Huffman problem. The goal is the same—minimize expected traversal depth—but because it's a search tree, we can't change the order of the leaves, and the greedy algorithm no longer works. Again, what we need is a parenthesization, corresponding to the tree structure.[17]

These three applications are quite different, but the problem is essentially the same: We want to segment the sequence hierarchically so that each segment contains two others, and we want to find such a partitioning that optimizes some cost or value (in the parsing case, the value is simply "valid"/"invalid"). The recursive decomposition works just like with a divide-and-conquer algorithm, as illustrated in Figure 8-6. A split point is chosen within the current interval, giving rise to two subintervals, which are partitioned recursively. If we were to create a balanced binary search tree based on a sorted sequence, that would be all there was to it. Use the middle element (or one of the two middle ones, for even-length intervals) as the split point (that is, root) and create the balanced left and right subtrees recursively.

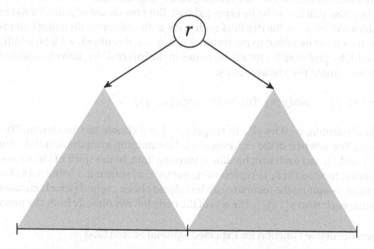

Figure 8-6. *Recursive sequence partitioning as it applies to optimal search trees. Each root in the interval gives rise to two subtrees corresponding to the optimal partitioning of the left and right subintervals*

Now we're going to have to step our game up, though, because the split point isn't given, like for the balanced divide-and-conquer example. No, now we need to try *multiple* split points, choosing the best one. In fact, in the general case, we need to try *every possible split point*. This is a typical DP problem—in some ways just as prototypical as finding shortest paths in DAGs. The DAG shortest path problem encapsulates the sequential decision perspective of DP; this sequence decomposition problem embodies the "recursive decomposition with overlap" perspective.

---

[16]If parsing is completely foreign to you, feel free to skip this bullet point. Or perhaps look into it?

[17]You can find more information about optimal search trees both in Section 15.5 in *Introduction to Algorithms* by Cormen et al., and in Section 6.2.2 of *The Art of Computer Programming*, volume 3, "Sorting and Searching," by Donald E. Knuth (see the "References" section of Chapter 1).

The subproblems are the various intervals, and unless we memoize our recursion, they will be solved an exponential number of times. Also note that we've got optimal substructure: If we split the sequence at the optimal (or correct) point initially, the two new segments must be partitioned optimally for us to get an optimal (correct) solution.[18]

As a concrete example, let's go with optimal search trees.[19] As when we were building Huffman trees in Chapter 7, each element has a *frequency*, and we want to minimize the expected traversal depth (or search time) for a binary search tree. In this case, though, the input is sorted, and we cannot change its ordering. For simplicity, let's assume that every query is for an element that is actually in the tree. (See Exercise 8-19 for a way around this.) Thinking inductively, we only need to find the right root node, and the two subtrees (over the smaller intervals) will take care of themselves (see Figure 8-6). Once again, to keep things simple, let's just worry about computing the optimal cost. If you want to extract the actual tree, you need to remember which subtree roots gave rise to the optimal subtree costs (for example, storing it in root[i,j]).

Now we need to figure out the recursive relationships; how do we calculate the cost for a given root, assuming that we know the costs for the subtrees? The contribution of a single node is similar to that in Huffman trees. There, however, we dealt only with leaves, and the cost was the expected depth. For optimal search trees, we can end up with any node. Also, so as not to give the root a cost of zero, let's count the expected number of nodes visited (that is, expected depth + 1). The contribution of node v is then $p(v) \times (d(v) + 1)$, where $p(v)$ is its relative frequency and $d(v)$ its depth, and we sum over all the nodes to get the total cost. (This is just 1 + sum of $p(v) \times d(v)$, because the $p(v)$ sums to 1.)

Let $e(i,j)$ be the expected search cost for the interval [i:j]. If we choose r as our root, we can decompose the cost into e(i,j) = e(i,r) + e(r+1,j) + something. The two recursive calls to e represent the expected costs of continuing the search in each subtree. What's the missing something, though? We'll have to add p[r], the probability of looking for the root, because that would be its expected cost. But how do we account for the extra edges down to our two subtrees? These edges will increase the depth of each node in the subtrees, meaning that each probability p[v] for every node v except the root must be added to the result. But, hey—as discussed, we'll be adding p[r] as well! In other words, we will need to add the probabilities for *all* the nodes in the interval. A relatively straightforward recursive expression for a given root r might then be as follows:

e(i,j) = e(i,r) + e(r+1,j) + sum(p[v] for v in range(i, j))

Of course, in the final solution, we'd try all r in range(i, j) and choose the maximum. There's a still more room for improvement, though: The sum part of the expression will be summing a quadratic number of overlapping intervals (one for every possible i and j), and each sum has linear running time. In the spirit of DP, we seek out the overlap: We introduce the memoized function s(i,j) representing the sum, as shown in Listing 8-14. As you can see, s is calculated in constant time, assuming the recursive call has already been cached (which means that a constant amount of time is spent calculating each sum s(i,j)). The rest of the code follows directly from the previous discussion.

Listing 8-14. Memoized Recursive Function for Expected Optimal Search Cost

```
def rec_opt_tree(p):
    @memo
    def s(i,j):
        if i == j: return 0
        return s(i,j-1) + p[j-1]
    @memo
    def e(i,j):
        if i == j: return 0
        sub = min(e(i,r) + e(r+1,j) for r in range(i,j))
        return sub + s(i,j)
    return e(0,len(p))
```

---

[18]You could certainly design some sort of cost function so this *wasn't* the case, but then we couldn't use dynamic programming (or, indeed, recursive decomposition) anymore. The induction wouldn't work.
[19]You should have a whack at the matrix chains yourself (Exercise 8-18), and perhaps even the parsing, if you're so inclined.

All in all, the running time of this algorithm is cubic. The asymptotic upper bound is straightforward: There is a quadratic number of subproblems (that is, intervals), and we have a linear scan for the best root inside each of them. In fact, the lower bound is also cubic (this is a bit trickier to show), so the running time is $\Theta(n^3)$.

As for the previous DP algorithms, the iterative version (Listing 8-15) is similar in many ways to the memoized one. To solve the problems in a safe (that is, topologically sorted) order, it solves all intervals of a certain length k before going on to the larger ones. To keep things simple, I'm using a dict (or, more specifically, a defaultdict, which automatically supplies the zeros). You could easily rewrite the implementation to use, say, a list of lists instead. (Note, though, that only a triangular half-matrix is needed—not the full n by n.)

Listing 8-15. An Iterative Solution to the Optimal Search Tree Problem

```
from collections import defaultdict

def opt_tree(p):
    n = len(p)
    s, e = defaultdict(int), defaultdict(int)
    for k in range(1,n+1):
        for i in range(n-k+1):
            j = i + k
            s[i,j] = s[i,j-1] + p[j-1]
            e[i,j] = min(e[i,r] + e[r+1,j] for r in range(i,j))
            e[i,j] += s[i,j]
    return e[0,n]
```

Summary

This chapter deals with a technique known as dynamic programming, or DP, which is used when the subproblem dependencies get tangled (that is, we have overlapping subproblems) and a straight divide-and-conquer solution would give an exponential running time. The term *dynamic programming* was originally applied to a class of sequential decision problems but is now used primarily about the solution technique, where some form of caching is performed, so that each subproblem need be computed only once. One way of implementing this is to add caching directly to a recursive function that embodies the recursive decomposition (that is, the induction step) of the algorithm design; this is called *memoization*. It can often be useful to invert the memoized recursive implementations, though, turning them into iterative ones. Problems solved using DP in this chapter include calculating binomial coefficients, finding shortest paths in DAGs, finding the longest increasing subsequence of a given sequence, finding the longest common subsequence of two given sequences, getting the most out of your knapsack with limited and unlimited supplies of indivisible items, and building binary search trees that minimize the expected lookup time.

If You're Curious …

Curious? About dynamic programming? You're in luck—there's a *lot* of rad stuff available about DP. A web search should turn up loads of coolness, including competition problems, for example. If you're into speech processing, or hidden Markov models in general, you could look for the Viterbi algorithm, which is a nice mental model for many kinds of DP. In the area of image processing, deformable contours (also known as *snakes*) are a nifty example.

If you think sequence comparison sounds cool, you could check out the books by Gusfield and Smyth (see the references). For a brief introduction to dynamic time warping and weighted edit distance—two important variations not discussed in this chapter—as well as the concept of *alignment*, you could have a look at the excellent tutorial

"Sequence comparison," by Christian Charras and Thierry Lecroq.[20] For some sequence comparison goodness in the Python standard library, check out the difflib module. If you have Sage installed, you could have a look at its knapsack module (http://sage.numerical.knapsack).

For more about how the ideas of dynamic programming appeared initially, take a look at Stuart Dreyfus's paper "Richard Bellman on the Birth of Dynamic Programming." For examples of DP problems, you can't really beat Lew and Mauch; their book on the subject discusses about 50. (Most of their book is rather heavy on the theory side, though.)

Exercises

8-1. Rewrite @memo so that you reduce the number of dict lookups by one.

8-2. How can two_pow be seen as using the "in or out" idea? What would the "in or out" correspond to?

8-3. Write iterative versions of *fib* and *two_pow*. This should allow you to use a constant amount of memory, while retaining the pseudolinear time (that is, time linear in the parameter n).

8-4. The code for computing Pascal's triangle in this chapter actually fills out an *rectangle*, where the irrelevant parts are simply zeros. Rewrite the code to avoid this redundancy.

8-5. Extend either the recursive or iterative code for finding the length of the shortest path in a DAG so that it returns an actual optimal path.

8-6. Why won't the pruning discussed in the sidebar "Varieties of DAG Shortest Path" have any effect on the asymptotic running time, even in the best case?

8-7. In the object-oriented *observer pattern*, several *observers* may register with an *observable* object. These observers are then notified when the observable changes. How could this idea be used to implement the DP solution to the DAG shortest path problem? How would it be similar to or different from the approaches discussed in this chapter?

8-8. In the *lis* function, how do we know that *end* is nondecreasing?

8-9. How would you reduce the number of calls to *bisect* in *lis*?

8-10. Extend either the recursive or one of the iterative solutions to the longest increasing subsequence problem so that it returns the actual subsequence.

8-11. Implement a function that computes the edit distance between two sequences, either using memoization or using iterative DP.

8-12. How would you find the underlying structure for LCS (that is, the actual shared subsequence) or edit distance (the sequence of edit operations)?

8-13. If the two sequences compared in lcs have different lengths, how could you exploit that to reduce the function's memory use?

8-14. How could you modify w and c to (potentially) reduce the running time of the unbounded knapsack problem?

8-15. The knapsack solution in Listing 8-13 lets you find the actual elements included in the optimal solution. Extend one of the other knapsack solutions in a similar way.

8-16. How can it be that we have developed efficient solutions to the integer knapsack problems, when they are regarded as hard, unsolved problems (see Chapter 11)?

---

[20]www-igm.univ-mlv.fr/~lecroq/seqcomp

8-17. The *subset sum* problem is one you'll also see in Chapter 11. Briefly, it asks you to pick a subset of a set of integers so that the sum of the subset is equal to a given constant, k. Implement a solution to this problem based on dynamic programming.

8-18. A problem closely related to finding optimal binary search trees is the *matrix chain multiplication* problem, briefly mentioned in the text. If matrices A and B have dimensions $n \times m$ and $m \times p$, respectively, their product AB will have dimensions $n \times p$, and we approximate the cost of this multiplication by the product nmp (the number of element multiplications). Design and implement an algorithm that finds a parenthetization of a sequence of matrices so that performing all the matrix multiplications has as low total cost as possible.

8-19. The optimal search trees we construct are based only on the frequencies of the elements. We might also want to take into account the frequencies of various queries that are *not* in the search tree. For example, we could have the frequencies for all words in a language available but store only some of the words in the tree. How could you take this information into consideration?

References

Bather, J. (2000). *Decision Theory: An Introduction to Dynamic Programming and Sequential Decisions*. John Wiley & Sons, Ltd.

Bellman, R. (2003). *Dynamic Programming*. Dover Publications, Inc.

Denardo, E. V. (2003). *Dynamic Programming: Models and Applications*. Dover Publications, Inc.

Dreyfus, S. (2002). Richard Bellman on the birth of dynamic programming. Operations Research, 50(1):48-51.

Fredman, M. L. (1975). On computing the length of longest increasing subsequences. Discrete Mathematics, 11(1):29-35.

Gusfield, D. (1997). Algorithms on Strings, Trees and Sequences: Computer Science and Computational Biology. Cambridge University Press.

Lew, A. and Mauch, H. (2007). *Dynamic Programming: A Computational Tool*. Springer.

Smyth, B. (2003). *Computing Patterns in Strings*. Addison-Wesley.

CHAPTER 9

∎ ∎ ∎

From A to B with Edsger and Friends

The shortest distance between two points is under construction.

— Noelie Altito

It's time to return to the second problem from the introduction:[1] How do you find the shortest route from Kashgar to Ningbo? If you pose this problem to any map software, you'd probably get the answer in less than a second. By now, this probably seems less mysterious than it (maybe) did initially, and you even have tools that could help you write such a program. You know that BFS would find the shortest path if all stretches of road had the same length, and you could use the DAG shortest path algorithm as long as you didn't have any cycles in your graph. Sadly, the road map of China contains both cycles and roads of unequal length. Luckily, however, this chapter will give you the algorithms you need to solve this problem efficiently!

And lest you think all this chapter is good for is writing map software, consider in what other contexts the abstraction of shortest paths might be useful. For example, you could use it in any situation where you'd like to efficiently navigate a network, which would include all kinds of routing of packets over the Internet. In fact, the 'net is *stuffed* with such routing algorithms, all working behind the scenes. But such algorithms are also used in less obviously graph-like navigation, such as having characters move about intelligently in computer games. Or perhaps you're trying to find the lowest number of moves to solve some form of puzzle? That would be equivalent to finding the shortest path in its state space—the abstract graph representing the puzzle states (nodes) and moves (edges). Or are you looking for ways to make money by exploiting discrepancies in currency exchange rates? One of the algorithms in this chapter will at least take you part of the way (see Exercise 9-1).

Finding shortest paths is also an important subroutine in other algorithms that need not be very graph-like. For example, one common algorithm for finding the best possible match between n people and n jobs[2] needs to solve this problem repeatedly. At one time, I worked on a program that tried to repair XML files, inserting start and end tags as needed to satisfy some simple XML schema (with rules such as "list items need to be wrapped in list tags"). It turned out that this could be solved easily by using one of the algorithms in this chapter. There are applications in operations research, integrated circuit manufacture, robotics—you name it. It's definitely a problem you want to learn about. Luckily, although some of the algorithm can be a bit challenging, you've already worked through many, if not most, of their challenging bits in the previous chapters.

The shortest path problem comes in several varieties. For example, you can find shortest paths (just like any other kinds of paths) in both directed and undirected graphs. The most important distinctions, though, stem from your starting points and destinations. Do you want to find the shortest from one node to all others (single source)? From one node to another (single pair, one to one, point to point)? From all nodes to one (single destination)? From all nodes to all others (all pairs)? Two of these—single source and all pairs—are perhaps the most important. Although we have some tricks for the single pair problem (see "Meeting in the Middle" and "Knowing Where You're Going," later),

---

[1]Don't worry, I'll revisit the "Sweden tour" problem in Chapter 11.
[2]The min-cost bipartite matching problem, discussed in Chapter 10.

there are no guarantees that will let us solve that problem any faster than the general single-source problem. The single destination problem is, of course, equivalent to the single-source version (just flip the edges for the directed case). The all-pairs problem can be tackled by using each node as a single source (and we'll look into that), but there are special-purpose algorithms for that problem as well.

Propagating Knowledge

In Chapter 4, I introduced the idea of relaxation and gradual improvement. In Chapter 8, you saw the idea applied to finding shortest paths in DAGs. In fact, the iterative shortest path algorithm for DAGs (Listing 8-4) is not just a prototypical example of dynamic programming; it also illustrates the fundamental structure of the algorithms in this chapter: we use relaxation over the edges of a graph to propagate knowledge about shortest paths.

Let's review what this looks like. I'll use a dict of dicts representation of the graph and use a dict D to maintain distance estimates (upper bounds), like in Chapter 8. In addition, I'll add a predecessor dict, P, as for many of the traversal algorithms in Chapter 5. These predecessor pointers will form a so-called shortest path tree and will allow us to reconstruct the actual paths that correspond to the distances in D. Relaxation can then be factored out in the relax function in Listing 9-1. Note that I'm treating nonexistent entries in D as if they were infinite. (I could also just initialize them all to be infinite in the main algorithms, of course.)

Listing 9-1. The Relaxation Operation

```
inf = float('inf')
def relax(W, u, v, D, P):
    d = D.get(u,inf) + W[u][v]      # Possible shortcut estimate
    if d < D.get(v,inf):            # Is it really a shortcut?
        D[v], P[v] = d, u           # Update estimate and parent
        return True                 # There was a change!
```

The idea is that we look for an improvement to the currently known distance to v by trying to take a shortcut through u. If it turns out not to be a shortcut, fine. We just ignore it. If it *is* a shortcut, we register the new distance and remember where we came from (by setting P[v] to u). I've also added a small extra piece of functionality: the return value indicates whether any change actually took place; that'll come in handy later (though you won't need it for all your algorithms).

Here's a look at how it works:

```
>>> D[u]
7
>>> D[v]
13
>>> W[u][v]
3
>>> relax(W, u, v, D, P)
True
>>> D[v]
10
>>> D[v] = 8
>>> relax(W, u, v, D, P)
>>> D[v]
8
```

As you can see, the first call to relax improves D[v] from 13 to 10 because I found a shortcut through u, which I had (presumably) already reached using a distance of 7 and which was just 3 away from v. Now I somehow discover that I can reach v by a path of length 8. I run relax again, but this time, no shortcut is found, so nothing happens.

As you can probably surmise, if I now set D[u] to 4 and ran the same relax again, D[v] *would* improve, this time to 7, propagating the improved estimate from u to v. This propagation is what relax is all about. If you randomly relax edges, any improvements to the distances (and their corresponding paths) *will* eventually propagate throughout the entire graph—so if you keep randomly relaxing forever, you know that you'll have the right answer. Forever, however, is a very long time ...

This is where the relax game (briefly mentioned in Chapter 4) comes in: we want to achieve correctness with as few calls to relax as possible. Exactly how few we can get away with depends on the exact nature of our problem. For example, for DAGs, we can get away with *one call per edge*—which is clearly the best we can hope for. As you'll see a bit later, we can actually get that low for more general graphs as well (although with a higher total running time and with no negative weights allowed). Before getting into that, however, let's take a look at some important facts that can be useful along the way. In the following, assume that we start in node s and that we initialize D[s] to zero, while all other distance estimates are set to infinity. Let $d(u,v)$ be the length of the shortest path from u to v.

- $d(s,v) <= d(s,u) + W[u,v]$. This is an example of the *triangle inequality*.

- $d(s,v) <= D[v]$. For v other than s, D[v] is initially infinite, and we reduce it only when we find actual shortcuts. We never "cheat," so it remains an upper bound.

- If there is no path to node v, then relaxing will never get D[v] below infinity. That's because we'll never find any shortcuts to improve D[v].

- Assume a shortest path to v is formed by a path from s to u and an edge from u to v. Now, if D[u] is correct (that is, D[u] == d(s,u)) at any time before relaxing the edge from u to v, then D[v] is correct at all times afterward. The path defined by P[v] will also be correct.

- Let [s, a, b, ... , z, v] be a shortest path from s to v. Assume all the edges (s,a), (a,b), ... , (z,v) in the path have been relaxed in order. Then D[v] and P[v] will be correct. It doesn't matter if other relax operations have been performed in between.

You should make sure you understand why these statements are true before proceeding. It will probably make the rest of the chapter quite a bit easier to follow.

Relaxing like Crazy

Relaxing at random is a bit crazy. Relaxing like crazy, though, might not be. Let's say that you relax *all* the edges. You can do it in a random order, if you like—it doesn't matter. Just make sure you get through all of them. Then you do it again—perhaps in another order—but you get through all the edges, once again. And again, and again. Until nothing changes.

■ **Tip** Imagine each node continuously shouting out bids for supplying short paths to its out-neighbors, based on the shortest path it has gotten itself, so far. If any node gets a better offer than what it already has, it switches its path supplier and lowers its bids accordingly.

It doesn't seem like such an unreasonable approach, at least for a first attempt. Two questions present themselves, though: How long will it take until nothing changes (if we ever get there), and can you be sure you've got the answer right when that happens?

Let's consider a simple case first. Assume that all edge weights are identical and nonnegative. This means that the `relax` operation can find a shortcut only if it finds a path consisting of fewer edges. What, then, will have happened after we relax all edges once? At the very least, all neighbors of s will have the correct answer and will have s set as their parent in the shortest path tree. Depending on the order in which we relaxed the edges, the tree may have spread further, but we have no guarantees of that. How about if we relax all edges once more? Well, if nothing else, the tree will at least have extended one more level. In fact, the shortest path tree will—in the worst case—spread level by level, as if we were performing some horribly inefficient BFS. For a graph with n nodes, the largest number of edges in any path is n-1, so we know that n-1 is the largest number of iterations we need.

In general, though, we can't assume this much about our edges (or if we could, we should rather just use BFS, which would do an excellent job). Because the edges can have different (possibly even negative) weights, the `relax` operations of later rounds may modify the predecessor pointers set in earlier rounds. For example, after one round, a neighbor v of s will have had P[v] set to s, but we cannot be sure that this is correct! Perhaps we'll find a shorter path to v via some other nodes, and then P[v] will be overwritten. What *can* we know, then, after one round of relaxing all the edges?

Think back to the last one of the principles listed in the previous section: if we relax all the edges—in order—along a shortest path from s to a node v, then our answer (consisting of D and P) will be correct for the path. In this case, specifically, we will have relaxed all edges along all shortest paths ... consisting of a single edge. We don't know where these paths *are*, mind you, because we don't (yet) know how many edges go into the various optimal paths. Still, although some of the P-edges linking s to its neighbors may very well not be final, we know that the ones that *are* correct must be there already.

And so the story goes. After k rounds of relaxing every edge in the graph, we know that all shortest paths of consisting of k edges have been completed. Following our earlier reasoning, for a graph with n nodes and m edges, it will require at most n-1 rounds until we're done, giving us a running time of $\Theta(nm)$. Of course, this need only be the worst-case running time, if we add a check: Has anything changed in the last round? If nothing changed, there's no point in continuing. We might even be tempted to drop the whole n-1 count and *only* rely on this check. After all, we've just reasoned that we'll never need more than n-1 rounds, so the check will eventually halt the algorithm. Right? No? No. There's one wrinkle: negative cycles.

You see, negative cycles are the enemy of shortest path algorithms. If we have no negative cycles, the "no change" condition will work just fine, but throw in a negative cycle, and our estimates can keep improving forever. So ... as long as we allow negative edges (and why wouldn't we?), we need the iteration count as a safeguard. The *good news* about this is that we can use the count to *detect* negative cycles: Instead of running n-1 rounds, we run n rounds and see whether anything changed in the last iteration. If we *did* get an improvement (which we shouldn't have), we immediately conclude "A negative cycle did it!" and we declare our answers invalid and give up.

■ **Note** Don't get me wrong. It's perfectly possible to find the shortest path even if there's a negative cycle. The answer isn't allowed to contain cycles anyway, so the negative cycles won't affect the answer. It's just that *finding* the shortest path while allowing negative cycles is an unsolved problem (see Chapter 11).

We have now arrived at the first proper algorithm of the chapter: Bellman-Ford (see Listing 9-2). It's a single-source shortest path algorithm allowing arbitrary directed or undirected graphs. If the graph contains a negative cycle, the algorithm will report that fact and give up.

Listing 9-2. The Bellman-Ford Algorithm

```
def bellman_ford(G, s):
    D, P = {s:0}, {}                    # Zero-dist to s; no parents
    for rnd in G:                       # n = len(G) rounds
        changed = False                 # No changes in round so far
        for u in G:                     # For every from-node...
```

```
        for v in G[u]:                    # ... and its to-nodes...
            if relax(G, u, v, D, P):      # Shortcut to v from u?
                changed = True            # Yes! So something changed
        if not changed: break             # No change in round: Done
    else:                                 # Not done before round n?
        raise ValueError('negative cycle')  # Negative cycle detected
    return D, P                           # Otherwise: D and P correct
```

Note that this implementation of the Bellman-Ford algorithm differs from many presentations precisely in that it includes the changed check. That check gives us two advantages. First, it lets us terminate early, if we don't need all the iterations; second, it lets us detect whether any change occurred during the last "superfluous" iteration, indicating a negative cycle. (The more common approach, without this check, is to add a separate piece of code implementing this last iteration, with its own change check.)

Because this algorithm is the foundation for several others, let's make sure it's clear how it works. Consider the weighted graph example from Chapter 2. We can specify it as a dict of dicts, as follows:

```
a, b, c, d, e, f, g, h = range(8)
G = {
    a: {b:2, c:1, d:3, e:9, f:4},
    b: {c:4, e:3},
    c: {d:8},
    d: {e:7},
    e: {f:5},
    f: {c:2, g:2, h:2},
    g: {f:1, h:6},
    h: {f:9, g:8}
}
```

See Figure 9-1 for a visual presentation of the graph. Let's say we call bellman_ford(G, a). What happens? If we want to find out in more detail, we can use a debugger, or perhaps the trace or logging packages. For simplicity, let's say we add a couple of print statements that show us the edges that are relaxed, as well as the assignments to D, if any. Let's say we also iterate over the nodes and neighbors in sorted order (using sorted), for deterministic results.

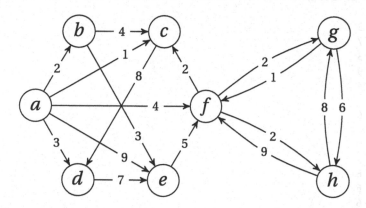

Figure 9-1. *An example weighted graph*

We then get a printout that starts something like the following:

```
(a,b)    D[b] = 2
(a,c)    D[c] = 1
(a,d)    D[d] = 3
(a,e)    D[e] = 9
(a,f)    D[f] = 4
(b,c)
(b,e)    D[e] = 5
(c,d)
(d,e)
(e,f)
(f,c)
(f,g)    D[g] = 6
(f,h)    D[h] = 6
(g,f)
(g,h)
(h,f)
(h,g)
```

This is the first round of Bellman-Ford; as you can see, it has gone through all the edges once. The printout will continue for another round, but no assignments will be made to D, and so the function returns. There is some sloppiness here: The distance estimate D[e] is first set to 9, which is the distance along the path directly from a to e. Only after relaxing (a,b) and then (b,e) will we discover a better option, namely, the path a, b, e, of length 5. However, we have gotten rather lucky, in that we needed only one pass through the edges. Let's see if we can make things more interesting and force the algorithm to do another round before settling down. See any ways of doing that? One way would be:

```
G[a][b] = 3
G[a][c] = 7
G[c][d] = -4
```

Now we have a good route to d via f, but we won't find that in the first round:

```
(a,b)    D[b] = 3
(a,c)    D[c] = 7
(a,d)    D[d] = 3
(a,e)    D[e] = 9
(a,f)    D[f] = 4
(b,c)
(b,e)    D[e] = 6
(c,d)
(d,e)
(e,f)
(f,c)    D[c] = 6
(f,g)    D[g] = 6
(f,h)    D[h] = 6
(g,f)
(g,h)
(h,f)
(h,g)
```

We've gotten D[c] down to 6 in the first round, but when we get to that point, we have already relaxed (c,d), at a time when that edge couldn't give us any improvement, because D[c] was 7 and D[d] was already 3. In the second round, however, you'd see

```
(c,d)     D[d] = 2
```

and in the third round, things would have settled down.

Before leaving the example, let's try to introduce a negative cycle. Let's use the original weights, with the following single modification:

```
G[g][h] = -9
```

Let's get rid of the relaxations that don't change D, and let's add some round numbers to the printout. We then get the following:

```
# Round 1:
(a,b)     D[b] = 2
(a,c)     D[c] = 1
(a,d)     D[d] = 3
(a,e)     D[e] = 9
(a,f)     D[f] = 4
(b,e)     D[e] = 5
(f,g)     D[g] = 6
(f,h)     D[h] = 6
(g,h)     D[h] = -3
(h,g)     D[g] = 5
# Round 2:
(g,h)     D[h] = -4
(h,g)     D[g] = 4
# Round 3:
(g,h)     D[h] = -5
(h,g)     D[g] = 3
# Round 4:
(g,h)     D[h] = -6
(h,f)     D[f] = 3
(h,g)     D[g] = 2
...

# Round 8:
(g,h)     D[h] = -10
(h,f)     D[f] = -1
(h,g)     D[g] = -2
Traceback (most recent call last):
  ...
ValueError: negative cycle
```

I've removed some of the rounds, but I'm sure you can see the pattern: After round 3, the distance estimates of g, h, and f repeatedly decrease by one. The fact that they did so even in round 8, given that there are only 8 nodes, alerts us to the presence of a negative cycle. This doesn't mean that there's no solution—it just means that continued relaxation won't find it for us, so we raise an exception.

Of course, a negative cycle is only a problem if we can actually *reach* it. Let's try to eliminate the edge (f,g), for example by using del G[f][g]. Now at least f won't participate in the cycle, but we still have g and h improving each others' estimates beyond what's correct. If, however, we also remove (f,h), our problem disappears!

```
(a,b)    D[b] = 2
(a,c)    D[c] = 1
(a,d)    D[d] = 3
(a,e)    D[e] = 9
(a,f)    D[f] = 4
(b,e)    D[e] = 5
```

The graph is still connected, and the negative cycle is still there, but our traversal never reaches it. If this makes you uncomfortable, rest assured: The distances to g and h are correct. They are both infinite, as they should be. If, however, you try to call either bellman_ford(G, g) or bellman_ford(G, h), though, the cycle is once again reachable, so you'll get a flurry of action, with several updates in each round, followed by the negative cycle exception at the end.

Pillow Talk. *Maybe I should've tried Wexler?* (http://xkcd.com/69)

Finding the Hidden DAG

The Bellman-Ford algorithm is great. In many ways it's the easiest to understand of the algorithms in this chapter: Just relax all the edges until we *know* everything must be correct. For arbitrary graphs, it's a good algorithm, but if we can make some assumptions, we can (as is usually the case) do better. As you'll recall, the single-source shortest path problem can be solved in *linear time* for DAGs. In this section, I'll deal with a different constraint, though. We can still have cycles, but *no negative edge weights*. (In fact, this is a situation that occurs in a great deal of practical applications, such as those discussed in the introduction.) Not only does this mean that we can forget about the negative cycle blues; it'll let us draw certain conclusions about when various distances are correct, leading to a substantial improvement in running time.

The algorithm I'm building up to here, designed by algorithm super-guru Edsger W. Dijkstra in 1959, can be explained in several ways, and understanding why it's correct can be a bit tricky. I think it can be useful to see it as a close relative to the DAG shortest path algorithm, with the important difference that it has to *uncover a hidden DAG*.

You see, even though the graph we're working with can have any structure it wants, we can think of some of the edges as irrelevant. To get things started, we can imagine that we already *know* the distances from the start node to each of the others. We don't, of course, but this imaginary situation can help our reasoning. Imagine ordering the nodes, left to right, based on their distance. What happens? For the general case—not much. However, we're assuming that we have no negative edge weights, and that makes all the difference.

Because all edges are positive, the only nodes that can contribute to a node's solution will lie to its *left* in our hypothetical ordering. It will be impossible to locate a node to the right that will help us find a shortcut because this node is further away and could give us a shortcut only if it had a *negative back edge*. The *positive* back edges are completely useless to us and aren't part of the problem structure. What remains, then, is a DAG, and the topological ordering we'd like to use is exactly the hypothetical ordering we started with: nodes sorted by their actual distance. See Figure 9-2 for an illustration of this structure. (I'll get back to the question marks in a minute.)

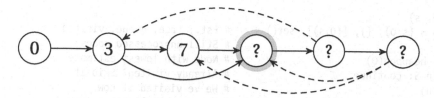

Figure 9-2. *Gradually uncovering the hidden DAG. Nodes are labeled with their final distances. Because weights are positive, the backward edges (dashed) cannot influence the result and are therefore irrelevant*

Predictably enough, we now hit the major gap in the solution: It's totally circular. In uncovering the basic problem structure (decomposing into subproblems or finding the hidden DAG), we've assumed that we've already solved the problem. The reasoning has still been useful, though, because we now have something specific to look for. We want to find the ordering—and we can find it with our trusty workhorse, induction!

Consider, again, Figure 9-2. Assume that the highlighted node is the one we're trying to identify in our inductive step (meaning that the earlier ones have been identified and already have correct distance estimates). Just like in the ordinary DAG shortest path problem, we'll be relaxing all out-edges for each node, as soon as we've identified it and determined its correct distance. That means that we've relaxed the edges out of all earlier nodes. We haven't relaxed the out-edges of *later* nodes, but as discussed, they can't matter: the distance estimates of these later nodes are upper bounds, and the back-edges have positive weights, so there's no way they can contribute to a shortcut.

This means (by the earlier relaxation properties or the discussion of the DAG shortest path algorithm in Chapter 8) that the next node *must have a correct distance estimate*. That is, the highlighted node in Figure 9-2 must by now have received its correct distance estimate, because we've relaxed all edges out of the first three nodes. This is very good news, and all that remains is to figure out *which node it is*. We still don't really know what the ordering is, remember? We're figuring out the topological sorting as we go along, step by step.

There is only one node that could possibly be the next one, of course:[3] the one with the *lowest distance estimate*. We know it's next in the sorted order, and we know it has a correct estimate; because these estimates are upper bounds, none of the later nodes could possibly have lower estimates. Cool, no? And now, by induction, we've solved the problem. We just relax all out-edges of each node in distance order—which means always taking the one with the lowest estimate next.

This structure is quite similar to that of Prim's algorithm: traversal with a priority queue. Just as in Prim's, we know that nodes we haven't discovered in our traversal will not have been relaxed, so we're not (yet) interested in them. And of the ones we *have* discovered (and relaxed), we always want the one with the lowest priority. In Prim's algorithm, the priority was the weight of the edge linking back to the traversal tree; in Dijkstra's, the priority is the distance estimate. Of course, the priority can change as we find shortcuts (just like new possible spanning tree edges could reduce the priority in Prim's), but just like in Listing 7-5, we can simply add the same node to our heap multiple times (rather than trying to modify the priorities of the heap entries), without compromising correctness or running time. The result can be found in Listing 9-3. Its running time is loglinear, or, more specifically, $\Theta((m+n) \lg n)$, where m is the number of edges and n the number of nodes. The reasoning here is that you need a (logarithmic) heap operation for (1) each node to be extracted from the queue and (2) each edge to be relaxed.[4] As long as you have $\Omega(n)$ edges, which you will for graphs where you can reach $\Theta(n)$ nodes from the start node, the running time can be simplified to $\Theta(m \lg n)$.

---

[3]Well, I'm assuming distinct distances here. If more than one node has the same distance, you could have more than one candidate. Exercise 9-2 asks you to show what happens then.

[4]You may notice that edges that go *back* into S are also relaxed here in order to keep the code simple. That has no effect on correctness or asymptotic running time, but you're free to rewrite the code to skip these nodes if you want.

Listing 9-3. Dijkstra's Algorithm

```
from heapq import heappush, heappop

def dijkstra(G, s):
    D, P, Q, S = {s:0}, {}, [(0,s)], set()   # Est., tree, queue, visited
    while Q:                                  # Still unprocessed nodes?
        _, u = heappop(Q)                     # Node with lowest estimate
        if u in S: continue                   # Already visited? Skip it
        S.add(u)                              # We've visited it now
        for v in G[u]:                        # Go through all its neighbors
            relax(G, u, v, D, P)              # Relax the out-edge
            heappush(Q, (D[v], v))            # Add to queue, w/est. as pri
    return D, P                               # Final D and P returned
```

Dijkstra's algorithm may be similar to Prim's (with another set of priorities for the queue), but it is also closely related to another old favorite: BFS. Consider the case where the edge weights are positive integers. Now, replace an edge that has weight *w* with *w*-1 unweighted edges, connecting a path of dummy nodes (see Figure 9-3). We're ruining what chances we had for an *efficient* solution (see Exercise 9-3), but we know that BFS will find a *correct* solution. In fact, it will do so in a way *very similar* to Dijkstra's algorithm: It will spend an amount of time on each (original) edge proportional to its weight, so it will reach each (original) node in order of distance from the start node.

Length = 3   Three edges

Figure 9-3. *An edge weight, or length, simulated by dummy nodes*

It's a bit like if you had set up a series of dominoes along each edge (the number of dominoes proportional to the weight), and you then tip the first domino in the start node. A node may be reached from multiple directions, but we can see which direction won, by looking at which dominoes lie below the others.

If we *started* with this approach, we could see Dijkstra's algorithm as a way of gaining performance by "simulating" BFS, or the dominoes (or flowing water or a spreading sound wave, or ...), without bothering to deal with each dummy node (or domino) individually. Instead, we can think of our priority queue as a timeline, where we mark various times at which we will reach nodes by following various paths. We look down the length of a newly discovered edge and think, "When could the dominoes reach that node by following this edge?" We add the time the edge would take (the edge weight) to the current time (the distance to the current node) and place the result on the timeline (our heap). We do this for each node that is reached for the first time (we're interested only in the *shortest* paths, after all), and we keep moving along the timeline to reach other nodes. As we reach the same node again, later in the timeline, we simply ignore it.[5]

I've been clear about how Dijkstra's algorithm is similar to the DAG shortest path algorithm. It is very much an application of dynamic programming, although the recursive decomposition wasn't quite as obvious as in the DAG case. To get a solution, it also uses greed, in that it always moves to the node that currently has the lowest distance estimate. With the binary heap as a priority queue, there's even a bit of divide and conquer going on in there; all in all, it's a beautiful algorithm that uses much of what you've learned so far. It's well worth spending some time on fully understanding it.

---

[5]In a more conventional version of Dijkstra's algorithm, where each node is just added once but its estimate is modified inside the heap, you could say this path is ignored if some better estimate comes along and overwrites it.

All Against All

In the next section, you'll see a really cool algorithm for finding the shortest distances between *all pairs of nodes*. It's a special-purpose algorithm that is effective even if the graph has a lot of edges. In this section, though, I'll have a quick look at a way to combine the two previous algorithms—Bellman-Ford and Dijkstra's algorithm—into one that really shines in *sparse* graphs (that is, ones with relatively few edges). This is Johnson's algorithm, one that seems to be neglected in many courses and books on algorithm design, but which is really clever and which you get almost for free, given what you already know.

The motivation for Johnson's algorithm is the following: When solving the all-pairs shortest paths problem for sparse graphs, simply using Dijkstra's algorithm from every node is, in fact, a really good solution. That in itself doesn't exactly motivate a *new* algorithm ... but the trouble is that Dijkstra's algorithm doesn't permit negative edges. For the single-source shortest path problem, there isn't much we can do about that, except use Bellman-Ford instead. For the all-pairs problem, though, we can permit ourselves some initial preprocessing to *make* all the weights positive.

The idea is to add a new node s, with zero-weight edges to all existing nodes, and then to run Bellman-Ford from s. This will give us a distance—let's call it $h(v)$—from s to each node v in our graph. We can then use h to adjust the weight of every edge: We define the new weight as follows: $w'(u,v) = w(u,v) + h(u) - h(v)$. This definition has two very useful properties. First, it guarantees us that every new weight $w'(u,v)$ is nonnegative (this follows from the triangle inequality, as discussed earlier in this chapter; see also Exercise 9-5). Second, we're not messing up our problem! That is, if we find the shortest paths with these *new* weights, those paths will also be shortest paths (with other lengths, though) with the *original* weights. Now, why is that?

This is explained by a sweet idea called *telescoping sums*: A sum like $(a - b) + (b - c) + ... + (y - z)$ will collapse like a telescope, giving us $a - z$. The reason is that every other summand is included once with a plus before it and once with a minus, so they all sum to zero. The same thing happens to every path with the modified edges in Johnson's algorithm. For any edge (u,v) in such a path, except for the first or last, the weight will be modified by adding $h(u)$ and subtracting $h(v)$. The *next* edge will have v as its first node and will *add* $h(v)$, removing it from the sum. Similarly, the previous edge will have subtracted $h(u)$, removing that.

The only two edges that are a bit different (in any path) are the first and the last. The first one isn't a problem, because $h(s)$ will be zero, and $w(s,v)$ was set to zero for all nodes v. But what about the last one? Not a problem. Yes, we'll end up with $h(v)$ subtracted for the last node v, but that will be true of *all* paths ending at that node—the shortest path will still be shortest.

The transformation doesn't discard any information either, so once we've found the shortest paths using Dijkstra's algorithm, we can inversely transform all the path lengths. Using a similar telescoping argument, we can see that we can get the real length of the shortest path from u to v by adding $h(v)$ and subtracting $h(u)$ from our answer based on the transformed weights. This gives us the algorithm implemented in Listing 9-4.[6]

Listing 9-4. Johnson's Algorithm

```
from copy import deepcopy

def johnson(G):                              # All pairs shortest paths
    G = deepcopy(G)                          # Don't want to break original
    s = object()                             # Guaranteed unused node
    G[s] = {v:0 for v in G}                  # Edges from s have zero wgt
    h, _ = bellman_ford(G, s)                # h[v]: Shortest dist from s
    del G[s]                                 # No more need for s
    for u in G:                              # The weight from u ...
```

---

[6]As you can see, I just instantiate object to create the node s. Each such instance is unique (that is, they aren't equal under ==), which makes them useful for added dummy nodes, as well as other forms of *sentinel* objects, which need to be different from all legal values.

```
        for v in G[u]:              # ... to v ...
            G[u][v] += h[u] - h[v]  # ... is adjusted (nonneg.)
    D, P = {}, {}                   # D[u][v] and P[u][v]
    for u in G:                     # From every u ...
        D[u], P[u] = dijkstra(G, u) # ... find the shortest paths
        for v in G:                 # For each destination ...
            D[u][v] += h[v] - h[u]  # ... readjust the distance
    return D, P                     # These are two-dimensional
```

■ **Note**   There is no need to check whether the call to `bellman_ford` succeeded or whether it found a negative cycle (in which case Johnson's algorithm won't work), because if there *is* a negative cycle in the graph, `bellman_ford` would raise an exception.

Assuming the $\Theta(m \lg n)$ running time for Dijkstra's algorithm, Johnson's is simply a factor of n slower, giving us $\Theta(mn \lg n)$, which is faster than the cubic running time of Floyd-Warshall (discussed in a bit), for sparse graphs (that is, for graphs with relatively few edges).[7]

The transform used in Johnson's algorithm closely related to the potential function of the A* algorithm (see "Knowing Where You're Going," later in this chapter), and it is similar to the transform used in the min-cost bipartite matching problem in Chapter 10. There, too, the goal is to ensure positive edge weights but in a slightly different situation (edge weights changing from iteration to iteration).

Far-Fetched Subproblems

While Dijkstra's algorithm is certainly based on the principles of dynamic programming, the fact is partly obscured by the need to discover the ordering of (or dependencies between) subproblems on the go. The algorithm I discuss in this section, discovered independently by Roy, Floyd, and Warshall, is a prototypical example of DP. It is based on a memoized recursive decomposition and is iterative in its common implementation. It is deceptively simple in form but devilishly clever in design. It is, in some ways, based on the "in or out" principle discussed in Chapter 8, but the resulting subproblems may, at least at first glance, seem highly artificial and far-fetched.

In many DP problems, we might need to hunt a bit for a set of recursively related subproblems, but once we find them, they often seem quite natural. Just think of the nodes in DAG shortest path, for example, or the prefix pairs of the longest common subsequence problem. The latter illustrates a useful principle that can be extended to less obvious structures, though: restricting which elements we're allowed to work with. In the LCS problem, we're restricting the lengths of prefixes, for example. In the knapsack problem, this is slightly more artificial: We invent an ordering for the objects and restrict ourselves to the k first ones. The subproblem is then parametrized by this "permitted set" and a portion of the knapsack capacity.

In the all-pairs shortest path problem, we can use this form of restriction, along with the "in or out" principle, to *design* a set of nonobvious subproblems: We arbitrarily order the nodes and restrict how many—that is, the k first—we're allowed to use as intermediate nodes in forming our paths. We have now parametrized our subproblems using three parameters:

- The starting node

- The ending node

- The highest node number we're allowed to pass through

---

[7]A common criterion for calling a graph *sparse* is that m is $O(n)$, for example. In this case, though, Johnson's will (asymptotically) match Floyd-Warshall as long as m is $O(n^2/\lg n)$, which allows for quite a lot of edges. On the other hand, Floyd-Warshall has very low constant overhead.

Unless you had *some* idea where we were going with this, adding the third item might seem totally unproductive—how could it help us to restrict what we're allowed to do? As I'm sure you can see, the idea is to *partition* the solution space, decomposing the problem into subproblems and then linking these into a subproblem graph. The linking is achieved by creating a recursive dependency based on the "in or out" idea: node k, in or out?

Let $d(u, v, k)$ be the length of the shortest path that exists from node u to node v if you're only allowed to use the k first nodes as intermediate nodes. We can decompose the problem as follows:

$$d(u, v, k) = \min(d(u, v, k-1), d(u, k, k-1) + d(k, v, k-1))$$

Like in the knapsack problem, we're considering whether to include k. If we don't include it, we simply use the existing solution, the shortest path we could find *without* using k, which is $d(u, v, k-1)$. If we *do* include it, we must use the shortest path *to* k (which is $d(u, k, k-1)$) as well as the shortest path *from* k (which is $d(k, v, k-1)$). Note that in all these three subproblems, we're working with the $k-1$ first nodes, because either we're excluding k or we're explicitly using it as an endpoint and not an intermediate node. This guarantees us a size-ordering (that is, a topological sorting) of the subproblems—no cycles.

You can see the resulting algorithm in Listing 9-5. (The implementation uses the memo decorator from Chapter 8.) Note that I'm assuming the nodes are integers in the range 1...n here. If you're using other node objects, you could have a list V containing the nodes in some arbitrary order and then use V[k-1] and V[k-2] instead of k and k-1 in the min part. Also note that the returned D map has the form D[u,v] rather than D[u][v]. I'm also assuming that this is a full weight matrix, so D[u][v] is inf if there is no edge from u to v. You could easily modify all of this, if you want.

Listing 9-5. A Memoized Recursive Implementation of the Floyd-Warshall Algorithm

```
def rec_floyd_warshall(G):                        # All shortest paths
    @memo                                          # Store subsolutions
    def d(u,v,k):                                  # u to v via 1..k
        if k==0: return G[u][v]                    # Assumes v in G[u]
        return min(d(u,v,k-1), d(u,k,k-1) + d(k,v,k-1))   # Use k or not?
    return {(u,v): d(u,v,len(G)) for u in G for v in G}    # D[u,v] = d(u,v,n)
```

Let's have a go at an iterative version. Given that we have three subproblem parameters (u, v, and k), we'll need three for loops to get through all the subproblems iteratively. It might seem reasonable to think that we need to store all subsolutions, leading to cubic memory use, but just like for the LCS problem, we can reduce this.[8] Our recursive decomposition only relates problems in stage k with those in stage $k-1$. This means that we need only *two* distance maps—one for the current iteration and one for the previous. But we can do better ...

Just like when using relax, we're looking for shortcuts here. The question at stage k is "Will going via node k provide a shortcut, compared to what we have?" If D is our current distance map and C is the previous one, we've got this:

```
D[u][v] = min(D[u][v], C[u][k] + C[k][v])
```

Now consider what would happen if we just used a single distance map throughout:

```
D[u][v] = min(D[u][v], D[u][k] + D[k][v])
```

The meaning is now *slightly* less clear and seemingly a bit circular, but there's no problem, really. We're looking for shortcuts, right? The values D[u][k] and D[k][v] will be the lengths of real paths (and therefore upper bounds to the shortest distances), so we're not cheating. Also, they'll be no greater than C[u][k] and C[k][v], because we never *increase* the values in our map. Therefore, the only thing that can happen is that D[u][v] moves faster toward the correct answer—which is certainly no problem. The result is that we need only a single, two-dimensional distance

---

[8]You could do the same memory saving in the memoized version, too. See Exercise 9-7.

map (that is, quadratic as opposed to cubic memory), which we'll keep updating by looking for shortcuts. In many ways, the result is *very* much (though not exactly) like a two-dimensional version of the Bellman-Ford algorithm (see Listing 9-6).

Listing 9-6. The Floyd-Warshall Algorithm, Distances Only

```
def floyd_warshall(G):
    D = deepcopy(G)                          # No intermediates yet
    for k in G:                              # Look for shortcuts with k
        for u in G:
            for v in G:
                D[u][v] = min(D[u][v], D[u][k] + D[k][v])
    return D
```

You'll notice that I start out using a copy of the graph itself as a candidate distance map. That's because we haven't tried to go via any intermediate nodes yet, so the only possibilities are direct edges, given by the original weights. Also notice that the assumption about the vertices being numbers is completely gone because we no longer need to explicitly parametrize which stage we're in. As long as we try creating shortcuts with each possible intermediate node, building on our previous results, the solution will be the same. I hope you'll agree that the resulting algorithm is super-simple, although the reasoning behind it may not be.

It would be nice to have a P matrix too, though, as in Johnson's algorithm. As in so many DP algorithms, constructing the actual solution piggybacks nicely on calculating the optimal value—you just need to record which choices are made. In this case, if we find a shortcut via k, the predecessor recorded in P[u][v] must be replaced with P[k][v], which is the predecessor belonging to the last "half" of the shortcut. The final algorithm can be found in Listing 9-7. The original P gets a predecessor for any distinct pair of nodes linked by an edge. After that, P is updated whenever D is updated.

Listing 9-7. The Floyd-Warshall Algorithm

```
def floyd_warshall(G):
    D, P = deepcopy(G), {}
    for u in G:
        for v in G:
            if u == v or G[u][v] == inf:
                P[u,v] = None
            else:
                P[u,v] = u
    for k in G:
        for u in G:
            for v in G:
                shortcut = D[u][k] + D[k][v]
                if shortcut < D[u][v]:
                    D[u][v] = shortcut
                    P[u,v] = P[k,v]
    return D, P
```

Note that it's important to use shortcut < D[u][v] here, and not shortcut <= D[u][v]. Although the latter would still give the correct distances, you could get cases where the last step was D[v][v], which would lead to P[u,v] = None.

The Floyd-Warshall algorithm can quite easily be modified to calculate the *transitive closure* of a graph (Warshall's algorithm). See Exercise 9-9.

Meeting in the Middle

The subproblems solutions of Dijkstra's algorithm—and of BFS, its unweighted special case—spread outward on a graph like ripples on a pond. If all you want is getting from A to B, or, using the customary node names, from *s* to *t*, this means that the "ripple" has to pass many nodes that you're not really interested, as in the left image in Figure 9-4. If, on the other hand, you start traversing from both your starting point *and* your end point (assuming you can traverse edges in reverse), the two ripples can, in some cases, meet up in the middle, saving you a lot of work, as illustrated in the right image.

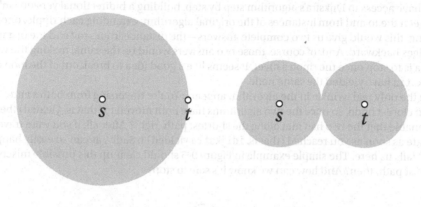

Traversing from *s*   Traversing both ways

Figure 9-4. *Unidirectional and bidirectional "ripples," indicating the work needed to find a path from s to t by traversal*

Note that while the "graphical evidence" of Figure 9-4 may be convincing, it is, of course, not a formal argument, and it gives no guarantees. In fact, although the algorithms of this section and the next provide practical improvements for the single-source, single-destination shortest path, no such a point-to-point algorithm is known to have a better asymptotic worst-case behavior than you could get for the ordinary single-source problem. Sure, two circles of half the original radius will have half the total area, but graphs don't necessarily behave like the Euclidean plane. We would certainly *expect* to get improvements in running time, but this is what's called a *heuristic* algorithm. Such algorithms are based on educated guesswork and are typically evaluated empirically. We can be sure it won't be *worse* than Dijkstra's algorithm, asymptotically—it's all about improving the practical running time.

To implement this bidirectional version of Dijkstra's algorithm, let's first adapt the original slightly, making it a generator, so we can extract only as many subsolutions as we need for the "meetup." This is similar to some of the traversal functions in Chapter 5, such as `iter_dfs` (Listing 5-5). This iterative behavior means that we can drop the distance table entirely and rely only on the distances kept in the priority queue. To keep things simple, I won't include the predecessor information here, but you could easily extend the solution by adding predecessors to the tuples in the heap. To get the distance table (like in the original `dijkstra`), you can simply call `dict(idijkstra(G, s))`. See Listing 9-8 for the code.

Listing 9-8. Dijkstra's Algorithm Implemented as a Generator

```
from heapq import heappush, heappop

def idijkstra(G, s):
    Q, S = [(0,s)], set()               # Queue w/dists, visited
    while Q:                            # Still unprocessed nodes?
        d, u = heappop(Q)               # Node with lowest estimate
        if u in S: continue             # Already visited? Skip it
```

```
        S.add(u)                          # We've visited it now
        yield u, d                        # Yield a subsolution/node
        for v in G[u]:                    # Go through all its neighbors
            heappush(Q, (d+G[u][v], v))   # Add to queue, w/est. as pri
```

Note that I've dropped the use of relax completely—it is now implicit in the heap. Or, rather, heappush is the new relax. Re-adding a node with a better estimate means it will take precedence over the old entry, which is equivalent to overwriting the old one with a relax operation. This is analogous to the implementation of Prim's algorithm in Chapter 7.

Now that we have access to Dijkstra's algorithm step by step, building a bidirectional version isn't too hard. We alternate between the to and from instances of the original algorithm, extending each ripple, one node at a time. If we just kept going, this would give us two complete answers—the distance from *s* to *t* and the distance from *t* to *s* if we follow the edges backward. And, of course, those two answers would be the same, making the whole exercise pointless. The idea is to stop once the ripples meet. It seems like a good idea to break out of the loop once the two instances of idijkstra have yielded the same node.

This is where the only real wrinkle in the algorithm appears: You're traversing from both *s* and *t*, consistently moving to the next closest node, so once the two algorithms have both moved to (that is, yielded) the same node, it would seem reasonable that the two had met along the shortest path, right? After all, if you were traversing only from *s*, you could terminate as soon as you reached (that is, idijkstra yielded) *t*. Sadly, as can so easily happen, our intuition (or, at least, mine) fails us here. The simple example in Figure 9-5 should clear up this possible misconception; but where *is* the shortest path, then? And how can we know it's safe to stop?

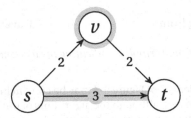

Figure 9-5. *The first meeting point (highlighted node) is not necessarily along the shortest path (highlighted edge)*

In fact, ending the traversal once the two instances meet is fine. To find the shortest path, however, we need to keep our eyes peeled, metaphorically speaking, while the algorithm is executing. We need to maintain the best distance found so far, and whenever an edge (*u*,*v*) is relaxed and we already have the distance to *u* from *s* (by forward traversal) and the distance from *v* to *t* (by backward traversal), we need to check whether linking up the paths with (*u*,*v*) will improve on our best solution.

In fact, we can tighten our stopping criterion a bit (see Exercise 9-10). Rather than waiting for the two instances to both visit the same node, we need to look only at how far they've come—that is, the latest distances they've yielded. These can't decrease, so if their sum is at least as great as the best path we've found so far, we can't find anything better, and we're done.

There's still a nagging doubt, though. The preceding argument might convince you that we can't possibly find any better paths by continuing, but how can we be sure that we haven't missed any? Let's say the best path we've found has length *m*. The two distances that caused the termination were *l* and *r*, so we know that $l + r \geq m$ (the stopping criterion). Now, let's say there is a path from *s* to *t* that is *shorter* than *m*. For this to happen, the path must contain an edge (*u*,*v*) such that $d(s,u) < l$ and $d(v,t) < r$ (see Exercise 9-11). This means that *u* and *v* are closer to *s* and *t*, respectively, than the current nodes, so both must have been visited (yielded) already. At the point when both had been yielded, our maintenance of the best solution so far should have found this path—a contradiction. In other words, the algorithm is correct.

This whole keeping track of the best path so far business requires us to have access to the innards of Dijkstra's algorithm. I prefer the abstraction that idijkstra gives me, so I'm going to stick with the simplest version of this algorithm: Stop once I've received the same node from both traversals and then scan for the best path *afterward*, examining all the edges that link the two halves. If your data set is of the kind that would profit from the bidirectional search, this scan is unlikely to be too much of a bottleneck, but feel free to break out the profiler and make your adjustments, of course. The finished code can be found in Listing 9-9. The cycle function from itertools gives us an iterator that will repeatedly give us the values from some other iterator, repeatedly yielding its values from start to finish. In this case, this means we're cycling between the forward and backward directions.

Listing 9-9. The Bidirectional Version of Dijkstra's Algorithm

```
from itertools import cycle

def bidir_dijkstra(G, s, t):
    Ds, Dt = {}, {}                             # D from s and t, respectively
    forw, back = idijkstra(G,s), idijkstra(G,t) # The "two Dijkstras"
    dirs = (Ds, Dt, forw), (Dt, Ds, back)       # Alternating situations
    try:                                        # Until one of forw/back ends
        for D, other, step in cycle(dirs):      # Switch between the two
            v, d = next(step)                   # Next node/distance for one
            D[v] = d                            # Remember the distance
            if v in other: break                # Also visited by the other?
    except StopIteration: return inf            # One ran out before they met
    m = inf                                     # They met; now find the path
    for u in Ds:                                # For every visited forw-node
        for v in G[u]:                          # ... go through its neighbors
            if not v in Dt: continue            # Is it also back-visited?
            m = min(m, Ds[u] + G[u][v] + Dt[v]) # Is this path better?
    return m                                    # Return the best path
```

Note that this code assumes that G is undirected (that is, all edges are available in both directions) and that G[u][u] = 0 for all nodes u. You could easily extend the algorithm so those assumptions aren't needed (Exercise 9-12).

Knowing Where You're Going

By now you've seen that the basic idea of traversal is pretty versatile, and by simply using different queues, you get several useful algorithms. For example, for FIFO and LIFO queues, you get BFS and DFS, and with the appropriate priorities, you get the core of Prim's and Dijkstra's algorithms. The algorithm described in this section, called A*, extends Dijkstra's, by tweaking the priority once again.

As mentioned earlier, the A* algorithm uses an idea similar to Johnson's algorithm, although for a different purpose. Johnson's algorithm transforms all edge weights to ensure they're positive, while ensuring that the shortest paths are still shortest. In A*, we want to modify the edges in a similar fashion, but this time the goal isn't to make the edges positive—we're assuming they already are (as we're building on Dijkstra's algorithm). No, what we want is to guide the traversal in the right direction, by using information of where we're going: We want to make edges moving away from our target node more expensive than those that take us closer to it.

■ **Note** This is similar to the best-first search used in the branch and bound strategy discussed in Chapter 11.

Of course, if we really knew which edges would take us closer, we could solve the whole problem by being greedy. We'd just move along the shortest path, taking no side routes whatsoever. The nice thing about the A* algorithm is that it fills the gap between Dijkstra's, where we have *no* knowledge of where we're going, and this hypothetical, ideal situation where we know *exactly* where we're going. It introduces a *potential function*, or *heuristic h(v)*, which is our best guess for the remaining distance, $d(v,t)$. As you'll see in a minute, Dijkstra's algorithm "falls out" of A* as a special case, when $h(v) = 0$. Also, if by magic we could set $h(v) = d(v,t)$, the algorithm would march directly from s to t.

So, how does it work? We define the modified edge weights to get a telescoping sum, like we did in Johnson's algorithm (although you should note that the signs are switched here): $w'(u,v) = w(u,v) - h(u) + h(v)$. The telescoping sum ensures that the shortest path will still be shortest (like in Johnson's) because all path lengths are changed by the same amount, $h(t) - h(s)$. As you can see, if we set the heuristic to zero (or, really, any constant), the weights are unchanged.

It should be easy to see how this adjustment reflects our intention to reward edges that go in the right direction and penalize those that don't. To each edge weight, we add the *drop in potential* (the heuristic), which is similar to how gravity works. If you let a marble loose on a bumpy table, it will start moving in a direction that will decrease its potential (that is, its potential energy). In our case, the algorithm will be steered in directions that cause a drop in the remaining distance—exactly what we want.

The A* algorithm is equivalent to Dijkstra's on the modified graph, so it's correct if h is *feasible*, meaning that $w'(u,v)$ is nonnegative for all nodes u and v. Nodes are scanned in increasing order of $D[v] - h(s) + h(v)$, rather than simply $D[v]$. Because $h(s)$ is a common constant, we can ignore it and simply add $h(v)$ to our existing priority. This sum is our best estimate for the shortest path from s to t via v. If $w'(u,v)$ is feasible, $h(v)$ will also be a *lower bound* on $d(v,t)$ (see Exercise 9-14).

One (very common) way of implementing all of this would be to use something like the original dijkstra and simply add $h(v)$ to the priority when pushing a node onto the heap. The original distance estimate would still be available in D. If we want to simplify things, however, *only* using the heap (as in idijkstra), we need to actually use the weight adjustment so that for an edge (u,v), we subtract $h(u)$ as well. This is the approach I've taken in Listing 9-10. As you can see, I've made sure to remove the superfluous $h(t)$ before returning the distance. (Considering the algorithmic punch that the a_star function is packing, it's pretty short and sweet, wouldn't you say?)

Listing 9-10. The A* Algorithm

```
from heapq import heappush, heappop
inf = float('inf')

def a_star(G, s, t, h):
    P, Q = {}, [(h(s), None, s)]        # Preds and queue w/heuristic
    while Q:                            # Still unprocessed nodes?
        d, p, u = heappop(Q)           # Node with lowest heuristic
        if u in P: continue            # Already visited? Skip it
        P[u] = p                       # Set path predecessor
        if u == t: return d - h(t), P  # Arrived! Ret. dist and preds
        for v in G[u]:                 # Go through all neighbors
            w = G[u][v] - h(u) + h(v)  # Modify weight wrt heuristic
            heappush(Q, (d + w, u, v)) # Add to queue, w/heur as pri
    return inf, None                   # Didn't get to t
```

As you can see, except from the added check for u == t, the only difference from Dijkstra's algorithm is really the adjustment of the weights. In other words, if you wanted, you could use a straight point-to-point version of Dijkstra's algorithm (that is, one that included the u == t check) on a graph where you had modified the weights, rather than having a separate algorithm for A*.

Of course, in order to get any benefit from the A* algorithm, you need a good heuristic. What this function should be will depend heavily on the exact problem you're trying to solve, of course. For example, if you're navigating a road map, you'd know that the Euclidean distance, as the crow flies, from a given node to your destination must be a valid heuristic (lower bound). This would, in fact, be a usable heuristic for any movement on a flat surface, such as monsters walking around in a computer game world. If there are lots of blind alleys and twists and turns, though, this lower bound may not be very accurate. (See the "If You're Curious …" section for an alternative.)

The A* algorithm is also used for searching solution spaces, which we can see as abstract (or implicit) graphs. For example, we might want to solve Rubik's Cube[9] or Lewis Carroll's so-called *word ladder* puzzle. In fact, let's have a whack at the latter puzzle (no pun intended).

Word ladders are built from a starting word, such as *lead*, and you want to end up with another word, say, *gold*. You build the ladder gradually, using actual words at every step. To get from one word to another, you can replace a single letter. (There are also other versions, which let you add or remove letters, or where you are allowed to swap the letters around.) So, for example, you could get from *lead* to *gold* via the words *load* and *goad*. If we interpret every word of some dictionary as a node in our graph, we could add edges between all words that differ by a single letter. We probably wouldn't want to explicitly build such a structure, but we could "fake" it, as shown in Listing 9-11.

Listing 9-11. An Implicit Graph with Word Ladder Paths

```python
from string import ascii_lowercase as chars

def variants(wd, words):              # Yield all word variants
    wasl = list(wd)                   # The word as a list
    for i, c in enumerate(wasl):      # Each position and character
        for oc in chars:              # Every possible character
            if c == oc: continue      # Don't replace with the same
            wasl[i] = oc              # Replace the character
            ow = ''.join(wasl)        # Make a string of the word
            if ow in words:           # Is it a valid word?
                yield ow              # Then we yield it
        wasl[i] = c                   # Reset the character

class WordSpace:                      # An implicit graph w/utils

    def __init__(self, words):        # Create graph over the words
        self.words = words
        self.M = dict()               # Reachable words

    def __getitem__(self, wd):        # The adjacency map interface
        if wd not in self.M:          # Cache the neighbors
            self.M[wd] = dict.fromkeys(self.variants(wd, self.words), 1)
        return self.M[wd]

    def heuristic(self, u, v):        # The default heuristic
        return sum(a!=b for a, b in zip(u, v))  # How many characters differ?

    def ladder(self, s, t, h=None):   # Utility wrapper for a_star
        if h is None:                 # Allows other heuristics
            def h(v):
                return self.heuristic(v, t)
        _, P = a_star(self, s, t, h)  # Get the predecessor map
        if P is None:                 # When no path exists
            return [s, None, t]
```

[9]Actually, as I was writing this chapter for the first edition, it was proven (using 35 years of CPU-time) that the most difficult positions of Rubik's Cube require 20 moves (see www.cube20.org).

205

```
    u, p = t, []
    while u is not None:              # Walk backward from t
        p.append(u)                  # Append every predecessor
        u = P[u]                     # Take another step
    p.reverse()                      # The path is backward
    return p
```

The main idea of the WordSpace class is that it works as a weighted graph so that it can be used with our a_star implementation. If G is a WordSpace, G['lead'] would be a dict with other words (such as 'load' and 'mead') as keys and 1 as weight for every edge. The default heuristic I've used simply counts the number of positions at which the words differ.

Using the WordSpace class is easy enough, as long as you have a word list of some sort. Many UNIX systems have a file called /usr/share/dict/words or /usr/dict/words, with a single word per line. If you don't have such a file, you could get one from http://ftp.gnu.org/gnu/aspell/dict/en. If you don't have this file, you could probably find it (or something similar) online. You could then construct a WordSpace like this, for example (removing whitespace and normalizing everything to lowercase):

```
>>> words = set(line.strip().lower() for line in open("/usr/share/dict/words"))
>>> G = WordSpace(words)
```

If you're getting word ladders that you don't like, feel free to remove some words from the set, of course.[10] Once you have your WordSpace, it's time to roll:

```
>>> G.ladder('lead', 'gold')
['lead', 'load', 'goad', 'gold']
```

Pretty neat, but not *that* impressive, perhaps. Now try the following:

```
>>> G.ladder('lead', 'gold', h=lambda v: 0)
```

I've simply replaced the heuristic with a completely uninformative one, basically turning our A* into BFS (or, rather, Dijkstra's algorithm running on an unweighted graph). On my computer (and with my word list), the difference in running time is pretty noticeable. In fact, the speedup factor when using the first (default) heuristic is close to 100![11]

Summary

A bit more narrowly focused than the previous ones, this chapter dealt with finding optimal routes in network-like structures and spaces—in other words, shortest paths in graphs. Several of the basic ideas and mechanisms used in the algorithms in this chapter have been covered earlier in the book, and so we could build our solutions gradually. One fundamental tactic common to all the shortest path algorithms is that of looking for *shortcuts*, either through a new possible next-to-last node along a path, using the relax function or something equivalent (most of the algorithms do this), or by considering a shortcut consisting of two subpaths, to and from some intermediate node (the strategy of Floyd-Warshall). The relaxation-based algorithms approach things differently, based on their assumptions about the graph. The Bellman-Ford algorithm simply tries to construct shortcuts with every edge in turn and repeats this procedure for at most n-1 iterations (reporting a negative cycle if there is still potential for improvement).

---

[10]For example, when working with my alchemical example, I removed words such as *algedo* and *dola*.
[11]That number is 100, not the factorial of 100. (And most certainly not the 11th power of the factorial of 100.)

You saw in Chapter 8 that it's possible to be more efficient than this; for DAGs, it's possible to relax each edge only *once*, as long as we visit the nodes in topologically sorted order. A topsort isn't possible for a general graph, but if we disallow negative edges, we can find a topological sorting that respects the edges that *matter*—namely, sorting the nodes by their distance from the starting node. Of course, we don't know this sorting to begin with, but we can build it gradually, by always picking the remaining node with the lowest distance estimate, as in Dijkstra's algorithm. We know this is the thing to do, because we've already relaxed the out-edges of all its possible predecessors, so the next one in sorted order must now have a correct estimate—and the only one this could be is the one with the lowest upper bound.

When finding distances between all pairs of nodes, we have a couple of options. For example, we could run Dijkstra's algorithm from every possible start node. This is quite good for rather sparse graphs, and, in fact, we can use this approach even if the edges aren't all positive! We do this by first running Bellman-Ford and then adjusting all the edges so that we (1) maintain the length-ranks of the paths (the shortest is still the shortest) and (2) make the edge weights positive. Another option is to use dynamic programming, as in the Floyd-Warshall algorithm, where each subproblem is defined by its start node, its end node, and the number of the other nodes (in some predetermined order) we're allowed to pass through.

There's no known method of finding the shortest path from one node to another that is better, asymptotically, than finding the shortest paths from the starting node to all the others. Still, there are some heuristic approaches that can give improvements in practice. One of these is to search *bidirectionally*, performing a traversal from both the start node and the end node "simultaneously," and then terminate when the two meet, thereby reducing the number of nodes that need be visited (or so we hope). Another approach is using a heuristic "best-first" approach, with a heuristic function to guide us toward more promising nodes before less promising ones, as in the A* algorithm.

If You're Curious ...

Most algorithm books will give you explanations and descriptions of the basic algorithms for finding shortest paths. Some of the more advanced heuristic ones though, such as A*, are more usually discussed in books on artificial intelligence. There you can also find thorough explanations on how to use such algorithms (and other, related ones) to search through complex solution spaces that look nothing like the explicit graph structures we've been working with. For a solid foundation in these aspects of artificial intelligence, I heartily recommend the wonderful book by Russell and Norvig. For ideas on heuristics for the A* algorithm, you could try to do a web search for "shortest path" along with "landmarks" or "ALT."

If you want to push Dijkstra's algorithm on the asymptotic front, you could look into Fibonacci heaps. If you swap out the binary heap for a Fibonacci heap, Dijkstra's algorithm gets an improved asymptotic running time, but chances are that your performance will still take a hit, unless you're working with really large instances, as Python's heap implementation is *really fast*, and a Fibonacci heap (a rather complicated affair) implemented in Python probably won't be. But still—worth a look.

Finally, you might want to combine the bidirectional version of Dijkstra's algorithm with the heuristic mechanism of A*. Before you do, though, you should research the issue a bit—there are pitfalls here that could invalidate your algorithm. One (slightly advanced) source of information on this and the use of landmark-based heuristics (as well as the challenges of a graph that changes over time) is the paper by Nannicini et al. (see "References").

Exercises

9-1. In some cases, discrepancies in exchange rates between currencies make it possible to exchange from one currency to another, continuing until one gets back to the original, having made a profit. How would you use the Bellman-Ford algorithm to detect the presence of such a situation?

9-2. What happens in Dijkstra's algorithm if more than one node has the same distance from the start node? Is it still correct?

9-3. Why is it a really bad idea to represent edge length using dummy nodes, like in Figure 9-3?

9-4. What would the running time of Dijkstra's algorithm be if you implemented it with an unsorted list instead of a binary heap?

9-5. Why can we be certain that the adjusted weights in Johnson's algorithm are nonnegative? Are there cases where things can go wrong?

9-6. In Johnson's algorithm, the h function is based on the Bellman-Ford algorithm. Why can't we just use an arbitrary function here? It would disappear in the telescoping sum anyway?

9-7. Implement the memoized version of Floyd-Warshall so it saves memory in the same way as the iterative one.

9-8. Extend the memoized version of Floyd-Warshall to compute a P table, just like the iterative one.

9-9. How would you modify the Floyd-Warshall algorithm so it detects the *presence* of paths, rather than finding the *shortest* paths (Warshall's algorithm)?

9-10. Why does correctness for the tighter stopping criterion for the bidirectional version of Dijkstra's algorithm imply correctness for the original?

9-11. In the correctness proof for the bidirectional version of Dijkstra's algorithm, I posited a hypothetical path that would be shorter than the best one we'd found so far and stated that it had to contain an edge (u,v) such that $d(s,u) < l$ and $d(v,t) < r$. Why is this the case?

9-12. Rewrite bidir_dijkstra so it doesn't require the input graph to be symmetric, with zero-weight self-edges.

9-13. Implement a bidirectional version of BFS.

9-14. Why is $h(v)$ a lower bound on $d(v,t)$ when w' is feasible?

References

Dijkstra, E. W. (1959). A note on two problems in connexion with graphs. *Numerische Mathematik*, 1(1):269-271.

Nannicini, G., Delling, D., Liberti, L., and Schultes, D. (2008). Bidirectional A* search for time-dependent fast paths. In *Proceedings of the 7th international conference on Experimental algorithms*, Lecture Notes in Computer Science, pages 334-346.

Russell, S. and Norvig, P. (2009). *Artificial Intelligence: A Modern Approach*, third edition. Prentice Hall.

CHAPTER 10

Matchings, Cuts, and Flows

A joyful life is an individual creation that cannot be copied from a recipe.

— Mihaly Csikszentmihalyi, *Flow: The Psychology of Optimal Experience*

While the previous chapter gave you several algorithms for a single problem, this chapter describes a single algorithm with many variations and applications. The core problem is that of finding maximum flow in a network, and the main solution strategy I'll be using is the augmenting path method of Ford and Fulkerson. Before tackling the full problem, I'll guide you through two simpler problems, which are basically special cases (they're easily reduced to maximum flow). These problems, bipartite matching and disjoint paths, have many applications themselves and can be solved by more specialized algorithms. You'll also see that the max-flow problem has a *dual*, the min-cut problem, which means that you'll automatically solve both problems at the same time. The min-cut problem has several interesting applications that seem very different from those of max-flow, even if they are really closely related. Finally, I'll give you some pointers on one way of extending the max-flow problem, by adding costs, and looking for the *cheapest* of the maximum flows, paving the way for applications such as min-cost bipartite matching.

The max-flow problem and its variations have almost endless applications. Douglas B. West, in his book *Introduction to Graph Theory* (see "References" in Chapter 2), gives some rather obvious ones, such as determining the total capacities of road and communication networks, or even working with currents in electrical circuits. Kleinberg and Tardos (see "References" in Chapter 1) explain how to apply the formalism to survey design, airline scheduling, image segmentation, project selection, baseball elimination, and assigning doctors to holidays. Ahuja, Magnanti, and Orlin have written one of the most thorough books on the subject and cover well over 100 applications in such diverse areas as engineering, manufacturing, scheduling, management, medicine, defense, communication, public policy, mathematics, and transportation. Although the algorithms apply to graphs, these application need not be all that graphlike at all. For example, who'd think of image segmentation as a graph problem? I'll walk you through some of these applications in the unsurprisingly named section "Some Applications" later in the chapter. If you're curious about how the techniques can be used, you might want to take a quick glance at that section before reading on.

The general idea that runs through this chapter is that we're trying to get the most out of a network, moving from one side to the other, pushing through as much of we can of some kind of substance—be it edges of a bipartite matching, edge-disjoint paths, or units of flow. This is a bit different from the cautious graph exploration in the previous chapter. The basic approach of incremental improvement is still here, though. We repeatedly find ways of improving our solutions slightly, until it can't get any better. You'll see that the idea of *canceling* is key—that we may need to remove parts of a previous solution in order to make it better overall.

■ Note   I'm using the labeling approach due to Ford and Fulkerson for the implementations in this chapter. Another perspective on the search for augmenting paths is that we're traversing a *residual network*. This idea is explained in the sidebar "Residual Networks" later in the chapter.

Bipartite Matching

I've already exposed you to the idea of bipartite matching, both in the form of the grumpy moviegoers in Chapter 4 and in the stable marriage problem in Chapter 7. In general, a *matching* for a graph is a node-disjoint subset of the edges. That is, we select some of the edges in such a way that no two edges share a node. This means that each edge matches two pairs—hence the name. A special kind of matching applies to bipartite graphs, graphs that can be partitioned into two independent node sets (subgraphs without edges), such as the graph in Figure 10-1. This is exactly the kind of matching we've been working with in the moviegoer and marriage problems, and it's much easier to deal with than the general kind. When we talk about bipartite matching, we usually want a *maximum* matching, one that consists of a maximum number of edges. This means, if possible, we'd like a *perfect* matching, one where all nodes are matched. This is a simple problem but one that can easily occur in real life. Let's say, for example, you're assigning people to projects, and the graph represents who'd like to work on what. A perfect matching would please everyone.[1]

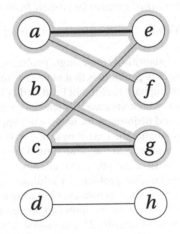

Figure 10-1. *A bipartite graph with a (non-maximal) matching (heavy edges) and an augmenting path from b to f (highlighted)*

We can continue to use the metaphor from the stable marriage problem—we'll just drop the stability and try to get everyone matched with someone they can accept. To visualize what's going on, let's say each man has an engagement ring. What we want is then to have each man give his ring to one of the women so that no woman has more than one ring. Or, if that's not possible, we want to move *as many rings as possible* from the men to the women, still prohibiting any woman from keeping more than one. As always, to solve this, we start looking for some form of reduction or inductive step. An obvious idea would be to somehow identify a pair of lovers destined to be together, thereby reducing the number of pairs we need to worry about. However, it's not so easy to guarantee that any single pair is part of a maximum matching, unless, for example, it's totally isolated, like *d* and *h* in Figure 10-1.

An approach that fits better in this case is *iterative improvement*, as discussed in Chapter 4. This is closely related to the use of relaxation in Chapter 9, in that we'll improve our solution step by step, until we can't improve it anymore. We also have to make sure that the only reason the improvement stops is that the solution is optimal—but I'll get back to that. Let's start by finding some step by step improvement scheme. Let's say that in each round we try to move one additional ring from the men to the women. If we're lucky, this would give us the solution straightaway—that is, if each man gives the ring to the woman he'd be matched to in the best solution. We can't let any romantic tendencies cloud our vision here, though. Chances are this approach won't work quite that smoothly. Consider, once again, the

---

[1] If you allow them to specify a degree of *preference*, this turns into the more general min-cost bipartite matching, or *the assignment problem*. Although a highly useful problem, it's a bit harder to solve—I'll get to that later.

graph in Figure 10-1. Let's say that in our first two iterations, *a* gives a ring to *e*, and *c* gives one to *g*. This gives us a tentative matching consisting of two pairs (indicated by the heavy black edges). Now we turn to *b*. What is he to do?

Let's follow a strategy somewhat similar to the Gale-Shapley algorithm mentioned in Chapter 7, where the women can change their minds when approached by a new suitor. In fact, let's mandate that they *always do*. So when *b* asks *g*, she returns her current ring to *c*, accepting the one from *b*. In other words, she *cancels* her engagement to *c*. (This idea of canceling is crucial to all the algorithms in this chapter.) But now *c* is single, and if we are to ensure that the iteration does indeed lead to improvement, we can't accept this new situation. We immediately look around for a new mate for *c*, in this case *e*. But if *c* passes his returned ring to *e*, she has to cancel her engagement to *a*, returning *his* ring. He in turn passes this on to *f*, and we're done. After this single zigzag swapping session, rings have been passed back and forth along the highlighted edges. Also, we now have increased the number of couples from two to three (*a* + *f*, *b* + *g*, and *c* + *e*).

We can, in fact, extract a general method from this ad hoc procedure. First, we need to find one unmatched man. (If we can't, we're done.) We then need to find some alternating sequence of engagements and cancellations so that we *end* with an engagement. If we can find that, we know that there must have been one more engagement than there were cancellations, increasing the number of pairs by one. We just keep finding such zigzags for as long as we can.

The zigzags we're looking for are *paths* that go from an unmatched node on the left side to an unmatched node on the right side. Following the logic of the engagement rings, we see that the path can only move to the *right* across an edge that is *not* already in the matching (a proposal), and it can only move *left* across one that *is* in the matching (a cancellation). Such a path (like the one highlighted in Figure 10-1) is called an *augmenting path*, because it augments our solution (that is, it increments the engagement count), and we can find augmenting paths by traversal. We just need to be sure we follow the rules—we can't follow matched edges to the right or unmatched edges to the left.

What's left is ensuring that we can indeed find such augmenting paths as long as there is room for improvement. Although this seems plausible enough, it's not immediately obvious why it *must* be so. What we want to show is that if there is room for improvement, we can find an augmenting path. That means that we have a current match *M* and that there is some greater matching *M'* that we haven't found yet. Now consider the edges in the *symmetric difference* between these two—that is, the edges that are in either one but not in both. Let's call the edges in *M* red and the ones in *M'* green.

This jumble of red and green edges would actually have some useful structure. For example, we know that each node would be incident to at most two edges, one of each color (because it couldn't have two edges from the same matching). This means that we'd have one or more connected components, each of which was a zigzagging path or cycle of alternating color. Because *M'* is bigger than *M*, we must have at least one component with more green than red edges, and the only way that could happen would be in a path—an odd-length one that started and ended with a green edge.

Do you see it yet? Exactly! This green-red-...-green path would be an augmenting path. It has odd length, so one end would be on the male side and one on the female. And the first and last edges were green, meaning they were *not* part of our original matching, so we're free to start augmenting. (This is essentially my take on what's known as Berge's lemma.)

When it comes to implementing this strategy, there is a lot of room for creativity. One possible implementation is shown in Listing 10-1. The code for the `tr` function can be found in Listing 5-10. The parameters X and Y are collections (iterable objects) of nodes, representing the bipartition of the graph G. The running time might not be obvious, because edges are switched on and off during execution, but we *do* know that one pair is added to the matching in each iteration, so the number of iterations is $O(n)$, for *n* nodes. Assuming *m* edges, the search for an augmenting path is basically a traversal of a connected component, which is $O(m)$. In total, then, the running time is $O(nm)$.

Listing 10-1. Finding a Maximum Bipartite Matching Using Augmenting Paths

```python
from itertools import chain

def match(G, X, Y):                                     # Maximum bipartite matching
    H = tr(G)                                           # The transposed graph
    S, T, M = set(X), set(Y), set()                     # Unmatched left/right + match
    while S:                                            # Still unmatched on the left?
        s = S.pop()                                     # Get one
        Q, P = {s}, {}                                  # Start a traversal from it
        while Q:                                        # Discovered, unvisited
            u = Q.pop()                                 # Visit one
            if u in T:                                  # Finished augmenting path?
                T.remove(u)                             # u is now matched
                break                                   # and our traversal is done
            forw = (v for v in G[u] if (u,v) not in M)  # Possible new edges
            back = (v for v in H[u] if (v,u) in M)      # Cancellations
            for v in chain(forw, back):                 # Along out- and in-edges
                if v in P: continue                     # Already visited? Ignore
                P[v] = u                                # Traversal predecessor
                Q.add(v)                                # New node discovered
        while u != s:                                   # Augment: Backtrack to s
            u, v = P[u], u                              # Shift one step
            if v in G[u]:                               # Forward edge?
                M.add((u,v))                            # New edge
            else:                                       # Backward edge?
                M.remove((v,u))                         # Cancellation
    return M                                            # Matching -- a set of edges
```

■ **Note**   König's theorem states that for bipartite graph, the dual of the maximum matching problem is the minimum vertex cover problem. In other words, the problems are equivalent.

Disjoint Paths

The augmenting path method for finding matchings can also be used for more general problems. The simplest generalization may be to count *edge-disjoint paths* instead of *edges*.[2] Edge-disjoint paths can share nodes but not edges. In this more general setting, we no longer need to restrict ourselves to bipartite graphs. When we allow general directed graphs, however, we can freely specify where the paths are to start and end. The easiest (and most common) solution is to specify two special nodes, s and t, called the *source* and the *sink*. (Such a graph is often called an *s-t* graph, or an *s-t*-network.) We then require all paths to start in t and end in t (implicitly allowing the paths to share these two nodes). An important application of this problem is determining the *edge connectivity* of a network—how many edges can be removed (or "fail") before the graph is disconnected (or, in this case, before s cannot reach t)?

Another application is finding communication paths on a multicore CPU. You may have lots of cores laid out in two dimensions, and because of the way communication works, it can be impossible to route two communication

---

[2]In some ways, this problem is similar to the path counting in Chapter 8. The main difference, however, is that in that case we counted *all possible paths* (such as in Pascal's Triangle), which would usually entail lots of overlap—otherwise the memoization would be pointless. That overlap is not permitted here.

channels through the same switching points. In these cases, finding a set of disjoint paths is critical. Note that these paths would probably be more naturally modeled as *vertex-disjoint*, rather than edge-disjoint. See Exercise 10-2 for more. Also, as long as you need to pair each source core with a specific sink core, you have a version of what's called the *multicommodity flow* problem, which isn't dealt with here. (See "If You're Curious ..." for some pointers.)

You could deal with multiple sources and sinks directly in the algorithm, just like in Listing 10-1. If each of these sources and sinks can be involved only in a single path and you don't care which source is paired with which sink, it can be easier to reduce the problem to the single-source, single-sink case. You do this by adding *s* and *t* as new nodes and introduce edges from *s* to all of your sources and from all your sinks to *t*. The number of paths will be the same, and reconstructing the paths you were looking for requires only snipping off *s* and *t* again. This reduction, in fact, makes the maximum matching problem a special case of the disjoint paths problem. As you'll see, the algorithms for solving the problems are also *very* similar.

Instead of thinking about complete paths, it would be useful to be able to look at smaller parts of the problem in isolation. We can do that by introducing two rules:

- The number of paths going *into* any node except *s* or *t* must equal the number of paths going *out of* that node.

- At most *one* path can go through any given edge.

Given these restrictions, we can use traversal to find paths from *s* to *t*. At some point, we can't find any more paths without overlapping with some of those we already have. Once again, though, we can use the augmenting path idea from the previous section. See, for example, Figure 10-2. A first round of traversal has established one path from *s* to *t* via *c* and *b*. Now, any further progress seems blocked by this path—but the augmenting path idea lets us improve the solution by *canceling* the edge from *c* to *b*.

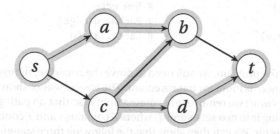

Figure 10-2. *An s-t network with one path found (heavy edges) and one augmenting path (highlighted)*

The principle of canceling works just like in bipartite matching. As we search for an augmenting path, we move from *s* to *a* and then to *b*. There, we're blocked by the edge *bt*. The problem at this point is that *b* has *two* incoming paths from *a* and *c* but only *one* outgoing path. By canceling the edge *cb*, we've solved the problem for *b*, but now there's a problem at *c*. This is the same kind of cascade effect we saw for the bipartite matching. In this case, *c* has an incoming path from *s*, but no outgoing path—we need to find somewhere for the path to go. We do that by continuing our path via *d* to *t*, as shown by the highlights in Figure 10-2.

If you either *add* an *incoming* edge or *cancel* an *outgoing* one at some node *u*, that node will be overcrowded. It will have more paths entering than leaving, which isn't allowed. You can fix this either by *adding* an *outgoing* edge or by *canceling* an *incoming* one. All in all, this works out to finding a path from *s*, following unused edges in their direction and used ones *against* their direction. Any time you can find such an augmenting path, you will also have discovered an additional disjoint path.

Listing 10-2 shows code for implementing this algorithm. As before, the code for the tr function can be found in Listing 5-10.

Listing 10-2. Counting Edge-Disjoint Paths Using Labeling Traversal to Find Augmenting Paths

```
from itertools import chain

def paths(G, s, t):                              # Edge-disjoint path count
    H, M, count = tr(G), set(), 0                # Transpose, matching, result
    while True:                                  # Until the function returns
        Q, P = {s}, {}                           # Traversal queue + tree
        while Q:                                 # Discovered, unvisited
            u = Q.pop()                          # Get one
            if u == t:                           # Augmenting path!
                count += 1                       # That means one more path
                break                            # End the traversal
            forw = (v for v in G[u] if (u,v) not in M)  # Possible new edges
            back = (v for v in H[u] if (v,u) in M)      # Cancellations
            for v in chain(forw, back):          # Along out- and in-edges
                if v in P: continue              # Already visited? Ignore
                P[v] = u                         # Traversal predecessor
                Q.add(v)                         # New node discovered
        else:                                    # Didn't reach t?
            return count                         # We're done
        while u != s:                            # Augment: Backtrack to s
            u, v = P[u], u                       # Shift one step
            if v in G[u]:                        # Forward edge?
                M.add((u,v))                     # New edge
            else:                                # Backward edge?
                M.remove((v,u))                  # Cancellation
```

To make sure we've solved the problem, we still need to prove the converse, though—that there always will *be* an augmenting path as long as there is room for improvement. The easiest way of showing this is by using the idea of connectivity: how many edges must we remove to separate *s* from *t* (so that no path goes from *s* to *t*)? Any such set represents an *s-t cut*, a partitioning into two sets *S* and *T*, where *S* contains *s* and *T* contains *t*. We call the edges going from *S* to *T* a directed *edge separator*. We can then show that the following three statements are equivalent:

- We have found *k* disjoint paths and there is an edge separator of size *k*.

- We have found the maximum number of disjoint paths.

- There are no augmenting paths.

What we primarily want to show is that the last two statements are equivalent, but sometimes it's easier to go via a third statement, such as the first one in this case.

It's pretty easy to see that the first implies the second. Let's call the separator *F*. Any *s-t* path must have at least one edge in *F*, which means that the size of *F* is at least as great as the number of disjoint *s-t* paths. If the size of the separator is the same as the number of disjoint paths we've found, clearly we've reached the maximum.

Showing that the second statement implies the third is easily done by contradiction. Assume there is no room for improvement but that we still have an augmenting path. As discussed, this augmenting path could be used to improve the solution, so we have a contradiction.

The only thing left to prove is that the last statement implies the first, and this is where the whole connectivity idea pays off as a stepping stone. Imagine you've executed the algorithm until you've run out of augmenting paths. Let *S* be the set of nodes you reached in your last traversal, and let *T* be the remaining nodes. Clearly, this is an *s-t* cut. Consider the edges across this cut. Any forward edge from *S* to *T* must be part of one of your discovered disjoint paths. If it wasn't, you would have followed it during your traversal. For the same reason, no edge from *T* to *S* can be part of one of the paths, because you could have canceled it, thereby reaching T. In other words, all edges across from S to T belong to your disjoint paths, and because none of the edges in the other direction do, the forward edges must all belong to a path of their own, meaning that you have k disjoint paths and a separator of size k.

This may be a bit involved, but the intuition is that if we can't find an augmenting path, there must be a bottleneck somewhere, and we must have filled it. No matter what we do, we can't get more paths through this bottleneck, so the algorithm must have found the answer. (This result is a version of Menger's theorem, and it is a special case of the max-flow min-cut theorem, which you'll see in a bit.)

What's the running time of all this, then? Each iteration consists of a relatively straightforward traversal from s, which has a running time of $O(m)$, for m edges. Each round gives us another disjoint path, and there are clearly at most $O(m)$, meaning that the running time is $O(m^2)$. Exercise 10-3 asks you to show that this is a tight bound in the worst case.

■ **Note**   Menger's theorem is another example of duality: The maximum number of edge-disjoint paths from s to t is equal to the minimum cut between s and t. This is a special case of the max-flow min-cut theorem, discussed later.

Maximum Flow

This is the central problem of the chapter. It forms a generalization of both the bipartite matching and the disjoint paths, and it is the mirror image of the minimum cut problem (next section). The only difference from the disjoint path case is that instead of setting the *capacity* for each edge to one, we let it be an arbitrary positive number. If the capacity is a positive integer, you could think of it as the number of paths that can pass through it. More generally, the metaphor here is some form of substance flowing through the network, from the source to the sink, and the capacity represents the limit for how many units can flow through a given edge. (You can think of this as a generalization of the engagement rings that were passed back and forth in the matching.) In general, the flow itself is an assignment of a number of flow units to each unit (that is, a function or mapping from edges to numbers), while the *size* or *magnitude* of the flow is the total amount pushed through the network. (This can be found by finding the net flow out of the source, for example.) Note that although flow networks are commonly defined as directed, you could find the maximum flow in an undirected network as well (Exercise 10-4).

Let's see how we can solve this more general case. A naïve approach would be to simply split edges, just like the naïve extension of BFS in Chapter 9 (Figure 9-3). Now, though, we want to split them *lengthwise*, as shown in Figure 10-3. Just like BFS with serial dummy nodes gives you a good idea of how Dijkstra's algorithm works, our augmenting path algorithm with parallel dummy nodes is very close to how the full Ford-Fulkerson algorithm for finding maximum flow works. As in the Dijkstra case, though, the actual algorithm can take care of greater chunks of flow in one go, meaning that the dummy node approach (which lets us saturate only one unit of capacity at a time) is hopelessly inefficient.

Capacity = 2   Two edges

Figure 10-3. *An edge capacity simulated by dummy nodes*

Let's walk through the technicalities. Just like in the zero-one case, we have two rules for how our flow interacts with edges and nodes. As you can see, they parallel the disjoint path rules closely:

- The amount of flow going *into* any node except *s* or *t* must equal the amount of flow going *out* of that node.

- At most *c(e)* units of flow can go through any given edge.

Here, *c(e)* is the *capacity* of edge *e*. Just like for the disjoint paths, we are required to follow the edge direction, so the flow *back* along an edge is always zero. A flow that respects our two rules is said to be *feasible*.

This is where you may need to take a breath and focus, though. What I'm about to say isn't really complicated, but it can get a bit confusing. I *am* allowed to push flow against the direction of an edge, as long as there's already some flow going in the right direction. Do you see how that would work? I hope the previous two sections have prepared you for this—it's all a matter of *canceling flow*. If I have one unit of flow going from *a* to *b*, I can *cancel* that unit, in effect pushing one unit in the other direction. The net result is zero, so there is no *actual* flow in the wrong direction (which is totally forbidden).

This idea lets us create augmenting paths, just like before: If you add *k* units of flow along an incoming edge or cancel *k* units on an outgoing one at some node *u*, that node will be overflowing. It will have more flow entering than leaving, which isn't allowed. You can fix this either by adding *k* units of flow along an outgoing edge or by canceling *k* units on an incoming one. This is exactly what you did in the zero-one case, except there *k* was always 1.

In Figure 10-4 two states of the same flow network are shown. In the first state, flow has been pushed along the path *s-c-b-t*, giving a total flow value of 2. This flow is blocking any further improvements along the *forward* edges. As you can see, though, the augmenting path includes a backward edge. By canceling one of the units of flow going from *c* to *b*, we can send one additional unit from *c* via *d* to *t*, reaching the maximum.

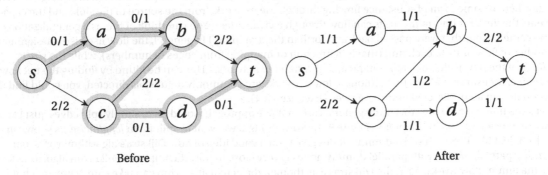

Before   After

Figure 10-4. A flow network before and after augmenting via an augmenting path (highlighted)

The general Ford-Fulkerson approach, as explained in this section, does not give any running time guarantees. In fact, if irrational capacities (containing square roots or the like) are allowed, the iterative augmentation may *never terminate*. For actual applications, the use of irrationals may not be very realistic, but even if we restrict ourselves to limited-precision floating-point numbers, or even *integers*, we can still run into trouble. Consider a really simple network with source, sink, and two other nodes, *u* and *v*. Both nodes have edges from the source and to the sink, all with a capacity of *k*. We also have a unit-capacity edge from *u* to *v*. If we keep choosing augmenting paths that go through the edge *uv*, adding and canceling one unit of flow in every iteration, that would give us 2*k* iterations before termination.

What's the problem with this running time? It's pseudopolynomial—exponential in the actual problem size. We can easily crank up the capacity, and hence the running time, without using much more space. And the annoying thing is that if we had chosen the augmenting paths more cleverly (for example, just avoiding the edge *uv* altogether), we would have finished in *two rounds*, regardless of the capacity *k*.

Luckily, there is a solution to this problem, one that gives us a polynomial running time, no matter the capacities (even irrational ones!). The thing is, Ford-Fulkerson isn't really a fully specified algorithm, because its traversal is completely arbitrary. If we settle on BFS as the traversal order (thereby always choosing the shortest augmenting path), we end up with what's called the Edmonds-Karp algorithm, which is exactly the solution we're looking for. For n nodes and m edges, Edmonds-Karp runs in $O(nm^2)$ time. That this is the case isn't entirely obvious, though. For a thorough proof, I recommend looking up the algorithm in the book by Cormen et al. (see "References" in Chapter 1). The general idea is as follows: Each shortest augmenting path is found in $O(m)$ time, and when we augment the flow along it, at least one edge is saturated (the flow reaches the capacity). Each time an edge is saturated, the distance from the source (along the augmenting path) must increase, and this distance is at most $O(n)$. Because each edge can be saturated at most $O(n)$ times, we get at $O(nm)$ iterations and a total running time of $O(nm^2)$.

For a *correctness* proof for the general Ford-Fulkerson method (and therefore also the Edmonds-Karp algorithm), see the next section, on minimum cuts. That correctness proof does assume termination, though, which is guaranteed if you avoid irrational capacities or if you simply use the Edmonds-Karp algorithm (which has a deterministic running time).

One augmentation traversal, based on BFS, is given in Listing 10-3. An implementation of the full Ford-Fulkerson method is shown in Listing 10-4. For simplicity, it is assumed that s and t are different nodes. By default, the implementation uses the BFS-based augmentation traversal, which gives us the Edmonds-Karp algorithm. The main function (ford_fulkerson) is pretty straightforward and really quite similar to the previous two algorithms in this chapter. The main while loop keeps going until it's impossible to find an augmenting path and then returns the flow. Whenever an augmenting path is found, it is traced backward to s, adding the capacity of the path to every forward edge and subtracting (canceling) it from every reverse edge.

The bfs_aug function in Listing 10-3 is similar to the traversal in the previous algorithms. It uses a deque, to get BFS, and builds the traversal tree using the P map. It only traverses forward edges if there is some remaining capacity (G[u][v]-f[u,v] > 0), and backward edges if there is some flow to cancel (f[v,u] > 0). The *labeling* consists both of setting traversal predecessors (in P) and in remembering how much flow could be transported to this node (stored in F). This flow value is the minimum of (1) the flow we managed to transport to the predecessor and (2) the remaining capacity (or reverse flow) on the connecting edge. This means that once we reach t, the total slack of the path (the extra flow we can push through it) is F[t].

■ **Note** If your capacities are integers, the augmentations will always be integral as well, leading to an integral flow. This is one of the properties that give the max-flow problem (and most algorithms that solve it) such a wide range of application.

Listing 10-3. Finding Augmenting Paths with BFS and Labeling

```
from collections import deque
inf = float('inf')

def bfs_aug(G, H, s, t, f):
    P, Q, F = {s: None}, deque([s]), {s: inf}   # Tree, queue, flow label
    def label(inc):                              # Flow increase at v from u?
        if v in P or inc <= 0: return            # Seen? Unreachable? Ignore
        F[v], P[v] = min(F[u], inc), u           # Max flow here? From where?
        Q.append(v)                              # Discovered -- visit later
    while Q:                                      # Discovered, unvisited
        u = Q.popleft()                          # Get one (FIFO)
        if u == t: return P, F[t]                # Reached t? Augmenting path!
        for v in G[u]: label(G[u][v]-f[u,v])     # Label along out-edges
        for v in H[u]: label(f[v,u])             # Label along in-edges
    return None, 0                               # No augmenting path found
```

Listing 10-4. The Ford-Fulkerson Method (by Default, the Edmonds-Karp Algorithm)

```
from collections import defaultdict

def ford_fulkerson(G, s, t, aug=bfs_aug):    # Max flow from s to t
    H, f = tr(G), defaultdict(int)           # Transpose and flow
    while True:                              # While we can improve things
        P, c = aug(G, H, s, t, f)            # Aug. path and capacity/slack
        if c == 0: return f                  # No augm. path found? Done!
        u = t                                # Start augmentation
        while u != s:                        # Backtrack to s
            u, v = P[u], u                   # Shift one step
            if v in G[u]: f[u,v] += c        # Forward edge? Add slack
            else:         f[v,u] -= c        # Backward edge? Cancel slack
```

RESIDUAL NETWORKS

One abstraction that is often used to explain the Ford-Fulkerson method and its relatives is *residual networks*. A residual network G_f is defined with respect to an original flow network G, as well as a flow f, and is a way of representing the traversal rules used when looking for augmenting paths. In G_f there is an edge from u to v if (and only if) either (1) there is an unsaturated edge (that is, one with residual capacity) from u to v in G or (2) there is a positive flow in G from v to u (which we are allowed to cancel).

In other words, our special augmenting traversal in G now becomes a *completely normal* traversal in G_f. The algorithm terminates when there is no longer a path from the source to the sink in the residual network. While the idea is primarily a formal one, making it possible to use ordinary graph theory to reason about the augmentation, you could also implement it explicitly, if you wanted (Exercise 10-5), as a dynamic view of the actual graph. That would allow you to use existing implementations of BFS, and (as you'll see later) Bellman-Ford and Dijkstra directly on the residual network.

Minimum Cut

Just like the zero-one flow gave rise to Menger's theorem, the more general flow problem gives us the *max-flow min-cut* theorem of Ford and Fulkerson, and we can prove it in a similar fashion.[3] If we assume that the only cuts we're talking about are *s-t* cuts and we let the *capacity* of a cut be the amount of flow that can be moved across it (that is, the sum of the forward-edge capacities), we can show that the following three statements are equivalent:

- We have found a flow of size k, and there is a cut with capacity k.

- We have found the maximum flow.

- There are no augmenting paths.

Proving this will give us two things: It will show that the Ford-Fulkerson method is correct, and it means that we can use it to also find a minimum cut, which is a useful problem in itself. (I'll get back to that.)

---

[3]Actually, the proof I used in the zero-one case was just a simplified version of the proof I use here. There are proofs for Menger's theorem that don't rely on the idea of flow as well.

As in the zero-one case, the first clearly implies the second. Every unit of flow must pass through any s-t cut, so if we have a cut of capacity k, that is an upper limit to the flow. If we have a flow that *equals* the capacity of a cut, that flow must be maximum, while the cut must be minimum. This is a case of what is called *duality*.

The implication from the second statement (we've reached the max) to the third (there are no augmenting paths) is once again provable by contradiction. Assume we have reached the maximum, but there is still an augmenting path. Then we could use that path to increase our flow, which is a contradiction.

The last step (no augmenting paths means we have a cut equaling the flow) is again shown using the traversal to construct a cut. That is, we let S be the set of nodes we can reach in the last iteration, and T is the remainder. Any forward edge across the cut must be saturated because otherwise we would have traversed across it. Similarly, any backward edge must be empty. This means that the flow going across the cut is exactly equal to its capacity, which is what we wanted to show.

Minimum cuts have several applications that don't really *look* like max-flow problems. Consider, for example, the problem of allocating processes to two processors in a manner that minimizes the communication between them. Let's say one of the processors is a GPU and that the processes have different running times on the two processors. Some fit the CPU better, while some should be run on the GPU. However, there might be cases where one fits on the CPU and one on the GPU, but where the two communicate extensively with each other. In that case, we might want to put them on the same processor, just to reduce the communication costs.

How would we solve this? We could set up an undirected flow network with the CPU as the source and the GPU as the sink, for example. Each process would have an edge to both source and sink, with a capacity equal to the time it would take to run on that processor. We also add edges between processes that communicate, with capacities representing the communication overhead (in extra computation time) of having them on separate processors. The minimum cut would then distribute the processes on the two processors in such a way that the total cost is as small as possible—a nontrivial task if we couldn't reduce to the min-cut problem.

In general, you can think of the whole flow network formalism as a special kind of algorithmic machine, and you can use it to solve other problems by reduction. The task becomes constructing some form of flow network where a maximum flow or minimum cut represents a solution to your original problem.

DUALITY

There are a couple of examples of duality in this chapter: Maximum bipartite matchings are the dual of minimum bipartite vertex covers, and maximum flows are the dual of minimum cuts. There are several similar cases as well, such as the *maximum tension* problem, which is the dual of the shortest path problem. In general, duality involves two optimization problems, the primal and the dual, where both have the same optimization cost, and solving one will solve the other. More specifically, for a maximization problem A and a minimization problem B, we have *weak duality* if the optimal solution for A is less than or equal to the optimal solution for B. If they are equal (as for the max-flow min-cut case), we have *strong duality*. If you want to know more about duality (including some rather advanced material), take a look at *Duality in Optimization and Variational Inequalities*, by Go and Yang.

Cheapest Flow and the Assignment Problem*

Before leaving the topic of flow, let's take a look at an important and rather obvious extension; let's find the *cheapest* maximum flow. That is, we still want to find the maximum flow, but if there is more than one way to achieve the same flow magnitude, we want the cheapest one. We formalize this by adding costs to the edges and define the total cost as the sum of $w(e) \cdot f(e)$ over all edges e, where w and f are the cost and flow functions, respectively. That is, the cost is *per unit of flow* over a given edge.

---

*This section is a bit hard and is not essential in order to understand the rest of the book. Feel free to skim it or even skip it entirely. You might want to read the first couple of paragraphs, though, to get a feel for the problem.

An immediate application of this is an extension of the bipartite matching problem. We can keep using the zero-one flow formulation but add costs to each of the edges. We then have a solution to the min-cost bipartite matching (or assignment) problem, hinted at in the introduction: By finding a maximum flow, we know we have a maximum matching, and by minimizing the cost, we get the matching we're looking for.

This problem is often referred to simply as *min-cost flow*. That means that rather than looking for the cheapest *maximum* flow, we're simply looking for the cheapest flow of a given magnitude. For example, the problem might be "give me a flow of size k, if such a flow exists, and make sure you construct it as cheaply as possible." You could, for example, construct a flow that is as great as possible, *up to the value k*. That way, finding the max-flow (or the min-cost max-flow) would simply involve setting k to a sufficiently large value. It turns out that simply focusing on maximum flow is sufficient, though; we can optimize to a specified flow value by a simple reduction, without modifying the algorithm (see Exercise 10-6).

The idea introduced by Busacker and Gowen for solving the min-cost flow problem was this: Look for the *cheapest augmenting path*. That is, use a shortest path algorithm for weighted graphs, rather than just BFS, during the traversal step. The only wrinkle is that edges traversed backward have their cost negated for the purpose of finding the shortest path. (They're used for canceling flow, after all.)

If we could assume that the cost function was positive, we could use Dijkstra's algorithm to find our augmenting paths. The problem is that once you push some flow from u to v, we can suddenly traverse the (fictitious) reverse edge vu, which has a *negative* cost. In other words, Dijkstra's algorithm would work just fine in the *first* iteration, but after that, we'd be doomed. Luckily, Edmonds and Karp thought of a neat trick to get around this problem—one that is quite similar to the one used in Johnson's algorithm (see Chapter 9). We can adjust all the weights in a way that (1) makes them all positive, and (2) forms telescoping sums along all traversal paths, ensuring that the shortest paths are still shortest.

Let's say we are in the process of performing the algorithm, and we have established some feasible flow. Let $w(u, v)$ be the edge weight, adjusted according to the rules of augmenting path traversal (that is, it's unmodified along edges with residual capacity, and it's negated along backward edges with positive flow). Let us once again (that is, just like in Johnson's algorithm) set $h(v) = d(s, v)$, where the distance is computed with respect to w. We can then define an *adjusted weight*, which we can use for finding our next augmenting path: $w'(u, v) = w(u, v) + h(u) - h(v)$. Using the same reasoning as in Chapter 9, we see that this adjustment will preserve all the shortest paths and, in particular, the shortest augmenting paths from s to t.

Implementing the basic Busacker-Gowen algorithm is basically a question of replacing BFS with, for example, Bellman-Ford (see Listing 9-2) in the code for bfs_aug (Listing 10-3). If you want to use Dijkstra's algorithm, you simply have to use the modified weights, as described earlier (Exercise 10-7). For an implementation based on Bellman-Ford, see Listing 10-5. (The implementation assumes that edge weights are given by a separate map, so W[u,v] is the weight, or cost, of the edge from u to v.) Note that the flow labeling from the Ford-Fulkerson labeling approach has been merged with the relax operation of Bellman-Ford—both are performed in the label function. To do anything, you must both have found a better path and have some free capacity along the new edge. If that is the case, both the distance estimate and the flow label are updated.

The running time of the Busacker-Gowen method depends on which shortest path algorithm you choose. We're no longer using the Edmonds-Karp-approach, so we're losing its running-time guarantees, but if we're using integral capacities and are looking for a flow of value k, we're guaranteed at most k iterations.[4] Assuming Dijkstra's algorithm, the total running time becomes $O(km \lg n)$. For the min-cost bipartite matching, k would be $O(n)$, so we'd get $O(nm \lg n)$.

In a sense, this is a greedy algorithm, where we gradually build the flow but add as little cost as possible in each step. Intuitively, this seems like it should work, and indeed it does, but *proving* as much can be a bit challenging—so much so, in fact, that I'm not going into details here. If you want to read the proof (as well as more details on the running time), have a look at the chapter on circulations in *Graphs, Networks and Algorithms*, by Dieter Jungnickel.[5] You can find a simpler proof for the special case of min-cost bipartite matching in *Algorithm Design*, by Kleinberg and Tardos (see "References" in Chapter 1).

---

[4]This is, of course, pseudopolynomial, so choose your capacities wisely.
[5]Also available online: http://books.google.com/books?id=NvuFAglxaJkC&pg=PA299

Listing 10-5. The Busacker-Gowen Algorithm, Using Bellman-Ford for Augmentation

```
def busacker_gowen(G, W, s, t):              # Min-cost max-flow
    def sp_aug(G, H, s, t, f):               # Shortest path (Bellman-Ford)
        D, P, F = {s:0}, {s:None}, {s:inf,t:0}  # Dist, preds and flow
        def label(inc, cst):                 # Label + relax, really
            if inc <= 0: return False        # No flow increase? Skip it
            d = D.get(u,inf) + cst           # New possible aug. distance
            if d >= D.get(v,inf): return False  # No improvement? Skip it
            D[v], P[v] = d, u                # Update dist and pred
            F[v] = min(F[u], inc)            # Update flow label
            return True                      # We changed things!
        for _ in G:                          # n = len(G) rounds
            changed = False                  # No changes in round so far
            for u in G:                      # Every from-node
                for v in G[u]:               # Every forward to-node
                    changed |= label(G[u][v]-f[u,v], W[u,v])  # Every forward to-node
                for v in H[u]:               # Every backward to-node
                    changed |= label(f[v,u], -W[v,u])  # Every backward to-node
            if not changed: break            # No change in round: Done
        else:                                # Not done before round n?
            raise ValueError('negative cycle')  # Negative cycle detected
        return P, F[t]                       # Preds and flow reaching t
    return ford_fulkerson(G, s, t, sp_aug)   # Max-flow with Bellman-Ford
```

Some Applications

As promised initially, I'll now sketch out a few applications of some of the techniques in this chapter. I won't be giving you all the details or actual code—you could try your hand at implementing the solutions if you'd like some more experience with the material.

Baseball elimination. The solution to this problem was first published by Benjamin L. Schwartz in 1966. If you're like me, you could forgo the baseball context and imagine this being about a round-robin tournament of jousting knights instead (as discussed in Chapter 4). Anyway, the idea is as follows: You have a partially completed tournament (baseball-related or otherwise), and you want to know if a certain team, say, the Mars Greenskins, can possibly win the tournament. That is, if they can at most win W games in total (if they win every remaining game), is it possible to reach a situation where no other team has more than W wins?

It's not obvious how this problem can be solved by reduction to maximum flow, but let's have a go. We'll build a network with integral flow, where each unit of flow represents one of the remaining games. We create nodes $x_1, \dots, x_n$ to represent the other teams, as well as nodes p_{ij} to represent each pair of nodes x_i and x_j. In addition, of course, we have the source s and the sink t. Add an edge from s to every team node, and one from every pair node to t. For a pair node p_{ij}, add edges from x_i and x_j with infinite capacity. The edge from pair node p_{ij} to t gets a capacity equal to the number of games left between x_i and x_j. If team x_i has won w_i games already, the edge from s to x_i gets a capacity of $W - w_i$ (the number it can win without overtaking the Greenskins).

As I said, each unit of flow represents one game. Imagine tracking a single unit from s to t. First, we come to a team node, representing the team that won this game. Then we come to a pair node, representing which team we were up against. Finally, moving along an edge to t, we gobble up a unit of capacity representing one match between the two teams in question. The only way we can saturate all the edges into t is if *all* the remaining games can be played under these conditions—that is, with no team winning more than W games in total. Thus, finding the maximum flow gives us our answer. For a more detailed correctness proof, either see Section 4.3 of *Introduction to Graph Theory* by Douglas B. West (see the references for Chapter 2) or take a look at the original source, *Possible winners in partially completed tournaments*, by B. L. Schwartz.

Choosing representatives. Ahuja et al. describe this amusing little problem. In a small town, there are n residents, $x_1, \ldots, x_n$. There are also m clubs, $c_1, \ldots, c_m$ and k political parties, $p_1, \ldots, p_k$. Each resident is a member of at least one club and can belong to exactly one political party. Each club must nominate one of its members to represent it on the town council. There is one catch, though: The number of representatives belonging to party p_i can be at most u_i. It is possible to find such a set of representatives? Again, we reduce to maximum flow. As is often the case, we represent the objects of the problem as nodes, and the constraints between them as edges and capacities. In this case, we have one node per resident, club, and party, as well as the source s and the sink t.

The units of flow represent the representatives. Thus, we give each club an edge from s, with a capacity of 1, representing the single person they can nominate. From each club, we add an edge to each of the people belonging to that club, as they form the candidates. (The capacities on these edges doesn't really matter, as long as it's at least 1.) Note that each person can have multiple in-edges (that is, belong to multiple clubs). Now add an edge from the residents to their political parties (one each). These edges, once again, have a capacity of 1 (the person is allowed to represent only a single club). Finally, add edges from the parties to t so that the edge from party p_i has a capacity of u_i, limiting the number of representatives on the council. Finding a maximum flow will now get us a valid set of nominations.

Of course, this max-flow solution gives only *a* valid set of nominations, not necessarily the one we *want*. We can assume that the party capacities u_i are based on democratic principles (some form of vote); shouldn't the choice of a representative similarly be based on the preferences of the club? Maybe they could hold votes to indicate how much they'd like each member to represent them, so the members get scores, say, equal to their percentages of the votes. We could then try to maximize the sum of these scores, while still ensuring that the nominations are valid, when viewed globally. See where I'm going with this? Exactly: We can extend the problem of Ahuja et al. by adding a *cost* to the edges from clubs to residents (equal to 100 – score, for example), and we solve the min-cost max-flow problem. The fact that we're getting a maximum flow will take care of the validity of the nominations, while the cost minimization will give us the best compromise, based on club preferences.

Doctors on vacation. Kleinberg and Tardos (see "References" in Chapter 1) describe a somewhat similar problem. Different objects and constraints, but the idea is somewhat similar still. The problem is assigning doctors to holiday days. At least one doctor must be assigned to each holiday day, but there are restrictions on how this can be done. First, each doctor is available on only some of the vacation days. Second, each doctor should be assigned to work on at most c vacation days in total. Third, each doctor should be assigned to work on only one day during each vacation period. Do you see how this can be reduced to maximum flow?

Once again, we have a set of objects with constraints between them. We need at least one node per doctor and one per vacation day, in addition to the sink s and the source t. We give each doctor an in-edge from s with a capacity c, representing the days that each doctor can work. Now we *could* start linking the doctors directly to the days, but how do we represent the idea of a vacation *period*? We could add one node for each, but there are individual constraints on each doctor for each period, so we'll need more nodes. Each doctor gets one node per vacation period and an out-edge to each one. For example, each doctor would have one Christmas node. If we set the capacity on these out-edges to 1, the doctors can't work more than one day in each period. Finally, we link these new period nodes to the days when the doctor is available. So if Dr Zoidberg can work only Christmas Eve and Christmas Day during the Christmas holiday, we add out-edges from his Christmas node to those two dates.

Finally, each vacation day gets an edge to t. The capacity we set on these depends on whether we want to find out how many doctors we can get or whether we want exactly one per vacation day. Either way, finding the maximum flow will give us the answer we're looking for. Just like we extended the previous problem, we could once again take preferences into account, by adding costs, for example on the edges from each doctor's vacation period node to the individual vacation days. Then, by finding the min-cost flow, we wouldn't find only a *possible* solution, we'd find the one that caused the least overall disgruntlement.

Supply and demand. Imagine that you're managing some form of planetary delivery service (or, if you prefer a less fanciful example, a shipping company). You're trying to plan out the distribution of some merchandise—*popplers*, for example. Each planet (or seaport) has either a certain supply or demand (measured in popplers per month), and your routes between these planets have a certain capacity. How do we model this?

In fact, the solution to this problem gives us a very nifty tool. Instead of just solving this specific problem (which is just a thinly veiled description of the underlying flow problem anyway), let's describe things a bit more generally. You have a network that's similar to the ones we've seen so far, except we no longer have a source or a sink. Instead, each node v has a *supply* $b(v)$. This value can also be negative, representing a *demand*. To keep things simple, we can assume that the supplies and demands sum to zero. Instead of finding the maximum flow, we now want to know if we can satisfy the demands using the available supplies. We call this a *feasible* flow with respect to b.

Do we need a new algorithm for this? Luckily, no. Reduction comes to the rescue, once again. Given a network with supplies and demands, we can construct a plain-vanilla flow network, as follows. First, we add a source s and a sink t. Then, every node v with a supply gets an in-edge from s with its supply as the capacity, while every node with a demand gets an out-edge to t, with its demand as the capacity. We now solve the maximum flow problem on this new network. If the flow saturates all the edges to the sink (and those from the source, for that matter), we have found a feasible flow (which we can extract by ignoring s and t and their edges).

Consistent matrix rounding. You have a matrix of floating-point numbers, and you want to round all the numbers to integers. Each row and column also has a sum, and you're also going to round those sums. You're free to choose whether to round up or down in each case (that is, whether to use math.floor or math.ceil), but you must make sure that the sum of the round numbers in each row and column is the same as the rounded column or row sum. (You can see this as a criterion that seeks to preserve some important properties of the original matrix after the rounding.) We call such a rounding scheme a *consistent rounding*.

This looks very numerical, right? You might not immediately think of graphs or network flows. Actually, this problem is easier to solve if we first introduce *lower bounds* on the flow in each edge, in addition to the capacity (which is an upper bound). This gives us a new initial hurdle: finding a feasible flow with respect to the bounds. Once we have a feasible flow, finding a maximum flow can be done with a slight modification of the Ford-Fulkerson approach, but how do we find this feasible initial flow? This is nowhere near as easy as finding a feasible flow with respect to supplies and demands. I'll just sketch out the main idea here—for details, consult Section 4.3 in *Introduction to Graph Theory*, by Douglas B. West, or Section 6.7 in *Network Flows*, by Ahuja et al.

The first step is to add an edge from t to s with infinite capacity (and a lower bound of zero). We now no longer have a flow network, but instead of looking for a flow, we can look for a *circulation*. A circulation is just like a flow, except that it has flow conservation at *every node*. In other words, there is no source or sink that is exempt from the conservation. The circulation doesn't appear somewhere and disappear somewhere else; it just "moves around" in the network. We still have both upper and lower bounds, so our task is now to find a *feasible circulation* (which will give us the feasible flow in the original graph).

If an edge e has lower and upper limits $l(e)$ and $u(e)$, respectively, we define $c(e) = u(e) - l(e)$. (The naming choice here reflects that we'll be using this as a capacity in a little while.) Now, for each node v, let $l^-(v)$ be the sum of the lower bounds on its in-edges, while $l^+(v)$ is the sum of the lower bounds on its out-edges. Based on these values, we define $b(v) = l^-(v) - l^+(v)$. Because each lower bound contributes both to its source and target node, the sum of b values is zero.

Now, magically enough, if we find a feasible flow with respect to the capacities c and the supplies and demands b (as discussed for the previous problem), we will also find a feasible circulation with respect to the lower and upper bounds l and u. Why is that? A feasible circulation must respect l and u, and the flow into each node much equal the flow out. If we can find *any* circulation with those properties, we're done. Now, let $f'(e) = f(e) - l(e)$. We can then enforce the lower and upper bounds on f by simply requiring that $0 \le f'(e) \le c(e)$, right?

Now consider the conservation of flow and circulation. We want to make sure that the circulation f into a node equals the circulation out of that node. Let's say the total flow f' into a node v minus the flow out of v equals $b(v)$—exactly the conservation requirement of our supply/demand problem. What happens to f? Let's say v has a single in-edge and a single out-edge. Now, say the in-edge has a lower bound of 3 and the out-edge has a lower bound of 2. This means that $b(v) = 1$.[6] We need one more unit of out-flow f' than in-flow. Let's say the in-flow is 0 and the out-flow is 1. When we transform these flows back to circulations, we have to add the lower bounds, giving us 3 for both the in-circulation and the out-circulation, so the sum is zero. (If this seems confusing, just try juggling the ideas about a bit, and I'm sure they'll "click.")

Now we know how to find a feasible flow with lower bounds (by first reducing to feasible circulations and then reducing again to feasible flows with supplies and demands). What does that have to do with matrix rounding?

---

[6]Note that the sum here is the *in-edge* lower bounds minus the *out-edge* lower bounds—the opposite of how we sum the flows. That's exactly the point.

Let $x_1, ..., x_n$ represent the rows of the matrix, and let $y_1, ..., y_m$ represent the columns. Also add a source s and a sink s. Give every row an in-edge from s, representing the row sums, and every column an out-edge to t, representing the column sums. Also, add an edge from every row to every column, representing the matrix elements. Every edge e then represents a real value r. Set $l(e) = \texttt{floor(r)}$ and $u(e) = \texttt{ceil(r)}$. A feasible flow from s to t with respect to l and u will give us exactly what we need—a consistent matrix rounding. (Do you see how?)

Summary

This chapter deals with a single core problem, finding maximum flows in flow networks, as well as specialized versions, such as maximum bipartite matching and finding edge-disjoint paths. You also saw how the minimum cut problem is the dual of the maximum flow problem, giving us two solutions for the price of one. Solving the minimum cost flow problem is also a close relative, requiring only that we switch the traversal method, using a shortest-path algorithm to find the cheapest augmenting path. The general idea underlying all of the solutions is that of iterative improvement, repeatedly finding an augmenting path that will let us improve the solution. This is the general Ford-Fulkerson method, which does not guarantee polynomial running time in general (or even termination, if you're using irrational capacities). Finding the augmenting path with the fewest number of edges, using BFS, is called the Edmonds-Karp algorithm and solves this problem nicely. (Note that this approach cannot be used in the min-cost case because there we have to find the shortest path with respect to the *capacities*, not the edge counts.) The max-flow problem and its relative are flexible and apply to quite a lot of problems. The challenge becomes finding the suitable reductions.

If You're Curious …

There is a truly vast amount of material out there on flow algorithm of various kinds. For example, there's Dinic's algorithm, which is a very close relative of the Edmonds-Karp algorithm (it actually predates it, and uses the same basic principles), with some tricks that improves the running time a bit. Or you have the push-relabel algorithm, which in most cases (except for sparse graphs) is faster than Edmonds-Karp. For the bipartite matching case, you have the Hopcroft-Karp algorithm, which improves on the running time by performing multiple *simultaneous* traversals. For min-cost bipartite matching, there is also the well-known *Hungarian algorithm*, as well as more recent heuristic algorithms that really fly, such as the cost scaling algorithm (CSA) of Goldberg and Kennedy. And if you want to dig into the foundations of augmenting paths, perhaps you'd like to read Berge's original paper, "Two Theorems in Graph Theory"?

There are more advanced flow problems, as well, involving lower bounds on edge flow, or so-called circulations, without sources or sinks. And there's the *multicommodity flow* problem, for which there are no efficient special-purpose algorithms (you need to solve it with a technique known as *linear programming*). And you have the matching problem—even the min-cost version—for general graphs. The algorithms for that are quite a bit more complex than the ones in this chapter.

A first stop for some gory details about flows might be a textbook such as *Introduction to Algorithms* by Cormen et al. (see the "References" section in Chapter 1), but if you'd like more breadth, as well as lots of example applications, I recommend *Network Flows: Theory, Algorithms, and Applications* by Ahuja, Magnanti, and Orlin. You may also want to check out the seminal work *Flows in Networks*, by Ford and Fulkerson.

Exercises

10-1. In some applications, such as when routing communication through switching points, it can be useful to let the *nodes* have capacities, instead of (or in addition to) the edges. How would you reduce this kind of problem to the standard max-flow problem?

10-2. How would you find vertex-disjoint paths?

10-3. Show that the worst-case running time of the augmenting path algorithm for finding disjoint paths is $\Theta(m^2)$, where m is the number of edges in the graph.

10-4. How would you find flow in an undirected network?

10-5. Implement a wrapper-object that looks like a graph but that dynamically reflects the residual network of an underlying flow network with a changing flow. Implement some of the flow algorithms in this chapter using plain implementations of the traversal algorithms to find augmenting paths.

10-6. How would you reduce the flow problem (finding a flow of a given magnitude) to the max-flow problem?

10-7. Implement a solution to the min-cost flow problem using Dijkstra's algorithm and weight adjustments.

10-8. In Exercise 4-3, you were inviting friends to a party and wanted to ensure that each guest knew at least k others there. You've realized that things are a bit more complicated. You like some friends more than others, represented by a real-valued *compatibility*, possibly negative. You also know that many of the guests will attend only if certain other guests attend (though the feelings need not be mutual). How would you select a feasible subset of potential guests that maximizes the sum of your compatibility to them? (You might also want to consider guests who *won't* come if certain others do. That's a bit harder, though—take a look at Exercise 11-19.)

10-9. In Chapter 4, four grumpy moviegoers were trying to figure out their seating arrangements. Part of the problem was that none of them would switch seats unless they could get their favorite. Let's say they were slightly less grumpy and were willing to switch places as required to get the best solution. Now, an optimal solution could be found by just adding edges to free seats until you run out. Use a reduction to the bipartite matching algorithm in this chapter to show that this is so.

10-10. You're having a team building seminar for n people, and you're doing two exercises. In both exercises, you want to partition crowd into groups of k, and you want to make sure that no one in the second round is in the same group as someone they were in a group with in the first round. How could you solve this with maximum flow? (Assume that n is divisible by k.)

10-11. You've been hired by an interplanetary passenger transport service (or, less imaginatively, an airline) to analyze one of its flight. The spaceship lands on planets $1...n$ in order and can pick up or drop off passengers at each stop. You know how many passengers want to go from planet every i to every other planet j, as well as the fare for each such trip. Design an algorithm to maximize the profit for the entire trip. (This problem is based on Application 9.4 in *Network Flows*, by Ahuja et al.)

References

Ahuja, R. K., Magnanti, T. L., and Orlin, J. B. (1993). *Network Flows: Theory, Algorithms, and Applications*. Prentice Hall.

Berge, C. (1957). Two theorems in graph theory. *Proceedings of the National Academy of Sciences of the United States of America* 43(9):842–844. http://www.pnas.org/content/43/9/842.full.pdf.

Busacker, R. G., Coffin, S. A., and Gowen, P. J. (1962). Three general network flow problems and their solutions. Staff Paper RAC-SP-183, Research Analysis Corporation, Operations Logistics Division. http://handle.dtic.mil/100.2/AD296365.

Ford, L. R. and Fulkerson, D. R. (1957). A simple algorithm for finding maximal network flows and an application to the hitchcock problem. Canadian Journal of Mathematics, 9:210–218. http://smc.math.ca/cjm/v9/p210.

Ford, L. R. and Fulkerson, D. R. (1962). *Flows in networks*. Technical Report R-375-PR, RAND Corporation. http://www.rand.org/pubs/reports/R375.

Jungnickel, D. (2007). *Graphs, Networks and Algorithms*, third edition. Springer.

Goh, C. J. and Yang, X. Q. (2002). *Duality in Optimization and Variational Inequalities*. Optimization Theory and Applications. Taylor & Francis.

Goldberg, A. V. and Kennedy, R. (1995). An efficient cost scaling algorithm for the assignment problem. *Mathematical Programming*, 71:153–178. http://theory.stanford.edu/~robert/papers/csa.ps.

Schwartz, B. L. (1966). Possible winners in partially completed tournaments. *SIAM Review*, 8(3):302–308. http://jstor.org/pss/2028206.

CHAPTER 11

■ ■ ■

Hard Problems and (Limited) Sloppiness

The best is the enemy of the good.

— Voltaire

This book is clearly about algorithmic problem solving. Until now, the focus has been on basic principles for algorithm design, as well as examples of important algorithms in many problem domains. Now, I'll give you a peek at the flip side of algorithmics: hardness. Although it is certainly possible to find efficient algorithms for many important and interesting problems, the sad truth is that most problems are really hard. In fact, most are so hard that there's little point in even trying to solve them. It then becomes important to recognize hardness, to show that a problem is intractable (or at least very likely so), and to know what alternatives there are to simply throwing your hands up.

There are three parts to this chapter. First, I'm going to explain the underlying ideas of one of the greatest unanswered questions in the world—and how it applies to you. Second, I'm going to build on these ideas and show you a bunch of monstrously difficult problems that you may very well encounter in one form or another. Finally, I'll show you how following the wisdom of Voltaire, and relaxing your requirements a bit, can get you closer to your goals than might seem possible, given the rather depressing news in the first two parts of the chapter.

As you read the following, you may wonder where all the code has gone. Just to be clear, most of the chapter is about the kind of problems that are simply *too hard*. It is also about how you uncover that hardness for a given problem. This is important because it explores the outer boundaries of what our programs can realistically *do*, but it doesn't really lead to any programming. Only in the last third of the chapter will I focus on (and give some code for) approximations and heuristics. These approaches will allow you to find usable solutions to problems that are too hard to solve optimally, efficiently, and in all generality. They achieve this by exploiting a loophole—the fact that in real life we may be content with a solution that is "good enough" along some or all of these three axes.

■ **Tip** It might be tempting to skip ahead to the seemingly more meaty part of the chapter, where the specific problems and algorithms live. If you are to make sense of that, though, I strongly suggest giving the more abstract parts a go and at least skimming the chapter from the beginning to get an overview.

Reduction Redux

From Chapter 4, I've been discussing reductions every now and then. Mostly, I've been talking about reducing to a problem you know how to solve—either smaller instances of the problem you're working on or a different problem entirely. That way, you've got a solution to this new, unknown problem as well, in effect proving that it's easy (or, at least, that you can solve it). Near the end of Chapter 4, though, I introduced a different idea: reducing in the other direction to prove *hardness*. In Chapter 6, I used this idea to give a lower bound on the worst-case running time of any algorithm solving the convex hull problem. Now we've finally arrived at the point where this technique is completely at home. Defining complexity classes (and problem hardness) is, in fact, what reductions are normally used for in most textbooks. Before getting into that, though, I'd like to really hammer home how this kind of hardness proof works, at the fundamental level. The concept is pretty simple (although the proofs themselves certainly need not be), but for some reason, many people (myself included) keep getting it backward. Maybe—just maybe—the following little story can help you when you try to remember how it works.

Let's say you've come to a small town where one of the main attractions is a pair of twin mountain peaks. The locals have affectionately called the two Castor and Pollux, after the twin brothers from Greek and Roman mythology. It is rumored that there's a long-forgotten gold mine on the top of Pollux, but many an adventurer has been lost to the treacherous mountain. In fact, so many unsuccessful attempts have been made to reach the gold mine that the locals have come to believe it can't be done. You decide to go for a walk and take a look for yourself.

After stocking up on donuts and coffee at a local roadhouse, you set off. After a relatively short walk, you get to a vantage point where you can see the mountains relatively clearly. From where you're standing, you can see that Pollux looks like a really hellish climb—steep faces, deep ravines, and thorny brush all around it. Castor, on the other hand, looks like a climber's dream. The sides slope gently, and it seems there are lots of handholds all the way to the top. You can't be sure, but it seems like it might be a nice climb. Too bad the gold mine isn't up there.

You decide to take a closer look and pull out your binoculars. That's when you spot something odd. There seems to be a small tower on top of Castor, with a zip line down to the peak of Pollux. Immediately, you give up any plans you had to climb Castor. Why? (If you don't immediately see it, it might be worth pondering for a bit.)[1]

Of course, we've seen the exact situation before, in the discussions of hardness in Chapters 4 and 6. The zip line makes it easy to get from Castor to Pollux, so if Castor were easy, someone would have found the gold mine already.[2] It's a simple contrapositive: If Castor were easy, Pollux would be too; Pollux is *not* easy, so Castor can't be either. This is exactly what we do when we want to prove that a problem (Castor) is hard. We take something we *know* is hard (Pollux) and show that it's easy to solve this hard problem using our new, unknown one (we uncover a zip line from Castor to Pollux).

As I've mentioned before, this isn't so confusing in itself. It can be easy to confuse things when we start talking about it in terms of reductions, though. For example, is it obvious to you that we're reducing Pollux to Castor here? The reduction is the zip line, which lets us use a solution to Castor as if it were a solution to Pollux. In other words, if you want to prove that problem X is hard, find some hard problem Y and reduce it to X.

■ **Caution**   The zip line goes in the *opposite direction of the reduction*. It's *crucial* that you don't get this mixed up, or the whole idea falls apart. The term *reduction* here means basically "Oh, that's easy, you just ..." In other words, if you reduce A to B, you're saying "You want to solve A? That's easy, you just solve B." Or in this case: "You want to scale Pollux? That's easy, just scale Castor (and take the zip line)." In other words, we've reduced the scaling of Pollux to the scaling of Castor (and *not* the other way around).

---

[1]You can assume that getting *down* from Pollux is easy enough. Perhaps there's a water slide? And that all of this was built before Pollux got so impregnable. Perhaps there was a rockslide?

[2]"An economics professor and a student were strolling through the campus. 'Look,' the student cried, 'there's a $100 bill on the path!' 'No, you are mistaken,' the wiser head replied. 'That cannot be. If there were actually a $100 bill, someone would have picked it up.'" (From *Compensation*, by G. T. Milkovich and J. M. Newman.)

A couple of things are worth noting here. First, we assume the zip line is *easy to use*. What if it wasn't a zip line but a horizontal line that you had to balance across? This would be really hard—so it wouldn't give us any information. For all we knew, people might easily get to the peak of Castor; they probably couldn't reach the gold mine on Pollux anyway, so what do we know? The other is that reducing in the opposite direction tells us nothing either. A zip line from Pollux to Castor wouldn't have impacted our estimate of Castor one bit. So, what if you could get to Castor from Pollux? You couldn't get to the peak of Pollux anyway!

Consider the diagrams of Figure 11-1. The nodes represent problems, and the edges represent easy reductions (that is, they don't matter, asymptotically). The thick line at the bottom is meant to illustrate "ground," in the sense that unsolved problems are "up in the sky," while solving them is equivalent to reducing them to nothing, or grounding them. The first image illustrates the case where an unknown problem u is reduced to a known, easy problem e. The fact that e is easy is represented by the fact that there's an easy reduction from e to the ground. Linking u to e, therefore, gives us a path from u to the ground—a solution.

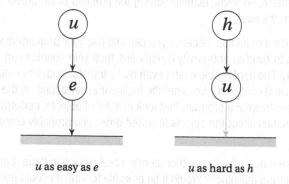

u as easy as e   *u as hard as h*

Figure 11-1. *Two uses of reduction: reducing an unknown problem to an easy one or reducing a hard problem to an unknown one. In the latter case, the unknown problem must be as hard as the known one*

Now look at the second image. Here, a known, hard problem is reduced to the unknown problem u. Can we have an edge from u to the ground (like the gray edge in the figure)? That would give us a path from h to the ground—but such a path cannot exist, or h wouldn't be hard!

In the following, I'll be using this basic idea not only to show that problems are hard but also to *define* some notions of hardness. As you may (or may not) have noticed, there is some ambiguity in the term *hard* here. It can basically have two different meanings:

- The problem is intractable—any algorithm solving it must be exponential.

- We don't know whether the problem is intractable, but no one has ever been able to find a polynomial algorithm for it.

The first of these means that the problem is hard for a computer to solve, while the second means that it's hard for people (and *maybe* computers as well). Take another look at the rightmost image in Figure 11-1. How would the two meaning of "hard" work here? Let's take the first case: We *know* that h is intractable. It's *impossible* to solve it efficiently. A solution to u (that is, a reduction to ground) would imply a solution to h, so no such solution can exist. Therefore, u must also be intractable.

The second case is a bit different—here the hardness involves a lack of knowledge. We don't *know* if problem h is intractable, although we know that it seems difficult to find a solution. The core insight is still that if we reduce h to u, then u is *at least as hard as h*. If h is intractable, then so is u. Also, the fact that many people have tried to find a solution to h makes it seem less likely that we'll succeed, which also means that it may be improbable that u is tractable. The more effort has been directed at solving h, the more astonishing it would be if u were tractable (because then so would h). This is, in fact, *exactly* the situation for a whole slew of practically important problems: We don't *know* if they're intractable, but most people are still highly convinced that they are. Let's take a closer look at these rascal problems.

REDUCTION BY SUBPROBLEM

While the idea of showing hardness by using reductions can be a bit abstract and strange, there is one special case (or, in some ways, a different perspective) that can be easy to understand: if your problem has a hard subproblem, then the problem as a whole is (obviously) hard. In other words, if solving your problem means that you also have to solve a problem that is known to be hard, you're basically out of luck. For example, if your boss asks you to create an antigravity hoverboard, you could probably do a lot of the work, such as crafting the board itself or painting on a nice pattern. However, actually solving the problem of circumventing gravity makes the whole endeavor doomed from the start.

So, how is this a reduction? It's a reduction, because you can still use your problem to solve the hard subproblem. In other words, if you're able to *build* an antigravity hoverboard, then your solution can (again, quite obviously) be used to circumvent gravity. The hard problem isn't even really transformed, as in most reductions; it's just embedded in a (rather irrelevant) context. Or consider the loglinear lower bound on the worst-case running time for general sorting. If you were to write a program that took in a set of objects, performed some operations on them, and then output information about the objects in sorted order, you probably couldn't do any better than loglinear in the worst case.

But why "probably"? Because it depends on whether there's a real reduction there. Could your program conceivably be used as a "sorting machine"? Would it be possible for me, if I could use your program as I wanted, to feed it objects that would let me sort any real numbers? If yes, then the bound holds. If no, then maybe it doesn't. For example, maybe the sorting is based on integers that can be sorted using counting sort? Or maybe you actually create the sorting keys yourself, so the objects can be output in any order you please? The question of whether your problem is *expressive* enough—whether it can express the general sorting problem. This is, in fact, one of the key insights of this chapter: that problem hardness is a matter of expressiveness.

Not in Kansas Anymore?

As I wrote this chapter for the first edition, the excitement had only just started dying down around the Internet after a scientific paper was published online, claiming to prove to have solved the so-called P versus NP problem, concluding that P does not equal NP.[3] Although the emerging consensus is that the proof is flawed, the paper created a tremendous interest—at least in computer science circles. Also, less credible papers with similar claims (or the converse, that P equals NP) keep popping up at regular intervals. Computer scientists and mathematicians have been working on this problem since the 1970s, and there's even a million-dollar prize for the solution.[4] Although much progress has been made in *understanding* the problem, no real solution seems forthcoming. Why is this so hard? And why is it so important? And what on Earth are P and NP?

---

[3]Vinay Deolalikar. *P is not equal to NP*. August 6, 2010.
[4]http://www.claymath.org/millennium-problems

The thing is, we don't really know what kind of a world we're living in. To use *The Wizard of Oz* as an analogy—we may *think* we're living in Kansas, but if someone were to prove that P = NP, we'd most definitely not be in Kansas anymore. Rather, we'd be in some kind of wonderland on par with Oz, a world Russel Impagliazzo has christened Algorithmica.[5] What's so grand about Algorithmica, you say? In Algorithmica, to quote a well-known song, "You never change your socks, and little streams of alcohol come trickling down the rocks." More seriously, life would be a lot less problematic. If you could state a mathematical problem, you could also solve it automatically. In fact, programmers no longer would have to tell the computer what to do—they'd only need to give a clear description of the desired output. Almost any kind of optimization would be trivial. On the other hand, cryptography would now be very hard because breaking codes would be so very, very easy.

The thing is, P and NP are seemingly *very different beasts*, although they're both classes of problems. In fact, they're classes of *decision problems*, problems that can be answered with *yes* or *no*. This could be a problem such as "Is there a path from s to t with a weight of at most w?" or "Is there a way of stuffing items in this knapsack that gives me a value of at least v?" The first class, P, is defined to consist of those problems we can *solve in polynomial time* (in the worst case). In other words, if you turn almost any of the problems we've looked at so far into a decision problem, the result would belong to P.

NP seems to have a much laxer definition[6]: It consists of any decision problems that can be solved in polynomial time by a "magic computer" called a *nondeterministic Turing machine*, or NTM. This is where the N in NP comes from—NP stands for "nondeterministically polynomial." As far as we know, these nondeterministic machines are super-powerful. Basically, at any time where they need to make a choice, they can just guess, and *by magic*, they'll always guess right. Sounds pretty awesome, right?

Consider the problem of finding the shortest path from s to t in a graph, for example. You already know quite a bit about how to do this with algorithms of the more … nonmagical kind. But what if you had an NTM? You'd just start in s and look at the neighbors. Which way should you go? Who knows—just take a guess. Because of the machine you're using, you'll always be right, so you'll just magically walk along the shortest path with no detours. For such a problem as the shortest path in a DAG, for example, this might not seem like such a huge win. It's a cute party trick, sure, but the running time would be linear either way.

But consider the first problem in Chapter 1: visiting all the towns of Sweden exactly once, as efficiently as possible. Remember how I said it took about 85 CPU-years to solve this problem with state-of-the-art technology a few years ago? If you had an NTM, you'd just need one computation step per town. Even if your machine were mechanical with a hand crank, it should finish the computation in a matter of seconds. This *does* seem pretty powerful, right? And magical?

Another way of describing NP (or, for that matter, nondeterministic computers) is to look at the difference between *solving* a problem and *checking* a solution. We already know what solving a problem means. If we are to *check* the solution to a decision problem, we'll need more than a "yes" or "no"—we also require some kind of proof, or *certificate* (and this certificate is required to be of polynomial size). For example, if we want to know whether there is a path from s to t, a certificate might be the actual path. In other words, if you solved the problem and found that the answer was "yes," you could use the certificate to convince me that this was true. To put it differently, if you managed to prove some mathematical statement, your proof could be the certificate.

The requirement, then, for a problem to belong to NP, is that I be able to check the certificate for any "yes" answers in polynomial time. A nondeterministic Turing machine can solve any such problem by simply guessing the certificate. Magic, right?

Well, maybe … You see, that's the thing. We know that P is *not* magical—it's full of problems we know very well how to solve. NP *seems* like a huge class of problems, and any machine that can solve all of them would be beyond this world. The thing is, in Algorithmica, there is such a thing as an NTM. Or, rather, our quite ordinary, humdrum computers (deterministic Turing machines) would turn out to be *just as powerful*. They had the magic in them all along! If P = NP, we could solve any (decision) problem that had a practical (verifiable) solution.

---

[5]Actually, Impagliazzo's definition of Algorithmica also permits some slightly different scenarios.
[6]Note the "seems to." We don't really know whether P = NP, so the definition might actually be equivalent.

Meanwhile, Back in Kansas …

All right, Algorithmica is a magical world, and it would be totally awesome if we turned out to be living in it—but chances are, we're not. In all likelihood, there is a very real difference between *finding* a proof and *checking* it—between *solving* a problem and simply *guessing* the right solution every time. So if we're still in Kansas, why should we care about all of this?

Because it gives us a very useful notion of hardness. You see, we have a bunch of mean-spirited little beasties that form a class called NPC. This stands for "NP-complete," and these are the *hardest problems in all of NP*. More precisely, each problem in NPC is *at least as hard as every other problem* in NP. We don't *know* if they're intractable, but if you were to solve just one of these tough-as-nails problems, you would automatically have transported us all to Algorithmica! Although the world population might rejoice at not having to change its socks anymore, this isn't a very likely scenario (which I hope the previous section underscored). It would be utterly amazing but seems totally unfeasible.

Not only would it be earth-shatteringly weird, but given the enormous upsides and the monumental efforts that have been marshaled to break just a single one of these critters, the four decades of failure (so far) would seem to bolster our confidence in the wager that you're not going to be the one to succeed. At least not anytime soon. In other words, the NP-complete problems *might* be intractable (hard for computers), but they've *certainly* been hard for humans so far.

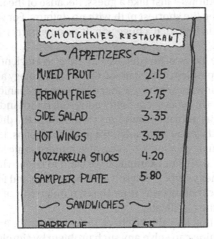

NP-Complete. General solutions get you a 50% tip. (`http://xkcd.com/287`)

But how does this all work? Why would slaying a single NPC monster bring all of NP crashing down into P and send us tumbling into Algorithmica? Let's return to our reduction diagrams. Take a look at Figure 11-2. Assume, for now, that all the nodes represent problems in NP (that is, at the moment we're treating NP as "the whole world of problems"). The left image illustrates the idea of completeness. Inside a class of problems, a problem c is *complete* if all problems in that class can "easily" be reduced to c.[7] In this case, the class we're talking about is NP, and reductions are "easy" if they're polynomial. In other words, a problem c is NP-complete if (1) c itself is in NP, and (2) every problem in NP can be reduced to c in polynomial time.

---

[7]Although I don't make a big fuss about it here, the fact that such problems exist is actually pretty weird.

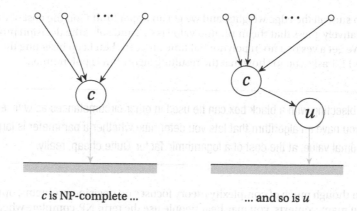

c is NP-complete ...   ... and so is u

Figure 11-2. *An NP-complete problem is a problem in NP that is at least as hard as all the others. That is, all the problems in NP can be reduced to it*

The fact that every problem (in NP) can be reduced to these tough-nut problems means that they're the hard core—if you can solve them, you can solve any problem in NP (and suddenly, we're not in Kansas anymore). The figure should help make this clear: Solving c means adding a solid arrow from c to the ground (reducing it to nothing), which immediately gives us a path from every *other* problem in NP to the ground, *via c*.

We have now used reductions to define the toughest problems in NP, but we can extend this idea slightly. The right image in Figure 11-2 illustrates how we can use reductions *transitively*, for hardness proofs such as the ones we've been discussing before (like the one on the right in Figure 11-1, for example). We know that c is hard, so reducing it to u proves that u is hard. We already know how this works, but this figure illustrates a slightly more technical reason for why it is true in this case. By reducing c to u, we have now placed u in the same position that c was in originally. We already knew that every problem in NP could be reduced to c (meaning that it was NP-complete). Now we also know that every problem can be reduced to u, via c. In other words, u also satisfies the definition of NP-completeness—and, as illustrated, if we can solve it in polynomial time, we will have established that P = NP.

Now, so far I've only been talking about decision problems. The main reason for this is that it makes quite a few things in the formal reasoning (much of which I won't cover here) a bit easier. Even so, these ideas are relevant for other kinds of problems, too, such as the many optimization problems we've been working with in this book (and will work with later in this chapter).

Consider, for example, the problem of finding the shortest tour of Sweden. Because it's not a decision problem, it's not in NP. Even so, it's a very difficult problem (in the sense "hard for humans to solve" and "most likely intractable"), and just like anything in NP, it would suddenly be easy if we found ourselves in Algorithmica. Let's consider these two points separately.

The term *completeness* is reserved for the hardest problems *inside* a class, so the NP-complete problems are the class bullies of NP. We can use the same hardness criterion for problems that might fall *outside* the class as well, though. That is, any problem that is at least as hard (determined by polynomial-time reduction) as any problem in NP, but that need not *itself* be in NP. Such problems are called *NP-hard*. This means that another definition of the class NPC, of NP-complete problems, is that it consists of all the NP-hard problems in NP. And, yes, finding the shortest route through a graph (such as through the towns of Sweden) is an NP-hard problem called the Traveling Salesman (or Salesrep) Problem, or often just TSP. I'll get back to that problem a bit later.

About the other point: Why would an optimization problem such as this be easy if P = NP? There are some technicalities about how a certificate could be used to find the actual route, and so on, but let's just focus on the difference between the yes-no nature of NP, and the numerical length we're looking for in the TSP problem. To keep things simple, let's say all edge weights are integers. Also, because P = NP, we can solve both the yes and no instances of our decision problems in polynomial time (see the sidebar "Asymmetry, Co-NP, and the Wonders of Algorithmica"). One way to proceed is then to use the decision problem as a black box and perform a binary search for the optimal answer.

For example, we can sum all the edge weights, and we get an upper limit C on the cost of the TSP tour, with 0 as a lower limit. We then tentatively guess that the minimum value is $C/2$ and solve the decision problem, "Is there a tour of length at most $C/2$?" We get a yes or a no in polynomial time and can then keep bisecting the upper or lower half of the value range. Exercise 11-1 asks you to show that the resulting algorithm is polynomial.

■ **Tip**   This strategy of bisecting with a black box can be used in other circumstances as well, even outside the context of complexity classes. If you have an algorithm that lets you determine whether a parameter is large enough, you can bisect to find the right/optimal value, at the cost of a logarithmic factor. Quite cheap, really.

In other words, even though much of complexity theory focuses on decision problems, optimization problems aren't all that different. In many contexts, you may hear people use the term NP-complete when what they really mean is NP-hard. Of course, you should be careful about getting things right, but whether you show a problem to be NP-hard or NP-complete is not all that crucial for the practical purpose of arguing its hardness. (Just make sure your reductions are in the right direction!)

ASYMMETRY, CO-NP, AND THE WONDERS OF ALGORITHMICA

The class of NP is defined asymmetrically. It consists of all decision problems whose *yes* instances can be solved in polynomial time with an NTM. Notice, however, that we don't say anything about the *no* instances. So, for example, it's quite clear that if there is a tour visiting each town in Sweden exactly once, an NTM would answer "yes" in a reasonable amount of time. If the answer is "no," however, it may take its sweet time.

The intuition behind this asymmetry is quite accessible, really. The idea is that in order to answer "yes," the NTM need only (by "magic") find a single set of choices leading to a computation of that answer. In order to answer "no," however, it needs to determine that no such computation exists. Although this does seem very different, we don't really know if it *is*, though. You see, here we have another one of many "versus questions" in complexity theory: NP versus co-NP.

The class co-NP is the class of the complements of NP problems. For every "yes" answer, we now want "no," and vice versa. If NP is truly asymmetric, then these two classes are different, although there is overlap between them. For example, all of P lies in their intersection, because both the yes and no instances in P can be solved in polynomial time with an NTM (and by a deterministic Turing machine, for that matter).

Now consider what would happen if an NP-complete problem FOO was found in the intersection of NP and co-NP. First of all, all problems in NP reduce to NPC, so this would mean that *all* of NP would be inside co-NP (because we could now deal with their complements, through FOO). Could there still be problems in co-NP outside of NP? Consider such a hypothetical problem, BAR. Its complement, co-BAR, would be in NP, right? But because NP was inside co-NP, co-BAR would *also* be in co-NP. That means that its complement, BAR, would be in NP. But, but, but ... we assumed it to be *outside* of NP—a contradiction!

In other words, if we find a single NP-complete problem in the intersection of NP and co-NP, we'll have shown that NP = co-NP, and the asymmetry has disappeared. As stated, all of P is in this intersection, so if P = NP, we'll also have NP = co-NP. That means that in Algorithmica, NP is pleasantly symmetric.

Note that this conclusion is often used to argue that problems that *are* in the intersection of NP and co-NP are probably *not* NP-complete, because it is (strongly) believed that NP and co-NP are different. For example, no one has found a polynomial solution to the problem of factoring numbers, and this forms the basis of much of cryptography. Yet the problem is in both NP and co-NP, so most computer scientists believe that it's *not* NP-complete.

But Where Do You Start? And Where Do You Go from There?

I hope the basic ideas are pretty clear now: The class NP consists of all decision problems whose "yes" answers can be verified in polynomial time. The class NPC consists of the hardest problems in NP; all problems in NP can be reduced to these in polynomial time. P is the set of problems in NP that we can solve in polynomial time. Because of the way the classes are defined, if there's the least bit of overlap between P and NPC, we have P = NP = NPC. We've also established that if we have a polynomial-time reduction from an NP-complete problem to some other problem in NP, that second problem must also be NP-complete. (Naturally, all NP-complete problems can be reduced to each other in polynomial time; see Exercise 11-2.)

This has given us what *seems* to be a useful notion of hardness—but so far we haven't even established that there *exists* such a thing as an NP-complete problem, let alone *found* one. How would we do that? Cook and Levin to the rescue!

In the early 1970s, Steven Cook proved that there is indeed such a problem, and a little later, Leonid Levin independently proved the same thing. They both showed that a problem called *boolean satisfiability*, or SAT, is NP-complete. This result has been named for them both and is now known as the Cook-Levin theorem. This theorem, which gives us our starting point, is quite advanced, and I can't give you a full proof here, but I'll try to outline the main idea. (A full proof is given by Garey and Johnson, for example; see the "References" section.)

The SAT problem takes a logical formula, such as (A or not B) and (B or C), and asks whether there is any way of making it true (that is, of *satisfying* it). In this case, of course, there is. For example, we could set A = B = True. To prove that this is NP-complete, consider an arbitrary problem FOO in NP and how you'd reduce it to SAT. The idea is to first construct an NTM that will solve FOO in polynomial time. This is possible by definition (because FOO is in NP). Then, for a given instance *bar* of FOO (that is, for a given input to the machine), you'd construct (in polynomial time) a logical formula (of polynomial size) expressing the following:

- The input to the machine was *bar*.

- The machine did its job correctly.

- The machine halts and answers "yes."

The tricky part is how you'd express this using Boolean algebra, but once you do, it seems clear that the NTM is, in fact, *simulated* by the SAT problem given by this logical formula. If the formula is satisfiable—that is, if (and only if) we can make it true by assigning truth values to the various variables (representing, among other things, the magical choices made by the machine), then the answer to the original problem should be "yes."

To recap, the Cook-Levin theorem says that SAT is NP-complete, and the proof basically gives you a way of simulating NTMs with SAT problems. This holds for the basic SAT problem and its close relative, Circuit-SAT, where we use a logical (digital) circuit, rather than a logical formula.

One important idea here is that all logical formulas can be written in what's called *conjunctive normal form* (CNF), that is, as a conjunction (a sequence of ands) of clauses, where each clause is a sequence of ors. Each occurrence of a variable can be either of the form A or its negation, not A. The formulas may not be in CNF to begin with, but they can be transformed automatically (and efficiently). Consider, for example, the formula A and (B or (C and D)). It is entirely equivalent with this other formula, which is in CNF: A and (B or C) and (B or D).

Because any formula can be rewritten efficiently to a (not too large) CNF version, it should not come as a surprise that CNF-SAT is NP-complete. What's interesting is that even if we restrict the number of variables per clause to k and get the so-called k-CNF-SAT (or simply k-SAT) problem, we can still show NP-completeness as long as $k > 2$. You'll see that many NP-completeness proofs are based on the fact that 3-SAT is NP-complete.

IS 2-SAT NP-COMPLETE? WHO KNOWS ...

When working with complexity classes, you need to be aware of special cases. For example, variations of the knapsack problem (or subset sum, which you'll encounter in a bit) are used for encryption. The thing is, many cases of the knapsack problem are quite easy to solve. In fact, if the knapsack capacity is bounded by a polynomial (as a function of the item count), the problem is in P (see Exercise 11-3). If one is not careful when constructing the problem instances, the encryption can be quite easy to break.

We have a similar situation with k-SAT. For $k \geq 3$, this problem is NP-complete. For $k = 2$, though, it can be solved in polynomial time. Or consider the longest path problem. It's NP-hard in general, but if you happen to know that your graph is a DAG, you can solve it in linear time. Even the shortest path problem is, in fact, NP-hard in the general case. The solution here is to assume the absence of negative cycles.

If you're not working with encryption, this phenomenon is good news. It means that even if you've encountered a problem whose general form is NP-complete, it might be that the specific instances you need to deal with are in P. This is an example of what you might call the *instability of hardness*. Tweaking the requirements of your problem *slightly* can make a huge difference, making an intractable problem tractable, or even an undecidable problem (such as the halting problem) decidable. This is the reason why approximation algorithms (discussed later) are so useful.

Does this mean that 2-SAT is not NP-complete? Actually, no. Drawing this conclusion is an easy trap to fall into. This is true only if P ≠ NP because otherwise all problems in P are NP-complete. In other words, our NP-completeness proof fails for 2-SAT, and we can show it's in P, but we do *not* know that it's *not* in NPC.

Now we have a place to start: SAT and its close friends, Circuit SAT and 3-SAT. There are still lots of problems to examine, though, and replicating the feat of Cook and Levin seems a bit daunting. How, for example, would you show that every problem in NP could be solved by finding a tour through a set of towns?

This is where we (finally) get to start working with reductions. Let's look at one of the rather simple NP-complete problems, that of finding a Hamilton cycle. I already touched upon this problem in Chapter 5 (in the sidebar "Island-Hopping in Kaliningrad"). The problem is to determine whether a graph with n nodes has a cycle of length n; that is, can you visit each node exactly once and return to your starting point, following the edges of the graph?

This doesn't immediately look as expressive as the SAT problem—there we had access to the full language of propositional logic, after all—so encoding NTMs seems like a bit much. As you'll see, it's not. The Hamilton cycle problem is every bit as expressive as the SAT problem. What I mean by this is that there is a polynomial-time reduction from SAT to the Hamilton cycle problem. In other words, we can use the machinery of the Hamilton cycle problem to create a SAT solving machine!

I'll walk you through the details, but before I do, I'd like to ask you to keep the big picture in the back of your mind: the general idea of what we're doing is that we're treating one problem as a sort of machine, and we're almost programming that machine to solve a different problem. The reduction, then, is the metaphorical programming. With that in mind, let's see how we can encode Boolean formulas as graphs so that a Hamilton cycle would represent satisfaction ...

To keep things simple, let's assume that the formula we want to satisfy is in CNF form. We can even assume 3-SAT (although that's not really necessary). That means we have a series of clauses we need to satisfy, and in each of these, we need to satisfy at least one of the elements, which can be variables (such as A) or their negations (not A). Truth needs to be represented by paths and cycles, so let's say we encode the truth value of each variable as a *direction* of a path.

This idea is illustrated in Figure 11-3. Each variable is represented by a single row of nodes, and these nodes are chained together with antiparallel edges so that we can move from left to right or from right to left. One direction (say, left to right) signifies that the variable is set to *true*, while the other direction means *false*. The number of nodes is immaterial, as long as we have enough.[8]

---

[8]We need to stick with a polynomial number of nodes, of course.

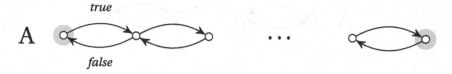

Figure 11-3. *A single "row," representing the variable A the Boolean expression we're trying to satisfy. If the cycle passes through from left to right, the variable is true; otherwise, it's false*

Before we start trying to encode the actual formula, we want to force our machine to set each variable to exactly one of the two possible logical values. That is, we want to make sure that any Hamilton cycle will pass through each row (with the direction giving us the truth value). We also have to make sure the cycle is free to switch direction when going from one row to the next, so the variables can be assigned independently of each other. We can do this by connecting each row to the next with two edges, at the anchor points at either end (highlighted in Figure 11-3), as shown in Figure 11-4.

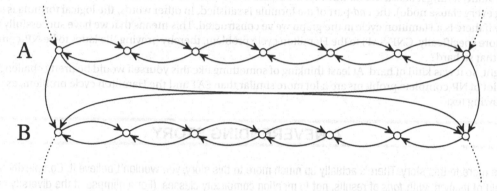

Figure 11-4. *The rows are linked so the Hamilton cycle can maintain or switch its direction when going from one variable to the next, letting A and B be true or false, independently of each other*

If we have only a set of rows connected as shown in Figure 11-4, there will be no Hamilton cycle in the graph. We can pass only from one row to the next and have no way of getting up again. The final touch to the basic row structure, then, is to add one source node *s* at the top (with edges to the left and right anchors of the first row) and a sink node *t* at the bottom (with edges from the left and right anchors of the last row) and then to add an edge from *t* to *s*.

Before moving on, you should convince yourself that this structure really does what we want it to. For *k* variables, the graph we have constructed so far will have 2^k different Hamilton cycles, one for each possible assignment of truth values to the variables, with the truth values represented by the cycle going left or right in a given row.

Now that we've encoded the idea of assigning truth values to a set of logical variables in our Hamilton machine, we just need a way of encoding the actual formula involving these variables. We can do that by introducing a single node for each clause. A Hamilton cycle will then have to visit each of these exactly one time. The trick is to hook these clause nodes onto our existing rows to make use of the fact that the rows already encode truth values. We set things up so that the cycle can take a detour from the path, via the clause node, but *only if it's going in the right direction*. So, for example, if we have the clause (A or not B), we'll add a detour to the A row that requires the cycle to be going left to right, and we add another detour (via the same clause node) to the B row, but this time from right to left (because of the not). The only thing we need to watch out for is that no two detours can be linked to the rows in the same places—that's why we need to have multiple nodes in each row, so we have enough for all the clauses. You can see how this would work for our example in Figure 11-5.

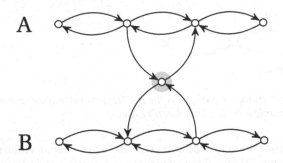

Figure 11-5. *Encoding the clause (A or not B) using a clause node (highlighted), and adding detours requiring A to be true (left to right) and B to be false (right to left) in order to satisfy the clause (that is, visit the node)*

After encoding the clauses in this way, each clause can be satisfied as long as at least one of its variables has the right truth value, letting it take a detour through the clause node. Because a Hamilton cycle must visit every node (including every clause node), the *and*-part of the formula is satisfied. In other words, the logical formula is satisfiable if and only if there is a Hamilton cycle in the graph we've constructed. This means that we have successfully reduced SAT (or, more specifically, CNF-SAT) to the Hamilton cycle problem, thereby proving the latter to be NP-complete! Now, was that so hard?

All right, so it was kind of hard. At least thinking of something like this yourself would be pretty challenging. Luckily, a lot of NP-complete problems are a lot more similar than SAT and the Hamilton cycle problem, as you'll see in the following text.

A NEVERENDING STORY

There's more to this story. There's actually so much more to this story, you wouldn't believe it. Complexity theory is a field of its own, with *tons* of results, not to mention complexity classes. (For a glimpse of the diversity of classes that are being studied, you could visit The Complexity Zoo, https://complexityzoo.uwaterloo.ca.)

One of the formative examples of the field is a problem that is *much* harder than the NP-complete ones: Alan Turing's halting problem (mentioned in Chapter 4). It simply asks you to determine whether a given algorithm will terminate with a given input. To see why this is actually impossible, imagine you have a function halt that takes a function and an input as its parameters so that halt(A, X) will return true if A(X) terminates and false otherwise. Now, consider the following function:

```
def trouble(A):
    while halt(A, A): pass
```

The call halt(A, A) determines whether A halts when applied to itself. Still comfortable with this? What happens if you evaluate trouble(trouble)? Basically, if it halts, it doesn't, and if it doesn't, it does ... We have a paradox (or a contradiction), meaning that halt cannot possibly exist. The halting problem is *undecidable*. In other words, solving it is impossible.

But you think impossible is hard? As a great boxer once said, impossible is nothing. There is, in fact, such a thing as *highly* undecidable, or "very impossible." For an entertaining introduction to these things, I recommend David Harel's *Computers Ltd: What They Really Can't Do*.

A Ménagerie of Monsters

In this section, I'll give you a brief glimpse of a few of the thousands of known NP-complete problems. Note that the descriptions here serve two purposes at once. The first, and most obvious, purpose is to give you an overview of lots of hard problems so that you can more easily recognize (and prove) hardness in whatever problems you may come across in your programming. I could have given you that overview by simply listing (and briefly describing) the problems. However, I'd also like to give you some examples of how hardness proofs work, so I'm going to describe the relevant reductions throughout this section.

Return of the Knapsack

The problems in this section are mostly about selecting subsets. This is a kind of problem you can encounter in many settings. Perhaps you're trying to choose which projects to finish within a certain budget? Or pack different-sized boxes into as few trucks as possible? Or perhaps you're trying to fill a fixed set of trucks with a set of boxes that will give you as much profit as possible? Luckily, many of these problems have rather efficient solutions in practice (such as the pseudopolynomial solutions to the knapsack problems in Chapter 8 and the approximations discussed later in this chapter), but if you want a polynomial algorithm, you're probably out of luck.[9]

■ **Note**   Pseudopolynomial solutions are known for only *some* NP-hard problems. In fact, for many NP-hard problems, you *can't* find a pseudopolynomial solution unless P = NP. Garey and Johnson call these *NP-complete in the strong sense*. (For more details, see Section 4.2 in their book, *Computers and Intractability*.)

The knapsack problem should be familiar by now. I discussed it with a focus on the fractional version in Chapter 7, and in Chapter 8 we constructed a pseudopolynomial solution using dynamic programming. In this section, I'll have a look at both the knapsack problem itself and a few of its friends.

Let's start with something seemingly simple,[10] the so-called *partition problem*. It's really innocent-looking—it's just about equitable distribution. In its simplest form, the partition problem asks you to take a list of numbers (integers, say) and partition it into two lists with equal sums. Reducing SAT to the partition problem is a bit involved, so I'm just going to ask you to trust me on this one (or, rather, see the explanation of Garey and Johnson, for example).

Moving from the partition problem to others is easier, though. Because there's seemingly so little complexity involved, using other problems to simulate the partition problem can be quite easy. Take the problem of *bin packing*, for example. Here we have a set of items with sizes in the range from 0 to k, and we want to pack them into bins of size k. Reducing from the partition problem is quite easy: We just set k to half the sum of the numbers. Now if the bin packing problem manages to cram the numbers into two bins, the answer to the partition problem is yes; otherwise, the answer is no. This means that the bin packing problem is NP-hard.

Another well-known problem that is simple to state is the so-called subset sum problem. Here you once again have a set of numbers, and you want to find a subset that sums to some given constant, k. Once again, finding a reduction is easy enough. For example, we can reduce from the partition problem, by (once again) setting k to half the sum of the numbers. A version of the subset sum problem locks k to zero—the problem is still NP-complete, though (Exercise 11-4).

---

[9]Both for this section and the following two, you might want to try to show that the examples in the initial paragraphs are, in fact, NP-hard.

[10]To make it easier to follow the arguments in these sections, I'll generally progress (using reductions) from seemingly simple problems to more expressive ones. In reality, of course, they're all just as expressive (and hard)—but some problems hide this better than others.

Now, let's look at the actual (integral, nonfractional) knapsack problem. Let's deal with the 0-1 version first. We can reduce from the partition problem again, if we want, but I think it's easier to reduce from subset sum. The knapsack problem can also be formulated as a decision problem, but let's say we're working with the same optimization version we've seen before: We want to maximize the sum of item values, while keeping the sum of item sizes below our capacity. Let each item be one of the numbers from the subset sum problem, and let both value and weight be equal to that number.

Now, the best possible answer we could get would be one where we match the knapsack capacity *exactly*. Just set the capacity to k, and the knapsack problem will give us the answer we seek: Whether we can fill up the knapsack completely is equivalent to whether we can find a sum of k.

To round up this section, I'll just briefly touch upon one of the most obviously expressive problems out there: *integer programming*. This is a version of the technique of *linear programming*, where a linear function is optimized, under a set of linear constraints. In integer programming, though, you also require the variables to take on only integral values—which breaks all existing algorithms. It also means that you can reduce from all kinds of problems, with these knapsack-style ones as an obvious example. In fact, we can show that 0-1 integer programming, which is special case, is NP-hard. Just let each item of the knapsack problem be a variable, which can take on the value of 0 or 1. You then make two linear functions over these, with the values and weights as coefficients, respectively. You optimize the one based on the values and constrain the one based on the weights to be below the capacity. The result will then give you the optimal solution to the knapsack problem.[11]

What about the unbounded integral knapsack? In Chapter 8, I worked out a pseudopolynomial solution, but is it really NP-hard? It does seem rather closely related to the 0-1 knapsack, for sure, but the correspondence isn't really close enough that a reduction is obvious. In fact, this is a good opportunity to try your hand at crafting a reduction—so I'm just going to direct you to Exercise 11-5.

Cliques and Colorings

Let's move on from subsets of numbers to finding structures in graphs. Many of these problems are about conflicts. For example, you may be writing a scheduling software for a university, and you're trying to minimize timing collisions involving teachers, students, classes, and auditoriums. Good luck with that one. Or perhaps you're writing a compiler, and you want to minimize the number of registers used by finding out which variables can share a register? As before, you may find acceptable solutions in practice, but you may not be able to optimally solve large instances in general.

I have talked about bipartite graphs several times already—graphs whose nodes can be partitioned into two sets so that all edges are *between* the sets (that is, no edges connect nodes in the same set). Another way of viewing this is as a *two-coloring*, where you color every node as either black or white (for example), but you ensure that no neighbors have the same color. If this is possible, the graph is bipartite.

Now what if you'd like to see whether a graph is *tripartite*, that is, whether you can manage a *three-coloring*? As it turns out, that's not so easy. (Of course, a k-coloring for $k > 3$ is no easier; see Exercise 11-6.) Reducing 3-SAT to three-coloring is, in fact, not so hard. It is, however, a bit involved (like the Hamilton cycle proof, earlier in this chapter), so I'm just going to give you an idea of how it works.

Basically, you build some specialized components, or widgets, just like the rows used in the Hamilton cycle proof. The idea here is to first create a triangle (three connected nodes), where one represents true, one false, and one is a so-called *base* node. For a variable A, you then create a triangle consisting of one node for A, one for not A, and the third being the base node. That way, if A gets the same color as the true node, then not A will get the color of the false node, and vice versa.

At this point, a widget is constructed for each clause, linking the nodes for either A or not A to other nodes, including the true and false nodes, so that the only way to find a three-coloring is if one of the variable nodes (of the form A or not A) gets the same color as the true node. (If you play around with it, you'll probably find ways of doing this. If you want the full proof, it can be found in several algorithm books, such as the one by Kleinberg and Tardos; see "References" in Chapter 1.)

---

[11]This paragraph is probably easier to understand if you already know a little bit about linear programming. If you didn't quite catch all of it, don't worry—it's not really essential.

Now, given that k-coloring is NP-complete (for $k > 2$), so is finding the *chromatic number* of a graph—how many colors you need. If the chromatic number is less than or equal to k, the answer to the k-coloring problem is yes; otherwise, it is no. This kind of problem may seem abstract and pretty useless, but nothing could be further from the truth. This is an essential problem for cases where you need to determine certain kinds of resource needs, both for compilers and for parallel processing, for example.

Let's take the problem of determining how many registers (a certain kind of efficient memory slots) a code segment needs. To do that, you need to figure out which variables will be used at the same time. The variables are nodes, and any conflicts are represented by edges. A conflict simply means that two variables are (or may be) used at the same time and therefore can't share a register. Now, finding the smallest number of registers that can be used is equivalent to determining the chromatic number of this graph.

A close relative of the k-coloring is the so-called *clique cover* problem (also known as *partitioning into cliques*). A clique is, as you may recall, simply a complete graph, although the term is normally used when referring to a complete *subgraph*. In this case, we want to split a graph into cliques. In other words, we want to divide the nodes into several (nonoverlapping) sets so that within each set, every node is connected to every other. I'll show you why this is NP-hard in a minute, but first, let's have a closer look at cliques.

Simply determining whether a graph has a clique of a given size is NP-complete. Let's say you're analyzing a social network and you want to see whether there's a group of k people, where every person is friends with every other. Not so easy … The optimization version, max-clique, is at least as hard, of course. The reduction from 3-SAT to the clique problem once again involves creating a simulation of logical variables and clauses. The idea here is to use three nodes for each clause (one for each literal, whether it be a variable or its negation) and then add edges between all nodes representing *compatible* literals, that is, those that can be true at the same time. (In other words, you add edges between all nodes except between a variable and its negation, such as A and not A.)

You do *not*, however, add edges *inside a clause*. That way, if you have k clauses and you're looking for a clique of size k, you're *forcing* at least one node from each clause to be in the clique. Such a clique would then represent a valid assignment of truth values to the variables, and you'd have solved 3-SAT by finding a clique. (Cormen et al. give a detailed proof; see "References" in Chapter 1.)

The clique problem has a very close relative—a yin to its yang, if you will—called the *independent set* problem. Here, the challenge is to find a set of k independent nodes (that is, nodes that don't have any edges to each other). The optimization version is to find the largest independent set in the graph. This problem has applications to scheduling resources, just like graph coloring. For example, you might have some form of traffic system where various lanes in an intersection are said to be in conflict if they can't be in use at the same time. You slap together a graph with edges representing conflicts, and the largest independent set will give you the largest number of lanes that can be in use at any one time. (More useful in this case, of course, would be to find a *partition* into independent sets; I'll get back to that.)

Do you see the family resemblance to clique? Right. It's exactly the same, except that instead of edges, we now want the *absence* of edges. To solve the independent set problem, we can simply solve the clique problem on the *complement* of the graph—where every edge has been removed and every missing edge has been added. (In other words, every truth value in the adjacency matrix has been inverted.) Similarly, we can solve the clique problem using the independent set problem—so we've reduced both ways.

Now let's return to the idea of a clique cover. As I'm sure you can see, we might just as well look for an *independent set cover* in the complement graph (that is, a partitioning of the nodes into independent sets). The point of the problem is to find a cover consisting of k cliques (or independent sets), with the optimization version trying to minimize k. Notice that there are no conflicts (edges) inside an independent set, so all nodes in the same set can receive the same color. In other words, finding a k-clique-partition is essentially equivalent to finding a k-coloring, which we know is NP-complete. Equivalently, both optimization versions are NP-hard.

Another kind of cover is a *vertex* (or *node*) cover, which consists of a subset of the nodes in the graph and covers the edges. That is, each edge in the graph is incident to at least one node in the cover. The decision problem asks you to find a vertex cover consisting of at most k nodes. What we'll see in a minute is that this happens exactly when the graph has an independent set consisting of at least $n-k$ nodes, where n is the total number of nodes in the graph. This gives us a reduction that goes both ways, just like the one between cliques and independent sets.

The reduction is straightforward enough. Basically, a set of nodes is a vertex cover if and only if the remaining nodes form an independent set. Consider any pair of nodes that are not in the vertex cover. If there were an edge between them, it would not have been covered (a contradiction), so there cannot be an edge between them. Because this holds for any pair of nodes outside the cover, these nodes form an independent set. (A single node would work on its own, of course.)

The implication goes the other way as well. Let's say you have an independent set—do you see why the remaining nodes must form a vertex cover? Of course, any edge not connected to the independent set will be covered by the remaining nodes. But what if an edge is connected to one of your independent nodes? Well, its other end can't be in the independent set (those nodes aren't connected), and that means that the edge is covered by an outside node. In other words, the vertex cover problem is NP-complete (or NP-hard, in its optimization version).

Finally, we have the *set covering problem*, which asks you to find a so-called set cover of size at most k (or, in the optimization version, to find the smallest one). Basically, you have a set S and another set F, consisting of subsets of S. The union of all the sets in F is equal to S. You're trying to find a small subset of F that covers all the elements of S. To get an intuitive understanding of this, you can think of it in terms of nodes and edges. If S were the nodes of a graph, and F, the edges (that is, pairs of nodes), you'd be trying to find the smallest number of edges that would cover (be incident to) all the nodes.

■ **Caution**   The example used here is the so-called edge cover problem. Although it's a useful illustration of the set covering problem, you should not conclude that the edge cover problem is NP-complete. It can, in fact, be solved in polynomial time.

It should be easy enough to see that the set covering problem is NP-hard, because the vertex cover problem is basically a special case. Just let S be the edges of a graph and F consist of the neighbor sets for every node, and you're done.

Paths and Circuits

This is our final group of beasties—and we're drawing near to the problem that started the book. This material mainly has to do with navigating efficiently, when there are requirements on locations (or states) you have to pass through. For example, you might try to work out movement patterns for an industrial robot, or the layout of some kinds of electronic circuits. Once more you may have to settle for approximations or special cases. I've already shown how finding a Hamilton cycle in general is a daunting prospect. Now let's see if we can shake out some other hard path and circuit-related problems from this knowledge.

First, let's consider the issue of direction. The proof I gave that checking for Hamilton cycles was NP-complete was based on using a directed graph (and, thus, finding a directed cycle). What about the undirected case? It might seem we lose some information, and the earlier proof doesn't hold here. However, with some widgetry, we can simulate direction with an undirected graph!

The idea is to split every node in the directed graph into three, basically replacing it by a length-two path. Imagine coloring the nodes: You color the original node blue, but you add a red in-node and a green out-node. All directed in-edges now become undirected edges linked to the red in-node, and the out-edges are linked to the green out-node. Clearly, if the original graph had a Hamilton cycle, the new one will as well. The challenge is getting the implication the other way—we need "if and only if" for the reduction to be valid.

Imagine that our new graph *does* have a Hamilton cycle. The node colors of this cycle would be either "... red, blue, green, red, blue, green ..." or "... green, blue, red, green, blue, red ..." In the first case, the blue nodes will represent a directed Hamilton cycle in the original graph, as they are entered only through their in-nodes (representing the original in-edges) and left through out-nodes. In the second case, the blue nodes will represent a *reverse* directed Hamilton cycle—which also tells us what we need to know (that is, that we have a usable directed Hamilton cycle in the other direction).

So, now we know that directed and undirected Hamilton cycles are basically equivalent (see Exercise 11-8). What about the so-called Hamilton *path* problem? This is similar to the cycle problem, except you're no longer required to end up where you started. Seems like it might be a bit easier? Sorry. No dice. If you can find a Hamilton path, you can use that to find a Hamilton cycle. Let's consider the directed case (see Exercise 11-9 for the undirected case). Take any node v with both in- and out-edges. (If there is no such node, there can be no Hamilton cycle.) Split it into two nodes, v and v', keeping all in-edges pointing to v and all out-edges starting at v'. If the original graph had a Hamilton cycle, the transformed one will have a Hamilton path starting at v' and ending at v (we've basically just snipped the cycle at v, making a path). Conversely, if the new graph has a Hamilton path, it *must* start at v' (because it has no in-edges), and, similarly, it must end at v. By merging these nodes back together, we get a valid Hamilton cycle in the original graph.

■ **Note** The "Conversely …" part of the previous paragraph ensures we have implication in both directions. This is important, so that both "yes" and "no" answers are correct when using the reduction. This does *not*, however, mean that I have reduced in both directions.

Now, perhaps you're starting to see the problem with the *longest path* problem, which I've mentioned a couple of times. The thing is, finding the longest path between two nodes will let you check for the presence of a Hamilton path! You might have to use every pair of nodes as end points in your search, but that's just a quadratic factor—the reduction is still polynomial. As we've seen, whether the graph is directed or not doesn't matter, and adding weights simply generalizes the problem. (See Exercise 11-11 for the acyclic case.)

What about the shortest path? In the general case, finding the shortest path is exactly equivalent to finding the longest path. You just need to negate all the edge weights. However, when we disallow negative cycles in the shortest path problem, that's like disallowing positive cycles in the longest path problem. In both cases, our reductions break down (Exercise 11-12), and we no longer know whether these problems are NP-hard. (In fact, we strongly believe they're *not* because we can solve them in polynomial time.)

■ **Note** When I say we disallow negative cycles, I mean *in the graph*. There's no specific ban on negative cycles in the paths themselves because they are assumed to be *simple paths* and therefore cannot contain any cycles at all, negative or otherwise.

Now, *finally*, I'm getting to the great (or, by now, perhaps not so great) mystery of why it was so hard to find an optimal tour of Sweden. As mentioned, we're dealing with the *traveling salesman problem*, or TSP. There are a few variations of this problem (most of which are also NP-hard), but I'll start with the most straightforward one, where you have a weighted undirected graph, and you want to find a route through all the nodes, so that the weight sum of the route is as small as possible. In effect, what we're trying to do is finding the *cheapest Hamilton cycle*—and if we're able to find that, we've also determined that there *is* a Hamilton cycle. In other words, TSP is just as hard.

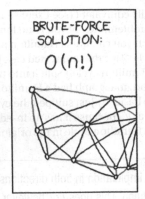

Travelling Salesman Problem. *What's the complexity class of the best linear programming cutting-plane techniques? I couldn't find it anywhere. Man, the Garfield guy doesn't have these problems ...* (http://xkcd.com/399)

But there's another common version of TSP, where the graph is assumed to be *complete*. In a complete graph, there will always be a Hamilton cycle (if we have at least three nodes), so the reduction doesn't really work anymore. What now? Actually, this isn't as problematic as it might seem. We can reduce the previous TSP version to the case where the graph must be complete by setting the edge weights of the superfluous edges to some very large value. If it's large enough (more than the sum of the other weights), we will find a route through the original edges, if possible.

The TSP problem might seem overly general for many real applications, though. It allows completely arbitrary edge weights, while many route planning tasks don't require such flexibility. For example, planning a route through geographical locations or the movement of a robot arm requires only that we can represent distances in Euclidean space.[12] This gives us a lot more information about the problem, which should make it easier to solve—right? Again, sorry. No. Showing that Euclidean TSP is NP-hard is a bit involved, but let's look at a more general version, which is still a lot more specific than the general TSP: *the metric TSP problem.*

A *metric* is a distance function $d(a,b)$, which measures the distance between two points, *a* and *b*. This need not be a straight-line, Euclidean distance, though. For example, when working out flight paths, you might want to measure distances along *geodesics* (curved lines along the earth's surface), and when laying out a circuit board, you might want to measure horizontal and vertical distance separately, adding the two (resulting in so-called *Manhattan distance* or *taxicab distance*). There are plenty of other distances (or distance-like functions) that qualify as metrics. The requirements are that they be symmetric, non-negative real-valued functions that yield a distance of zero only from a point to itself. Also, they need to follow the *triangular inequality*: $d(a,c) \leq d(a,b) + d(b,c)$. This just means that the shortest distance between two points is given directly by the metric—you can't find a shortcut by going through some other points.

Showing that this is still NP-hard isn't too difficult. We can reduce from the Hamilton cycle problem. Because of the triangular inequality, our graph has to be complete.[13] Still, we can let the original edges get a weight of one, and the added edges, a weight of, say, two (still doesn't break things). The metric TSP problem will give us a minimum-weight Hamilton cycle of our metric graph. Because such a cycle always consists of the same number of edges (one per node), it will consist of the original (unit-weight) edges if and only if there is a Hamilton cycle in the original, arbitrary graph.

Even though the metric TSP problem is also NP-hard, you will see in the next section that it differs from the general TSP problem in a very important way: We have polynomial *approximation algorithms* for the metric case, while approximating general TSP is itself an NP-hard problem.

---

[12]Unless we want to take relativity or the curvature of the earth into account ...
[13]Any infinite distances would break it, unless it was completely without edges or consisted of only two nodes.

When the Going Gets Tough, the Smart Get Sloppy

As promised, after showing you that a lot of rather innocent-looking problems are actually unimaginably hard, I'm going to show you a way out: sloppiness. I mentioned earlier the idea of "the instability of hardness," that even small tweaks to the problem requirements can take you from utterly horrible to pretty nice. There are many kinds of tweaks you can do—I'm going to cover only two. In this section, I'll show you what happens if you allow a certain percentage of sloppiness in your search for optimality; in the next section, we'll have a look at the "fingers crossed" school of algorithm design.

Let me first clarify the idea of approximation. Basically, we'll be allowing the algorithm to find a solution that may not be optimal, but whose value is at most a given percentage off. More commonly, this percentage is given as a factor, or *approximation ratio*. For example, for a ratio of 2, a minimization algorithm would guarantee us a solution at most twice the optimum, while a maximization problem would give us one at least half the optimum.[14] Let's see how this works, by returning to a promise I made back in Chapter 7.

What I said was that the unbounded integer knapsack problem can be approximated to within a factor of two using greed. As for exact greedy algorithms, designing the solution here is trivial (just use the same greedy approach as for fractional knapsack); the problem is showing that it's correct. How can it be that, if we keep adding the item type with the highest unit value (that is, value-to-weight ratio), we're guaranteed to achieve at least half the optimum value? How on Earth can we know this when we have no idea what the optimum value *is*?

This is the crucial point of approximation algorithms. We don't know the exact ratio of the approximation to the optimum—we give only a guarantee for how bad it can get. This means that if we get an estimate on *how good the optimum can get*, we can work with that instead of the actual optimum, and our answer will still be valid. Let's consider the maximization case. If we know that the optimum will never be *greater* than A and we know our approximation will never be *smaller* than B, we can be certain that the ratio of the two will never be greater than A/B.[15]

For the unbounded knapsack, can you think of some upper limit to the value you can achieve? Well, we can't get anything better than filling the knapsack to the brim with the item type with the highest unit value (sort of like an unbounded fractional solution). Such a solution might very well be impossible, but we certainly can't do *better*. Let this optimistic bound be A.

Can we give a lower bound B for our approximation, or at least say something about the ratio A/B? Consider the first item you add. Let's say it uses up more than half the capacity. This means we can't add any more of this type, so we're already worse off than the hypothetical A. But we *did* fill at least *half* the knapsack with the best item type, so even if we stop right now, we know that A/B is at most 2. If we manage to add more items, the situation can only improve.

What if the first item *didn't* use more than half the capacity?[16] Good news, everyone: We can add another item of the same kind! In fact, we can keep adding items of this kind until we've used at least half the capacity, ensuring that the bound on the approximation ratio still holds.

There are tons and tons of approximation algorithms out there—with plenty of books about this topic alone. If you want to learn more about the topic, I suggest getting one of those (both *The Design of Approximation Algorithms* by Williamson and Shmoys and *Approximation Algorithms* by Vijay V. Vazirany are excellent choices). I will show you one particularly pretty algorithm, though, for approximating the metric TSP problem.

What we're going to do is, once again, to find some kind of invalid, optimistic solution and then tweak that until we get a valid (but probably not optimal) solution. More specifically, we're going to aim for *something* (not necessarily a valid Hamilton cycle) that has a weight of at most twice the optimum solution and then tweak and repair that something using shortcuts (which the triangle inequality guarantees won't make things worse), until we actually get a Hamilton cycle. That cycle will then also be at most twice the length of the optimum. Sounds like a plan, no?

---

[14]Note that we always divide the larger of the two (optimum and approximation) by the smaller.
[15]For the minimization case, just reverse the logic, and consider the ratio B/A.
[16]Notice the use of "proof by cases" here. It's a really useful technique.

What, though, would be only a few shortcuts away from a Hamilton cycle and yet be at most twice the length of the optimum solution? We can start with something simpler: What's guaranteed to have a weight that is no greater than the shortest Hamilton cycle? Something we know how to find? A minimum spanning tree! Just think about it. A Hamilton cycle connects all nodes, and the absolutely cheapest way of connecting all nodes is using a minimum spanning tree.

A tree is not a cycle, though. The idea of the TSP problem is that we're going to *visit* every node, walking from one to the next. We could certainly visit every node following the edges of a tree, as well. That's exactly what Trémaux might do, if he were a salesman (see Chapter 5).[17] In other words, we could follow the edges in a depth-first manner, backtracking to get to other nodes. This gives us a *closed walk* of the graph but not a *cycle* (because we're revisiting nodes and edges). Consider the weight of this closed walk, though. We're walking along each edge exactly twice, so it's twice the weight of the spanning tree. Let this be our optimistic (yet invalid) solution.

The great thing about the metric case is that we can skip the backtracking and take shortcuts. Instead of going back along edges we've already seen, visiting nodes we've already passed through, we can simply make a beeline for the next unvisited node. Because of the triangular inequality, we're guaranteed that this won't degrade our solution, so we end up with an approximation ratio bound of two! (This algorithm is often called the "twice around the tree" algorithm, although you could argue that the name doesn't really make that much sense because we're going around the tree only once.)

Implementing this algorithm might not seem entirely straightforward. It kinda is, actually. Once we have our spanning tree, all we need is to traverse it and avoid visiting nodes more than once. Just reporting the nodes as they're discovered during a DFS would actually give us the kind of solution we want. You can find an implementation of this algorithm in Listing 11-1. You can find the implementation of prim in Listing 7-5.

Listing 11-1. The "Twice Around the Tree" Algorithm, a 2-Approximation for Metric TSP

```
from collections import defaultdict

def mtsp(G, r):                          # 2-approx for metric TSP
    T, C = defaultdict(list), []         # Tree and cycle
    for c, p in prim(G, r).items():      # Build a traversable MSP
        T[p].append(c)                   # Child is parent's neighbor
    def walk(r):                         # Recursive DFS
        C.append(r)                      # Preorder node collection
        for v in T[r]: walk(v)           # Visit subtrees recursively
    walk(r)                              # Traverse from the root
    return C                             # At least half-optimal cycle
```

There is one way of improving this approximation algorithm that is conceptually simple but quite complicated in practice. It's called Christofides' algorithm, and the idea is that instead of walking the edges of the tree twice, it creates a *min-cost matching* among the odd-degree nodes of the spanning tree.[18] This means that you can get a closed walk by following the edges of the tree once, and the edges of the matching once (and then fixing the solution by adding shortcuts, as before). We already know that the spanning tree is no worse than the optimum cycle. It can also be shown that the weight of the minimum matching is no greater than *half* the optimum cycle (Exercise 11-15), so in sum, this gives us a 1.5-approximation, the best bound known so far for this problem. The problem is that the algorithm for finding a min-cost matching is pretty convoluted (it's certainly a *lot* worse than finding a min-cost *bipartite* matching, as discussed in Chapter 10), so I'm not going to go into details here.

---

[17]I'm guessing he'd think of something better, though.
[18]You might want to verify for yourself that the number of odd-degree nodes in any graph is even.

Given that we can find a solution for the metric TSP problem that is a factor of 1.5 away from the optimum, even though the problem is NP-hard, it may be a bit surprising that finding such an approximation algorithm—or *any* approximation within a fixed factor of the optimum—is itself an NP-hard problem for TSP in general (even if the TSP graph is complete). This is, in fact, the case for several problems, which means that we can't necessarily rely on approximation as a practical solution for all NP-hard optimization problems.

To see why approximating TSP is NP-hard, we do a reduction from the Hamilton cycle problem to the approximation. You have a graph, and you want to find out whether it has a Hamilton cycle. To get the complete graph for the TSP problem, we add any missing edges, but we make sure we give them *huge* edge weights. If our approximation ratio is k, we make sure these edge weights are greater than km, where m is the number of edges in the original graph. Then an optimum tour of the new graph would be at most m if we could find a Hamilton tour of the original, and if we included even *one* of the new edges, we'd have broken our approximation guarantee. That means that if (and only if) there were a Hamilton cycle in the original graph, the approximation algorithm for the new one would find it—meaning that the approximation is at least as hard (that is, NP-hard).

Desperately Seeking Solutions

We've looked at one way that hardness is unstable—sometimes finding near-optimal solutions can be *vastly* easier than finding optimal ones. There is another way of being sloppy, though. You can create an algorithm that is basically a brute-force solution but that uses guesswork to try to avoid as much computation as possible. With a little luck, if the instance you're trying to solve isn't one of the really hard ones, you may actually be able to find a solution pretty quickly! In other words, the sloppiness here is not about the quality of the solution but about the running time guarantees.

This is a bit like with quicksort, which has a quadratic worst-case running time but which is loglinear in the average case, with very low constant factors. Much of the reasoning about hard problems deals with what guarantees we can give about the worst-case performance, but in practice, that may not be all we care about. In fact, even if we're not in Russel Impagliazzo's fantasy world, Algorithmica, we may be in one of his *other* worlds, which he calls Heuristica. Here, NP-hard problems are still intractable in the worst case, but they're tractable in the *average* case. And even if this isn't the case, it certainly *is* the case that by using heuristic methods, we can often solve problems that might seem impossible.

There are plenty of methods in this vein. The A* algorithm discussed in Chapter 9, for example, can be used to search through a space of solutions in order to find a correct or optimal one. There are also such heuristic search techniques as artificial evolution and simulated annealing (see "If You're Curious ..." later in this chapter). In this section, though, I'll show you a really cool and actually pretty simple idea, which can be applied to hard problems such as those discussed in this chapter but which can also serve as a quick-and-dirty way of solving any kind of algorithmic problem, even ones for which there are polynomial solutions. This could be useful either because you can't think of a custom algorithm or because your custom algorithm is too slow.

The technique is called *branch and bound* and is particularly well-known in the field of artificial intelligence. There's even a special version of it (called *alpha-beta pruning*) used in programs playing games. (For example, if you have a chess program, chances are there's some branch and bound going on inside it.) In fact, branch and bound is one of the main tools for solving NP-hard problems, including such general and expressive ones as integer programming. Even though this awesome technique follows a very straightforward schema, it can be hard to implement in a completely general fashion. Chances are, if you're going to use it, you'll have to implement a version that is customized to your problem.

Branch and bound, or B&B, is based on gradually building solutions, sort of like a lot of greedy algorithms (see Chapter 7). In fact, which new building block to consider is often chosen greedily, resulting in so-called best-first branch and bound. However, instead of fully committing to this new building block (or this way of extending the solution), all possibilities are considered. At the core, we're dealing with a brute-force solution. The thing that can make it all work, though, is that whole avenues of exploration can be pruned away, by reasoning about how promising (or, rather, unpromising) they are.

To make this more concrete, let's consider a specific example. In fact, let's revisit one we've worked with in several ways before, the 0-1 knapsack problem. In 1967, Peter J. Kolesar published the paper "A branch and bound algorithm for the knapsack problem," where he describes exactly this approach. As he puts it, "A branch and bound algorithm proceeds by repeatedly partitioning the class of all feasible solutions into smaller and smaller subclasses in such a way that ultimately an optimal solution is obtained." These "classes" are what we get by constructing partial solutions.

For example, if we decide to include item x in our knapsack, we have implicitly constructed the class of all solutions including x. There is, of course, also the complement of this class, all solutions that do *not* include x. We will need to examine both of these classes, unless we can somehow reach the conclusion that one of them cannot contain the optimum. You can picture this as a tree-shaped state space, a concept mentioned in Chapter 5. Each node is defined by two sets: the items that are *included* in the knapsack, and the items that are *excluded* from it. Any remaining items are as yet undetermined.

In the root of this (abstract, implicit) tree structure, no objects are included or excluded, so all are undetermined. To expand a node into two child nodes (the *branching* part), we decide on one of the undecided objects and *include* it to get one child and *exclude* it to get the other. If a node has no undecided items, it's a leaf, and we can get no further.

It should be clear that if we explore this tree fully, we will examine every possible combination of included and excluded objects (a brute-force solution). The whole idea of branch and bound algorithms is to add *pruning* to our traversal (just like in bisection and search trees), so we visit as little as possible of the search space. As for approximation algorithms, we introduce upper and lower bounds. For a maximization problem, we use a *lower* bound on the optimum (based on what we've found so far) and use an *upper* bound on the solutions in any given subtree (based on some heuristic).[19] In other words, we're comparing a *conservative* estimate of the optimum with an *optimistic* estimate of what we can find in a given subtree. If the conservative bound is better than the optimistic bound on what a subtree contains, that subtree cannot hold the optimum, and so it is pruned (the *bounding* part).

In the basic case, the conservative bound for the optimum is simply the best value we've found so far. It can be extremely beneficial to have this bound be as high as possible when the B&B starts running, so we might want to spend some time on that first. (For example, if we were looking for a metric TSP tour, which is a minimization problem, we could set the initial upper bound to the result of our approximation algorithm.) To keep things simple for our knapsack example, though, let's just keep track of the best solution, starting out with a value of zero. (Exercise 11-16 asks you to improve on this.)

The only remaining conundrum is how to find an upper bound for a partial solution (representing a subtree of the search space). If we don't want to lose the actual solution, this bound has to be a true upper bound; we don't want to exclude a subtree based on overly gloomy predictions. Then again, we shouldn't be too optimistic ("This might have *infinite* value! Yay!") because then we'd never get to exclude anything. In other words, we need to find an upper bound that is as tight (low) as we can make it. One possibility (and the one used by Kolesar) is to pretend we're dealing with the *fractional* knapsack problem and then use the greedy algorithm on that. This solution can never be worse than the actual optimum we're looking for (Exercise 11-17), and it turns out it's a pretty tight bound for practical purposes.

You can see one possible implementation of the 0-1 knapsack B&B in Listing 11-2. To keep things simple, the code calculates only the *value* of the optimum solution. If you want the actual solution structure (which items are included), you'll need to add some additional bookkeeping. As you can see, instead of explicitly managing two sets for each node (included and excluded items), only the weight and value sums of items included so far are used, with a counter (m) indicating which items have been considered (in order). Each node is a generator, which will (when prompted) generate any promising children.

---

[19]If you were minimizing, the bounds would, of course, be swapped.

■ **Note** The `nonlocal` keyword, which is used in Listing 11-2, lets you modify a variable in a surrounding scope, just like `global` lets you modify the global scope. However, this feature was new in Python 3.0. If you want similar functionality in earlier Pythons, simply replace the initial `sol = 0` by `sol = [0]` and later access the value using the expression `sol[0]` instead of just `sol`. (For more information, see PEP 3104, available at `http://legacy.python.org/dev/peps/pep-3104`.)

And the Moral of the Story Is ...

All right. This chapter may not be the easiest one in the book, and it may not be entirely obvious how to use some of the topics here in your day-to-day coding. To clarify the main points of the chapter, I thought I'd try to give you some advice on what to do when a monster problem crosses your path.

- First, follow the first two pieces of problem solving advice in Chapter 4. Are you sure you really understand the problem? Have you looked *everywhere* for a reduction (for example, do you know of any algorithms that seem even remotely relevant)?

- If you're stumped, look again for reductions, but this time *from* some known NP-hard problems, rather than *to* problems you know how to solve. If you find one, at least you know the problem is hard, so there's no reason to beat yourself up.

- Consider the last bit of problem solving advice from Chapter 4: Are there any extra assumptions you can exploit to make the problem less monstrous? The longest path problem is NP-hard in general, but in a DAG, you can solve it easily.

- Can you introduce some slack? If your solution needn't be 100 percent optimal, perhaps there is an approximation algorithm you can use? You could either design one or research the literature on the subject. If you don't need polynomial worst-case guarantees, perhaps something like branch and bound could work?

Listing 11-2. Solving the Knapsack Problem with the Branch and Bound Strategy

```
from __future__ import division
from heapq import heappush, heappop
from itertools import count

def bb_knapsack(w, v, c):
    sol = 0                                          # Solution so far
    n = len(w)                                       # Item count

    idxs = list(range(n))
    idxs.sort(key=lambda i: v[i]/w[i],               # Sort by descending unit cost
        reverse=True)

    def bound(sw, sv, m):                            # Greedy knapsack bound
        if m == n: return sv                         # No more items?
        objs = ((v[i], w[i]) for i in idxs[m:])      # Descending unit cost order
        for av, aw in objs:                          # Added value and weight
            if sw + aw > c: break                    # Still room?
            sw += aw                                 # Add wt to sum of wts
```

```
        sv += av                              # Add val to sum of vals
        return sv + (av/aw)*(c-sw)            # Add fraction of last item

    def node(sw, sv, m):                      # A node (generates children)
        nonlocal sol                          # "Global" inside bb_knapsack
        if sw > c: return                     # Weight sum too large? Done
        sol = max(sol, sv)                    # Otherwise: Update solution
        if m == n: return                     # No more objects? Return
        i = idxs[m]                           # Get the right index
        ch = [(sw, sv), (sw+w[i], sv+v[i])]   # Children: without/with m
        for sw, sv in ch:                     # Try both possibilities
            b = bound(sw, sv, m+1)            # Bound for m+1 items
            if b > sol:                       # Is the branch promising?
                yield b, node(sw, sv, m+1)    # Yield child w/bound

    num = count()                             # Helps avoid heap collisions
    Q = [(0, next(num), node(0, 0, 0))]       # Start with just the root
    while Q:                                  # Any nodes left?
        _, _, r = heappop(Q)                  # Get one
        for b, u in r:                        # Expand it ...
            heappush(Q, (b, next(num), u))    # ... and push the children

    return sol                                # Return the solution
```

If all else fails, you could implement an algorithm that *seems* reasonable and then use experiments to see whether the results are good enough. For example, if you're scheduling lectures to minimize course collisions for students (a kind of problem that's easily NP-hard), you may not need a guarantee that the result will be optimal, as long as the results are good enough.[20]

Summary

This chapter has been about hard problems and some of the things you can do to deal with them. There are many classes of (seemingly) hard problems, but the most important one in this chapter is NPC, the class of NP-complete problems. NPC forms the hard core of NP, the class of decision problems whose solutions can be verified in polynomial time—basically every decision problem of any real practical use. Every problem in NP can be reduced to every problem in NPC (or to any so-called NP-hard problem) in polynomial time, meaning that if any NP-complete problem can be solved in polynomial time, *every* problem in NP can be, as well. Most computer scientists find this scenario highly unlikely, although no proof as yet exists either way.

The NP-complete and NP-hard problems are legion, and they crop up in many contexts. This chapter gave you a taste of these problems, including brief proof sketches for their hardness. The basic idea for such proofs is to rely on the Cook-Levin theorem, which says that the SAT problem is NP-complete, and then to reduce in polynomial time either from that, or from some other problem we have already shown to be NP-complete or NP-hard.

The strategies hinted at for actually *dealing* with these hard problems are based on controlled sloppiness. Approximation algorithms let you control precisely how far your answer will be from the optimum, while heuristic search methods such as branch and bound guarantee you an optimal solution but can take an unspecified amount of time to finish.

---

[20]And if you want to get fancy, you could always research some of the many heuristic search methods originating in the field of artificial intelligence, such as genetic programming and tabu search. See the "If You're Curious ..." section for more.

If You're Curious …

There are lots of books out there that deal with computational complexity, approximation algorithms, and heuristic algorithms; see the "References" section for some ideas.

One area that I haven't touched upon at all is that of so-called *metaheuristics*, a form of heuristic search that gives few guarantees but that can be surprisingly powerful. For example, there is artificial evolution, with so-called genetic programming, or GP, as one of its most well-known techniques. In GP, you maintain a virtual population of structures, usually interpreted as little computer programs (although they could be Hamilton cycles in the TSP problem, for example, or whatever structure you'd like to build). In each generation, you evaluate these individual (for example, computing their length when solving the TSP problem). The most promising ones are allowed to have offspring—new structures in the next generation, based on the parents, but with some random modifications (either simple mutation, or even combinations of several parent structures). Other metaheuristic methods are based on how melted materials behave when cooled down slowly (simulated annealing), how you might search for things when avoiding areas where you've recently looked (tabu search), or even how a swarm of insect-like solutions might move around in the state space (particle swarm optimization).

Exercises

11-1. We've seen several cases where the running time of an algorithm depends on one of the values in the input, rather than the actual size of the input (for example, the dynamic programming solution to the 0-1 knapsack problem). In these cases, the running time has been called *pseudopolynomial*, and it has been exponential as a function of problem size. Why is bisecting for a specific integer value an exception to this?

11-2. Why can every NP-complete problem be reduced to every other?

11-3. If the capacity of the knapsack problem is bounded by a function that is polynomial in the number of items, the problem is in P. Why?

11-4. Show that the subset sum problem is NP-complete even if the target sum, k, is fixed at zero.

11-5. Describe a polynomial-time reduction from the subset sum problem with positive integers to the unbounded knapsack problem. (This can be a bit challenging.)

11-6. Why is a four-coloring, or any k-coloring for $k > 3$, no easier than a three-coloring?

11-7. The general problem of *isomorphism*, finding out whether two graphs have the same structure (that is, whether they're equal if you disregard the labels or identities of the nodes), is not known to be NP-complete. The related problem of *subgraph isomorphism* is, though. This problem asks you to determine whether one graph has a subgraph that is isomorphic to another. Show that this problem is NP-complete.

11-8. How would you simulate the undirected Hamilton cycle problem using the directed version?

11-9. How would you reduce the undirected Hamilton cycle problem (directed or undirected) to the undirected Hamilton path problem?

11-10. How would you reduce the Hamilton path problem to the Hamilton cycle problem?

11-11. Why don't the proofs given in this section let us conclude that finding the longest path in a DAG is NP-complete? Where do the reductions break down?

11-12. Why haven't we shown that the longest path problem without positive cycles is NP-complete?

11-13. In the greedy 2-approximation for the unbounded knapsack problem, why can we be certain that we can fill more than half the knapsack (assuming that at least some objects will fit in it)?

11-14. Let's say you have a directed graph and you want to find the largest subgraph without cycles (the largest sub-DAG, so to speak). You'll measure the size in the number of edges involved. You think the problem seems a bit challenging, though, so you've decided that you'll settle for a 2-approximation. Describe such an approximation.

11-15. In Christofides' algorithm, why is there a matching of the odd-degree nodes with a total weight equal to at most half that of the optimum Hamilton cycle?

11-16. Devise some improvement on the starting-value for lower bound on the optimum in the branch and bound solution for the 0-1 knapsack.

11-17. Why is the greedy fractional solution never worse than the actual optimum in 0-1 knapsack?

11-18. Consider the optimization problem MAX-3-SAT (or MAX-3-CNF-SAT), where you're trying to make as many of the clauses in a 3-CNF formula true. This is clearly NP-hard (because it can be used to solve 3-SAT), but there is a curiously effective and oddly simple randomized approximation algorithm for it: Just flip a coin for each variable. Show that in the average case, this is an 8/7-approximation (assuming that no clause contains both a variable and its negation).

11-19. In Exercises 4-3 and 10-8, you started building a system for selecting friends to invite to a party. You have a numerical compatibility with each guest, and you want to select a subset that gives you a highest possible sum of compatibilities. Some guests would come only if certain others were present, and you managed to accommodate this constraint. You realize, however, that some of the guests will *refuse* to come if certain others are present. Show that solving the problem suddenly got a lot harder.

11-20. You're writing a system for parallel processing that distributes batch jobs to different processors in order to get all the work done as quickly as possible. You have the processing times for n jobs, and you are to divide these among m identical processors so that the final completion time is minimized. Show that this is NP-hard, and describe and implement an algorithm that solves the problem with approximation ratio 2.

11-21. Use the branch and bound strategy and write a program that finds an optimal solution to the scheduling problem in Exercise 11-20.

References

Arora, S. and Barak, B. (2009). *Computational Complexity: A Modern Approach*. Cambridge University Press.

Crescenzi, G. A., Gambosi, G., Kann, V., Marchetti-Spaccamela, A., and Protasi, M. (1999). *Complexity and Approximation: Combinatorial Optimization Problems and Their Approximability Properties*. Springer. Appendix online: ftp://ftp.nada.kth.se/Theory/Viggo-Kann/compendium.pdf.

Garey, M. R. and Johnson, D. S. (2003). *Computers and Intractability: A Guide to the Theory of NP-Completeness*. W. H. Freeman and Company.

Goldreich, O. (2010). *P, NP, and NP-Completeness: The Basics of Computational Complexity*. Cambridge University Press.

Harel, D. (2000). *Computers Ltd: What They Really Can't Do*. Oxford University Press.

Hemaspaandra, L. A. and Ogihara, M. (2002). *The Complexity Theory Companion*. Springer.

Hochbaum, D. S., editor (1997). *Approximation Algorithms for NP-Hard Problems*. PWS Publishing Company.

Impagliazzo, R. (1995). A personal view of average-case complexity. In *Proceedings of the 10th Annual Structure in Complexity Theory Conference* (SCT '95), pages 134–147. http://cseweb.ucsd.edu/~russell/average.ps.

Kolesar, P. J. (1967). A branch and bound algorithm for the knapsack problem. *Management Science*, 13(9):723–735. http://www.jstor.org/pss/2628089.

Vazirani, V. V. (2010). *Approximation Algorithms*. Springer.

Williamson, D. P. and Shmoys, D. B. (2011). *The Design of Approximation Algorithms*. Cambridge University Press. http://www.designofapproxalgs.com.

APPENDIX A

■ ■ ■

Pedal to the Metal: Accelerating Python

Make it work, make it right, make it fast.

— Kent Beck

This appendix is a tiny peek at some of the options for tweaking the constant factors of your implementations. Although this kind of optimization in many cases won't take the place of proper algorithm design—especially if your problems can grow large—making your program run ten times as fast can indeed be useful.

Before calling for external help, you should make sure you're using Python's built-in tools to their full potential. I've given you some pointers throughout the book, including the proper uses of list versus deque and how bisect and heapq can give you a great performance boost under the right circumstances. As a Python programmer, you're also lucky enough to have easy access to one of the most advanced and efficient (and efficiently implemented) sorting algorithms out there (list.sort), as well as a really versatile and fast hash table (dict). You might even find that itertools and functools can give your code a performance boost.[1]

Also, when choosing your technology, make sure you optimize only what you must. Optimizations do tend to make either your code or your tool setup more complicated, so make sure it's worth it. If your algorithm scales "well enough" and your code is "fast enough," introducing the extension modules in another language such as C might not be worth it. What is enough is, of course, up to you to determine. (For some hints on timing and profiling your code, see Chapter 2.)

Note that the packages and extensions discussed in this appendix are mainly about optimizing single-processor code, either by providing efficiently implemented functionality, by letting you create or wrap extension modules, or by simply speeding up your Python interpreter. Distributing your processing to multiple cores and processors can certainly also be a big help. The multiprocessing module can be a place to start. If you want to explore this approach, you should be able to find a lot of third-party tools for distributed computing as well. For example, you could have a look at the Parallel Processing page in the Python Wiki.

In the following pages, I describe a selection of acceleration tools. There are several efforts in this area, and the landscape is of course a changing one: New projects appear from time to time, and some old ones fade and die. If you think one of these solutions sounds interesting, you should check out its web site and consider the size and activity of its community—as well, of course, as your own needs. For web site URLs, see Table A-1 later in the appendix.

NumPy, SciPy, Sage, and Pandas. NumPy is a package with a long lineage. It is based on older projects such as Numeric and numarray, and at its core it implements a multidimensional array of numbers. In addition to this data structure, NumPy has several efficiently implemented functions and operators that work on the entire array so that when you use them from Python, the number of function calls is minimized, letting you write highly efficient

---

[1]Though, if you're writing iterator-laden, functional code and you *do* want an external boost, you might want to look at CyToolz.

numeric computations without compiling any custom extensions. As a supplement to NumPy, Theano can optimize mathematical expressions on numeric arrays. SciPy and Sage are much more ambitious projects (although with NumPy as one of their building blocks), collecting several tools for scientific, mathematical, and high-performance computing (including some of the ones mentioned later in this appendix). Pandas is more geared toward data analysis, but if its data model fits your problem instances, it is both powerful and fast. A related toolkit is Blaze, which can help if you're working with large amounts of semistructured data.

PyPy, Pyston, Parakeet, Psyco, and Unladen Swallow. One of the least intrusive approaches to speeding up your code is to use a just-in-time (JIT) compiler. In the olden days, you could use Psyco together with your Python installation. After installing Psyco, you would simply import the psyco module and call psyco.full() to get a potentially quite noticeable speedup. Psyco would compile parts of your Python program into machine code while your program was running. Because it could watch what happens to your program at runtime, it could make optimizations that a static compiler could not. For example, a Python list can contain arbitrary values. If, however, Psyco noticed that a given list of yours only ever seems to contain integers, it could assume that this would be the case also in the future and compile that part of the code as if your list were an array of integers. Sadly, like several of the Python acceleration solutions, Psyco is, to quote its web site, "unmaintained and dead." Its legacy lives on in PyPy, though.

PyPy is a more ambitious project: a reimplementation of Python *in Python*. This does not, of course, give a speedup directly, but the idea behind the platform is to put a lot of infrastructure in place for analyzing, optimizing, and translating code. Based on this framework, it is then possible to do JIT compilation (techniques used in Psyco are being ported to PyPy), or even translation to some high-performance language such as C. The core subset of Python used in implementing PyPy is called RPython (for *restricted Python*), and there are already tools for statically compiling this language into efficient machine code.

Unladen Swallow is also a JIT compiler for Python, in a way. More precisely, it's a version of the Python interpreter that uses the so-called Low Level Virtual Machine (LLVM). The goal of the project has been a speedup factor of 5 compared to the standard interpreter. This target has not yet been reached, though, and the activity of the project seems to have stopped.

Pyston is a similar, more recent LLVM-based JIT compiler for Python being developed by Dropbox. At the time of writing, Pyston is still a young project, supporting only a subset of the language, and there is as yet no support for Python 3. However, it already beats the standard Python implementation in many cases and is under active development. Parakeet is also a rather young project, which, to quote the web page, "uses type inference, data parallel array operators, and a lot of black magic to make your code run faster."

GPULib, PyStream, PyCUDA, and PyOpenCL. These four packages let you use graphics processing units (GPUs) to accelerate your code. They don't provide the kind of drop-in acceleration that a JIT compiler such as Psyco would, but if you have a powerful GPU, why not use it? Of the projects, PyStream is older, and the efforts of Tech-X Corporation have shifted to the newer GPULib project. It gives you a high-level interface for various forms of numeric computation using GPUs. If you want to use GPUs to speed up your code, you might also want to try PyCUDA or PyOpenCL.

Pyrex, Cython, Numba, and Shedskin. These four projects let you translate Python code into C, C++ or LLVM code. Shedskin compiles plain Python code into C++, while Pyrex and Cython (which is a fork of Pyrex) primarily target C. In Cython (and Pyrex, its predecessor), you can add optional type declarations to your code, stating that a variable is (and will always be) an integer, for example. In Cython, there is also interoperability support for NumPy arrays, letting you write low-level code that accesses the array contents efficiently. I have used this in my own code, achieving speedup factors of up to 300–400 for suitable code. The code that is generated by Pyrex and Cython can be compiled directly to an extension module that can be imported into Python. If you want to generate C code from your Python, Cython is a safe bet. If you're just looking for the speedup, particularly for array-oriented and math-heavy code, you should look into Numba, which generates LLVM code at import time. With the premium features available in NumbaPro, there's even GPU support.

SWIG, F2PY, and Boost.Python. These tools let you wrap C/C++, Fortran, and C++ code, respectively. Although you could write your own wrapper code for accessing your extension modules, using a tool like one of these takes a lot of the tedium out of the job—and makes it more likely that the result will be correct. For example, when using SWIG, you run a command-line tool on your C (or C++) header files, and wrapper code is generated. A bonus to using SWIG is that it can generate wrappers for a lot of other languages, beside Python, so your extension could be available for Java or PHP as well, for example.

ctypes, llvm-py, and CorePy2. These are modules that let you manipulate low-level code objects in your Python code. The ctypes module lets you build C objects in memory and call C functions in shared libraries (such as DLLs) with those objects as parameters. The llvm-py package gives you a Python API to the LLVM, mentioned earlier, which lets you build code and then compile it efficiently. If you wanted, you could use this to build your own compiler (perhaps for a language of your own?) in Python. CorePy2 also lets you manipulate and efficiently run code objects, although it works at the assembly level. (Note that ctypes is part of the Python standard library.)

Weave, Cinpy, and PyInline. These three packages let you use C (or some other languages) directly in your Python code. This is done quite cleanly, by keeping the C code in multiline Python strings, which are then compiled on the fly. The resulting code object is then available to your Python code, using facilities such as ctypes for the interfacing.

Other tools. Clearly there are plenty of other tools out there, which may be of more use to you than these, depending on your needs. For example, if you want to reduce memory use rather than time, a JIT is not for you—JITs generally need a lot of memory. Instead, you might want to check out Micro Python, which is designed to have a minimal memory footprint and to be suited for using Python on microcontrollers and in embedded devices. And, who knows, maybe you don't even require the use of Python. Perhaps you're working in a Python environment, and you want a high-level language, but you want all of your code to be really fast. Though it might be Pythonic heresy, I suggest looking at Julia. While it's a different language, its syntax should be familiar enough to any Python programmer. It also has support for calling Python libraries, which means that the Julia team is cooperating with Python projects such as IPython,[2] and it has even been the subject of a SciPy conference lecture already.[3]

Table A-1. *URLs for Acceleration Tool Web Sites*

Tool	Web Site
Blaze	`http://blaze.pydata.org`
Boost.Python	`http://boost.org`
Cinpy	`http://www.cs.tut.fi/~ask/cinpy`
CorePy2	`https://code.google.com/p/corepy2`
ctypes	`http://docs.python.org/library/ctypes.html`
Cython	`http://cython.org`
CyToolz	`https://github.com/pytoolz/cytoolz`
F2PY	`http://cens.ioc.ee/projects/f2py2e`
GPULib	`http://txcorp.com/products/GPULib`
Julia	`http://julialang.org`
llvm-py	`http://mdevan.org/llvm-py`
Micro Python	`http://micropython.org`
Numba	`http://numba.pydata.org`
NumPy	`http://www.numpy.org`

(continued)

---

[2]See, for example, `http://jupyter.org`.
[3]`https://conference.scipy.org/scipy2014/schedule/presentation/1669`.

Table A1-1. (*continued*)

Tool	Web Site
Pandas	http://pandas.pydata.org
Parakeet	http://www.parakeetpython.com
Parallel Processing	https://wiki.python.org/moin/ParallelProcessing
Psyco	http://psyco.sf.net
PyCUDA	http://mathema.tician.de/software/pycuda
PyInline	http://pyinline.sf.net
PyOpenCL	http://mathema.tician.de/software/pyopencl
PyPy	http://pypy.org
Pyrex	http://www.cosc.canterbury.ac.nz/greg.ewing/python/Pyrex
PyStream	http://code.google.com/p/pystream
Pyston	https://github.com/dropbox/pyston
Sage	http://sagemath.org
SciPy	http://scipy.org
Shedskin	http://code.google.com/p/shedskin
SWIG	http://swig.org
Theano	http://deeplearning.net/software/theano
Unladen Swallow	http://code.google.com/p/unladen-swallow
Weave	http://docs.scipy.org/doc/scipy/reference/weave.html

APPENDIX B

■ ■ ■

List of Problems and Algorithms

If you're having hull problems, I feel bad for you, son; I've got 99 problems, but a breach ain't one.

— Anonymous[1]

This appendix does not list every problem and algorithm mentioned in the book because some algorithms are discussed only to illustrate a principle and some problems serve only as examples for certain algorithms. The most important problems and algorithms, however, are sketched out here, with some references to the main text. If you're unable to find what you're looking for by consulting this appendix, take a look in the index.

In most descriptions in this appendix, *n* refers to the problem size (such as the number of elements in a sequence). For the special case of graphs, though, *n* refers to the number of nodes, and *m* refers to the number of edges.

Problems

Cliques and independent sets. A *clique* is a graph where there is an edge between every pair of nodes. The main problem of interest here is finding a clique in a larger graph (that is, identifying a clique as a subgraph). An independent set in a graph is a set of nodes where no pair is connected by an edge. In other words, finding an independent set is equivalent to taking the complement of the edge set and finding a clique. Finding a *k*-clique (a clique of *k* nodes) or finding the largest clique in a graph (the max-clique problem) is NP-hard. (For more information, see Chapter 11.)

Closest pair. Given a set of points in the Euclidean plane, find the two points that are closest to each other. This can be solved in loglinear time using the divide-and-conquer strategy (see Chapter 6).

Compression and optimal decision trees. A Huffman tree is a tree whose leaves have weights (frequencies), and the sum of their weights multiplied by their depth is as small as possible. This makes such trees useful for constructing compression codes and as decision trees when a probability distribution is known for the outcomes. Huffman trees can be built using Huffman's algorithm, described in Chapter 7 (Listing 7-1).

Connected and strongly connected components. An undirected graph is connected if there is a path from every node to every other. A directed graph is connected if its underlying undirected graph is connected. A connected component is a maximal subgraph that is connected. Connected components can be found using traversal algorithms such as DFS (Listing 5-5) or BFS (Listing 5-9), for example. If there is a (directed) path from every node to every other in a directed graph, it is called *strongly* connected. A strongly connected component (SCC) is a maximal subgraph that is strongly connected. SCCs can be found using Kosaraju's algorithm (Listing 5-10).

Convex hulls. A convex hull is the minimum convex region containing a set of points in the Euclidean plane. Convex hulls can be found in loglinear time using the divide-and-conquer strategy (see Chapter 6).

---

[1]Facetiously attributed to Lt. Cdr. Geordi La Forge of *Star Trek: The Next Generation*.

Finding the minimum/maximum/median. Finding the minimum and maximum of a sequence can be found in linear time by a simple scan. Repeatedly finding and extracting the maximum or minimum in constant time, given linear-time preparation, can be done using a binary heap. It is also possible to find the kth smallest element of a sequence (the median for $k = n/2$) in linear (or expected linear) time, using the select or randomized select. (For more information, see Chapter 6.)

Flow and cut problems. How many units of flow can be pushed through a network with flow capacities on the edges? That is the max-flow problem. An equivalent problem is finding the set of edge capacities that most constrain the flow; this is the min-cut problem. There are several versions of these problems. For example, you could add costs to the edges and find the cheapest of the maximum flows. You could add a lower bound on each edge and look for a feasible flow. You could even add separate supplies and demands in each node. These problems are dealt with in detail in Chapter 10.

Graph coloring. Try to color the nodes of a graph so that no neighbors share a color. Now try to do this with a given number of colors, or even to find the lowest such number (the *chromatic number* of the graph). This is an NP-hard problem in general. If, however, you're asked to see whether a graph is two-colorable (or bipartite), the problem can be solved in linear time using simple traversal. The problem of finding a clique cover is equivalent to finding an independent set cover, which is an identical problem to graph coloring. (See Chapter 11 for more on graph coloring.)

The halting problem. Determine whether a given algorithm will terminate with a given input. The problem is undecidable (that is, unsolvable) in the general case (see Chapter 11).

Hamilton cycles/paths and TSP … and Euler tours. Several path and subgraph problems can be solved efficiently. If, however, you want to visit every node exactly once, you're in trouble. Any problem involving this constraint is NP-hard, including finding a Hamilton cycle (visit every node once and return), a Hamilton path (visit every node once, without returning), or a shortest tour of a complete graph (the Traveling Salesman/Salesrep problem). The problems are NP-hard both for the directed and undirected case (see Chapter 11). The related problem of visiting every *edge* exactly once, though—finding a so-called Euler tour—is solvable in polynomial time (see Chapter 5). The TSP problem is NP-hard even for special cases such as using Euclidean distances in the plane, but it can be efficiently approximated to within a factor of 1.5 for this case, and for any other metric distance. Approximating the TSP problem in general, though, is NP-hard. (See Chapter 11 for more information.)

The knapsack problem and integer programming. The knapsack problem involves choosing a valuable subset of a set of items, under certain constraints. In the (bounded) fractional case, you have a certain amount of some substances, each of which has a unit value (value per unit of weight). You also have a knapsack that can carry a certain maximum weight. The (greedy) solution is to take as much as you can of each substance, starting with the one with the highest unit value. For the integral knapsack problem, you can take only entire items—fractions aren't allowed. Each item has a weight and a value. For the bounded case (also known as 0-1 knapsack), you have a limited number of objects of each type. (Another perspective would be that you have a fixed set of objects that you either take or not.) In the unbounded case, you can take as many as you want from each of a set of object types (still respecting your carrying capacity, of course). A special case known as the subset sum problem involves selecting a subset of a set of numbers so that the subset has a given sum. These problems are all NP-hard (see Chapter 11), but admit pseudopolynomial solutions based on dynamic programming (see Chapter 8). The fractional knapsack case, as explained, can even be solved in polynomial time using a greedy strategy (see Chapter 7). Integer programming is, in some ways, a generalization of the knapsack problem (and is therefore obviously NP-hard). It is simply linear programming where the variables are constrained to be integers.

Longest increasing subsequence. Find the longest subsequence of a given sequence whose elements are in increasing order. This can be solved in loglinear time using dynamic programming (see Chapter 8).

Matching. There are many matching problems, all of which involve linking some object to others. The problems discussed in this book are bipartite matching and min-cost bipartite matching (Chapter 10) and the stable marriage problem (Chapter 7). Bipartite matching (or maximum bipartite matching) involves finding the greatest subset of edges in a bipartite graph so that no two edges in the subset share a node. The min-cost version does the same but minimizes the sum of edge costs over this subset. The stable marriage problem is a bit different; there, all men and women have preference rankings of the members of the opposite sex. A stable set of marriages is characterized by the fact that you can't find a pair that would rather have each other than their current mates.

Minimum spanning trees. A spanning tree is a subgraph whose edges form a tree over all the nodes of the original graph. A minimum spanning tree is one that minimizes the sum of edge costs. Minimum spanning trees can be found using Kruskal's algorithm (Listing 7-4) or Prim's algorithm (Listing 7-5), for example. Because the number of edges is fixed, a maximum spanning tree can be found by simply negating the edge weights.

Partitioning and bin packing. Partitioning involves dividing a set of numbers into two sets with equal sums, while the bin packing problem involves packing a set of numbers into a set of "bins" so that the sum in each bin is below a certain limit and so that the number of bins is as small as possible. Both problems are NP-hard. (See Chapter 11.)

SAT, Circuit-SAT, k-CNF-SAT. These are all varieties of the satisfaction problem (SAT), which asks you to determine whether a given logical (Boolean) formula can ever be true, if you're allowed to set the variables to whatever truth values you want. The circuit-SAT problem simply uses logical circuits rather than formulas, and k-CNF-SAT involves formulas in conjunctive normal form, where each clause consists of k literals. The latter can be solved in polynomial time for $k = 2$. The other problems, as well as k-CNF-SAT for $k > 2$, are NP-complete. (See Chapter 11.)

Searching. This is a very common and extremely important problem. You have a key and want to find an associated value. This is, for example, how variables work in dynamic languages such as Python. It's also how you find almost anything on the Internet these days. Two important solutions are hash tables (see Chapter 2) and binary search or search trees (see Chapter 6). Given a probability distribution for the objects in the data set, optimal search trees can be constructed using dynamic programming (see Chapter 8).

Sequence comparison. You may want to compare two sequences to know how similar (or dissimilar) they are. One way of doing this is to find the longest subsequence the two have in common (longest common subsequence) or to find the minimum number of basic edit operations to go from one sequence to the other (so-called edit distance, or Levenshtein distance). These two problems are more or less equivalent; see Chapter 8 for more information.

Sequence modification. Inserting an element into the middle of a linked list is cheap (constant time), but finding a given location is costly (linear time); for an array, the opposite is true (constant lookup, linear insert, because all later elements must be shifted). Appending can be done cheaply for both structures, though (see the "Black Box" sidebar on list in Chapter 2).

Set and vertex covers. A vertex cover is a set of vertices that cover (that is, are adjacent to) all the edges of the graph. A set cover is a generalization of this idea, where the nodes are replaced with subsets, and you want to cover the entire set. The problem lies in constraining or minimizing the number of nodes/subsets. Both problems are NP-hard (see Chapter 11).

Shortest paths. This problem involves finding the shortest path from one node to another, from one node to all the others (or vice versa), or from all nodes to all others. The one-to-one, one-to-all, and all-to-one cases are solved the same way, normally using BFS for unweighted graphs, DAG shortest path for DAGs, Dijkstra's algorithm for nonnegative edge weights, and Bellman–Ford in the general case. To speed up things in practice (although without affecting the worst-case running time), you can also use bidirectional Dijkstra, or the A* algorithm. For the all pairs shortest paths problem, the algorithms of choice are probably Floyd–Warshall or (for sparse graphs) Johnson's algorithm. If the edges are nonnegative, Johnson's algorithm is (asymptotically) equivalent to running Dijkstra's algorithm from every node (which may be more effective). (For more information on shortest path algorithms, see Chapters 5 and 9.) Note that the *longest* path problem (for general graphs) can be used to find Hamilton paths, which means that it is NP-hard. This, in fact, means that the shortest path problem is *also* NP-hard in the general case. If we disallow negative cycles in the graph, however, our polynomial algorithms will work.

Sorting and element uniqueness. Sorting is an important operation and an essential subroutine for several other algorithms. In Python, you would normally sort by using the list.sort method or the sorted function, both of which use a highly efficient implementation of the timsort algorithm. Other algorithms include insertion sort, selection sort, and gnome sort (all of which have a quadratic running time), as well as heapsort, mergesort, and quicksort (which are loglinear, although this holds only in the average case for quicksort). For information on the quadratic sorting algorithms, see Chapter 5; for the loglinear (divide-and-conquer) algorithms, see Chapter 6. Deciding whether a set of real numbers contains duplicates cannot (in the worst case) be solved with a running time better than loglinear. By reduction, neither can sorting.

Topological sorting. Order the nodes of a DAG so that all the edges point in the same direction. If the edges represent dependencies, a topological sorting represents an ordering that respects the dependencies. This problem can be solved by a form of reference counting (see Chapter 4) or by using DFS (see Chapter 5).

Traversal. The problem here is to visit all the objects in some connected structure, usually represented as nodes in a graph or tree. The idea can be either to visit every node or to visit only those needed to solve some problem. The latter strategy of ignoring parts of the graph or tree is called *pruning* and is used (for example) in search trees and in the branch and bound strategy. For a lot on traversal, see Chapter 5.

Algorithms and Data Structures

2-3-trees. Balanced tree structure, allowing insertions, deletions, and search in worst-case $\Theta(\lg n)$ time. Internal nodes can have two or three children, and the tree is balanced during insertion by splitting nodes, as needed. (See Chapter 6.)

A*. Heuristically guided single source shortest path algorithm. Suitable for large search spaces. Instead of choosing the node with the lowest distance estimate (as in Dijkstra's), the node with the lowest heuristic value (sum of distance estimate and guess for remaining distance) is used. Worst-case running time identical to Dijkstra's algorithm. (See Listing 9-10.)

AA-tree. 2-3-trees simulated using node rotations in a binary tree with level-numbered nodes. Worst-case running times of $\Theta(\lg n)$ for insertions, deletions, and search. (See Listing 6-6.)

Bellman–Ford. Shortest path from one node to all others in weighted graphs. Looks for a shortcut along every edge n times. Without negative cycles, correct answer guaranteed after $n-1$ iterations. If there's improvement in the last round, a negative cycle is detected, and the algorithm gives up. Running time $\Theta(nm)$. (See Listing 9-2.)

Bidirectional Dijkstra. Dijkstra's algorithm run from start and end node simultaneous, with alternating iterations going to each of the two algorithms. The shortest path is found when the two meet up in the middle (although some care must be taken at this point). The worst-case running time is just like for Dijkstra's algorithm. (See Listings 9-8 and 9-9.)

Binary search trees. A binary tree structure where each node has a key (and usually an associated value). Descendant keys are partitioned by the node key: Smaller keys go in the left subtree, and greater keys go in the right. On the average, the depth of any node is logarithmic, giving an expected insertion and search time of $\Theta(\lg n)$. Without extra balancing, though (such as in the AA-tree), the tree can become unbalanced, giving linear running times. (See Listing 6-2.)

Bisection, binary search. A search procedure that works in a manner similar to search trees, by repeated halving the interval of interest in a sorted sequence. The halving is performed by inspecting the middle element and deciding whether the sought value must lie to the left or right. Running time $\Theta(\lg n)$. A very efficient implementation can be found in the bisect module. (See Chapter 6.)

Branch and bound. A general algorithmic design approach. Searches a space of solutions in a depth-first or best-first order by building and evaluating partial solutions. A conservative estimate is kept for the optimal value, while an optimistic estimate is computed for a partial solution. If the optimistic estimate is worse than the conservative one, the partial solution is not extended, and the algorithm backtracks. Often used to solve NP-hard problems. (See Listing 11-2 for a branch-and-bound solution to the 0-1 knapsack problem.)

Breadth-first search (BFS). Traversing a graph (possibly a tree) level by level, thereby also identifying (unweighted) shortest path. Implemented by using a FIFO queue to keep track of discovered nodes. Running time $\Theta(n+m)$. (See Listing 5-9.)

Bucket sort. Sort numerical values that are evenly (uniformly) distributed in a given interval by dividing the interval into n equal-sized buckets and placing the values in them. Expected bucket size is constant, so they can be sorted with (for example) insertion sort. Total running time $\Theta(n)$. (See Chapter 4.)

Busacker–Gowen. Finds the cheapest max-flow (or the cheapest flow with a given flow value) in a network by using the cheapest augmenting paths in the Ford–Fulkerson approach. These paths are found using Bellman–Ford or (with some weight adjustments) Dijkstra's algorithm. The running time in general depends on the maximum flow value and so is pseudopolynomial. For a maximum flow of k, the running time is (assuming Dijkstra's algorithm is used) $O(km \lg n)$. (See Listing 10-5.)

Christofides' algorithm. An approximation algorithm (with an approximation ratio bound of 1.5) for the metric TSP problem. Finds a minimum spanning tree and then a minimum matching[2] among the odd-degree nodes of the tree, short-circuiting as needed to make a valid tour of the graph. (See Chapter 11.)

Counting sort. Sort integers with a small value range (with at most $\Theta(n)$ contiguous values) in $\Theta(n)$ time. Works by counting occurrences and using the cumulative counts to directly place the numbers in the result, updating the counts as it goes. (See Chapter 4.)

DAG shortest path. Finds the shortest path from one node to all others in a DAG. Works by finding a topological sorting of the nodes and then relaxing all out-edges (or, alternatively, all in-edges) at every node from left to right. Can (because of the lack of cycles) also be used to find *longest* paths. Running time $\Theta(n+m)$. (See Listing 8-4.)

Depth-first search (DFS). Traversing a graph (possibly a tree) by going in depth and then backtracking. Implemented by using a LIFO queue to keep track of discovered nodes. By keeping track of discover- and finish-times, DFS can also be used as a subroutine in other algorithms (such as topological sorting or Kosaraju's algorithm). Running time $\Theta(n+m)$. (See Listings 5-4, 5-5, and 5-6.)

Dijkstra's algorithm. Find the shortest paths from one node to all others in a weighted graph, as long as there are no negative edge weights. Traverses the graph, repeatedly selecting the next node using a priority queue (a heap). The priority is the current distance estimate of the node. These estimates are updated whenever a shortcut is found from a visited node. The running time is $\Theta((m+n) \lg n)$, which is simply $\Theta(m \lg n)$ if the graph is connected.

Double-ended queues. FIFO queues implemented using linked lists (or linked lists of arrays), so that inserting and extracting objects at either end can be done in constant time. An efficient implementation can be found in the collections.deque class. (See the "Black Box" sidebar on the topic in Chapter 5.)

Dynamic arrays, vectors. The idea of having extra capacity in an array, so appending is efficient. By relocating the contents to a bigger array, growing it by a constant factor, when it fills up, appends can be constant in average (amortized) time. (See Chapter 2.)

Edmonds–Karp. The concrete instantiation of the Floyd–Warshall method where traversal is performed using BFS. Finds min-cost flow in $\Theta(nm^2)$ time. (See Listing 10-4.)

Floyd–Warshall. Finds shortest paths from each node to all others. In iteration k, only the first k nodes (in some ordering) are allowed as intermediate nodes along the paths. Extending from $k-1$ involves checking whether the shortest paths to and from k via the first $k-1$ nodes is shorter than simply going directly via these nodes. (That is, node k is either used or not, for every shortest path.) Running time is $\Theta(n^3)$. (See Listing 9-6.)

Ford–Fulkerson. A general approach to solving max-flow problems. The method involves repeatedly traversing the graph to find a so-called augmenting path, a path along which the flow can be increased (augmented). The flow can be increased along an edge if it has extra capacity, or it can be increased *backward* across an edge (that is, canceled) if there is flow along the edge. Thus, the traversal can move both forward and backward along the directed edges, depending on the flow across them. The running time depends on the traversal strategy used. (See Listing 10-4.)

Gale–Shapley. Finds a stable set of marriages given preference rankings for a set of men and women. Any unengaged men propose to the most preferred woman they haven't proposed to. Each woman will choose her favorite among her current suitors (possibly staying with her fiancé). Can be implemented with quadratic running time. (See the sidebar "Eager Suitors and Stable Marriages" in Chapter 7.)

---

[2]Note that finding matchings in general (possibly nonbipartite) graphs is not covered in this book.

Gnome sort. A simple sorting algorithm with quadratic running time. Probably not an algorithm you'll use in practice. (See Listing 3-1.)

Hashing, hash tables. Look up a key to get the corresponding value, just like in a search tree. Entries are stored in an array, and their positions are found by computing a (pseudorandom, sort of) *hash value* of the key. Given a good hash function and enough room in the array, the expected running time of insertion, deletion and lookup is $\Theta(1)$. (See Chapter 2.)

Heaps, heapsort. Heaps are efficient priority queues. With linear-time preprocessing, a min- (max-) heap will let you find the smallest (largest) element in constant time and extract or replace it in logarithmic time. Adding an element can also be done in logarithmic time. Conceptually, a heap is a full binary tree where each node is smaller (larger) than its children. When modifications are made, this property can be repaired with $\Theta(\lg n)$ operations. In practice, heaps are usually implemented using arrays (with nodes encoded as array entries). A very efficient implementation can be found in the heapq module. Heapsort is like selection sort, except that the unsorted region is a heap, so finding the largest element n times gives a total running time of $\Theta(n \lg n)$. (See the "Black Box" sidebar on heaps, heapq, and heapsort in Chapter 6.)

Huffman's algorithm. Builds Huffman trees, which can be used for building optimal prefix codes, for example. Initially, each element (for example, character in an alphabet) is made into a single-node tree, with a weight equal to its frequency. In each iteration, the two lightest trees are picked, combining them with a new root and giving the new tree a weight equal to the sum of the original two tree weights. This can be done in loglinear time (or, in fact, in linear time if the frequencies are presorted). (See Listing 7-1.)

Insertion sort. A simple sorting algorithm with quadratic running time. It works by repeatedly inserting the next unsorted element in an initial sorted segment of the array. For small data sets, it can actually be preferable to more advanced (and optimal) algorithms such as merge sort or quicksort. (In Python, though, you should use list.sort or sorted if at all possible.) (See Listing 4-3.)

Interpolation search. Similar to ordinary binary search, but linear interpolation between the interval endpoints is used to guess the correct position, rather than simply looking at the middle element. The worst-case running time is still $\Theta(\lg n)$, but the average-case running time is $O(\lg \lg n)$ for uniformly distributed data. (Mentioned in the "If You're Curious ..." section of Chapter 6.)

Iterative deepening DFS. Repeated runs of DFS, where each run has a limit to how far it can traverse. For structures with some fanout, the running time will be the same as for DFS or BFS (that is, $\Theta(n+m)$). The point is that it has the advantages of BFS (it finds shortest paths and explores large state spaces conservatively), with the smaller memory footprint of DFS. (See Listing 5-8.)

Johnson's algorithm. Finds shortest paths from every node to all others. Basically runs Dijkstra's from every node. However, it uses a trick so that it also works with negative edge weights: It first runs Bellman–Ford from a new start node (with added edges to all existing nodes) and then uses the resulting distances to modify the edge weights of the graph. The modified weights are all nonnegative but are set so that the shortest paths in the original graph will also be the shortest paths in the modified graph. Running time $\Theta(mn \lg n)$. (See Listing 9-4.)

Kosaraju's algorithm. Finds strongly connected components, using DFS. First, nodes are ordered by their finish times. Then the edges are reversed, and another DFS is run, selecting start nodes using the first ordering. Running time $\Theta(n+m)$. (See Listing 5-11.)

Kruskal's algorithm. Finds a minimum spanning tree by repeatedly adding the smallest remaining edge that doesn't create a cycle. This cycle checking can (with some cleverness) be performed very efficiently, so the running time is dominated by sorting the edges. All in all, the running time is $\Theta(m \lg n)$. (See Listing 7-4.)

Linked lists. An alternative to arrays for representing sequences. Although linked lists are cheap (constant time) to modify once you've found the right entries, finding those normally takes linear time. Linked lists are implemented sort of like a path, with each node pointing to the next. Note that Python's list type is implemented as an array, not a linked list. (See Chapter 2.)

Merge sort. The archetypal divide-and-conquer algorithm. It divides the sequence to be sorted in the middle, sorts the two halves recursively, and then merges the two sorted halves in linear time. The total running time is $\Theta(n \lg n)$. (See Listing 6-5.)

Ore's algorithm. An algorithm for traversing actual mazes in person, by marking passage entries and exits. In many ways similar to iterative deepening DFS or BFS. (See Chapter 5.)

Prim's algorithm. Grows a minimum spanning tree by repeatedly adding the node closest to the tree. It is, at core, a traversal algorithm and uses a priority queue, just like Dijkstra's algorithm. (See Listing 7-5.)

Radix sort. Sorts numbers (or other sequences) by digit (element), starting with the least significant one. As long as the number of digits is constant and the digits can be sorted in linear time (using, for example, counting sort), the total running time is linear. It's important that the sorting algorithm used on the digits is *stable*. (See Chapter 4.)

Randomized select. Finds the median, or, in general, the *k*th order statistic (the *k*th smallest element). Works sort of like "half a quicksort." It chooses a *pivot* element at random (or arbitrarily) and partitions the other elements to the left (smaller elements) or right (greater elements) of the pivot. The search then continues in the right portion, more or less like binary search. Perfect bisection is not guaranteed, but the expected running time is still linear. (See Listing 6-3.)

Select. The rather unrealistic, but guaranteed linear, sibling of randomized select. It works as follows: Divide the sequence into groups of five. Find the median in each using insertion sort. Find the median of these medians recursively, using select. Use this median of medians as a pivot and partition the elements. Now run select on the proper half. In other words, it's similar to randomized select—the difference is that it can guarantee that a certain percentage will end up on either side of the pivot, avoiding the totally unbalanced case. Not really an algorithm you're likely to use in practice, but it's important to know about. (See Chapter 6.)

Selection sort. A simple sorting algorithm with quadratic running time. Very similar to insertion sort, but instead of repeatedly inserting the next element into the sorted section, you repeatedly find (that is, select) the largest element in the unsorted region (and swap it with the last unsorted element). (See Listing 4-4.)

Timsort. A super-duper in-place sorting algorithm based on mergesort. Without any explicit conditions for handling special cases, it is able to take into account partially sorted sequences, including segments that are sorted in reverse, and can therefore sort many real-world sequences faster than what would seem possible. The implementation in `list.sort` and `sorted` is also really fast, so if you need to sort something, that's what you should use. (See the "Black Box" sidebar on timsort in Chapter 6.)

Topological sorting by reference counting. Orders the nodes of a DAG so that all edges go from left to right. This is done by counting the number of in-edges at each node. The nodes with an in-degree of zero are kept in a queue (could just be a set; the order doesn't matter). Nodes are taken from the queue and placed in the topological sorted order. As you do so, you decrement the counts for the nodes that this node has edges to. If any of them reaches zero, they are placed in the queue. (See Chapter 4.)

Topological sorting with DFS. Another algorithm for sorting DAG nodes topologically. The idea is simple: perform a DFS and sort the nodes by inverse finish time. To easily get a linear running time, you can instead simply append nodes to your ordering as they receive their finish times in DFS. (See Listing 5-7.)

Tremaux's algorithm. Like Ore's algorithm, this is designed to be executed in person, while walking through a maze. The pattern traced by a person executing Tremaux's algorithm is essentially the same as that of DFS. (See Chapter 5.)

Twice around the tree. An approximation algorithm for the metric TSP problem, guaranteed to yield a solution with a cost of at most twice the optimum. First it builds a minimum spanning tree (which is less than the optimum), and then it "walks around" the tree, taking shortcuts to avoid visiting the same edge twice. Because of the metricity, this is guaranteed to be cheaper than walking each edge twice. This last traversal can be implemented by a preorder DFS. (See Listing 11-1.)

APPENDIX C

■ ■ ■

Graph Terminology

He offered a bet that we could name any person among earth's one and a half billion inhabitants and through at most five acquaintances, one of which he knew personally, he could link to the chosen one.

— Frigyes Karinthy, *Láncszemek*[1]

The following presentation is loosely based on the first chapters of *Graph Theory* by Reinhard Diestel and *Digraphs* by Bang-Jensen and Gutin, and on the appendixes of *Introduction to Algorithms* by Cormen et al. (Note that the terminology and notation may differ between books; it is not completely standardized.) If you think it seems like there's a lot to remember and understand, you probably needn't worry. Yes, there may be many new words ahead, but most of the concepts are intuitive and straightforward, and their names usually make sense, making them easier to remember.

So ... A *graph* is an abstract network, consisting of *nodes* (or *vertices*), connected by *edges* (or *arcs*). More formally, we define a graph as a pair of sets, $G = (V, E)$, where the node set V is any finite set, and the edge set E is a set of (unordered) node pairs.[2] We call this a graph *on V*. We sometimes also write $V(G)$ and $E(G)$, to indicate which graph the sets belong to.[3] Graphs are usually illustrated with network drawings, like those in Figure C-1 (just ignore the gray highlighting for now). For example, the graph called G_1 in Figure C-1 can be represented by the node set $V = \{a,b,c,d,e,f\}$ and the edge set $E = \{\{a,b\},\{b,c\},\{b,d\},\{d,e\}\}$.

You don't always have to be totally strict about distinguishing between the graph and its node and edge sets. For example, we might talk about a node u in a graph G, really meaning in $V(G)$, or equivalently, an edge $\{u,v\}$ in G, meaning in $E(G)$.

■ **Note** It is common to use the sets V and E directly in asymptotic expressions, such as $\Theta(V+E)$, to indicate linearity in the graph size. In these cases, the sets should be interpreted as their *cardinalities* (that is, sizes), and a more correct expression would be $\Theta(|V| + |E|)$, where $|\cdot|$ is the cardinality operator.

---

[1]As quoted by Albert-László Barabási in his book *Linked: TheNew Science of Networks* (Basic Books, 2002).
[2]You probably didn't even think of it as an issue, but you can assume that V and E don't overlap.
[3]The functions would still be called V and E, even if we give the sets other names. For example, for a graph $H = (W,F)$, we would have $V(H) = W$ and $E(H) = F$.

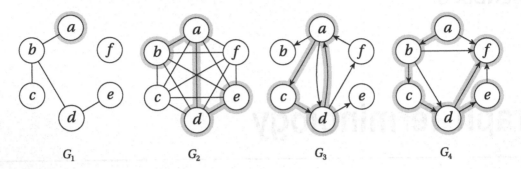

Figure C-1. *Various types of graphs and digraphs*

The basic graph definition gives us what is often called an *undirected* graph, which has a close relative: the *directed* graph, or *digraph*. The only difference is that the edges are no longer *unordered* pairs but *ordered*: An edge between nodes u and v is now either an edge (u,v) from u to v or an edge (v,u) from v to u. In other words, in a digraph G, $E(G)$ is a relation over $V(G)$. The graphs G_3 and G_4 in Figure C-1 are digraphs where the edge directions are indicated by arrowheads. Note that G_3 has what is called *antiparallel* edges between a and d, that is, edges going both ways. This is OK because (a,d) and (d,a) are different. Parallel edges, though (that is, the same edge, repeated) are not allowed—neither in graphs nor digraphs. (This follows from the fact that the edges form a set.) Note also that an undirected graph cannot have an edge between a node and itself, and even though this is possible in a digraph (so-called *self-loops*), the convention is to disallow it.

■ **Note**   There are other relatives of the humble graph that *do* permit such things as parallel edges and self-loops. If we construct our network structure so that we can have multiple edges (that is, the edges now form a *multiset*), and self-loops, we call it a (possibly directed) *pseudograph*. A pseudograph without self-loops is simply a *multigraph*. There are also more exotic versions, such as the *hypergraph*, where each edge can have multiple nodes.

Even though graphs and digraphs are quite different beasts, many of the principles and algorithms we deal with work just as well on either kind. Therefore, it is common to sometimes use the term *graph* in a more general sense, covering both directed and undirected graphs. Note also that in many contexts (such as when *traversing* or "moving around in" a graph), an undirected graph can be simulated by a directed one, by replacing each undirected edge with a pair of antiparallel directed edges. This is often done when actually implementing graphs as data structures (discussed in more detail in Chapter 2). If it is clear whether an edge is directed or undirected or if it doesn't matter much, I'll sometimes write uv instead of $\{u,v\}$ or (u,v).

An edge is *incident on* its two nodes, called its *end nodes*. That is, uv is incident on u and v. If the edge is directed, we say that it *leaves* (or is *incident from*) u and that it *enters* (or is *incident to*) v. We call u and v its *tail* and *head*, respectively. If there is an edge uv in an undirected graph, the nodes u and v are *adjacent* and are called *neighbors*. The set of neighbors of a node v, also known as the *neighborhood* of v, is sometimes written as $N(v)$. For example, the neighborhood $N(b)$ of b in G_1 is $\{a,c,d\}$. If all nodes are pairwise adjacent, the graph is called *complete* (see G_2 in Figure C-1). For a directed graph, the edge uv means that v is *adjacent to* u, but the converse is true only if we also have an antiparallel edge vu. (In other words, the nodes adjacent to u are those we can "reach" from u by following the edges incident from it in the right direction.)

The number of (undirected) edges incident on a node v (that is, the size of $N(v)$) is called its *degree*, often written $d(v)$. For example, in G_1 (Figure C-1), the node b has a degree of 3, while f has a degree of 0. (Zero-degree nodes are called *isolated*.) For directed graphs we can split this number into the *in-degree* (the number of incoming edges) and *out-degree* (the number of outgoing edges). We can also partition the neighborhood of a node into an *in-neighborhood*, sometimes called *parents*, and an *out-neighborhood*, or *children*.

One graph can be *part of* another. We say that a graph $H = (W,F)$ is a *subgraph* of $G = (V, E)$ or, conversely, that G is a *supergraph* of H, if W is a subset of V and F is a subset of E. That is, we can get H from G by (maybe) removing some nodes and edges. In Figure C-1, the highlighted nodes and edges indicate some example subgraphs that will be discussed in more detail in the following. If H is a subgraph of G, we often say that *G contains H*. We say that *H spans G* if $W = V$. That is, a *spanning* subgraph is one that covers all the nodes of the original graph (such as the one in graph G_4 in Figure C-1).

Paths are a special kind of graphs that are primarily of interest when they occur as subgraphs. A *path* is often identified by an sequence of (distinct) nodes, such as $v_1, v_2, \ldots, v_n$, with edges (only) between pairs of successive nodes: $E = \{v_1 v_2, v_2 v_3, \ldots, v_{n-1} v_n\}$. Note that in a directed graph, a path has to follow the directions of the edges; that is, all the edges in a path point forward. The *length* of a path is simply its edge count. We say that this is a path between v_1 to v_n (or, in the directed case, from v_1 to v_n). In the sample graph G_2, the highlighted subgraph is a path between b and e, for example, of length 3. If a path P_1 is a subgraph of another path P_2, we say that P_1 is a *subpath* of P_2. For example, the paths b, a, d and a, d, e in G_2 are both subpaths of b, a, d, e.

A close relative of the path is the *cycle*. A cycle is constructed by connecting the last node of a path to the first, as illustrated by the (directed) cycle through a, b, and c in G_3 (Figure C-1). The length of a cycle is also the number of edges it contains. Just like paths, cycles must follow the directions of the edges.

■ **Note** These definitions do not allow paths to cross themselves, that is, to contain cycles as subgraphs. A more general path-like notion, often called a *walk*, is simply an alternating sequence of nodes and edges (that is, not a graph in itself), which would allow nodes and edges to be visited multiple times and, in particular, would permit us to "walk in cycles." The equivalent to a cycle is a *closed walk*, which starts and ends on the same node. To distinguish a path without cycles from a general walk, the term *simple path* is sometimes used.

A common generalization of the concepts discussed so far is the introduction of *edge weights* (or *costs* or *lengths*). Each edge $e = uv$ is assigned a real number, $w(e)$, sometimes written $w(u,v)$, usually representing some form of cost associated with the edge. For example, if the nodes are geographic locations, the weights may represent driving distances in a road network. The weight $w(G)$ of a graph G is simply the sum of $w(e)$ for all edges e in G. We can then generalize the concept of path and cycle length to $w(P)$ and $w(C)$ for a path P and cycle C, respectively. The original definitions correspond to the case where each edge has a weight of 1. The *distance* between two nodes is the length of the shortest path between them. (Finding such shortest paths is dealt with extensively in the book, primarily in Chapter 9.)

A graph is *connected* if it contains a path between every pair of nodes. We say that a digraph is connected if the so-called *underlying undirected graph* (that is, the graph that results if we ignore edge directions) is connected. In Figure C-1, the only graph that is not connected is G_1. The maximal subgraphs of a graph that *are* connected are called its *connected components*. In Figure C-1, G_1 has two connected components, while the others have only one (each), because the graphs themselves are connected.

■ **Note** The term *maximal*, as it is used here, means that something cannot be extended and still have a given property. For example, a connected component is maximal in the sense that it is not a subgraph of a *larger* graph (one with more nodes or edges) that is also connected.

One family of graphs in particular is given a lot of attention, in computer science and elsewhere: graphs that do not contain cycles, or *acyclic graphs*. Acyclic graphs come in both directed and undirected variants, and these two versions have rather different properties. Let's focus on the undirected kind first.

Another term for an undirected, acyclic graph is *forest*, and the connected components of a forest are called *trees*. In other words, a tree is a connected forest (that is, a forest consisting of a single connected component). For example, G_1 is a forest with two trees. In a tree, nodes with a degree of one are called *leaves* (or *external nodes*),[4] while all others are called *internal* nodes. The larger tree in G_1, for example, has three leaves and two internal nodes. The smaller tree consists of only an internal node, although talking about leaves and internal nodes may not make much sense with fewer than three nodes.

■ **Note**   Graphs with 0 or 1 nodes are called *trivial* and tend to make definitions trickier than necessary. In many cases, we simply ignore these cases, but sometimes it may be important to remember them. They can be quite useful as a starting point for induction, for example (covered in detail in Chapter 4).

Trees have several interesting and important properties, some of which are dealt with in relation to specific topics throughout the book. I'll give you a few right here, though. Let T be an undirected graph with n nodes. Then the following statements are equivalent (Exercise 2-9 asks you to show that this is, indeed, the case):

1. T is a tree (that is, it is acyclic and connected).

2. T is acyclic and has n–1 edges.

3. T is connected and has n–1 edges.

4. Any two nodes are connected by exactly one path.

5. T is acyclic, but adding any new edge to it will create a cycle.

6. T is connected, but removing any edge yields two connected components.

In other words, any one of these statements of T, on its own, characterizes it as well as any of the others. If someone tells you that there is exactly one path between any pair of nodes in T, for example, you immediately know that it is connected and has n–1 edges and that it has no cycles.

Quite often, we anchor our tree by choosing a *root node* (or simply *root*). The result is called a *rooted tree*, as opposed to the *free* trees we've been looking at so far. (If it is clear from the context whether a tree has a root or not, I will simply use the unqualified term *tree* in both the rooted and free case.) Singling out a node like this lets us define the notions of *up* and *down*. Paradoxically, computer scientists (and graph theorists in general) tend to place the root at the top and the leaves at the bottom. (We probably should get out more …). For any node, *up* is in the direction of the root (along the single path between the node and the root). *Down* is then any other direction (automatically in the direction of the leaves). Note that in a rooted tree, the root is considered an internal node, *not* a leaf, *even if it happens to have a degree of one*.

Having properly oriented ourselves, we now define the *depth* of a node as its distance from the root, while its *height* is the length of longest downward path to any leaf. The height of the tree then is simply the height of the root. For example, consider the larger tree in G_1 in Figure C-1 and let a (highlighted) be the root. The height of the tree is then 3, while the depth of, say, c and d is 2. A *level* consists of all nodes that have the same depth. (In this case, level 0 consists of a, level 1 of b, level 2 of c and d, and level 3 of e.)

These directions also allow us to define other relationships, using rather intuitive terms from family trees (with the odd twist that we have only single parents). Your neighbor on the level above (that is, closer to the root) is your *parent*, while your neighbors on the level below are your *children*.[5] (The root, of course, has no parent, and the leaves, no children.) More generally, any node you can reach by going upward is an *ancestor*, while any node you can reach by going down is a *descendant*. The tree spanning a node v and all its descendants is called the *subtree rooted at v*.

---

[4]As explained later, though, the root is not considered a leaf. Also, for a graph consisting of only two connected nodes, calling them both leaves sometimes doesn't make sense.

[5]Note that this is the same terminology as for the in- and out-neighborhoods in digraphs. The two concepts coincide once we start orienting the tree edges.

■ **Note** As opposed to subgraphs in general, the term *subtree* usually does *not* apply to all subgraphs that happen to be trees—especially not if we are talking about rooted trees.

Other similar terms generally have their obvious meanings. For example, *siblings* are nodes with a common parent. Sometimes siblings are *ordered* so that we can talk about the "first child" or "next sibling" of a node, for example. In this case, the tree is called an *ordered tree*.

As explained in Chapter 5, many algorithms are based on *traversal*, exploring graphs systematically, from some initial starting point (a start node). Although the way graphs are explored may differ, they have something in common. As long as they traverse the entire graph, they all give rise to *spanning trees*.[6] (Spanning trees are simply spanning subgraphs that happen to be trees.) The spanning tree resulting from a traversal, called the *traversal tree*, is rooted at the starting node. The details of how this works will be revisited when dealing with the individual algorithms, but graph G_4 in Figure C-1 illustrates the concept. The highlighted subgraph is such a traversal tree, rooted at *a*. Note that all paths from *a* to the other nodes in the tree follow the edge directions; this is always the case for traversal trees in digraphs.

■ **Note** A digraph whose underlying graph is a rooted tree and where all the directed edges point away from the root (that is, all nodes can be reached by directed paths from the root) is called an *arborescence*, even though I'll mostly talk about such graphs simply as trees. In other words, traversal in a digraph really gives you a *traversal arborescence*. The term *oriented tree* is used about both rooted (undirected) trees and arborescences because the edges of a rooted tree have an implicit direction away from the root.

Terminology fatigue setting in yet? Cheer up—only one graph concept left. As mentioned, directed graphs can be acyclic, just as undirected graphs can. The interesting thing is that these graphs don't generally look much like forests of directed trees. Because the underlying undirected graph can be as cyclic as it wants, a *directed acyclic graph*, or DAG, can have an arbitrary structure (see Exercise 2-11), as long as the edges point in the right directions—that is, they are pointing so that no *directed* cycles exist. An example of this can be seen in sample graph G_4.

DAGs are quite natural as representations for dependencies because cyclic dependencies are generally impossible (or, at least, undesirable). For example, the nodes might be college courses, and an edge (u,v) would indicate that course u was a prerequisite for v. Sorting out such dependencies is the topic of the section on topological sorting in Chapter 5. DAGs also form the basis for the technique of dynamic programming, discussed in Chapter 8.

---

[6]This is true only if all nodes can be reached from the start node. Otherwise, the traversal may have to restart in several places, resulting in a *spanning forest*. Each component of the spanning forest will then have its own root.

■ ■ ■

Hints for Exercises

To solve any problem, here are three questions to ask yourself: First, what could I do? Second, what could I read? And third, who could I ask?

— Jim Rohn

Chapter 1

1-1. As machines get faster and get more memory, they can handle larger inputs. For poor algorithms, this will eventually lead to disaster.

1-2. A simple and quite scalable solution would be to sort the characters in each string and compare the results. (In theory, counting the character frequencies, possibly using collections.Counter, would scale even better.) A really *poor* solution would be to compare all possible orderings of one string with the other. I can't overstate how poor this solution is; in fact, algorithms don't get much worse than this. Feel free to code it up and see how large anagrams you can check. I bet you won't get far.

Chapter 2

2-1. You would be using the same list ten times. Definitely a bad idea. (For example, try running a[0][0] = 23; print(a).)

2-2. One possibility is to use *three* arrays of size n; let's call them A, B, and C, along with a count of how many entries have been assigned yet, m. A is the actual array, and B, C, and m form the extra structure for checking. Only the first m entries in C are used, and they are all indices into B. When you perform A[i] = x, you also set B[i] = m and C[m] = i and then increment m (that is, m += 1). Can you see how this gives you the information you need? Extending this to a two-dimensional adjacency array should be quite straightforward.

2-3. If f is $O(g)$, then there is a constant c so that for $n > n_0$, $f(n) \leq cg(n)$. This means that the conditions for g being $\Omega(f)$ are satisfied by using the constant $1/c$. The same logic holds in reverse.

2-4. Let's see how it works. By definition, $b^{\log_b n} = n$. It's an equation, so we can take the logarithm (base a) on both sides and get $\log_a (b^{\log_b n}) = \log_a n$. Because $\log x^y = y \log x$ (standard logarithm rule), we can write this as $(\log_a b)(\log_b n) = \log_a n$, which gives us $\log_b n = (\log_a n)$. The takeaway from this result is that the difference between $\log_a n$ and $\log_b n$ is just a constant factor ($\log_a b$), which disappears when we use asymptotic notation.

2-5. We want to find out whether, as n increases, the inequality $k^n \geq c \cdot n^j$ is eventually true, for some constant c. For simplicity, we can set $c = 1$. We can take the logarithm (base k) on both sides (it won't flip the inequality because it is an increasing function), and we're left with finding out whether $n \geq j \log_k n$ at some point, which is given by the fact that (increasing) linear functions dominate logarithms. (You should verify that yourself.)

2-6. This can be solved easily using a neat little trick called *variable substitution*. Like in Exercise 1-5, we set up a tentative inequality, $n^k \geq \lg n$, and want to show that it holds for large n. Again, we take the logarithm on both sides and get $k \lg n \geq \lg(\lg n)$. The double logarithm may seem scary, but we can sidestep it quite elegantly. We don't care about how *fast* the exponential overtakes the polynomial, only that it happens at some point. This means we can substitute our variable—we set $m = \lg n$. If we can get the result we want by increasing m, we can get it by increasing n. This gives us $km \geq \lg m$, which is just the same as in Exercise 2-5!

2-7. Anything that involves finding or modifying a certain position will normally take constant time in Python lists because their underlying implementation is arrays. You have to traverse a linked list to do this (on average, half the list), giving a linear running time. Swapping things around, once you know the positions, is constant in both. (See whether you can implement a linear-time linked list reversal.) Modifying the list structure (by inserting or deleting element, except at the end) is generally linear for arrays (and Python lists) but can in many cases be done in constant time for linked lists.

2-8. For the first result, I'll stick to the upper half here and use O notation. The lower half (Ω) is entirely equivalent. The sum $O(f) + O(g)$ is the sum of two functions, say, F and G, such that (for large enough n, and some c) $F(n) \leq cf(n)$ and $G(n) \leq cg(n)$. (Do you see why it's OK to use the same c for both?) That means that, for large enough n, we will have $F(n) + G(n) \leq c \cdot (f(n) + g(n))$, which simply means that $F(n) + G(n)$ is $O(f(n) + g(n))$, which is what we wanted to prove. The $f \cdot g$ case is mostly equivalent (with a little wrinkle related to the c). Showing that $\max(\Theta(f), \Theta(g)) = \Theta(\max(f, g))$ follows a similar logic. The most surprising fact may be that $f + g$ is $O(\max(f, g))$, or $\max(f, g)$ is $\Omega(f + g)$—that is, that maximum grows at least as fast as a sum. This is easily explained by the fact that $f + g \leq 2 \cdot \max(f, g)$.

2-9. When showing equivalence of statements like this, it's common to show implication from one to the next through the list and then from the last to the first. (You might want to try to show some of the other implications directly as well; there are 30 to choose from.) Here are a couple of hints to get you started. $1 \Rightarrow 2$: Imagine that the tree is oriented. Then every edge represents a parent–child relationship, and each node except the root has a parent edge, giving $n - 1$ edges. $2 \Rightarrow 3$: Build T gradually by adding the $n - 1$ edges one by one. You aren't allowed to connect nodes already in T (it's acyclic), so each edge must be used to connect a new node to T, meaning that it will be connected.

2-10. This is sort of an appetizer for the counting in Chapter 3, and you can prove the result by induction (a technique discussed in depth in Chapter 4). There is an easy solution, though (which is quite similar to the presentation in Chapter 2). Give each parent (internal node) two imaginary ice cream cones. Now, every parent gives its children one ice cream cone each. The only one stuck without ice cream is the root. So, if we have n leaves and m internal nodes, we can now see that $2m$ (the number of ice cream cones, as specified initially) is equal to $m + n - 1$ (all nodes except the root, with one cone each), which means that $m = n - 1$. And this is the answer we're looking for. Neat, huh? (This is an example of a nice counting technique, where we count the same thing in two different ways and use the fact that the two counts—in this case, the number of ice cream cones—must be equal.)

2-11. Number the nodes (arbitrarily). Orient all edges from lower to higher numbers.

2-12. The advantages and disadvantages depend on what you're using it for. It works well for looking up edge weights efficiently but less well for iterating over the graph's nodes or a node's neighbors, for example. You could improve that part by using some extra structures (for example, a global list of nodes, if that's what you need or a simple adjacency list structure, if that's required).

Chapter 3

3-1. You could try doing this with induction or even recursion!

3-2. Start by rewriting to $(n^2-n)/2$. Then first drop the constant factor, leaving n^2-n. After that, you can drop the n, because it is dominated by n^2.

3-3. Binary encoding shows us which powers of two are included in a sum, and each is included only once. Let's say that the first k powers (or binary digits) let us represent any number up to $2^k - 1$ (our inductive hypothesis; clearly true for $k = 1$). Now try to use the property mentioned in the exercise to show another digit (that is, being allowed to add in the next power of two) will let you represent any number up to $2^{k+1} - 1$.

3-4. One of these is basically a for loop over the possible values. The other one is bisection, which is discussed in more detail in Chapter 6.

3-5. This is quite obvious from the symmetry in the numerator of the formula. Another way of seeing it is that there are as many ways of *removing* k elements as there are of *leaving* k elements.

3-6. The act of extracting sec[1:] requires copying $n-1$ elements, meaning that the running time of the algorithm turns into the handshake sum.

3-7. This quickly yields the handshake sum.

3-8. When unraveling the recursion, you get $2\{2T(n-2) + 1\} + 1 = 2^2T(n-2) + 2 + 1$, which eventually turns into a doubling sum, $1 + 2 + \ldots + 2^i$. To get to the base case, you need to set $i = n$, which gives you a sum of powers up to 2^n, which is $\Theta(2^n)$.

3-9. Similar to Exercise 3-8, but here the unraveling gives you $2\{2T(n-2)+(n-1)\}+n = 2^2T(n-2)+2(n-1)+n$. After a while, you end up with a rather tricky sum, which has $2^iT(n-i)$ as its dominating summand. Setting $i = n$ gives you 2^i. (I hope this sketchy reasoning didn't completely convince you; you should check it with induction.)

3-10. This is a neat one: take the logarithm on both sides, yielding $\log x^{\log y} = \log y^{\log x}$. Now, simply note that both of these are equal to $\log x \cdot \log y$. (See why?)

3-11. What's happening outside the recursive calls is basically that the two halves of the sequence are merged together to a single sequence. First, let's just assume that the sequences returned by the recursive calls have the same length as the arguments (that is, lft and rgt don't change length). The while loop iterates over these, popping off elements until one of them is empty; this is at most linear. The reverse is also at most linear. The res list now consists of elements popped off from lft and rgt, and finally, the rest of the elements (in lft or rgt) are combined (linear time). The only thing remaining is to show that the length of the sequence returned from mergesort has the same length as its argument. You could do this using induction in the length of seq. (If that still seems a bit challenging, perhaps you could pick up some tricks in Chapter 4?)

3-12. This would give us the handshake sum inside $f(n)$, meaning that the recurrence is now $T(n) = 2T(n/2) + \Theta(n^2)$. Even a basic familiarity with the master theorem should tell you that the quadratic part dominates, meaning that $T(n)$ is now $\Theta(n^2)$—drastically worse than the original!

Chapter 4

4-1. Try induction on E, and do the induction step "backward," as in the internal node count example. The base case ($E = 0$ or $E = 1$) is trivial. Assume the formula is true for $E - 1$, and consider an arbitrary connected planar graph with E edges. Try to remove an edge, and assume (for now) that the smaller graph is still connected. Then the edge removal has reduced the edge count by one, and it must have merged two regions, reducing the region count by one. The formula holds for this, meaning that $V - (E - 1) + (F - 1) = 2$, which is equivalent to the formula we want to prove. Now see if you can tackle the case when removing an edge *disconnects* the graph. (Hint: You can apply the induction hypothesis to each of the connected components, but this counts the infinite region twice, so you must compensate for that.) Also try to use induction on V and F. Which version suits your tastes?

4-2. This is actually sort of a trick question, because any sequence of breaks will give you the same "running time" of $n-1$. You can show this by induction, as follows (with $n=1$ giving a trivial base case): the first break will give you one rectangle with k squares and one with $n-k$ (where k depends on where you break). Both of these are smaller than n, so by strong induction, we assume that the number of breaks for each of them is $k-1$ and $n-k-1$, respectively. Adding these, along with the initial break, we get $n-1$ for the entire chocolate.

4-3. You can represent this as a graph problem, where an edge uv means that u and v know each other. You're trying to find the largest subgraph (that is, with the greatest number of nodes) where each node v has a degree $d(v) \geq k$. Once again, induction comes to the rescue. The base case is $n = k + 1$, where you can solve the problem only if the graph is complete. The reduction (inductive hypothesis) is, as you might have guessed, that you can solve the problem for $n-1$, and the way to solve it for n is to either (1) see that all nodes have degrees greater than or equal to k (we're done!) or (2) find a single node to remove and solve the rest (by the induction hypothesis). It turns out that you can remove any node you like that has a degree smaller than k, because it could never be part of a solution. (This is a bit like the permutation problem—if it's *necessary* to remove a node, just go ahead and remove it.)

Hint for bonus question: Note that $d/2$ is the ratio of edges to nodes (in the full graph), and as long as you delete nodes with a degree of less than or equal to $d/2$, that ratio (for remaining subgraph) will not decrease. Just keep deleting until you hit this limit. The remaining graph has a nonzero edge-to-node ratio (because it's at least as great as for the original), so it must be non-empty. Also, because we couldn't remove any more nodes, each node has a degree greater than $d/2$ (that is, we've removed all nodes with smaller degrees).

4-4. Although there are many ways of showing that there can be only two central nodes, the easiest way is, perhaps, to construct the algorithm first (using induction) and then use that to complete the proof. The base cases for $V = 0$, 1, or 2 are quite easy—the available nodes are all central. Beyond that, we want to reduce the problem from V to $V - 1$. It turns out that we can do that by removing a leaf node. For $V > 2$, no leaf node can be central (its neighbor will always be "more central" because its longest distance will be lower), so we can just remove it and forget about it. The algorithm follows directly: keep removing leaves (possibly once again implemented by maintaining degrees/counts) until all remaining nodes are equally central. It should now be quite obvious that this occurs when V is at most 2.

4-5. This is a *bit* like topological sorting, except that we may have cycles, so there's no guarantee we'll have nodes with an in-degree of zero. This is, in fact, equivalent to finding a directed Hamiltonian path, which may not even exist in a general graph (and finding out is really hard; see Chapter 11), but for a complete graph with oriented edges (what is actually called a *tournament* in graph theory), such a path (that is, one that visits each node once, following the directions of the edges) will always exist. We can do a single-element reduction directly—we remove a node and order the rest (which is OK by inductive hypothesis; the base case is trivial). The question now becomes whether (and how) we can insert this last node, or knight. The easiest way to see that this is possible is to simply insert the knight before the *first* opponent he (or she) defeated (if there is such an opponent; otherwise, place him last). Because we're choosing the first one, the knight before must have defeated him, so we're preserving the desired type of ordering.

4-6. This shows how important it is to pay attention to detail when doing induction. The argument breaks down for $n=2$. Even though the inductive hypothesis is true for $n-1$ (the base case, $n=1$), in this case there *is no overlap* between the two sets, so the inductive step breaks down! Note that if you could somehow show that any *two* horses had the same color (that is, set the base case to $n=2$), then the induction would (obviously) be valid.

4-7. The point isn't that it should work for any tree with $n-1$ leaves, because we had already assumed that to be the case. The important thing is that the argument hold for *any* tree with n leaves, and it does. No matter which tree with n leaves you choose, you can delete a leaf and its parent and construct a valid binary tree with $n-1$ leaves and $n-2$ internal nodes.

4-8. This is just a matter of applying the rules directly.

4-9. Once we get down to a single person (if we ever do), we know that this person couldn't have been pointing to anyone else, or that other person would not have been removed. Therefore, he (or she) must be pointing to himself (or, rather, his own chair).

4-10. A quick glance at the code should tell you that this is the handshake recurrence (with the construction of B taking up linear time in each call).

4-11. Try sorting sequences (of "digits"). Use counting sort as a subroutine, with a parameter telling you which digit to sort by. Then just loop over the digits from the last to the first, and sort your numbers (sequences) once for each digit. (Note: You could use induction over the digits to prove radix sort correct.)

4-12. Figure out how big each interval (value range) must be. You can then divide each value by this number, rounding down, to find out which bucket to place it in.

4-13. We assume (as discussed in Chapter 2) that we can use constant-time operations on numbers that are large enough to address the entire data set, and that includes d_i. So, first, find these counts for all strings, adding them as a separate "digit." You can then use counting sort to sort the numbers by this new digit, for a total running time so far of $\Theta(\sum d_i + n) = \Theta(\sum d_i)$. Each "block" of numbers with equal digit length can now be sorted individually (with radix sort). (Do you see how this still gives a total running time of $\Theta(\sum d_i)$ and how we actually get all the numbers sorted correctly in the end?)

4-14. Represent them as two-digit numbers, where each digit has a value range of $1\ldots n$. (Do you see how to do this?) You can then use radix sort, giving you a linear running time in total.

4-15. The list comprehension has a quadratic running time complexity.

4-16. See Chapter 2 for some hints on running experiments.

4-17. It cannot be placed *before* this point, and as long as we don't place it any later, it cannot end up after anything that depends on it (because there are no cycles).

4-18. You could generate DAGs by, for example, randomly ordering the nodes, and add a random number of forward-pointing edges to each of them.

4-19. This is quite similar to the original. You now have to maintain the out-degrees of the remaining nodes, and insert each node *before* the ones you have already found. (Remember not to insert anything in the beginning of a list, though; rather, append, and then reverse it at the end, to avoid a quadratic running time.)

4-20. This is a straightforward recursive implementation of the algorithm idea.

4-21. A simple inductive solution would be to remove one interval, solving the problem for the rest, and then checking whether the initial interval should be added back. The problem is that you'd have to check this interval against all the others, giving a quadratic running time overall. You can improve this running time, however. First, sort the intervals by their left endpoints, and use the induction hypothesis that you can solve the problem for the $n-1$ first intervals. Now, extend the hypothesis: Assume that you can also find the largest right endpoint among the $n-1$ intervals. Do you see how the inductive step can now be performed in constant time?

4-22. Instead of randomly selecting pairs u, v, simply go through every possible pair, giving a quadratic running time. (Do you see how this necessarily gives you the right answer for each town?)

4-23. To show that *foo* was hard, you would have to reduce *bar* to *foo*. To show that *foo* was easy, you would have to reduce *foo* to *baz*.

Chapter 5

5-1. The asymptotic running time would be the same, but you'd probably get more overhead (that is, a higher constant factor) because instead of adding lots of objects with a built-in operation, you'd run slower, custom Python code for each object.

5-2. Try turning the induction proof into a recursive algorithm. (You might also want to look up Fleury's algorithm.)

5-3. Try to reconstruct the inductive argument (and recursive algorithm) that's used for undirected graphs—it's virtually identical. The link to Trémaux's algorithm is the following: Because you're allowed to traverse each maze passage once in each direction, you can treat the passage as two directed edges, with opposite directions. This means that all intersections (nodes) will have equal in- and out-degrees, and you're guaranteed that you can find a tour that walks every edge twice, one in each direction. (Note that you couldn't use Trémaux's algorithm in the more general case presented in this exercise.)

5-4. This is just a simple matter of traversing the grid that consists of pixels, with adjacent pixels acting as neighbors. It is common to use DFS for this, but any traversal would do.

5-5. I'm sure there would be many ways of using this thread, but one possibility would be to use it like the stack of DFS (or IDDFS), if you're unable to make any other kinds of marks. You would probably end up visiting the same rooms multiple times, but at least you'd never walk in a cycle.

5-6. It's not really represented at all in the iterative version. It just implicitly occurs once you've popped off all your "traversal descendants" from the stack.

5-7. As explained in Exercise 5-6, there is point in the code where backtracking occurs in the iterative DFS, so we can't just set the finish time at some specific place (like in the recursive one). Instead, we'd need to add a marker to the stack. For example, instead of adding the neighbors of u to the stack, we could add edges of the form (u, v), and before all of them, we'd push (u, None), indicating the backtracking point for u.

5-8. Let's say node u must come before v in a topological sorting. If we run DFS from (or through) v first, we could never reach u, so v would finish before we (at some later point) start a new DFS that is run either from or through u. So far, we're safe. If, on the other hand, we pass u first. Then, because there is a (direct or indirect) dependency (that is, a path) between u and v, we will reach v, which will (once again) finish before u.

5-9. You could just supply some functions as optional arguments here, for example.

5-10. If there is a cycle, DFS will always traverse the cycle as far as it can (possibly after backtracking from some detours). This means it'll eventually get to where it entered the cycle, creating a back edge. (Of course, it could already have traversed this edge by following some *other* cycle, but that would still make it a back edge.) So if there are no back edges, there can't be any cycles.

5-11. Other traversal algorithms would also be able to detect cycles by finding an edge from a visited node to one of its ancestors in the traversal tree (a back edge). However, determining when this happens (that is, distinguishing back edges from cross edges) wouldn't necessarily be quite as easy. In undirected graphs, however, all you need in order to find a cycle is to reach a node twice, and detecting that is easy, no matter what traversal algorithm you're using.

5-12. Let's say you *did* find a forward and cross edge to some node u. Because there are no direction restrictions, DFS would never have backtracked beyond u without exploring all its out-edges, which means it would already have traversed the hypothetical forward/cross edge in the other direction!

5-13. This is just a matter of keeping track of the distance for each node instead of its predecessor, beginning with zero for the start node. Instead of remembering a predecessor, you simply add 1 to the predecessor's distance, and remember that. (You could certainly do both, of course.)

5-14. The nice thing about this problem is that for an edge uv, if you color u white, v must be black (or vice versa). This is an idea we've seen before: If the constraints of the problem *force* you to do something, it must be a safe step to take when building a solution. Therefore, you can simply traverse the graph, making sure you're coloring neighbors in different colors; if, at some point, you can't, there is no solution. Otherwise, you've successfully created a bipartitioning.

5-15. In a strong component, every node can reach every other, so there must be at least one path in each direction. If the edges are reversed, there still will be. On the other hand, any pair that is *not* connected by two paths like this won't be after the reversal either, so no new nodes will be added to the strong components either.

5-16. Let's say the DFS starts somewhere in X. Then, at some point, it will migrate over to Y. We already know it can't get back to X without backtracking (the SCC graph is acyclic), so every node in Y must receive a finishing time before we get back to X. In other words, at least one node in X will be finished *after* all the nodes in Y are finished.

5-17. Try finding a simple example where this would give the wrong answer. (You can do it with a really small graph.)

Chapter 6

6-2. The asymptotic running time would be the same. The number of comparison goes *up*, however. To see this, consider the recurrences $B(n) = B(n/2) + 1$ and $T(n) = T(n/3) + 2$ for binary and ternary search, respectively (with base cases $B(1) = T(1) = 0$ and $B(2) = T(2) = 1$). You can show (by induction) that $B(n) < \lg n + 1 < T(n)$.

6-3. As shown in Exercise 6-2, the number of comparisons won't go down; however, there can be other advantages. For example, in the 2-3-tree, the 3-nodes help us with balancing. In the more general B-tree, the large nodes help reduce the number of disk accesses. Note that it is common to use binary search *inside* each node in a B-tree.

6-4. You could just traverse the tree and print or yield each node key between the recursive calls to the left and right subtrees (*inorder* traversal).

6-5. First you find it the node; let's call it v. If it's a leaf, just remove it. If it's an internal node with a single child, just replace it with its child. If the node has *two* children, find the largest (rightmost) node in the left subtree or the smallest (leftmost) in the right subtree—your choice. Now replace the key and value in v with those of this descendant and then delete the descendant. (To avoid making the tree unnecessarily unbalanced, you should switch between the left and right versions.)

6-6. We're inserting n random values, so each time we insert a value, the probability of it being the smallest among the k inserted so far (including this value) is $1/k$. If it is, the depth of the leftmost node increases by 1. (For simplicity, let's say the depth of the root is 1, rather than 0, as is customary.) This means that the node depth is $1 + 1/2 + 1/3 + \ldots + 1/n$, a sum known as the n-th harmonic number, or H_n. Interestingly, this sum is $\Theta(\lg n)$.

6-7. Let's say you switch place with your left child, and it turns out to be greater than your right child. You've just broken the heap property.

6-8. Each parent has two children, so you need to move two steps to get to the children of the next one; hence, the children of node i are at $2i + 1$ and $2i + 2$. If you're having trouble seeing how this works, try drawing the nodes in a sequence, as they're placed in the array, with tree edges arcing between parents and children.

6-9. It can be a bit tricky to see how building a heap is linear when considering the standard implementation, which goes through the nodes level by level, from just above the leaves, performing a logarithmic operation on each node as it goes. This almost looks loglinear. However, we can reformulate this into an equivalent divide-and-conquer algorithm, which is a bit more familiar: Make a heap out of the left subtree, then of the right subtree, and then repair the root. The recurrence becomes $T(n) = 2T(n/2) + \Theta(\lg n)$, which we know (for example, by the master theorem) is linear.

6-10. First, heaps give you direct access to the minimum (or maximum) node. This could, of course, be implemented by maintaining a direct pointer to the leftmost (or rightmost) node in a search tree as well. Second, the heaps allows you to maintain balance easily, and because it is perfectly balanced, it can be represented compactly, leading to very low overhead (you save one reference per node, and you can keep the values located in the same memory area, for example). Finally, building a (balanced) search tree takes loglinear time, while building a heap takes linear time.

6-13. For random input, it wouldn't really make any difference (except the cost of the extra function call). In general, though, it would mean that no single input would be guaranteed to always elicit worst-case behavior.

6-15. Here you can use the pigeonhole principle (if you try to fit more than n pigeons into n pigeonholes, at least one hole will hold at least two pigeons). Divide the square into four of side $n/2$. If you have more than four points, one of these must hold at least two points. By simple geometry, the diagonal of these squares is less than d, so this is impossible.

6-16. Just do a pass over the data before you start, removing co-located points. They're already sorted, so finding duplicates would only be a linear-time operation. Now, when running the algorithm, the slices along the midline can, at most, hold *six* points (do you see why?), so you now need to compare to at most five following points in the y-sequence.

6-17. This is similar to how the lower bound for sorting is used to prove the lower bound for the convex hull problem: You can reduce the element uniqueness for real numbers to the closest pair problem. Just plot your numbers as points on the x-axis (linear time, which is asymptotically less than the bound at hand) and find the closest pair. If the two points are identical, the elements aren't unique; otherwise, they are. Because uniqueness *cannot* be determined in less than loglinear time, it would be *impossible* for the closest pair problem to be any more efficient.

6-18. The crucial observation is that there's never any point in including an initial portion of the slice whose sum is zero or negative (you could always discard it and get the same or a higher sum). Also, there's never any point in *discarding* an initial portion whose sum is *positive* (including it will give a higher sum). Thus, we can start summing from the left side, always keeping the best sum (and corresponding interval) so far. Once the sum goes negative, we move i (the starting index) to the next position and start our sum afresh from there. (You should convince yourself that this really works; perhaps prove it by induction?)

Chapter 7

7-1. There are many possibilities here (such as dropping a few coins from the U.S. system). One significant example is the old British system (1, 2, 6, 12, 24, 48, 60).

7-2. This is just a way of viewing how a base-k number system works. This is especially easy to see with $k = 10$.

7-3. When you consider whether to include the greatest remaining element or not, it will *always* pay to include it because if you don't, the sum of the remaining elements can't make up for the lost value.

7-4. Let's say Jack is the first one to get rejected by his best feasible wife, Jill, and that she rejects him for Adam. By assumption, Adam has not yet been rejected by *his* best feasible wife, Alice, which means that he likes Jill at least as well as her. Consider a stable pairing where Jack and Jill *are* together. (This must exist because Jill is a feasible wife for Jack.) In this pairing, Jill would still prefer Adam, of course. However, we know that Adam prefers Jill over Alice—or any other feasible wife—so this matching wouldn't be stable after all! In other words, we have a contradiction, invalidating our assumption that some man was not paired with his best feasible wife.

7-5. Let's say Jack was married to Alice and Jill to Adam in a stable pairing. Because Jill is Jack's best feasible wife, he will prefer her to Alice. Because the pairing is stable, Jill must prefer Adam. This holds for *any* stable pairing where Jill has another husband—meaning that she'd prefer *any* other feasible husband to Jack.

7-6. A greedy algorithm would certainly work if the capacity of your knapsack was divisible by all the various increments. For example, if one item was breakable in increments of 2.3 and another in increments of 3.6 and your knapsack capacity was divisible by 8.28, you'd be OK, because you have a "resolution" that is good enough. (Do you see any further variations we could allow? Other implications of this idea?)

7-7. This follows rather directly from the tree structure. Because the codes all give us unique, deterministic instructions on how to navigate from the root to a leaf, there is never any doubt when we have arrived, or *where* we have arrived.

7-8. We know that a and b are the two items with the lowest frequencies; that means the frequency of a is lower than (or equal to) the one of c, and the same holds for b and d. If a and d have equal frequencies, we'd sandwich all the inequalities (including $a \leq b$ and $c \leq d$), and all four frequencies are equal.

7-9. Take the case where all files are of equal, constant size. Then a balanced merge tree would give us a loglinear merging time (typical divide and conquer). However, if we make the merge tree completely unbalanced, we'd get a quadratic running time (just like insertion sort, for example). Now consider a set of files whose sizes are the powers of two up to $n/2$. The last file would have linear size, and in a balanced merge tree, it would be involved in a logarithmic number of merges, meaning that we'd get (at least) loglinear time. Now consider what Huffman's algorithm would do: It would always merge the two smallest files, and they'd always sum to about (that is, one less than) the size of the next. We get a sum of powers and end up with a *linear* merge time.

7-10. You would need to have at least edges with the same weight that both are viable as part of a solution. For example, if the lowest weight was used twice, on two different edges, you'd have (at least) two solutions.

7-11. Because the number of edges in all spanning trees is the same, we could do this by simply negating the weights (that is, if an edge had weight w, we'd change it to $-w$) and finding the *minimum* spanning tree.

7-12. We need to show this for the general case where we have a set of edges that we *know* are going into the solution. The subproblem is then the remaining graph, and we want to show that finding a minimum spanning tree in the rest that's compatible with what we have (no cycles) will give us an optimal solution globally. As usual, we show this by contradiction, assuming that we could find a nonoptimal solution to this subproblem that would give us a *better* global solution. Both subsolutions would be compatible with what we had, so they would be interchangeable. Clearly, swapping out the nonoptimal solution with the optimal one would improve the global sum, which gives us our contradiction.

7-13. Kruskal's algorithm invariably finds a minimum spanning *forest*, which in the case of connected graphs turns into a minimum spanning tree. Prim's algorithm could be extended with a loop, like depth-first search, so that it would restart in all components.

7-14. It will still run, but it won't necessarily find the cheapest traversal (or *min-cost arborescence*).

7-15. Because you can use this to sort real numbers, which has a loglinear lower bound. (This is similar to the case with convex hulls.) You just use the numbers as x-coordinates and use identical y-coordinates. The minimum spanning tree would then be a path from the first number to the last, giving you the sorted order.

7-16. All we need to show is that the component trees have (at most) logarithmic height. The height of a component tree is equal to the highest rank in the component. This rank is increased only if two component tree of equal height are merged, and then it is increased by one. The only way to increase *some* rank in every union would be to merge the components in a balanced way, giving a logarithmic final rank (and height). Going some rounds *without* incrementing any ranks won't help because we're just "hiding" nodes in trees without changing their ranks, giving us less to work with. In other words, there is no way to get more than a logarithmic height for the component trees.

7-17. It's all hidden by the logarithmic operations of the heap. In the worst case, if we added each node only once, these operations would be logarithmic in the number of nodes. Now, they could be logarithmic in the number of *edges*, but since the number of edges is polynomial (quadratic) in the number of nodes, that amounts only to a constant difference: $\Theta(\lg m) = \Theta(\lg n^2) = \Theta(\lg n)$.

7-18. The interval with the earliest starting time could, potentially, cover the entire reminder of the set, which could all be nonoverlapping. If we wanted to go with the *highest* starting time, we'd be equally doomed to failure, by always getting only a single element.

7-19. We'd have to sort them all, but after that, the scanning and elimination can be performed in linear time in total (do you see how?). In other words, the total running time is dominated by the sorting, which is loglinear in general.

Chapter 8

8-1. Instead of checking whether the parameter tuple is already in the cache, just retrieve it and catch the KeyError that might occur if it's *not* there. Using some nonexistent value (such as None) along with get might give even better performance.

8-2. One way of viewing this might be counting subsets. Each element is either in the subset or not.

8-3. For fib, you just need the two previous values at each step, while for two_pow, you only need to keep doubling the value you have.

8-5. Just use the "predecessor pointer" idea from Chapter 5. If you're doing the forward version, store which choice you made (that is, which out-edge you followed) in each node. If you're doing the reverse version, store where you came from to each node.

8-6. Because the topological sorting still has to visit every edge.

8-7. You could let each node observe its predecessors and then explicitly trigger an update in the estimate in the start node (giving it a value of zero). The observers would be notified of changes and could update their own estimates accordingly, triggering new updates in their observers. This is in many ways quite similar to the relaxation-based solution in this chapter. The solution would be a bit "over-eager," though. Because cascades of updates are triggered instantly (instead of letting each node finish its out- or in-updates at a time), the solution could, in fact, have exponential running time. (Do you see how?)

8-8. This can be shown in many ways—but one is simply to look at how the list is constructed. Each object is added (either appended or overwriting an old element) using bisect, which finds the right place to put it, in sorted order. By induction, end will be sorted. (Can you think of other ways of seeing that this list must be sorted?)

8-9. You don't need bisect when the new element is larger than the last element or if end is empty. You could add an if statement to check for that. It *might* make the code faster, but it would probably make it a bit less readable.

8-10. Just like in the DAG shortest path problem, this would involve remembering "where you came from," that is, keeping track of predecessors. For the quadratic version, you could—instead of using predecessor pointers—simply copy the list of predecessors at each step. It wouldn't affect the asymptotic running time (copying all those lists would be quadratic, but that's what you already have), and the impact on actual running time and memory footprint should be negligible.

8-11. This is quite similar to the LCS code in many ways. If you need more help, you could do a web search for *levenshtein distance python*, for example.

8-12. Just like the other algorithms, you'd keep track of which choices were made, corresponding to which edges you followed in the "subproblem DAG."

8-13. You could swap the sequences and their lengths.

8-14. You could divide c and all the elements in w by their greatest common divisor.

8-16. The running time is pseudopolynomial—meaning that it is still exponential. You could easily crank up the knapsack capacity so that the running time became unacceptable, while keeping the actual problem instance size low.

8-19. You could add a set of dummy leaf nodes representing failed searches. Each leaf node would then represent all the nonexistent elements between two that were actually in the tree. You'd have to treat these separately in the sums.

Chapter 9

9-1. You have to somehow modify the algorithm or the graph so the detection mechanism for negative additive cycles can be used to find multiplicative cycles where the product of the exchange rates ends up above 1. The easiest solution is to simply take transform all the weights by taking their logarithms and negating them. You could then use the standard version of Bellman–Ford, and a negative cycle would give you what you needed. (Do you see how?) Of course, to actually *use* this for anything, you should work out how to output which nodes are involved in this cycle.

9-2. This isn't a problem, no more than it is in the DAG shortest path problem. It doesn't matter which one of them ends up first in the ordering because the other one (which then comes later) can't be used to create a shortcut anyway.

9-3. It gives you a pseudopolynomial running time, all of a sudden (with respect to the original problem instance). Do you see why?

9-4. This can depend on how you do it. Adding nodes multiple times is no longer a good idea, and you should probably set things up so you can access and modify entries directly in your queue when you run relax. You could then do this part in constant time, while the extraction from the queue would now be linear, and you'd end up with a quadratic running time. For a dense graph, that's actually quite OK.

9-5. Things can go wrong if there are negative cycles—but the Bellman–Ford algorithm would have raised an exception in that case. Barring this, we can turn to the triangular inequality. We know that $h(v) \leq h(u) + w(u, v)$ for all nodes u and v. This means that $w'(u, v) = w(u, v) + h(u) - h(v) \geq 0$, as required.

9-6. We might preserve the shortest paths, but we couldn't necessarily guarantee that the weights would be nonnegative.

9-9. This requires few changes. You'd use a (binary, Boolean) adjacency matrix instead of a weight matrix. When seeing if you could improve a path, you would not use addition and minimum; instead, you would see whether there was a new path there. In other words, you would use A[u, v] = A[u, v] or A[u, k] and A[k, v].

9-10. The tighter stopping criterion tells us to stop as soon as $l + r$ is greater than the shortest path we've found so far, and we've already established that that is correct. At the point when both directions have yielded (and therefore visited) the same node, we know the shortest path going through that node has been explored; because it is itself one of those we have explored, it must be greater than or equal to the *smallest* one of those we have explored.

9-11. No matter which edge you pick we know that $d(s,u) + w(u,v) + d(v,t)$ is smaller than the length of the shortest path found so far, which is, again, shorter than or equal to $l + r$. This means that both l and r would go past the midpoint of the path, wherever that is. If the midpoint is inside an edge, just choose that; if it's exactly on a node, choosing either adjacent edge on the path would do the trick.

9-14. Consider the shortest path from v to t. The modified cost can be expressed in two ways. The first is as $d(v,t) - h(v) + h(t)$, which is the same as $d(v,t) - h(v)$ because $h(t) = 0$. The other way of expressing this modified cost is as the sum of the individual modified edge weights; by assumptions, these are all nonnegative (that is, h is feasible). Therefore, we get $d(v,t) - h(v) \geq 0$, or $d(v,t) \geq h(v)$.

Chapter 10

10-1. Simply split each node v into two nodes, v and v', and add the edge vv' with the desired capacity. All in-edges would then stay with v, while all out-edges from v would be moved to v'.

10-2. You could modify the algorithm, or you could modify your data. For example, you could split each node into two, with a unit-capacity edge between them, and give all remaining edges infinite capacity. Then the maximum flow would let you identify the vertex-disjoint paths.

10-3. We know the running time is $O(m^2)$, so all we need to do is construct a situation where the quadratic running time occurs. One possibility is to have $m/2$ nodes in addition to s and t, each with an edge from s and to t. In the worst case, the traversal would visit all the unsaturated out-edges from s, which (by the handshake sum) gives us a quadratic running time.

10-4. Simply replace each edge uv by uv and vu, both with the same capacity. In this case, you could, of course, end up with flow going both ways at the same time. This isn't really a problem—to find out the actual flow through the undirected edge, just subtract one from the other. The sign of the result will indicate the direction of flow. (Some books avoid having edges in both directions between nodes in order to simplify the use of residual networks. This can be done by splitting one of the two directed edges in two, with a dummy node.)

10-6. For example, you could give the source a capacity (as described in Exercise 10-1) equal to the desired flow value. If feasible, the maximum flow would then have that value.

10-8. You can solve this by finding a minimum cut, as follows. If guest A will attend only if B also attends, add the edge (A,B) to your network, with an infinite capacity. This edge will then never cross a cut (in the forward direction), if it can be avoided. The friends you invite will be on the source side of the cut, while the others will be on the sink side. Your compatibilities can be modeled as follows: any positive compatibility is used as a capacity for an edge from the source, while any negative compatibility is used, *negated*, as a capacity for an edge to the source. The algorithm will then minimize the sum of such edges crossing the cut, keeping the ones you like on the source side and the ones you don't on the sink side (to the extent possible).

10-9. Because each person has a single favorite seat, each node on the left side has a single edge to the right. That means that the augmenting paths all consist of single unsaturated edges—so the behavior described is equivalent to the augmenting path algorithm, which we know will give an optimal answer (that is, it'll pair as many people as possible to their favorite seats).

10-10. Represent the groups for both rounds as nodes. Give the first groups in-edges from the source, with a capacity of k. Similarly, give the second groups out-edges to the sink, also with capacity k. Then add edges from all the first groups to all the second groups, all with capacity 1. Each flow unit is then a person, and if you're able to saturate the edges from the source (or to the sink), you've succeeded. Each group will then have k persons, and each of the second groups will at most have one person from each of the first.

10-11. This solution combines the supply/demand idea with min-cost flow. Represent each planet by a node. Also add a node for every passenger type (that is, for each valid combination of passenger origin and destination). Link every planet to $i < n$ to planet $i +1$ with a capacity equal to the actual carrying capacity of the spaceship. The passenger type nodes are given supplies equal to the number of passenger of that type (that is, the number of passengers wanting to go from i to j). Consider the node v, representing passengers wanting to go from planet i to planet j. These can either make the trip or not. We represent that fact by adding an edge (with infinite capacity) from v to i and another to j. We then add a demand to node j equal to the supply at v. (In other words, we make sure that each planet has a demand that will account for all passengers who want to go there.) Finally, we add a cost on (v,i) equal to the fare for the trip from i to j, except it's negative. This represents the amount we'll make for each of the passengers at v that we take on. We now find a min-cost flow that is feasible with respect to these supplies and demands. This flow will make sure that either each passenger is routed to their desired origin (meaning that they'll take the trip) and then via the planet-to-planet edges to their destination, adding to our revenue, or they are routed directly to their destination (meaning they won't take the trip) along a zero-cost edge.

Chapter 11

11-1. Because the running time of bisection is logarithmic. Even if the size of the value range in question is exponential as a function of the problem size, the actual running time will only be *linear*. (Do you see why?)

11-2. Because they are all in NP, and all problems in NP can be reduced to any NP-complete problem (by the definition of NP-completeness).

11-3. Because the running time is $O(nW)$, where W is the capacity. If W is polynomial in n, then so is the running time.

11-4. The reduction from the version with an arbitrary k is simple enough: Simply add $-k$ as an element.

11-5. It should be clear that we could reduce an unbounded version of the subset sum problem to unbounded knapsack (just set weights and values equal to the numbers in question). The challenge is getting from the unbounded to the bounded case. This is basically a matter of juggling numbers, and there are several elements to this juggling. We still want to keep the weights so that the optimization maximizes them. In addition, however, we need to add some kind of constraints to make sure at most one of each number is used. Let's look at this constraint thing separately. For n numbers, we can try to create n "slots" using powers of two, representing number i by 2^i. We could then have a capacity of $2^1 + \ldots + 2^n$, and run our maximization. This isn't quite enough, though; the maximization wouldn't care if we have one instance of 2^n or two instances of 2^{n-1}. We can add another constraint: We represent number i by $2^i + 2^{n+1}$ and set the capacity to $2^1 + \ldots + 2^n + n2^{n+1}$. For the maximization, it will still pay to fill every slot from 1 to n, but now it can include only n occurrences of 2^{n+1}, so a single instance of $2n$ will be preferable to two instances of 2^{n-1}. But we're not done yet ... this only lets us force the maximization to take exactly one of each number, and that's not really what we want. Instead, we want *two versions* of each item, one representing that the number is included and one representing that it is excluded. If number i is included, we will add w_i, and if it is excluded, we will add 0. We will also have a the original capacity, k. These constraints are subordinate to the "one item per slot" stuff, so we'd really like to have two "digits" in our representation. We can do that by multiplying the slot constraint number by a huge constant. If the largest of our numbers is B, we can multiply the constraints with nB, and we should be on the safe side. The resulting scheme, then, is to represent number w_i from the original problem by the following two new numbers, representing inclusion and exclusion, respectively: $(2^{n+1} + 2^i)nB + w_i$ and $(2^{n+1} + 2i)nB$. The capacity becomes $(n2^{n+1} + 2^n + \ldots + 2^1)nB + k$.

11-6. It's easy to reduce three-coloring to any k-coloring for $k > 3$; you simply conflate two or more of the colors.

11-7. Here you can reduce from any number of things. A simple example would be to use subgraph isomorphisms to detect cliques.

11-8. You can simply simulate undirected edges by adding directed ones in both directions (antiparallel edges).

11-9. You can still use the red-green-blue scheme to simulate direction here and then use the previous reduction from directed Hamilton cycle to directed Hamilton path (you should verify how and why this would still work). Here's another option, though. Consider how to reduce the undirected Hamilton cycle problem to the undirected Hamilton path problem. Choose some node u, and add three new nodes, u', v and v', as well as the (undirected) edges (v,v') and (u,u'). Now add an edge between v and every neighbor of u. If the original graph has a Hamilton cycle, this new one will obviously have a Hamilton path (just disconnect u from one of its neighbors in the cycle, and add u' and v' at either end). More importantly, the implication works both ways: A Hamilton path in the new graph must have u' and v' as its end points. If we remove u', v, and v', we're left with a Hamilton path from u to a neighbor of u, and we can link them up to get a Hamilton cycle.

11-10. This is (unsurprisingly) sort of the opposite of the reduction in the other direction. Instead of splitting an existing node, you can add a new one. Connect this node to every other. You will then have a Hamilton cycle in the new graph if and only if there is a Hamilton path in the original one.

11-11. We can trace things up the chain. Longest paths in DAGs can be used to find Hamilton paths, but only in DAGs. This will, again, let us find directed Hamilton cycles in digraphs that become DAGs when we split them at a single node (or, by fiddling with the reduction, something very close to that). However, the digraph we used for reducing 3-SAT to the directed Hamilton cycle was nothing like this. True, we could see a hint of this structure in the s and t nodes, and the general downward direction of edges from s to t, but every row was *full* of antiparallel edges, and the ability to go in either direction was crucial to the proof. Therefore, things break down here if we assume acyclicity further down.

11-12. The reasoning here is quite similar to that in Exercise 11-11.

11-13. As discussed in the main text, if the object is bigger than half the knapsack, we're done. If it's slightly less (but not as small as a quarter of the knapsack), we can include two and again have filled more than half. The only remaining case is if it's even smaller. In either case, we can just keep piling on, until we get past the midline—and because the objects is so small, it won't extend far enough across the midline to get us into trouble.

11-14. This is actually easy. First, randomly order the nodes. This will give you two DAGs, consisting of the edges going left-to-right and those going right-to-left. The largest of these must consist of at least half the edges, giving you a 2-approximation.

11-15. Let's say *all* the nodes are of odd degree (which will give the matching as large a weight as possible). That means the cycle will consist only of these nodes, and every second edge of the cycle will be part of the matching. Because we're choosing the *minimum* matching, we of course choose the smallest of the two possible alternating sequences, ensuring that the weight is at most half the total of the cycle. Because we know the triangle inequality holds, relaxing our assumption and dropping some nodes won't make the cycle—or the matching—more expensive.

11-16. Feel free to be creative here. You could, perhaps, just try to add each of the objects individually, or you could add some random objects? Or you could run the greedy bound initially—although that will happen already in one of the first expansions ...

11-17. Intuitively, you're getting the most possible value out of the items. See whether you can come up with a more convincing proof, though.

11-18. This requires some knowledge of probability theory, but it's not that hard. Let's look at a single clause, where each literal (either a variable or its negation) is either true or false, and the probability of either outcome is 1/2. This means that the probability of the entire clause being true is $1-(1/2)^3 = 7/8$. This is also the expected number of clauses that will be true, if we have only a single clause. If we have m clauses, we can expect to have $7m/8$ true clauses. We know that m is an upper bound on the optimum, so our approximation ratio becomes $m/(7m/8) = 8/7$. Pretty neat, don't you think?

11-19. The problem is now expressive enough to solve (for example) the maximum independent set problem, which is NP-hard. Therefore, your problem is also NP-hard. One reduction goes as follows: Set the compatibility for each guest to 1 and add conflicts for each edge in the original graph. If you can now maximize the compatibility sum without inviting guests who dislike each other, you have found the largest independent set.

11-20. The NP-hardness can easily be established, even for $m = 2$, by reducing from the partition problem. If we can distribute the jobs so that the machines finish at the same time, that will clearly minimize the completion time—and if we can minimize the completion time, we will also know whether they can finish simultaneously (that is, whether the values can be partitioned). The approximation algorithm is easy, too. We consider each job in turn (in some arbitrary order) and assign it to the machine that currently has the earliest finish time (that is, the lowest workload). In other words, it's a straightforward greedy approach. Showing that it's a 2-approximation is a little bit harder. Let t be the optimum completion time. First, we know that no job duration is greater than t. Second, we know that the average finish time cannot exceed t, as a completely even distribution is the best we can get. Let M be the machine to finish last in our greedy scheme, and let j be the last job on that machine. Because of our greedy strategy, we know that at the starting time of j, all the other machines were busy, so this starting time was before the average finish time and therefore before t. The duration of j must *also* be lower than t, so adding this duration to its starting time, we get a value lower than $2t$ ... and this value is, indeed, our completion time.

11-21. You could reuse the basic structure of Listing 11-2, if you'd like. A straightforward approach would be to consider each job in turn and try to assign it to each machine. That is, the branching factor of your search tree will be m. (Note that the ordering of the jobs within a machine doesn't matter.) At the next level of the search, you then try to place the second job. The state can be represented by a list of the finish times of the m machines. When you tentatively add a job to a machine, you simply add its duration to the finish time; when you backtrack, you can just subtract the duration again. Now you need a bound. Given a partial solution (some scheduled jobs), you need to give an optimistic value for the final solution. For example, we can never finish earlier than the latest finish time in the partial solution, so that's one possible bound. (Perhaps you can think of better bounds?) Before you start, you must initialize your solution value to an upper bound on the optimum (because we're minimizing). The tighter you can get this, the better (because it increases your pruning power). Here you could use the approximation algorithm from Exercise 11-20.

Index

Get the eBook for only $10!

Now you can take the weightless companion with you anywhere, anytime. Your purchase of this book entitles you to 3 electronic versions for only $10.

This Apress title will prove so indispensible that you'll want to carry it with you everywhere, which is why we are offering the eBook in 3 formats for only $10 if you have already purchased the print book.

Convenient and fully searchable, the PDF version enables you to easily find and copy code—or perform examples by quickly toggling between instructions and applications. The MOBI format is ideal for your Kindle, while the ePUB can be utilized on a variety of mobile devices.

Go to www.apress.com/promo/tendollars to purchase your companion eBook.

Apress®
THE EXPERT'S VOICE™